THE
PSYCHOLOGY
OF
QUESTIONS

THE
PSYCHOLOGY
OF
QUESTIONS

Edited By

Arthur C. Graesser
John B. Black

LEA LAWRENCE ERLBAUM ASSOCIATES, PUBLISHERS
1985   Hillsdale, New Jersey   London

Lawrence Erlbaum Associates, Inc., Publishers
365 Broadway
Hillsdale, New Jersey 07642

Library of Congress Cataloging in Publication Data

Main entry under title:

The Psychology of questions.

Includes bibliographies and indexes.
1. Reasoning (Psychology)   2. Question (Logic)
3. Cognition.   I. Graesser, Arthur C.   II. Black, John B.
(John Benjamin), 1947–   . [DNLM: 1. Problem Solving.
BF 441 P974]
BF441.P83   1985   153.4'3   85-1591
ISBN 0-89859-444-8

Printed in the United States of America
10   9   8   7   6   5   4   3   2   1

Contents

v

1 An Introduction to the Study of Questioning

Arthur C. Graesser
California State University, Fullerton

INTRODUCTION

J. T. Dillon recently reviewed 15 books on the topic of questioning (Dillon, 1982). The books were published during the last decade and spanned many different fields: philosophy, logic, linguistics, semantics, cognitive psychology, anthropology, sociolinguistics, survey research, education, counseling, personnel interviewing, psychotherapy, library science, and cross-examination techniques. Dillon had several informative observations after completing this broad survey. Listed below are three of the more general observations.

1. *When considering the different fields collectively, there is a growing and widening interest in the study of questioning.* Obviously, questioning has attracted the attention of scholars since Aristotle (or before). However, serious studies of questioning have escalated during the last decade.
2. *The different fields are rather isolated from one another.* Multidisciplinary approaches are rare even though each field would benefit from the contributions of other fields. As usual, there is a natural tendency for fields to be insulated (if not encapsulated).
3. *A multidisciplinary study of questioning seems imminent.* There are some common interests, unresolved issues, and contradictory conclusions among the fields. The stage has been set for some multidisciplinary efforts.

Dillon's survey included Lehnert's book, *The Process of Question Answering* (1978), as the representative contribution from cognitive psychol-

1

ogy. Lehnert's book introduced a detailed model that specified symbolic procedures for 13 categories of questions (e.g., causal antecedent questions, goal orientation questions, concept completion questions, requests). The model (called QUALM) has been implemented in the form of a computer program. Lehnert's work has had a profound impact on the question-answer research that I have conducted in recent years (Graesser, 1981). The fact that Lehnert's book was selected to represent cognitive psychology is appropriate because her goal was to capture the mechanisms that humans invoke when they answer questions. At the same time, however, it is informative to note that Lehnert is not a prototypical cognitive psychologist; her background and primary research interests are in computer science and artificial intelligence.

Cognitive psychology has never really treated questioning as a primary object of inquiry. Questioning has always had a secondary status. Researchers have usually collected answers to questions as a data base for investigating and testing some other, more "primary" cognitive component or mechanism (e.g., memory organization, memory retrieval, natural language comprehension, problem solving, social attribution). The mechanisms that underly question comprehension, question answering, and question asking have rarely been under direct scrutiny. Consequently, cognitive psychology's image is rather fuzzy in the multidisciplinary arena.

In light of this historical context, John Black and I thought that it would be useful to edit a book on the psychology of questions. The contributors to this volume are cognitive psychologists who have investigated question comprehension, question answering, and question asking either directly or indirectly. It is hoped that this volume will create a more salient impression of cognitive psychology's contributions and will stimulate more focused efforts in the study of questioning. The time is ripe for cognitive psychologists to develop serious, well-articulated theories.

How do other fields approach the study of questioning? A complete answer to this question would require several books because there are many fields with quite different theoretical frameworks and methodologies. Nevertheless, I thought that it would be helpful to summarize briefly some of the highlights. The next few sections describe major objectives, perspectives, and contributions in other fields. The coverage is selective rather than exhaustive. For most of the fields, I have cited some recent references for curious readers who want to reconstruct the literature.

RATIONAL APPROACHES TO THE STUDY OF QUESTIONING

The "rational" approaches to the study of questioning are pursued in philosophy, logic, and linguistics. The critical issues in these fields involve language events, i.e., the nature, structure, and meaning of sentences. There is a special logic called *erotetic logic* which applies to all sentences that call for a reply (Harrah, in press). Scholars who pursue these rational approaches worry about (a) expressing questions and responses in a formal manner; (b) elucidating well-formed relationships between questions and responses; and (c) solving problems of truth, reference, presupposition, and other traditional problems as they apply to questioning.

An erotetic logic must somehow deal with the fact that expressions in a logical theory have a truth value, yet questions do not seem to have a truth value. For example, it would be silly to assign a truth value to the following questions:

1. Is the number of trees that border Canada and the United States even?
2. Why did that professor write that paper?
3. When did you stop beating your spouse?

An early solution to this problem was the *set-of-answers* methodology (see Harrah, in press; Kiefer, 1983). According to this methodology, the logical meaning of a question is the set of all possible answers to the question (or alternatively, the set of all true answers). Truth values were assigned to questions by virtue of the truth values assigned to answers.

The set-of-answers methodology suffers from a number of shortcomings (Kiefer, 1983). Two major problems involve context and pragmatics. A complete theory of questioning requires a contextually restricted notion of possible answers (or true answers). The meaning of a question and the possible answers to it depend critically on the relevant context or world under consideration. A complete theory of questioning must also incorporate the pragmatic level of language usage, i.e., properties of the social interaction between the questioner and answerer. This pragmatic component would specify the questioner's knowledge, the answerer's knowledge, the intentions of the questioner and answerer, and perhaps other properties of the speech participants. In other words, a theory of questioning is a special case of a more general theory of conversation (Hobbs & Robinson, 1979). An inappropriate answer or question involves a lack of cooperation between the questioner and answerer. Specifically, inappropriate speech acts violate some implicit conversational maxim or rule for achieving a smooth conversation, e.g., be sincere, be truthful, be informative, be relevant, be clear (see Grice, 1975). The problem of generating a pragmatically significant answer to a question cannot be satisfactorily solved by appealing to the set-of-answers methodology (Grewendorf, 1983).

More recent rational approaches to the study of questioning have indeed acknowledged the pragmatic level of conversational interaction (see Harrah, in press). In fact, researchers in this field have identified many of the alternative *pragmatic modes*. One pragmatic mode is called "Tell Me Truly." In this mode the speech participants may or may not know the answers to questions, but there is a ground rule that the questioner expects the answerer to supply true, sincere answers. A second pragmatic mode is called "Make it the Case that I Know." In this mode there is the expectation that (a) the answerer is more knowledgable than the questioner about the information referenced in the question and (b) the questioner wants the answer to supply the needed information. This second mode is appropriate when the questioner has a problem to solve and needs critical information. A third pragmatic mode is called "Make Me Know that You Know." In this mode it is expected that (a) the questioner is more knowledgable than the answerer about the information referenced in the question and (b) the questioner wants the answerer to demonstrate that the answerer knows the information. A good example of this third mode is in a teacher-student dialogue where the teacher asks the student questions even though the teacher already knows the answers to the questions. A fourth pragmatic mode is called "Give Me an Answer and Claim that it is True." This mode would occur in a cross-examination context. It is expected that both the questioner (policeman, judge, lawyer) and the answerer (witness, client) know the answer to a question, but the speech acts are performed to satisfy certain legal objectives. Other pragmatic modes include rhetorical questions, indirect requests, and gripes (see Bach & Harnish, 1979). In these modes, speech acts are questions syntactically, but functionally they are not questions because replies are not expected. A different erotetic logic would apply to each of the pragmatic modes and it is the task of the researcher to uncover their logical properties.

Kaplan (1983) has pointed out that a pragmatically cooperative answer may not be a direct answer to a question, but rather an indirect answer that corrects a misconception on the part of the questioner. Consider the question and the set of answers below.

How many beers did Jack have at Bill's party?

    (a) zero
    (b) Jack did not have any beers at Bill's party
    (c) There was no beer at the party

The question presupposes that Jack had beer at the party and it presumes that beer was available at the party (see Kaplan for the distinction between presuppositions and presumptions). It is quite possible, however, that Jack never had beer at the party and that there was no beer available. How would the answerer reply if no beer was available at the party? All three answers (a, b, and c) would be acceptable, technically speaking, but answer c would be the only pragmatically cooperative answer. Answer a would involve *stonewalling*. Stonewalling occurs when the answerer gives an uncooperative and often misleading answer that is nevertheless direct and technically correct. Pragmatically cooperative answers should correct erroneous presuppositions and presumptions that the questioner believes are true. A complete theory of questioning must address not only the explicit information in the questions and answers, but also the implicit knowledge that underlies the social interaction.

ARTIFICIAL INTELLIGENCE APPROACHES TO THE STUDY OF QUESTIONING

Researchers in artifical intelligence (AI) have developed computer systems that answer questions that users type into the system. Generally speaking, a question answering (Q/A) mechanism displays intelligence to the extent that it can search efficiently through a large data base, derive answers that are not directly stored in the data base, and formulate responses both quickly and accurately. Of course, developing an intelligent Q/A mechanism is no small task. Part of the key to achieving this goal is to organize and represent data base knowledge in a manner that caters to the constraints of the proposed Q/A mechanism. In other words, the data base and the Q/A mechanism work together in producing replies to questions. Just as it makes sense to evaluate the intelligence of a Q/A mechanism, it also makes sense to evaluate the intelligence of a data base.

There are three basic strategies to developing intelligent data bases and Q/A procedures. The first strategy is strictly analytical. The AI researcher uses proofs, algorithms, formulas, and other computational/mathematical tools for determining a system design that minimizes retrieval time and maximizes the accuracy of responses to queries. The second strategy capitalizes on what is known about human intelligence. The AI researcher incorporates the data base organization that humans allegedly possess and the Q/A heuristics that humans allegedly use. The belief underlying this second strategy is that AI should mimic human intelligence because it seems to be the most flexible and effective system available. Cognitive psychologists have had the most direct contact with AI researchers who adopt this second strategy (Lehnert, Dyer, Johnson, Yang, & Harley, 1983; Schank & Riesbeck, 1981; Williams, Hollan, & Stevens, 1983). The third and most recent strategy is to develop an expert system (Hayes-Roth, Waterman, & Lenat, 1983). The AI reseacher incorporates data base knowledge and retrieval heuristics of experts in a specific area (e.g., medicine, law, engineering). The expert systems presumably capitalize on the advantages of both machine intelligence and expert human intelligence.

The most successful AI systems have had restricted semantic domains (see Waltz, 1982, for a review). Thus, the properties of the data base and the Q/A procedures have depended on the semantic domain under investigation. AI researchers have collectively covered a broad range of semantic domains, including simple stories, arches, blocks (with different sizes, shapes, and colors), scientific information about moonrocks, aircraft flight and maintenance data, the operation of a steam engine, medical diagnosis and treatment, South American geography, and psychological problems (paranoia). AI reseacher have found it feasible to develop a Q/A system that is customized to the unique constraints of a specific semantic domain. There presently is no "portable" Q/A module that can be successfully integrated wth any semantic domain (although see Kaplan, 1983).

Available AI systems are not developed to the point where the computer can comprehend and formulate good answers to any question that a user happens to type into the system. Virtually all of the systems handle a restricted set of inputs which must be entered in a syntactically rigid way. Alternatively, there is a preliminary dialogue between the user and the computer, which eventually converges on the true question that the user intends to ask. Researchers in AI acknowledge that natural language is very complex, varied, and dependent on the pragmatic goals of the user-computer dialogue. Moreover, solutions to these problems will require decades of research.

There are several lessons that I have learned from the research projects in AI. One lesson is that a key to developing an intelligent Q/A procedure is to organize the data base in an intelligent way. A second lesson is that there is not a single way to organize a data base. There should be several organizational schemes that can be used at different times for different purposes. A third lesson is that it is important to study how different components, structural levels, and representations interact symbolically. Finally, AI has introduced important formalisms and system architectures that cognitive psychologists might consider when they develop their own theories of questioning.

PRACTICAL APPROACHES TO THE STUDY OF QUESTIONING

If a complete theory of questioning were ever achieved, there would be a staggering number of practical applications. On the other side of the coin, practical approaches to the study of questioning have had an impact on many of the theoretical approaches. The practical approaches have sometimes provided a refreshing perspective to the theoretical puzzles.

There are many practical approaches to the study of questioning. Survey researchers have investigated the influence of question wording, question structure, and question sequencing on answer profiles in public opinion polls and interviews (Sudman & Bradburn, 1983). Researchers in library science are developing search procedures and organizations for large data bases that provide efficient retrieval of references that are relevant to specific queries (Karlgren & Walker, 1983). Researchers in the area of computer-human interactions are investigating how computer users are influenced by characteristics of command and query languages in computers (Black & Sebrechts, 1981; Carroll, 1982; Dumais & Landauer, 1982).

Researchers have examined the role of questions in interviews. Among the different types of interviews are personnel interviews, counseling, psychotherapy, and legal cross-examinations. The goals and guidelines for effective questioning are hardly uniform among these different types of interviews. In personnel interviewing the goal is to acquire as much relevant information about the applicant as possible in the minimum amount of time. A good interviewer asks many questions and the questions probe information that is relevant to the job. In counseling and psychotherapy, however, it is sometimes appropriate to refrain from asking the client questions; questions tend to discourage a passive client from engaging in active self-discovery and problem solving. Questions must be carefully constructed in legal cross-examinations (Loftus, 1979). There are documented stories of lawyers losing cases because they asked one bad question in the entire litigation. One kind of bad question provokes an answer that hurts the client's case. Another kind of bad question may lead to a mistrial because it violates a legal technicality. One of the interesting maxims for lawyers is "never ask a question unless you know the answer" (see Dillon, 1982).

The role of questioning in education has received a great deal of attention. Researchers had examined the extent to which text comprehension is influenced by adjunct questions that are inserted either before, after, or throughout the text (Anderson & Biddle, 1975; Reynolds & Anderson, 1982; Rickards, 1979; Rothkopf, 1965). The adjunct question paradigm has inspired hundreds of empirical studies and research questions in the field of educational psychology. Educational researchers have also investigated the amount, nature, and pattern of questions produced by teachers and students in the classroom (Singer & Donlan, 1982). I will not elaborate further on the role of questioning in educational research, however, because this research is covered in some chapters in this volume.

CONTRIBUTIONS FROM COGNITIVE PSYCHOLOGY

Cognitive psychology has had its share of contributions to the study of questions. Indeed, most psychological studies involve questioning in some form or another. Psychologists have conducted experiments that measure the errors, the decision latencies, and the quality of answers that subjects give to questions. Psychologists have tested hypotheses about the cognitive mechanisms that exist during question comprehension, question answering, and question asking. As I mentioned earlier, however, this research is fragmented and scattered haphazardly throughout the literature in cognitive psychology. This fact inspired us to organize this volume.

Human question answering is not simply a matter of fetching information that is explicitly stored in long-term memory. Most adults can quickly answer questions even though the answers are not directly stored in memory.

Is San Francisco in North America?
Is there a gas station in New Haven?
Does it snow in San Diego?

Answers to these questions are typically derived from various fragments of knowledge in long-term memory. The answer to the first question would probably be derived from the following set of stored facts and pattern of reasoning: (1) San Francisco is in California; (2) California is in the United States; and (3) the United States is in North America; so (4) San Francisco is indeed in North America—the answer is YES. (This pattern of reasoning would probably not be accomplished consciously.) The answer to the second question would probably be derived as follows: New Haven is a city and cities have gas stations so New Haven has a gas station—the answer is YES. Obviously, we do not have a directly stored fact for each city specifying that the city has a gas station. Now consider the probable reasoning pattern for the third question: San Diego is in southern California, southern California is hot, snow is cold, and snow does not exist in hot climates, so there is a contradiction—the answer is NO. We probably do not directly store in long-term memory a large number of negative facts about people, objects, and regions. As we wander through the world, we do not encode ridiculous negative expressions, e.g., *this chair is not purple, this chair is not a turtle,* and *the chair is not under the refrigerator.* These examples illustrate the importance of reasoning and knowledge in human question answering.

During the last decade cognitive psychologists have been developing a catalog of reasoning heuristics (strategies) that exist in the cognitive system (Clark, 1979; Clark & Clark, 1977; Collins, 1977; Kahneman, Slovic, & Tversky, 1982; Wyer & Carlston, 1979). Researchers have conducted experiments to assess the components, scope, processing characteristics, and inferences generated by each reasoning heuristic. Inferences are generated by induction, deduction, analogy, default assignments, and other more subtle heuristics. However, it is quite beyond the scope of this introduction to describe all these reasoning heuristics and the inferences they generate. There seems to be a fundamental difference between reasoning heuristics in closed worlds (where there is a complete specification of the objects and their properties) and reasoning heuristics in open worlds (where only fragments of knowledge are stored in memory). For example, a closed world is involved when answering the question *How many states in the U.S. are on the Pacific Ocean?;* most adults have memorized all 50 states and their approximate locations. An open world is involved in the question *How many cities in the*

U.S. are on the Pacific Ocean?; most adults do not keep an exhaustive inventory of all the cities and their locations. The reasoning heuristics in an open world rely on human knowledge, which is normally incomplete, imprecise, uncertain, open-ended and fuzzy. Nevertheless, many of the inferences generated from open worlds are quite on the mark. Consider the following two questions.

Is Santa Clara a U.S. city on the Pacific Ocean?
Is Goofball a U.S. city on the Pacific Ocean?

Since the correct answer to both of these questions is NO, there presumably are no facts in memory that match the queried statements. Yet most people give either POSSIBLY or I DON'T THINK SO as an answer to the first question and NO to the second. These answers are derived from fragments of knowledge in memory. For example, the reasoning pattern for the second question might be: Goofball is a very bizarre name, most people want to be proud of the city they live in, and it is difficult to be proud of a city with a bizarre name, so the answer is NO.

Cognitive psychologists have vigorously investigated the structure, organization, and representation of knowledge in long-term memory. Researchers have examined many different representational systems, including feature lists, sets of exemplars, concept hierarchies, templates, propositional structures, schemas (including scripts and frames), and semantic networks. Each representational system has formal properties that can be tested in psychology experiments (Anderson, 1980; Keil, 1979; Mandler, 1983; Smith & Medin, 1981). Examples of data collected in these experiments are: (1) decision latencies for verifying the truth or falsity test statements (e.g., *a robin is a bird, birds can fly*), (2) decision latencies for deciding whether test words are a member of a specific category, (3) similarity ratings for pairs of concepts, and (4) patterns of memory errors. These data have been explained by cognitive models that are well articulated and precisely quantified.

Nearly all of the cognitive research on questioning has involved answers that are unidimensional, as opposed to answers with complex verbal responses. In the typical experiment, the subject comprehends stimulus material and then formulates a response on some dimension with a very restricted number of alternatives, e.g., YES versus NO, or a number on a rating scale. There are a number of advantages to collecting unidimensional responses. First, they involve objective measurements in the sense that there is very little measurement error. Second, they can be analyzed with standard statistical tools. Third, it is a comparatively straightforward task to build quantitative models of the data. Fourth, unidimensional answers are familiar to the colleagues who review the research for journals. Nevertheless, most questions invite answers with complex verbal descriptions. In this sense, it is disappointing that cognitive psychologists have an underdeveloped understanding of complex questions (e.g., *why, how, what are the consequences of*).

During the last few years some cognitive psychologists have started to investigate how people answer complex questions. In fact, many of the contributors to this volume have headed in this direction. Cognitive psychologists are ready to tackle complex questions because they have the conceptual and methodological tools to do so. Some of these tools have been borrowed from other disciplines, such as linguistics, philosophy, logic, and artificial intelligence, whereas others have been developed in the interdisciplinary field of cognitive science. Exactly where the tools came from is perhaps unimportant. The important fact is that the tools are here. There are sophisticated methods for analyzing verbal protocols. There are theoretical systems for representing complex information structures, such as text, world knowledge schemas, plans, and real world scenes. There are computer systems that can simulate complex cognitive mechanisms. Now that all these tools are available, the study of complex questions is well within the grasp of cognitive psychology.

CONTRIBUTIONS IN THIS VOLUME

The contributors to this volume are cognitive psychologists who have studied questioning. The chapters collectively approach the phenomenon of questioning from many perspectives. There are studies on question comprehension, question answering, question asking, and the influence of adjunct questions on text comprehension and memory. The chapters cover different theories, models, methods, and practical applications. Some contributors focus exclusively on adult subjects, whereas others examine cognitive development in children. The study of questioning is very heterogeneous at this point in history, so it was difficult to arrive at a good scheme for categorizing the chapters. However, the order of the chapters is not altogether arbitrary. The earlier chapters in the book have a "pure science" emphasis, whereas the later chapters have an "applied" emphasis. Of course, the distinction between science and application has become very fuzzy in recent years.

Chapter 2.   Graesser and Murachver describe a model that specifies the symbolic procedures that adults execute when they answer complex questions (including *why, how, what enabled, when, where, what are the consequences of,* and *what is the significance of*). The Q/A procedures were discovered by analyzing answers to questions about events and actions in simple stories. According to the model, passages (and generic knowledge packets) are represented as networks of categorized statement nodes (including inferences) that are interconnected by directed, relational arcs. The symbolic procedure for a question category specifies (a) the legal paths of arcs and nodes when searching through a knowledge structure and (b) constraints on those nodes that are potential answers.

Chapter 3. Murachver, Murray, and Graesser report research that tests the Graesser-Murachver model of question answering. The chapter summarizes the experimental support for the network representations that were adopted by the model. Murachver et al. report an experiment that assesses the extent to which the Q/A procedures can explain goodness-of-answer ratings. Finally, the chapter describes a computer program that implements part of the Graesser-Murachver model.

Chapter 4. Singer describes and evaluates a model of question answering called VAIL. VAIL is an additive stage process model that generates predictions for decision latencies when individuals judge the truth of statements. In a typical experiment, subjects read context sentences and then decide whether a test statement is a true assertion or implication. In some of the experiments there are DON'T KNOW and PROBABLY response options in addition to the standard YES and NO options. The VAIL model is a natural extension of the stage models in the information processing tradition.

Chapter 5. Galambos and Black analyze answers to why-questions for component actions in scripts and familiar activities (e.g., *shopping for groceries* and *changing a flat*). In addition to performing qualitative analyses on the Q/A protocols, they collected ratings on the distinctiveness, centrality, standardness, and sequential position of the actions in the activities. The rich data base and analyses provided insights about Q/A processes and characteristics of the underlying knowledge structures.

Chapter 6. Robertson, Black, and Lehnert examine how memory for narrative passages is altered by questions with misleading presuppositions. Their experiments revealed that the modifiability of actions and states differ substantially, perhaps because actions play a more central role in narrative representations. Robertson et al. also argue that question comprehension and information retrieval are not separate stages of processing, but rather two facets of the same integrated mechanism.

Chapter 7. Olson, Duffy, and Mach report a study that traces the questions that come to a subject's mind during text comprehension. They performed qualitative analyses on question-asking protocols that were collected as the subjects comprehended text, sentence by sentence. Olson et al. examine the extent to which sentence recall and sentence reading times can be predicted by the profile of questions from the question-asking task.

Chapter 8.   Kemper, Otalvaro, Estill, and Schadler examine the role of causal knowledge in comprehension, inference generation, and question answering. Sentence reading times were collected when subjects comprehended narrative text. When subjects later answered questions about the narrative passages, the accuracy and latencies of the answers were recorded. The experiments supported the claim that readers infer missing causal connections in causal event chains. When the text triggers familiar schemas (scripts and cultural stereotypes) the speed of inferring the causal connections is facilitated. Familiar background knowledge also facilitates the speed and accuracy of question answering.

Chapter 9.   Goldman compared children's and adults' answers to why-questions for actions in multi-episode stories. The stories had different episode structures (i.e., goal embedded versus outcome embedded). After performing qualitative analyses on the Q/A protocols, she found informative trends in cognitive development. For example, children have a basic understanding of characters' motives and intentions at a very early age. In fact, children tend to overapply goal-oriented interpretations of behavior and end up having to learn when it is *not* appropriate to apply such interpretations. Children also have difficulty understanding the abstract themes and morals that are suggested by stories.

Chapter 10.   Pressley and Forrest-Pressley review the child development research that has examined whether question answering increases memory for materials that children are asked to learn. There are documented learning gains produced by questions, but questioning effects depend on how the task is presented to children. The chapter covers teacher questions, text questions, child-generated questions, and metacognition. Pressley and Forrest-Pressley describe a new area of research involving "interrogative MAPs" (metacognition acquisition procedures). Interrogative MAPs are questions designed to increase metamemory, so that children might have more self-control of their cognitive strategies.

Chapter 11.   Nix describes a training procedure called LINKS which explicitly teaches children about inferences in reading comprehension and about metacomprehension skills. Children learn how to "link" together propositions in a text by making use of prior knowledge and conceptual relations. Nix has identified approximately 40 categories of links, which children eventually learn how to recognize, generate, describe, and apply during comprehension. The teacher asks questions in order to guide the children in their acquisition of the links. Nix reports some studies that assess the impact of the LINKS training procedure on children's reading comprehension.

Chapter 12.   Bean reviews the literature on classroom questioning and points out some directions for future applications. The chapter covers teacher-guided questions, student-guided questions, and the pseudo-Socratic method of classroom questioning. Systematic research on classroom questioning is very challenging because there is so much going on — often simultaneously. Bean introduces a "discussion map" analysis that includes background information and a detailed record of classroom discussion. The discussion maps are collected in order to analyze the impact of educational methods on classroom interaction.

Chapter 13.   Shwartz and Lehnert discuss computer-human interface problems that exist when users query a data base in a computer. Most of the available user-friendly interfaces have been either query languages (English-like languages which usually have a rigid syntax) or menus (lists specifying alternative directions that the user can take). Shwartz and Lehnert have pursued a third type of interface in which information is accessed by queries in natural language. Their computer interface, called EXPLORER, analyzes natural language queries that untrained users type into the computer. So far, EXPLORER has been customized for a data base involving geological rock formations and oil wells.

REFERENCES

Anderson, J. R. *Cognitive psychology and its implications.* San Francisco: Freeman, 1980.

Anderson, R., & Biddle, W. On asking people questions about what they are reading. In G. H. Bower (Ed.), *The psychology of learning and motivation,* (Vol. 9). New York: Academic Press, 1975.

Bach, K., & Harnish, R. M. *Linguistic communication and speech acts.* Cambridge, MA: MIT Press, 1979.

Black, J. B., & Sebrechts, M. M. Facilitating human-computer communication. *Applied Psycholinguistics,* 1981, *2,* 149–177.

Carroll, J. M. Learning, using, and designing command paradigms. *Human Learning: Journal of Practical Research and Applications,* 1982, *1,* 31–62.

Clark, H. H. Responding to indirect speech acts. *Cognitive Psychology,* 1979, *11,* 430–477.

Clark, H. H., & Clark, E. V. *Psychology and language.* New York: Harcourt Brace Jovanovich, 1977.

Collins, A. M. Processes in acquiring knowledge. In R. C. Anderson, R. J. Spiro, & W. E. Montague (Eds.), *Schooling and the acquisition of knowledge.* Hillsdale, N.J.: Lawrence Erlbaum Associates, 1977.

Dillon, J. T. The multidisciplinary study of questioning. *Journal of Educational Psychology,* 1982, *74,* 147–165.

Dumais, S. T., & Landauer, T. K. Psychological investigations of natural terminology for command and query languages. In A. Badre & B. Shneiderman (Eds.), *Directions in human-computer interaction.* Norwood, NJ: Ablex, 1982.

Graesser, A. C. *Prose comprehension beyond the word.* New York: Springer-Verlag, 1981.

Grewendorf, G. What answers can be given? In F. Kiefer (Ed.), *Questions and answers.* Boston: Reidel, 1983.

Grice, H. P. Logic and conversation. In P. Cole & J. L. Morgan (Eds.), *Syntax and semantics (Vol. 3): Speech acts.* New York: Seminar Press, 1975.

Harrah, D. The logic of questions. In F. Guenthner & D. Gabbay (Eds.), *Handbook of philosophical logic* (Vol. 2). Boston: Reidel, in press.

Hayes-Roth, F., Waterman, D. A., & Lenat, D. B. *Building expert systems.* Reading, MA: Addison-Wesley, 1983.

Hobbs, J. B., & Robinson, J. J. Why ask? *Discourse Processes,* 1979, *2,* 251–281.

Kahneman, D., Slovic, P., & Tversky, A. (Eds.) *Judgment under uncertainty: Heuristics and biases.* New York: Cambridge University Press, 1982.

Kaplan, J. Cooperative responses from a portable natural language data base query system. In M. Brady & R. C. Berwick (Eds.), *Computational models of discourse.* Cambridge, MA: MIT Press, 1983.

Karlgren, H., & Walker, D. E. The polytext system: A new design for a text retrieval system. In F. Kiefer (Ed.), *Questions and answers.* Boston: Reidel, 1983.

Keil, F. *Semantic and conceptual development.* Cambridge, MA: Harvard University Press, 1979.

Kiefer, F. Introduction. In F. Kiefer (Ed.), *Questions and answers.* Boston: Reidel, 1983.

Lehnert, W. G. *The process of question answering.* Hillsdale, NJ: Lawrence Erlbaum Associates, 1978.

Lehnert, W. G., Dyer, M. G., Johnson, P. N., Yang, C. J., & Harley, S. BORIS: An experiment in in-depth understanding of narratives. *Artificial Intelligence,* 1983, *20,* 15–62.

Loftus, E. F. *Eyewitness testimony.* Cambridge, MA: Harvard University Press, 1979.

Mandler, J. M. Representation. In J. H. Flavell & E. M. Markman (Eds.), *Cognitive development, Vol. 2 of Mussen (Ed.), Manual of child psychology.* New York: Wiley, 1983.

Reynolds, R., & Anderson, R. C. Influence of questions on the allocation of attention during reading. *Journal of Educational Psychology,* 1982, *74,* 623–632.

Rickards, J. Adjunct post-questions in text: A critical review of methods and processes. *Review of Educational Research,* 1979, *49,* 181–196.

Rothkopf, E. Some theoretical and experimental approaches to problems in written instruction. In J. Krummboltz (Ed.), *Learning and the educational process.* Chicago: Rand McNally, 1965.

Schank, R. C., & Riesbeck, C. K. (Eds.) *Inside computer understanding: Five programs plus miniatures.* Hillsdale, NJ: Lawrence Erlbaum Associates, 1981.

Singer, H., & Donlan, D. Active comprehension: Problem solving schema with question generation for comprehension of complex short stories. *Reading Quarterly,* 1982, *17,* 166–186.

Smith, E. E., & Medin, D. L. *Categories and concepts.* Cambridge, MA: Cambridge University Press, 1981.

Sudman, S., & Bradburn, N. M. *Asking questions: A practical guide to questionnaire design.* San Francisco: Jossey-Bass, 1983.

Waltz, D. L. The state of the art in natural language understanding. In W. G. Lehnert & M. H. Ringle (Eds.), *Strategies for natural language processing.* Hillsdale, NJ: Lawrence Erlbaum Associates, 1982.

Williams, M. D., Hollan, J. D., & Stevens, A. L. Human reasoning about a simple physical system. In D. Gentner & A. L. Stevens (Eds.), *Mental models.* Hillsdale, NJ: Lawrence Erlbaum Associates, 1983.

Wyer, R. S., & Carlston, D. E. *Social cognition, inference, and attribution.* Hillsdale, NJ: Lawrence Erlbaum Associates, 1979.

2 Symbolic Procedures of Question Answering

Arthur C. Graesser
California State University, Fullerton

Tamar Murachver
University of California, San Diego

INTRODUCTION

This chapter explores the symbolic procedures that humans execute when they answer complex questions. Complex questions invite elaborate verbal descriptions. For example, we could ask a number of complex questions about President Reagan cutting the research budget: *Why did Reagan cut the budget? How did Reagan cut the budget? What enabled Reagan to cut the budget? What is the consequence of Reagan's cutting the budget? When did Reagan cut the budget? Where did Reagan cut the budget?* and *What is the significance of Reagan's cutting the budget?* These complex questions may be contrasted with simple questions that involve discrete or continuous judgments on some dimension. For example, simple questions include truth verification questions and "rating scale" type questions: *Did Reagan cut the research budget?* and *How much do you like Reagan's cutting the budget?*

Psychologists know very little about the symbolic procedures of complex questions. Psychologists have vigorously investigated simple questions during the last two decades (Clark & Clark, 1977; Collins & Loftus, 1975; Collins & Quillian, 1969; Kintsch, 1974; McCloskey & Glucksberg, 1979; Reder, 1982; Singer, 1980; Smith & Medin, 1981; Smith, Shoben, & Rips, 1974). However, complex questions have only recently attracted the attention of psychologists (Collins, 1977; Galambos & Black, 1981; Graesser, 1981a; Nicholas & Trabasso, 1980; Nix, 1983; Stein & Glenn, 1979; Trabasso, Secco, & van den Broek, 1983; Trabasso & Stein, 1981; Warren, Nicholas,

& Trabasso, 1979). Psychologists should understand how humans answer complex questions. They are much too important for psychologists to ignore.

The standard methodological tools in experimental psychology are not adequate for discovering the symbolic procedures of complex questions. Psychologists are well equipped for measuring and manipulating variables, but their skills are rather underdeveloped when it comes to analyzing complex verbal protocols. We will need to pursue new methods of collecting and analyzing verbal protocols before any substantial progress will be made (see Graesser, 1981a; Olson, Mack, & Duffy, 1980). We will need to develop and verify our understanding of complex questions by simulating human conceptual processes on computers (see Dyer & Lehnert, 1980; Lehnert, 1977, 1978; Luria, 1982; Schank, Goldman, Rieger, Riesbeck, 1973; Scragg, 1975; Winograd, 1972).

Complex questions can be classified into different question categories. For each question category there is a specific symbolic procedure that operates on knowledge structures. In this chapter we represent this knowledge in the form of conceptual graph structures. A conceptual graph structure consists of a set of categorized statement nodes that are interrelated by directed, relational arcs. The symbolic procedure for a question category specifies (1) the specific relational arcs that are followed when searching through a knowledge structure and (2) constraints on those nodes that are accessed by this arc search procedure. However, before we describe these symbolic procedures any further, we will discuss question answering at a more general level.

AN ARCHITECTURE FOR STUDYING QUESTION ANSWERING

Question answering is not an easy phenomenon to study because there are many knowledge sources that contribute to the process. This is a trite claim but we do have to acknowledge it. In this section we offer an architecture for studying question answering. The purpose of presenting this architecture is to identify the knowledge sources and basic processes that contribute to question answering. In other words, we divide the problem into subproblems. The proposed architecture should not be literally construed as a flow chart of the psychological processes in question answering. The architecture is simply a useful context for the analyses discussed in this chapter.

Figure 2.1 presents our proposed architecture for question answering. The architecture has five active processing components which together produce answers to a question. These five active processing components involve the following respective goals:

1. Interpret the question
2. Select the appropriate question category

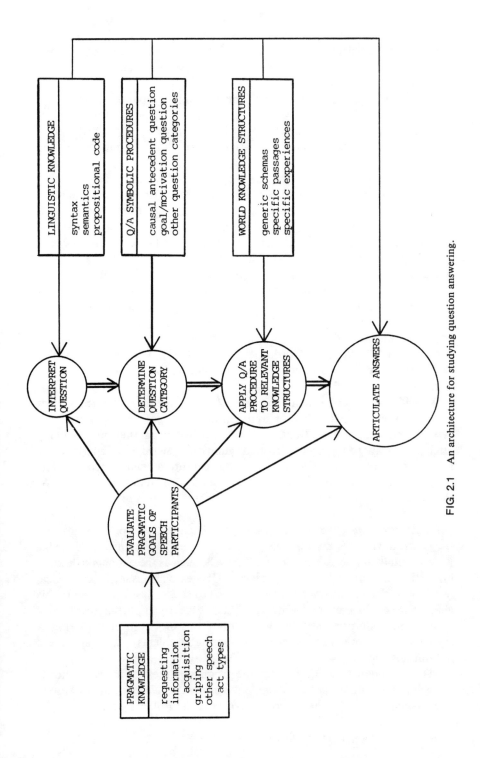

FIG. 2.1   An architecture for studying question answering.

17

3. Apply the selected question-answering procedure to relevant knowledge structures
4. Articulate answers to the question
5. Evaluate the pragmatic goals of the speech participants

According to the Q/A architecture in Fig. 2.1, pragmatic goal evaluation governs the processing characteristics of the other four processing components.

For each active processor, there is a corresponding knowledge base that critically influences the activities of the processor. For example, linguistic knowledge is obviously tapped during question interpretation. World knowledge structures are tapped when Q/A procedures are applied to relevant knowledge structures. The fact that we have associated specific knowledge to specific processors is a convenient, but erroneous, simplification. A processor undoubtedly draws information from each of the four knowledge bases at some time or another. For example, it may be impossible to interpret a question without accessing world knowledge structures (Lehnert, 1978; Lehnert, Robertson, & Black, 1983). Similarly, linguistic knowledge is one important knowledge base for evaluating the pragmatic goals of the speech participants (Clark, 1979; Gordon & Lakoff, 1971). We have attached to each processor the knowledge that predominantly contributes to that processor.

We will now describe each component in more detail. Our discussion of each component presupposes some commitments to specific representational systems and computational devices. We acknowledge that there may be many alternative ways to represent a given domain of knowledge. Similarly, there may be several computational devices that capture a given processor. The proposed representations and computational devices reflect our biases. At the same time, they are useful in the sense that they seem to work.

Interpreting the Question.   When comprehenders interpret a question, they must obviously have knowledge of language. This linguistic knowledge is traditionally segregated into different levels, such as the phonemic, lexical, syntactic, semantic, and pragmatic levels. Of these various levels, the lexical level and the semantic level are most central to the analyses reported in this chapter. The phonemic and syntactic levels are clearly important ingredients for question interpretation, but we do not focus on question answering at these levels. The pragmatic level presents special problems that are addressed later in this chapter.

In our proposed Q/A mechanism, the product of question interpretation is an expression with a *question function,* a *statement element,* and a *knowledge structure element.* For example, consider the following question.

Why did Reagan cut the budget?

This question would be segmented into the question function and elements listed below.

Question function: WHY
Statement element: < Reagan cut the budget >
Knowledge structure element: < ? >

The product of question interpretation would be an expression in the following format.

WHY (< Reagan cut the budget > < ? >)

The question function may be construed as a higher-order function with the statement element and the knowledge structure element serving as arguments (or slots, variables, etc.). Obviously, the semantic content of the question critically determines the content of the statement element. At the same time, however, we should point out that the content and meaning of the statement element is in part constrained by the relevant knowledge structure and the pragmatic context. The knowledge structure element is left unspecified (i.e., < ? >) at the stage of question interpretation; this element is specified more completely when other components of the question-answering mechanism are executed.

The semantic content of a statement element consists of one or more statement nodes (Graesser, 1981a; Graesser & Goodman, 1984b; Graesser, Robertson, & Anderson, 1981). A statement node is akin to the FACT unit proposed by van Dijk (1980) in the sense that it refers to a single state, process, event, or action. A statement node is also similar to a proposition unit (Anderson & Bower, 1973; Kieras & Bovair, 1982; Kintsch, 1974; Norman & Rumelhart, 1975) in the sense that a statement node contains one predicate (e.g., verb) and a number of arguments (e.g., nouns and embedded statement nodes). Statement nodes are also similar to propositions in the sense that they are bounded by time and location indices. However, unlike propositions, sets of statement nodes are related structurally by relational arcs. Statement nodes and relational arcs are discussed in more detail in a later section. Until then, an example is presented that conveys the general flavor of how linguistic expressions are segmented into statement nodes.

Listed below is an expression and the way it would be translated into statement nodes.

After Reagan cut the budget, psychologists became depressed.

< Reagan cut budget >

↓C

< Psychologists became depressed >

There are two statement nodes in this example. The statement nodes are connected by a C arc, which refers to a Consequence relation. The psychologists became depressed *as a consequence of* Reagan cutting the budget. In the statement node *Reagan cut budget, cut* is the predicate whereas *Reagan* and *budget* are arguments. This statement node refers to an intentional action. The statement node also has time and location arguments that are left unspecified. In the statement node *psychologists became depressed,* the predicate is *depressed* whereas *psychologists* is the argument. This statement node refers to an event (i.e., a change of state), that is not intentionally achieved. Again, time and location arguments are left unspecified.

In some questions a statement element contains more than one statement node. Consider the following question.

Why were the psychologists depressed after Reagan cut the budget?

The statement element of this question contains two statement nodes: < Psychologists became depressed > and < Reagan cut the budget >. During question interpretation, the comprehender must determine which statement node is the *focus* of the query. The primary focus in the question involves the psychologists becoming depressed. Whenever the statement element has more than one statement node, the question interpreter must determine which statement node receives primary focus.

The question particle that is explicitly stated usually announces the question function that is relevant to the speech context. Thus, *WHY* would normally be the question function in the question *why did Reagan cut the budget*? However, the relevant question function is not always dictated by the explicit question particle. The relevant knowledge structures and pragmatic constraints may impart a different question function than the explicit question particle. In either case, the relevant question function is determined during question interpretation.

Selecting the Question Category.   According to the Q/A architecture in Fig. 2.1, there are a number of different question categories. Each question category has a unique symbolic procedure that specifies how the relevant world knowledge structures are to be searched for answers. Our classifying questions into different categories is compatible with Lehnert's Q/A system, which has been implemented on computer (Dyer & Lehnert, 1980; Lehnert, 1977, 1978). Lehnert identified 13 different question categories:

1. Causal antecedent (What caused the psychologists to become depressed?).
2. Goal orientation (Why did Reagan cut the budget?).
3. Enablement (What enabled the recession to occur?).

4. Causal consequent (What are the consequences of the budget cut?).
5. Verification (Did Reagan increase the military budget?).
6. Disjunctive (Is the president Republican or Democrat?).
7. Instrument/procedural (How did the people survive?).
8. Concept completion (Who shot Reagan?).
9. Expectational (Why didn't the U.S. invade Russia?).
10. Judgmental (What do you think about Reagan?).
11. Quantification (How much money are you in debt?).
12. Feature specification (What does Reagan's ranch look like?).
13. Requests (Why don't you write your Congressional representative a letter?).

Lehnert's Q/A system is very comprehensive in the sense that it handles many different questions. Moreover, the symbolic procedure of each question category has been tested by implementing the procedure on computer and observing whether the computer's answers to specific questions are intuitively plausible. However, Lehnert's Q/A procedures have not been rigorously tested on humans. Despite her lack of systematic experimental research on humans, many of her insights proved to be useful in our investigations of complex questions.

There presently is little or no research in psychology that reveals the functional question categories in humans. Consequently, we adopted a simple, but rigid, device for determining the question category. Question categories are identified on the basis of two criteria. The first criterion is the question function that is passed from the question interpreter. In this chapter we investigated seven question functions: WHY, HOW, ENABLE, CONS (i.e., what is the consequence of), WHEN, WHERE, and SIG (i.e., what is the significance of). The second criterion pertains to the node category of the statement element. Statement nodes were classified into three types: intentional actions, events, and states. Consequently, WHY < action >, WHY < event >, and WHY < state > are different question categories which have different symbolic procedures. Since there are 7 question functions and 3 statement element categories, there are 21 different question categories. Of course, the symbolic procedures of some question categories might be identical or similar. Once the 21 categories are fairly well understood, some categories might eventually be combined.

In order to select the appropriate question category, the answerer must evaluate whether the queried statement node is an action, event, or state. States are ongoing characteristics of an entity in a social world, physical world, or mind of an animate being (*the tree is tall, the woman is worried, the child believes in magic*). Events are state changes in the physical world, social world, or mind of an animate being (*the tree fell, the woman became divorced, the child forgot the song*). Actions involve an agent who does something in order to achieve a desired state or state change (*the girl slapped the sailor, the student sold his car, the child memorized songs*). Actions are always goal oriented. We discuss the action/event/state distinction further in a later section.

In order to determine whether a statement node is an action, event, or state, the comprehender often needs to consult relevant knowledge structures. Statement nodes are sometimes ambiguous with respect to the action/event/state distinction. The relevant world knowledge structure usually resolves such ambiguities. For example, *the woman was married* may be either an event or a state. In the context of a wedding, this statement node would be an event. In the context of the woman filling out her income tax forms, the statement node would be a state.

The product of selecting the appropriate question category consists of a question function (e.g., WHY, HOW) and a categorized statement node (e.g., action, event, or state). Once the appropriate question category is determined (e.g., WHY-action, WHERE-event), the symbolic procedure for that question category is applied to the relevant knowledge structures.

The symbolic procedure for a question category accomplishes two objectives. First, the symbolic procedure specifies an arc search procedure. The arc search procedure designates which relational arcs are followed when searching through a knowledge structure for an answer. Second, the symbolic procedure specifies node constraints. Nodes that are accessed by the arc search procedure must meet the node constraints if they are to be generated as answers to the question. A major goal of this chapter is to specify the symbolic procedures for different question categories.

Applying the Q/A Procedure to Relevant Knowledge Structures. Once the question category is determined, the symbolic procedure for that question category is applied to relevant knowledge structures. In order to convey some impression of how this is accomplished, we will briefly describe what knowledge structures are and then discuss how the symbolic procedures are applied to them.

As presented in Fig. 2.1, world knowledge structures correspond to generic schemas, specific passages, and specific experiences. The comprehender possesses a vast storehouse of world knowledge structures. Some knowledge structures are created when the comprehender perceives or participates in a specific activity at a specific time and place. For example, a knowledge structure was constructed when we watched the San Francisco 49ers win the Super Bowl in 1982. Similarly, a knowledge structure is created when the comprehender reads a specific passage. In contrast to these specific knowledge structures, there are generic world knowledge structures. Generic knowledge structures include schemas (Graesser, 1981a; Mandler, 1983; Rumelhart & Ortony, 1977), scripts (Abelson, 1981; Bower, Black, &

Turner, 1979; Graesser & Nakamura, 1982; Schank & Abelson, 1977), person stereotypes (Taylor & Crocker, 1981), frames (Minsky, 1975), and other generic knowledge packets that have recently been introduced in the cognitive sciences. We refer to schemas as a covering term for all of these types of generic knowledge structures. Schemas are abstractions or summaries of several specific knowledge structures. The content of a schema contains properties that are typical of the specific knowledge structures. For example, there is a schema for PLAYING FOOTBALL, which includes such actions as *throwing the football, catching the football,* and *lining up.* There is a COWBOY schema, which includes such properties as *wears a hat* and *rides horses.* The schema construct has been extensively discussed by cognitive scientists, so we need not discuss it in detail here. The important point to keep in mind is the distinction between generic knowledge structures (schemas) and specific knowledge structures that are constructed when an individual comprehends a specific experience or passage.

World knowledge structures are represented in the form of conceptual graph structures. Conceptual graph structures are described later so we will avoid an extensive discussion of them at this point. It suffices to say that a conceptual graph structure consists of a set of categorized statement nodes that are interrelated by directed, relational arcs. There are different categories of statement nodes (e.g., Goal, Physical Event, Internal State). There are different categories of arcs (e.g., Consequence, Reason, Property) and the arcs are directed (i.e., forward versus backward direction). Our proposed conceptual graph structures are similar to the structures created by Schank's Conceptual Dependency Theory (Schank, 1973, Schank & Abelson, 1977) and psychological theories that have attempted to integrate or interface text representations with world knowledge representations (de Beaugrande, 1980; Black & Bower, 1980; Nicholas & Trabasso, 1980; Trabasso et al., 1983; Warren et al., 1979).

The symbolic procedures of the question categories are applied to world knowledge structures. Stated differently, at least one knowledge structure must be accessed and used in order to apply a symbolic procedure for a question. As we discussed earlier, a question always has a question function, a statement element, and a knowledge structure element, as shown below.

Question function (<Statement element> <Knowledge structure element>)

If the question is *Why does John carry a briefcase?* and the relevant world knowledge structure is an EDUCATION schema, then the question would be represented as follows:

WHY (<John carry briefcase> <EDUCATION schema>)

The statement element is an intentional action so the symbolic procedure for a WHY-action question would be applied to the EDUCATION schema.

When individuals answer a particular question, they might access and, in fact, use more than one world knowledge structure. Our example question might also tap an EXECUTIVE schema.

WHY (< John carry briefcase > < EXECUTIVE schema >)

The answerer might also access a knowledge structure involving a personal experience; the answerer remembers watching a movie about a kidnapper carrying a briefcase with a bomb in it.

WHY (< John carry briefcase > < movie about a kidnapper >)

There are two important points to be gained here. First, a world knowledge structure must be accessed and referenced in order to answer a particular question. Second, several world knowledge structures might be accessed when a particular question is answered.

According to our proposed Q/A mechanism, the symbolic procedure for a question category contains three stages.

Stage 1: Node matching.   The statement nodes in the world knowledge structure are examined in search of a statement node that matches the statement element in the question. We will call the matching node in the world knowledge structure the *entry statement node.*

Stage 2: Arc search procedure.   A search is executed starting from the entry statement node. The arc search procedure for a question category specifies what relational arcs and paths are pursued in order to access potential answer nodes. Nodes that are accessed by the arc search procedure are called *candidate answer nodes.*

Stage 3: Checking node constraints.   The candidate answer nodes (that are accessed through the arc seaarch procedure) are evaluated as to whether they satisfy specific node constraints. In other words, a candidate answer node is not automatically produced as an answer; it is produced only if it satisfies the designated node constraints.

According to this three-stage mechanism, a statement node will be produced as an answer if and only if (a) there is a node in a world knowledge structure that matches the queried statement node, (b) the answer statement node is accessed through the arc search procedure, and (c) the answer node satisfies the node constraints of the Q/A procedure.

A simple example will now be presented in order to illustrate the operations executed when a question is answered. Suppose that the structure in Fig. 2.2

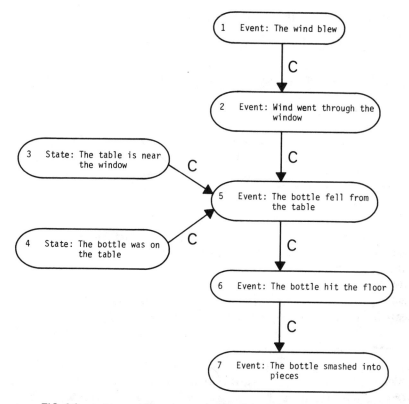

FIG. 2.2   A conceptual graph structure involving BOTTLE BREAKING.

is the relevant knowledge structure that is eventually tapped when a particular question is answered. This BOTTLE-BREAKING structure represents a specific experience that the answerer had constructed in memory sometime in the past. Suppose further that the symbolic procedure for a WHEN-event question contains the following stages.

SYMBOLIC PROCEDURE FOR A WHEN-EVENT QUESTION

1. *Node matching.*   Find an entry node in the world knowledge structure that matches the queried statement node.
2. *Arc search procedure.*   Generate nodes that radiate from the entry statement node via paths of backward consequence arcs (C).
3. *Node constraints.*   Produce as answers the candidate statement nodes generated in step 2 that are either events or actions (i.e., not the state nodes).

Consider what would occur when the following question is asked.

When did the bottle fall from the table?

The question interpreter would translate the query into the expression below.

WHEN (<bottle fall from table> < ? >)

Since *bottle fall from table* is an event, the question would be categorized as a WHEN-event question and the symbolic procedure for a WHEN-event question would be applied. Since the relevant world knowledge structure is the BOTTLE BREAKING structure, the following expression would be generated for the query.

WHEN (<bottle fall from table> <BOTTLE BREAKING
structure>)

The first stage of the WHEN-event procedure is to find an entry node in the relevant knowledge structure. The BOTTLE–BREAKING structure does contain a matching statement node, namely Event 5. The arc search procedure in stage 2 generates nodes that radiate from the entry node by paths of backward Consequence arcs. The candidate answer nodes generated from stage 2 would be Event 1, Event 2, State 3 and State 4. Event 6 and Event 7 would not be generated because they radiate from the entry node by forward Consequence arcs instead of backward Consequence arcs. According to stage 3, there are node constraints on what nodes will be produced as answers. Specifically, the answer node can be an event or action, but not a state. Since State 3 and State 4 are states, they would not be produced as answers. Event 1 and Event 2 would be the only two statement nodes in the structure that would be theoretical answers. Therefore, if the question *When did the bottle fall from the table?* were asked, the following answers would be produced.

When the wind blew.
When the wind went through the window.

The following statement nodes from the structure would not be produced as answers.

When the table was near the window.
When the bottle was on the table.
When the bottle hit the floor.
When the bottle smashed into pieces.

The node-matching stage of the Q/A procedures may not always involve exact matches, as was the case in our example. There may not be an exact match in the arguments of statement nodes that are compared. When a schema is accessed as the relevant knowledge structure, the entry node usually has an argument that is more abstract than the corresponding argument of the queried statement node. For example, consider the question *why did Reagan cut the budget?* If a NATIONAL BUDGET schema were accessed, it might contain the node *president cut budget*. *President cut budget* would be the entry node even though the *president* argument does not exactly match the *Reagan* argument in the queried node. Thus, the node match processes would involve *argument substitution* (see Graesser, 1981b). Of course, there are semantic constraints on argument substitutions.

Articulating the Answers.   A major goal of this chapter is to uncover the Q/A procedures that determine what answers are generated by questions. We are not directly concerned with the problem of how these answers are expressed in language. Nevertheless, we point out obvious trends regarding the articulation of answers to questions. A given question category produces answers with specific connectives (e.g., *because, in order to, so that*). The tense and syntax of a statement node may be transformed when an answer is articulated. A statement node may be "decomposed" in order to isolate subunits. Two or more statement nodes may be "amalgamated" in order to derive a new expression that can be expressed in language more naturally. A complete theory of question answering will obviously need to address the problem of articulation very seriously. However, it is beyond the scope of this chapter to address and solve all of the articulation problems.

Evaluating the Pragmatic Goals of the Speech Participants.   When individuals ask questions and answer questions, they are performing speech acts in a social context (Bach & Harnish, 1979; Clark, 1979; Grice, 1975; Searle, 1969). Asking and answering questions serve a variety of conversational goals. The conversational goals generally guide the course of a speech interchange in a coherent fashion. A theory of question answering must obviously address this pragmatic level of discourse. For example, a speech utterance that is articulated as a question syntactically may functionally not be a question at all. Instead, it may be a request, a gripe, or a rhetorical comment. A complete theory of question answering needs to explain when speech utterances are genuine questions rather than some other type of speech act. More generally, a theory of question answering must eventually be integrated with a theory of conversation (see Agar & Hobbs, 1982; Bruce & Newman, 1978; Cohen, Perrault, & Allen, 1982; Fetler, 1979; Fine, 1978; Freedle & Duran, 1979; Gamst, 1982; Hobbs & Robinson, 1979; Levin & Moore, 1977; Nelson & Gruendel, 1979; Robertson, Black, & Johnson, 1981; Sadock, 1974).

According to the Q/A architecture in Fig. 2.1, the pragmatic goals of the speech participants influence the other four components of the question-answering mechanism. Unfortunately, we are not ready to specify completely *how* the pragmatic goals influence the other four components. Our most informative comments will address the node constraints of the Q/A symbolic procedures. Nevertheless, we need to seriously acknowledge the importance of pragmatics in a complete theory of question answering.

It is hoped that our discussion of the Q/A architecture provides an adequate framework for understanding the subsequent sections of this chapter. The next section describes our system for representing world knowledge structures. The subsequent section reports a study in which Q/A protocols were collected from college students. The chapter eventually specifies the symbolic procedures for several question categories and assesses how well they explain the answers that the subjects gave.

CONCEPTUAL GRAPH STRUCTURES

World knowledge structures are represented as conceptual graph structures. Conceptual graph structures consist of a set of categorized statement nodes that are structurally interrelated by directed, relational arcs. In previous studies (Graesser, 1981a; 1981b; Graesser & Goodman, 1984a, 1984b; Graesser, Robertson, & Anderson, 1981) we described what conceptual graph structures are and how they are utilized in different behavioral tasks. The behavior tasks include question answering, recall, and truth verification. We have recently revised our representaton system in light of the data we have collected over the years. Our present representational system contains more statement node categories and arc categories than our earlier representational system did.

Our discussion of conceptual graph structures is divided into five parts which address the following five aspects: (1) statement nodes; (2) statement node categories; (3) arc categories and composition rules; (4) amalgamation rules; and (5) decomposition rules.

Statement Nodes. We have already discussed some of the properties of statement nodes. A statement node refers to an action, event, or a state. A statement node contains one predicate, one or more argument elements, a time index, and a location index. When the statement node is a state, the predicate ascribes properties to the argument (e.g., *the daughters are lovely, the forest is green*) or specifies how two or more arguments are conceptually related (e.g., *the tree is in the forest, the Czar has a wife*). When the statement node is an action or event, the predicate specifies (a) some information about the nature of a state change, (b) some information about the manner in which the state change occurs, and (c) the role that each argument plays in the state change. For example, consider the event *the bomb burned down the house*. During this event the house changes from the state of being erect and sturdy to the state of not being erect and sturdy. The house ends up in a collapsed state with its parts transformed to ashes. The manner in which this state change occurs involves an explosion and a fire. The bomb causes the explosion, whereas the house is the object destroyed.

We should point out that the example statement could be decomposed further to capture details of the event (see Norman & Rumelhart, 1975; Schank, 1972, 1973). However, we found that statement nodes served as a natural unit for investigating the complex questions in this chapter. Moreover, we can always develop decomposition procedures to unpack statement nodes when we need to.

Actions always contain an agent that intentionally does something that eventually causes a state change. In contrast, events may or may not be intentionally inspired. Intention is a critical dimension in our representational system. Some event sequences are driven by causal mechanisms that are not initiated, maintained, or altered by animate agents. The event sequences that occur when a person washes a car are driven by the goals and behavior of the agent. The event sequences that occur when the rain washes the car are driven by causal mechanisms rather than an agent's plan.

Statement nodes have time indices and location indices. Physical events occur at a specific time and place in the physical world. Cognitive events occur at a specific time in the mind of a specific agent. In fact, there are other indices, such as a truth value and an index that specifies who knows about or believes the statement node (see Fodor, 1981; Lewis, 1972). However, these additional indices are not discussed in this chapter because they are not critical for developing the Q/A procedures that we report.

All linguistic descriptions can be segmented and transformed into a set of statement nodes. However, we will not discuss further the issues and details regarding how the segmentation is accomplished. This information is reported elsewhere (Graesser, 1981a; Graesser & Goodman, 1984b). It is hoped the statement node unit will become sufficiently understood by the examples presented throughout this chapter.

Node Categories.   Each statement node is assigned to a node category. We believe the proposed categories impart useful distinctions for organizing world knowledge and using this knowledge during question answering. Altogether, there are 20 statement node categories. These node categories are listed in Table 2.1 along with the abbreviations for the node categories and example statement nodes.

The first 16 node categories in Table 2.1 refer to states and events. Half of these 16 node categories are ongoing states whereas the other 8 are events,

TABLE 2.1
Node Categories

Node Category	Example
General Physical State (GPS)	trees have leaves
Specific Physical State (SPS)	the tree had leaves
General Physical Event (GPE)	fires destroy trees
Specific Physical Event (SPE)	the fire destroyed the tree
General Internal State (GIS)	children believe in magic
Specific Internal State (SIS)	the child believed in magic
General Internal Event (GIE)	professors get depressed
Specific Internal Event (SIE)	the professor became depressed
General Social State (GSS)	children have mothers
Specific Social State (SSS)	the woman was the hero's mother
General Social Event (GSE)	politicians retire
Specific Social Event (SSE)	the politician retired
General Meta State (GMS)	stories have a main character
Specific Meta State (SMS)	the heroes were the main characters
General Meta Event (GME)	stories excite readers
Specific Meta Event (SME)	the story excited the child
General Goal (GG)	daughters want to be free
Specific Goal (SG)	the daughters wanted to be free
General Style (GS)	(people run) quickly
Specific Style (SS)	(the boy walked) quickly

i.e., state changes. Orthogonal to the state/event dimension is the general/specific dimension. Specific events and states refer to contextually specific occurrences and characteristics. Specific statement nodes have specific time indices, such as a specific experience on a specific day or a specific set of occurrences conveyed in a narrative passage. General statement nodes are bounded by universal time indices, spanning sets of experiences, passages, characters, objects, locations, and so forth. *Trees have leaves* is general because it refers to many trees that exist at many times and places. *The tree has leaves* is specific because it refers to a specific tree at a contextually specific time and place. Knowledge structures for narrative passages and experiences would contain predominately specific nodes. Structures for expository passages would have more general nodes.

Among the first 16 node categories, there is a third dimension that distinguishes physical, internal, social, and "meta" worlds. These worlds are not entirely mutually exclusive; a given statement node may involve two or more worlds (e.g., both physical and social). Physical nodes refer to events and states in the external, material world. We also categorize references to time as physical nodes (e.g., *X* occurred *in the morning*). Physicists would be able to measure physical events and states. Internal nodes refer to knowledge, beliefs, cognitions, sentiments, and emotions in an animate agent. Internal events include sensation and perception, i.e., an agent's mind changes from not knowing to knowing. Social nodes refer to kinship relationships, possession of objects, legal matters, and other socially significant events and states. Communication events (e.g., talking, asking, griping) are categorized as social nodes.

The meta nodes are more esoteric. Meta nodes refer to a level of knowledge that is outside of another knowledge structure. Meta nodes ascribe properties to an embedded knowledge structure. For example, consider a story passage in which a set of characters interact according to some plot sequence in a specific setting. The social, physical, and internal nodes in this plot and setting would be defined as knowledge structure KS1. Meta nodes would include pragmatic information about the storyteller's experience and the listener's experience in the speech interchange, e.g., *the story excited the listener, the storyteller likes the story*. Meta nodes also include assertions about and properties of the story structure KS1, e.g., *this information is part of the setting, the dragon is the villain in this story*. It is possible to have "meta meta" nodes. If KS2 refers to the knowledge structure involving the story-telling experience, then KS3 might include assertions about and properties of story-telling performance, i.e., *John doesn't like the way Bill told Mary the Czar story*. There may also be "meta meta meta" nodes (see Bruce & Newman, 1978), but we will not examine these levels of recursion. Meta nodes are quite satisfactory for the analyses reported in this chapter. In fact, there were very few meta nodes in the story passage structures that we analyzed.

The last four node categories in Table 2.1 are Goal and Style nodes. As with the above 16 node categories, Goal and Style nodes are either specific or general. Goal nodes refer to desired states or events that an animate agent wants to achieve (e.g., *the daughters wanted to be safe*). These Goal nodes refer to intentions. Style nodes modify events, actions, and occasionally Goals. Style nodes refer to the intensity, force, speed, and some qualitative manner in which an event or action occurs (e.g., the event occurred *quickly, gently, in circles.*). Sometimes Goal nodes are modified by Style nodes (e.g., the child wanted the ice cream *a lot*).

An observant reader may wonder where intentional *actions* fit into our categorization scheme. Actions are derived from a pair of statement nodes in our representational system. An action is an amalgamation of (a) a Goal node and (b) an Event or State node that satisfies the Goal node. For example, suppose that there is a Goal node *the heroes wanted the daughters to be safe,* an Event node *the daughters became safe,* and the heroes did something that led to the daughters' safety. Then the following action description would be derived: *the heroes saved the daughters.* We describe an action amalgamation rule later in this section.

Arc Categories and Composition Rules.   An arc specifies a relation between two nodes. There are eight categories of directed, relational arcs in our representational system. The arcs are listed in Table 2.2. For each arc category in Table 2.2, there are constraints on what node categories may be related by such an arc. We have also designated the temporal relationship between two nodes that are related by a given arc category. The node and time constraints for the arc categories are called the *rules of composition* for our conceptual graph structures.

Reason arcs relate Goal nodes. When Goal X is connected to Goal Y by a forward Reason arc, Goal Y is a motive for Goal X. For example, consider the two Goal nodes below.

Goal 1: The heroes wanted the daughters to be safe.
Goal 2: The heroes wanted to fight the dragon.

Saving the daughters is a motive for *the heroes wanting to fight*. The two nodes would be related as follows.

< Goal 2 > – – –R– – – > < Goal 1 >

The direction of the arc is not arbitrary and carries with it a number of implications. First, there is an *in order to test*. It makes sense to say the heroes fought the dragon *in order* to save the daughters, but it does not make sense to say the heroes saved the daughters in order to fight the dragon (the reader should read the Czar story in Table 2.5 in order to understand the relevant context). Second, there is a *because* test. It makes sense to say that the heroes wanted to fight the dragon *because* the heroes wanted the daughters to be safe, but not vice versa. Third, Goal 1 is hierarchically *superordinate* to Goal 2; Goal 2 is hierarchically *subordinate* to Goal 1. Fourth, Goal 2 must be achieved either *before or during* the achievement of Goal 1; Goal 1 is not achieved before Goal 2. The heroes must fight the dragon before the daughters achieve safety. In summary, there are systematic semantic/conceptual constraints that determine the direction of the Reason arc that relates the two Goal nodes.

Goal nodes and Reason arcs form the heart of goal/plan hierarchies. Many researchers have proposed that goal/plan hierarchies organize sequences of intentional actions performed by an agent (Black & Bower, 1980; Charniak, 1977; Graesser, 1978, 1981a; Lichtenstein & Brewer, 1980; Miller, Galanter, & Pribram; 1960; Newell & Simon, 1972; Rumelhart, 1977; Schank & Abelson, 1977; Schmidt, Sridharan, & Goodson, 1978; Stefik, 1981; Wilensky, 1983). One or more goal structures are created for each character in a narrative passage. In interesting narratives, the goal structures of different characters may conflict as they are enacted (Lehnert, 1981, 1982; Wilensky, 1978).

An agent's goal structure must obviously be inspired by certain events and states in the world. Goals are generated from cognitive, physiological, and

TABLE 2.2
Arc Categories and Composition Rules

Arc Category	Abbreviation	Direction and Node Constraints	Temporal Relationship
REASON	R	$\langle$Goal 1$\rangle$ $\xrightarrow{\text{R}}$ $\langle$Goal 2$\rangle$	Goal 1 is achieved *before* or at *same time* as Goal 2
INITIATE	I	$\left\{\begin{array}{l}\text{State}\\\text{Event}\\\text{Style}\end{array}\right\}$ $\xrightarrow{\text{I}}$ $\langle$Goal$\rangle$	$\left\{\begin{array}{l}\text{State}\\\text{Event}\\\text{Style}\end{array}\right\}$ *before* Goal
OUTCOME	O	$\langle$Goal$\rangle$ $\xrightarrow{\text{O}}$ $\left\{\begin{array}{l}\text{State}\\\text{Event}\end{array}\right\}$	Goal *before* $\left\{\begin{array}{l}\text{State}\\\text{Event}\end{array}\right\}$
MANNER	M	$\left\{\begin{array}{l}\text{Goal}\\\text{Event}\\\text{Style}\end{array}\right\}$ $\xrightarrow{\text{M}}$ $\left\{\begin{array}{l}\text{Style}\\\text{Event}\end{array}\right\}$	$\left\{\begin{array}{l}\text{Style}\\\text{Event}\end{array}\right\}$ *during* $\left\{\begin{array}{l}\text{Goal}\\\text{Event}\\\text{Style}\end{array}\right\}$
		$\langle$Goal 1$\rangle$ $\xrightarrow{\text{M}}$ $\langle$Goal 2$\rangle$	Goal 2 is achieved *during* the achievement of Goal 1
CONSEQUENCE	C	$\left\{\begin{array}{l}\text{Event}\\\text{State}\\\text{Style}\end{array}\right\}$ $\xrightarrow{\text{C}}$ $\left\{\begin{array}{l}\text{Event}\\\text{State}\end{array}\right\}$	$\left\{\begin{array}{l}\text{Event}\\\text{State}\\\text{Style}\end{array}\right\}$ *before* or *during* $\left\{\begin{array}{l}\text{Event}\\\text{State}\end{array}\right\}$
IMPLIES	Im	$\left\{\begin{array}{l}\text{Event 1}\\\text{State 1}\end{array}\right\}$ $\xrightarrow{\text{Im}}$ $\left\{\begin{array}{l}\text{Event 2}\\\text{State 2}\end{array}\right\}$	$\left\{\begin{array}{l}\text{Event 1}\\\text{State 1}\end{array}\right\}$ at *same time as* $\left\{\begin{array}{l}\text{Event 2}\\\text{State 2}\end{array}\right\}$
PROPERTY	P	$\left\{\begin{array}{l}\text{argument}\\\text{of node}\end{array}\right\}$ $\xrightarrow{\text{P}}$ $\langle$State$\rangle$	State exists at *same time* as the argument exists
SET MEMBERSHIP	S	$\left\{\begin{array}{l}\text{argument}\\\text{of node}\end{array}\right\}$ $\xrightarrow{\text{S}}$ $\langle$State$\rangle$	State exists at *same time* as the argument of node exists

social mechanisms (see Carbonell, 1982; Schank & Abelson, 1977). An Initiate arc connects a Goal node with an Event, State, or Style node that directly invokes the Goal, as shown in Table 2.2. The State, Event, or Style node that is connected to the Goal is called the *goal initiator*. There is a forward Initiate arc between the goal initiator and the goal. Consider the nodes below.

Event: The daughters were in danger.
Goal: The heroes wanted the daughters to be safe.

The daughters being in danger is the goal initiator for the heroes wanting the daughters to be safe. The nodes would be related as follows.

< Event > — — —I— — — > < Goal >

There are two semantic/conceptual considerations when Initiate arcs exist. First, there is the *because* test. It makes sense to say the heroes wanted the daughters to be safe *because* the daughters were in danger, but not vice versa. Second, there is a temporal relationship. The goal initiator must exist or occur before the goal is created.

Sometimes goals are achieved and sometimes goals are not achieved. The Outcome arc relates a Goal node with an Event or State that specifies whether or not the Goal node is achieved. For example, consider the statement nodes below.

Goal: The heroes wanted the daughters to be safe.
Event: The daughters became safe.

These two nodes would be related by an Outcome arc, as shown below.

< Goal > — — —O— — — > <Event >

In this example, the Event node satisfies the Goal node. If the daughters had not become safe, then the Goal would not be satisfied. The *outcome* of a Goal node is that node directly connected to the Goal node by an Outcome arc. Whenever the outcome node satisfies the Goal, the outcome node is called the *achievement node*. An intentional *action* is an amalgamation of a Goal node and its corresponding achievement node. However, actions are discussed later. There obviously are semantic/conceptual constraints on the statement nodes that are related by Outcome arcs. First, the outcome node must either satisfy or directly clash with the Goal node. Second, there is a *because* test. It makes sense to say that the daughters became safe because the heroes wanted the daughters to be safe, but not vise versa. Third, the Goal node must be created before the outcome node.

The composition rules for Manner arcs are relatively complicated. Sometimes two Goal nodes are related by a Manner arc, as shown below.

<Goal 1: The heroes wanted to fight the dragon>

$$\downarrow M$$

<Goal 2: The heroes wanted to push the dragon>

These two Goal nodes would not be related by a Reason arc because they fail to satisfy the semantic/conceptual constraints of Reason arcs. Consider the achievement of these two Goal nodes. Pushing the dragon is achieved during the course of fighting the dragon. Also, it does not make sense to say that the heroes fought the dragon *in order to* push the dragon; it does not make sense to say that the heroes pushed the dragon *in order to* fight the dragon. Pushing conveys the manner in which fighting was achieved.

There are other uses of the Manner arc. Style nodes modify Goals, achieved Goal nodes, Events, and other Style nodes by virtue of the Manner arcs. For example, *the wave violently hit the shore* would be represented by the structure below.

<Event: The wave hit the shore>

$$\downarrow M$$

<Style: The wave's hitting the shore was violent>

Style nodes are event and action modifiers. A style node is always connected to the node it modifies by a Manner arc.

Consequence arcs relate State and Event nodes in a causal manner. The notion of causality in the present context is a very weak sense of causality. Our Consequence arcs include Lehnert's Enable, Result, and Leadsto relations. A Consequence arc is used when an ongoing state enables an event, as shown below.

<State: The tree was in the forest>

$$\downarrow C$$

<Event: The daughters saw the tree>

A Consequence arc is used when one event directly causes or indirectly leads to another event, as shown below.

<Event: The daughters forgot the time>

$$\downarrow C$$

<Event: The daughters stayed too late>

The Consequence arc is used when a state results from another event or state, as shown below.

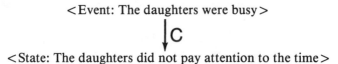

The direction of the Consequence arc has semantic/conceptual implications. First, there is the *because* test. It makes sense to say that the daughters did not pay attention to the time *because* they were busy, but not vice versa. Second, the daughters being busy must occur *before* they failed to pay attention to the time. Whenever Event/State 1 is linked to Event/State 2 by a forward Consequence arc, Event/State 1 is called an antecedent node of Event/State 2. We should point out again that Consequence arcs do not presuppose strict causality in the sense that an event is a necessary and sufficient cause of another event. Human conceptualizations are not that rigid and rigorous.

Event and State nodes may also be related by an Implies arc. One Event/State may logically imply another Event/State, as shown below.

<State: The daughters were in the forest>

$\downarrow$ Im

<State: The daughters were not in the palace>

When nodes are related by an Implies arc, both nodes occur or exist at the same time. The daughters were in the forest at the same time that they were not in the palace. The direction of the Implies arc is not always arbitrary. It makes sense to say that the daughters were not in the palace *because* they were in the forest; it does not make sense to say that the daughters were in the forest *because* they were not in the palace (they could have been by the fountain outside).

Property arcs occur when a State node ascribes a characteristic to an argument of another node. For example, consider the nodes below.

<State: The Czar had daughters>

$\downarrow$ P

<State: The daughters were lovely>

The *daughters* argument of the *Czar had daughters* node is modified by the other node, *the daughters were lovely*. Whenever two nodes are connected by a Property arc, at least one argument of each node must overlap. Kintsch and van Dijk (1978) have proposed that this argument overlap constraint is an important principle for text cohesion. Of course, there are other critical factors that contribute to text cohesion, such as causal connectivity in event sequences (Abbot & Black, 1982; Black & Bern, 1981; Haberlandt & Bingham, 1978; Reiser & Black, 1983; Trabasso, Secco, & van den Broek, 1983). Property arcs are prevalent in the expository passages that psychologists have analyzed in the recent past (Kieras, 1981; Kinsch & van Dijk, 1978; Meyer, 1975). When two nodes are related by a Property arc, they exist simultaneously.

Set Membership arcs occur when an argument of a node represents a class of animate agents, objects, locations, or concepts. For example, consider the nodes below.

<Goal: The heroes wanted to use weapons>

S   S

<State: Weapons include swords>   <State: Weapons include guns>

There is a "set membership amalgamation rule" which derives expressions from pairs of nodes that are connected by a set membership arc. We describe this rule later in this chapter. The set membership amalgamation rule would generate the following expression from the above structure.

The heroes wanted to use swords.
The heroes wanted to use guns.

We have described all of the arc categories and the composition rules for constructing conceptual graph structures. We are ready to present a conceptual graph structure with several nodes and arcs. Figures 2.3 and 2.4 show two subgraphs from the story *The Czar and His Daughters* (see Table 2.5).

The conceptual graph structure in Figure 2.3 is a cause-driven structure. Cause-driven structures contain events and states that unfold over time in a causal manner and are driven by mechanisms that exist in nature, technology, or the mental world of an animate being. Stated differently, the event/state chains are not always goal-driven. Cause-driven structures have a high proportion of Consequence arcs. There is an event chain in Figure 2.3, namely nodes 1, 2, and 4. Nodes 5, 6, and 7 are enabling states that allow the event chain to unfold.

The conceptual graph structure in Fig. 2.4 is a goal-driven structure. Just as in Fig. 2.3, there is an event chain shown in Fig 2.4: <node 8>--C--> <node 9> --C--> <node 6> --Im--> <node 3>. Unlike in Fig 2.3, however, this event chain is driven by a goal hierarchy

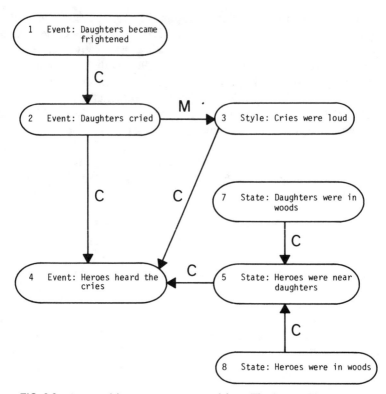

FIG. 2.3   A cause-driven structure extracted from *The Czar and his Daughters.*

(nodes 2, 5, and 7). Node 2 (*heroes wanted the daughters to be safe*) is the most superordinate Goal and Node 7 (*heroes want to fight dragon*) is the most subordinate Goal. This goal hierarchy is invoked by the goal initiator nodes 1 and 4. Goal-driven structures tend to have many Reason, Initiate, and Outcome arcs.

Amalgamation Rules.   Amalgamation rules systematically generate additional statements when they are applied to a conceptual graph structure. These new statements are normally derived from a pair of statement nodes in the structure. There are three amalgamation rules that were frequently applied in our story passages: (1) an action amalgamation rule; (2) a causal amalgamation rule; and (3) a set membership amalgamation rule. These derived nodes were not usually included in the conceptual graph structures. However, they were always available when needed.

The action amalgamation rule is presented in Table 2.3. The action amalgamation rule derives an action statement from (a) a Goal node and (b) an achievement node that is linked directly to the Goal node by an Outcome arc. Certain conditions must be met in order to apply an action amalgamation

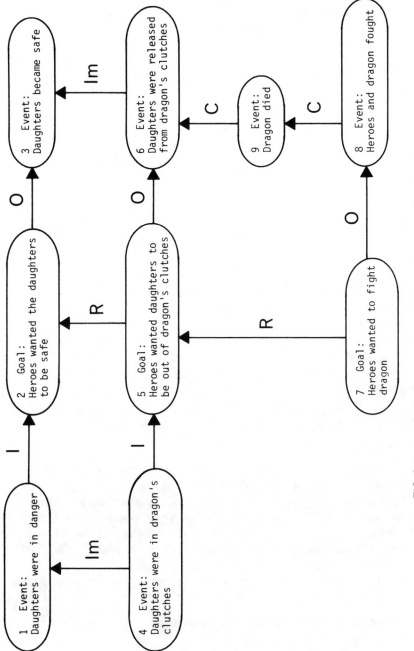

FIG. 2.4   A goal-driven structure extracted from *The Czar and his Daughters.*

TABLE 2.3
Action Amalgamation Rule: Converting an Achieved Goal to an
Action Statement

(1) IF	(a)	Agent has Goal X &
	(b)	There is a node Y directly emanating from Goal X via a forward Outcome arc &
	(c)	Node Y satisfies Goal X &
	(d)	The agent invokes a set of subordinate Goals that are achieved &
	(e)	The outcomes of the agent's subordinate Goals causally leads to node Y
THEN	[Agent cause Y]	
(2) IF	(a)	Agent cause Y &
	(b)	There is a verb that naturally captures the expression in 2a in the form of an action
THEN	[Use the action verb in 2b]	

rule. One condition (1c) is that the outcome node must satisfy the Goal node. Another condition (1d and 1e) is that the agent of the Goal must do something that causally leads to the outcome node. Thus, it is not sufficient for the agent to sit and wait for the world to generate the desired outcome. When the action amalgamation rule is applied to Fig. 2.4, the following action statements are produced.

The heroes saved the daughters.
The heroes got the daughters out of the dragon's clutches.
The heroes fought the dragon.

We should note that the subordinate goals and outcomes (1d and 1e) are implicit when deriving *the heroes fought the dragon*.

The causal amalgamation creates additional causal statements from causal event/state chains. The causal amalgamation rule is presented in Table 2.4. The derived causal statement may capture information in a pair of adjacent nodes. Alternatively, the causal statements capture the beginning and ending nodes of a causal chain.

For example, the following statements are causal statements derived from Fig. 2.3.

The daughters being frightened made them cry.
Fright made the daughters cry.
The heroes being in the woods caused them to be near the daughters.

The following statements are some of the causal statement nodes derived from Fig 2.4.

The heroes killed the dragon.
Fighting killed the dragon.
The fight caused the dragon to die.
The fight saved the daughters.
The daughters being in the dragon's clutches endangered them.

Still other causal statement nodes could be derived from structures in Figs. 2.3 and 2.4. Causal statements sometimes serve as summaries of a long chain of actions, events, and states. The derived causal statement might capture information from the first and last node of a chain. In this sense, causal statements provide an abstraction of a causal chain.

The set membership amalgamation rule does not require much discussion. In fact, our earlier discussion of this rule is quite satisfactory. Consider the node structure below.

TABLE 2.4
Causal Amalgamation Rule: Abstracting a Causal Statement
from a Consequence Chain

(1) IF
    (a) There exists a causally driven chain of Action/Event/ State nodes: Action/Event/State X1, Action/Event/ State X2, . . . Action/Event/State Xn &

    (b) The subject argument of Action/Event/State X1 is a plausible cause of Action/Event/State Xn OR

    (c) Action/Event/State X1 is a plausible cause of Action/Event/State Xn

THEN
    (the subject of) Action/Event/State X1 cause Action/Event/State Xn

(2) IF
    (a) (the subject of) Action/Event/State X1 cause Action/Event/State Xn &
    (b) There is a verb that naturally captures the causal expression

THEN
    Use the causal verb

(3) IF
    (a) Action/Event/State X1 cause Action/Event/State Xn &
    (b) There is a noun that naturally captures Action/Event/ State X1

THEN
    Use the noun that captures Action/Event/State X1

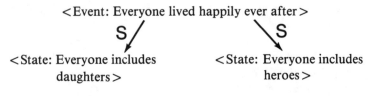

The following statements would be derived from this structure when the set membership amalgamation rule is applied.

The daughters lived happily ever after.
The heroes lived happily ever after.

The three amalgamation rules we have introduced hardly exhaust the set of possible amalgamation rules. These are simply the three rules that were frequently applied to the stories we have analyzed. There are more global amalgamation rules that derive statements from complex configurations of nodes. For example, consider the statement, *there was a conflict between the daughters and the dragon*. This statement would be derived from (a) a Goal structure associated with the daughters, (b) a Goal structure associated with the dragon, and (c) incompatibilities between these two structures. Lehnert (1982) has analyzed plot structures and how abstract summary statements can be derived from complex configurations of goal structures that motivate actions of different story characters. Such analyses present a fruitful direction for future research, but are beyond the scope of the present chapter.

Decomposition Rules. The statement nodes may be decomposed when certain elements or features from a node are needed. Decomposition rules specify how nodes are unpacked when certain information from the nodes is sought. For example, the agent of an action statement or the location of an event may be required for particular symbolic procedure to be executed. Case structure grammars and computational theories in artificial intelligence (Lehnert, 1978; Schank, 1972, 1973), psychology (Gentner, 1981; Norman & Rumelhart, 1975), and linguistics (Fillmore, 1968) would provide useful guides for specifying detailed decomposition rules. However, we do not emphasize this level of analysis in this chapter.

There was one type of decomposition rule that we frequently needed in our analysis of story passages. Sometimes we needed to evaluate whether there was any overlap in arguments from two nodes. Isolating argument elements from statement nodes is a relatively straightforward decomposition rule. There were other occasions in which statement node arguments were extracted and evaluated. Time and location indices were extracted in our analyses of WHEN and WHERE questions.

Statement nodes could be decomposed in more complex ways. For example, the semantic/conceptual properties of the predicate (e.g., verb) were analyzed when assessing some node constraints in the Q/A procedures. When assessing whether statement node X is relevant to statement node Y, the predicate of Y is critical for assessing relevance. The predicate would be decomposed into its semantic/conceptual properties in order to assess relevance.

DATA COLLECTION AND PRELIMINARY ANALYSES

Data Collection.   Question-answering protocols were collected for two story passages, *The Czar and His Daughters* and *The Ant and the Dove*. These passages are presented in Table 2.5. College students read these passages and later answered a number of questions about them. There were 14 groups of subjects, with 8 subjects assigned to each group. Half of the subjects read and answered questions about *The Czar and His Daughters,* whereas the other half received *The Ant and the Dove*. Among the 7 groups assigned to each passage, one group was assigned to each of the question types we investigated: WHY, HOW, WHEN, WHERE, ENABLE, CONS (i.e., what is the consequence of), and SIG (i.e., what is the significance of).

The subjects received a booklet with two sections. The first section contained the story passage. The second section contained a list of questions. The subjects first read the passage and then answered the questions. For each question, there were four lines available for subjects to write down their answers. Subjects were instructed to fill up all four lines for each question. Thus, subjects were encouraged to give detailed answers.

TABLE 2.5
The Czar and His Daughters

Once there was a Czar who had three lovely daughters. One day, the three daughters went walking in the woods. They were enjoying themselves so much that they forgot the time and stayed too long. A dragon kidnapped the three daughters. As they were being dragged off they called for help. Three heroes heard the cries and set off to rescue the daughters. The heroes came and fought the dragon and rescued the maidens. Then the heroes returned the daughters to their palace. When the Czar heard of the rescue, he rewarded the heroes.

The Ant and the Dove

A thirsty ant went to a river. He became carried away by the rush of the stream and was about to drown. A dove was sitting in the tree overhanging the water. The dove plucked a leaf and let it fall. The leaf fell into the stream close to the ant and the ant climbed onto it. The ant floated safely to the bank. Shortly afterwards, a birdcatcher came and laid a trap in the tree. The ant saw his plan and stung him on the foot. In pain the birdcatcher threw down his trap. The noise made the bird fly away.

The selection and preparation of the questions were straightforward. Each passage was segmented into statement units, i.e., an action, event, or state description. Each explicit statement in the passage was transformed into a question. For example, one explicit statement in the Czar story was *the dragon kidnapped the daughters.* This statement would be transformed into the following questions: *Why did the dragon kidnap the daughters? How did the dragon kidnap the daughters? What enabled the dragon to kidnap the daughters? What was the consequence of the dragon kidnapping the daughters? When did the dragon kidnap the daughters? Where did the dragon kidnap the daughters?* and *What is the significance of the dragon kidnapping the daughters?* A particular group of subjects received only one question type (e.g., WHY); all explicit statements in the passage were queried with the assigned question type. When considering all groups of subjects, each explicit statement was queried with all seven types of questions.

Coding the Question–Answering (Q/A) Protocols. A list of answers was prepared for each specific question. A specific question is defined as a particular queried statement (e.g., *the dragon kidnapped the daughters*) that is queried with a particular type of question (e.g., WHY). Hence, *Why did the dragon kidnap the daughters?* is a specific question. There were eight answer protocols to analyze for each specific question, one protocol for each subject. The answer protocols were segmented into statement node units. A list of answer statements was then prepared. Associated with each answer statement was a frequency score reflecting the number of subjects (out of eight) who produced the answer in the Q/A protocols.

Table 2.6 provides an example of the way we coded the answers for a specific question. There were seven answers that the eight subjects gave to *Why did the dragon kidnap the daughters?* The first two answers in Table 2.6 were given by four subjects whereas the other five answers were given by two sub-

TABLE 2.6
Answers Given to *Why Did the Dragon Kidnap the Daughters?*

Distinct Answer Statement	Frequency
(1) The dragon wanted to eat the daughters	4
(2) Dragons like to kidnap people	4
(3) The dragon was hungry	2
(4) The dragon was lonely	2
(5) The dragon wanted to hurt the Czar	2
(6) The daughters stayed in the forest too long	2
(7) The dragon wanted to keep the daughters	2

jects. An observant reader may have noticed that there are no answers that had a frequency of 1. This is not an accidental outcome. We eliminated all answers to a specific question that were emitted by only one subject. This criterion eliminates bizarre, cute, and off-the-wall answers. We wanted to isolate the serious answers that a person would typically produce. The listing in Table 2.6 is the answer distribution for a specific question.

The scorers of the Q/A protocols obviously had to make semantic/conceptual judgments when they coded the protocols. The scorers had to decide how to segment the verbal descriptions into statement units. The scorers had to determine when statements from two or more protocols overlapped in meaning sufficiently to count them as the answer. The scorers had to decide on how to articulate each statement node when an answer distribution was prepared for a specific question. A college student who is moderately trained in our representation system can perform these analyses (see Graesser, 1981a, for a discussion of scoring and interjudge reliability).

An answer distribution was prepared for each specific question. The average question elicited six answers. There were some differences among the question types. For example, HOW questions elicited roughly seven answers whereas SIG questions elicited roughly four answers. On the average, a specific answer was given by 38% of the subjects, i.e., three out of eight subjects. Most of the answers (86%) were inferences derived from the stories as opposed to verbatim passage statements.

List of Distinct Statements.   We prepared a list of distinct statements for each passage. Each list included (a) the set of statements that were explicitly mentioned in the passage and (b) the set of distinct inferences that came from the answer distributions of *all* specific questions. Thus, the inferences were empirically generated from the Q/A protocols. A distinct statement was often elicited as an answer to more than one specific question. In fact, 64% of the distinct statements were produced as answers to two or more specific questions; 36% of the distinct statements were produced as answers to only one specific question. In other words, there was a substantial amount of overlap in the answers elicited from different specific questions.

Preparing the Passage Structures.   The conceptual graph structure for each passage was constructed containing information about all of the distinct statements previously described. The conceptual graph structures therefore contained a large number of inference nodes. When preparing the conceptual graph structures, we followed the analytical procedures discussed earlier in this chapter. First we translated the list of distinct statements to statement nodes. Second, we assigned each statement node to a node category (see Table 2.1). Third, we interrelated the statement nodes by relational arcs (see Table 2.2).

The conceptual graph structures for each passage had literally hundreds of statement nodes. The Czar story had 401 statement nodes whereas the Ant and Dove story had 427 statement nodes. Of the 828 statement nodes in the two stories, 26% were Goals, 6% were Style nodes, 34% were State nodes, and 34% were Event nodes. Nearly all of the statement nodes were in the Specific categories (98%) as opposed to the General node categories. The fact that the structures had very few General nodes was expected because stories involve actions and events unfolding at a specific time and location. Expository passages would have more General nodes. Among the State and Event nodes, 73% were Physical, 17% were Internal, 9% were Social, and 1% were Meta nodes. The distribution of nodes among the statement node categories was very similar for the two stories.

The conceptual graph structures for each passage had hundreds of arcs. There were 642 arcs in the Czar story and 577 arcs in the Ant and Dove story. The distribution of arcs among the eight arc categories was very similar for the two stories. Of the 1219 arcs, 14% were Reason arcs, 9% were Initiate arcs, 14% were Outcome arcs, 7% were Manner arcs, 31% were Consequence arcs, 15% were Implies arcs, 9% were Property arcs, and 1% were Set Membership arcs.

We computed the number of arcs directly radiating from a node in either the forward or backward direction. An average node in the Czar story had 3.2 arcs directly radiating from it, whereas the Ant and Dove story had 2.7 arcs. When the two stories were combined, an average node had 2.9 radiating arcs. It follows that an average node is directly connected to 2.9 nodes. Number of radiating arcs serves as a measure of node centrality. A very central node would have many arcs directly radiating from it. A dead end node would have only one arc directly radiating from it and would have low centrality. The centrality of a node varied from 1 to 21 among the 828 nodes. State nodes and Style nodes had relatively low centrality, with means of 1.9 and 1.6, respectively. Goals and Events had higher centrality, with means of 4.1 and 3.3, respectively. Hence, Goal and Event nodes are more central structurally than State and Style nodes. This finding supports some conclusions that other researchers have reported (Lehnert et al., 1983; Seifert, Robertson, & Black, 1982).

Discovering Symbolic Procedures of Question Answering.   A Q/A symbolic procedure operates on the conceptual graph structure for a passage. The next section describes in detail the Q/A procedures for different categories of questions. Before we discuss these Q/A procedures, however, we should say a few words about how we discovered them.

In an earlier section, we proposed that a Q/A procedure has three stages: a node-matching stage, an arc search procedure stage, and a stage that checks the node restrictions. The node-matching stage is relatively trivial. The conceptual graph structure is examined in order to find a statement node that matches the queried statement. Assuming that a match is found, the matching node in the conceptual graph structure is the entry statement node. The arc search procedure (stage 2) and the checking of node restrictions (stage 3) are far more complex.

How would we discover the arc search procedure for a specific question category, such as a WHY-event question? The method we adopted is to examine the shortest path of arcs between a queried statement (i.e., the entry statement node) and an obtained answer. We will call this the "shortest path analysis." For example, suppose that the structure in Fig. 2.3 was the relevant knowledge structure and the question was *Why did the heroes hear the cries?* Suppose further that one of the answers was *because the daughters cried.* Node 4 is the entry statement node and Node 2 is the answer node. The shortest path involves one arc, a backward Consequence arc when going from the entry node to the answer node. There is another path that involves two arcs, a backward Consequence arc and a backward Manner arc (e.g., $\overleftarrow{CM}$). Since this second path has more arcs than the first path, we would adopt the first as the shortest path and ignore the second path. For each obtained answer to a specific question, we isolated the shortest path. We then performed analyses on the set of shortest paths that exist when considering all of the answers for a question category.

After we isolated the set of shortest paths for a question category, we prepared a frequency distribution for the arc categories (segregating arc directions). In other words, we examined what arc categories are traversed when moving along the shortest paths. For WHY-event questions, 197 arcs were traversed when examining the shortest paths. The arc distribution analysis revealed that 84% of these arcs were backward Consequence arcs ($\overleftarrow{C}$), 5% were backward Implies arcs ($\overleftarrow{Im}$), 5% were forward Property arcs ($\overrightarrow{P}$), 4% were backward Reason arcs ($\overleftarrow{R}$), and 2% were forward Reason arcs ($\overrightarrow{R}$). There were no arcs in the other arc categories. One would conclude, therefore, that the backward Consequence arcs are pursued in the arc search procedures of WHY-event questions. Backward Consequence arcs access causal antecedents to the entry statement node.

The shortest path analyses provided the critical clues for discovering the arc search procedures. However, the final arc search procedure for a question category was not based entirely on the analyses of shortest paths. In some instances, the shortest path involved a strange combination of arcs; a longer path would provide a more systematic route. The shortest path analyses merely provided critical clues. These clues directed our hypotheses as to what was the most plausible and elegant arc search procedure for a question category.

How would we discover the node restrictions for the symbolic procedures of a particular question category? Our discovery of the node restrictions involved two steps. In the first step, we generated all answer nodes that would be accessed by the arc search procedure for a specific question. This set of nodes is called the set of candidate answer nodes. For example, suppose that we adopted the following arc search procedure for WHY-event questions.

Generate nodes that radiate from the entry statement node via paths of backward Consequence ($\overline{C}$) arcs.

If we applied this arc search procedure to the question *Why did the heroes hear the cries?* then all of the nodes in Fig. 2.3 would be generated as candidate answer nodes. If we applied this arc search procedure to the question *Why did the daughters cry?* then only one node (Node 1) would be generated as a candidate answer node. For each specific question, there is a set of candidate answer nodes that would be generated by the arc search procedure.

In the second step of discovering node restrictions, we examined the candidate answers and intuitively judged which of the candidate answers would be plausible answers to the question. Consider the following candidate answers for *Why did the heroes hear the cries?*

because the daughters became frightened (Node 1)
because the daughters cried (Node 2)
because the cries were loud (Node 3)
because the heroes were near the daughters (Node 5)
because the daughters were in the woods (Node 7)
because the heroes were in the woods (Node 6)

Most of these candidate answers are plausible answers to the specific question. Node 1 seems suspect, however. Why is Node 1 a funny answer? By inspecting which candidates are good answers and which are bad answers, we could eventually induce general principles that could serve as node restrictions.

The Status of Inferred Statement Nodes.   Two working assumptions that we have adopted are (1) Q/A symbolic procedures operate on world knowledge structures and (2) there is one large passage structure that serves as the relevant knowledge structure when passage statements are questioned. Moreover, we have reported that the lion's share of the statement nodes in a passage structure consists of inferences.

The status of the inferences has concerned some of our colleagues who have followed our work. For example, there is the question of whether the inferences were made during comprehension or whether they were derived only at the time of questioning (see Chaffin, 1979; Dunay, Balzer, & Yekovich, 1981; McKoon & Ratcliff, 1981; Singer, 1980). There is the issue of whether the act of answering a question modifies the passage structure (Granger, 1982; Lehnert et al., 1983; Loftus, 1979).

If the inferences were derived only at questioning, then perhaps it is inappropriate to assume that there is only one relevant knowledge structure that represents the passage. Instead, there may be several relevant knowledge structures: (1) a passage structure that contains a relatively small number of inferences and (2) several generic schema structures that are relevant to the passage structure. Hence, the relevant schemas may be accessed during question answering and serve as relevant world knowledge structures for the Q/A procedures to operate on.

The above concerns of our colleagues are important issues that a theory of question answering should eventually address. However, we do not believe that these issues *must be* entirely resolved at this stage of the enterprise. From our perspective, these issues are interesting but do not seriously undermine the usefulness of our working assumptions and the validity of our project. It is informative to consider the alternatives. Suppose that all of the inferences were made during passage comprehension. If this is a valid claim, then our working assumption (that there is a single passage structure) would be appropriate; our Q/A symbolic procedures would be more or less complete. Suppose, alternatively, that many of the inferences were made at question answering but not during passage comprehension. If this alternative is correct, the Q/A symbolic procedures would operate on generic schemas in addition to the passage structure. However, while the Q/A procedures operate on the generic schemas, the passage structure would need to be continuously consulted in order to ensure that the accessed generic nodes are relevant to the passage. Our working assumption of there being one relevant knowledge structure would be incorrect. However, our Q/A procedures would not be entirely useless and invalid. Our Q/A procedures would probably operate on schema structures in the same way (or a very similar way) that they operate on passage structures. The Q/A procedures could be naturally expanded by adding on a stage that assesses whether an accessed schema node is compatible with the passage content.

According to a third alternative, generic schemas embellish the passage structure during question answering and create additional inferences. This embellishment process occurs before the Q/A symbolic procedures are applied to the passage structure. If this third alternative is correct, then our notion of a single passage structure would be a plausible working assumption and our Q/A symbolic procedures would be complete (more or less). Of course, we would need to specify that a "passage structure embellishment" stage is executed before the Q/A symbolic procedures are applied to a revised passage structure.

In summary, the above alternative possibilities support two general conclusions. First, our Q/A symbolic procedures are theoretically useful and plausible processes if either all or only some of the inferences are made at comprehension. Second, it is not necessary to resolve the question of when inferences are made (i.e., at comprehension versus at question answering) before we can explore the symbolic procedures of question answering.

SYMBOLIC PROCEDURES FOR FOURTEEN QUESTION CATEGORIES

In this section, we present Q/A procedures for 14 question categories, altogether. There are separate Q/A procedures for queried actions and queried events. Orthogonal to the action/event distinction are the seven question functions: WHY, HOW, ENABLE, CONS (i.e., what is the consequence of), WHEN, WHERE, and SIG (i.e., what is the significance of). We did not analyze Q/A procedures for State nodes because the stories did not have enough explicit State nodes to warrant such an analysis.

Our discussion of the Q/A procedures covers both theory and data. When we present evidence for a Q/A procedure, both the power and sufficiency of the procedure are evaluated. A very sufficient and powerful Q/A procedure would generate all of the obtained answers to a question, and only the obtained answers to the question. There would be a perfect match between theoretical answers and obtained answers. Alternatively, a Q/A procedure could be very sufficient but not very powerful. Such a procedure would theoretically generate all of the obtained answers to the question, but there would be many theoretical answers that were not obtained from that question. The worst of all possible worlds is a Q/A procedure that is insufficient and lacks power. Such a procedure would not theoretically generate the answers that were in fact obtained.

Among the two passages, we examined 10 events and 16 actions. The events and actions are listed in Table 2.7. The list in Table 2.7 does not include all of the explicit statement nodes in the passages. Specifically, the list does not include State nodes, Style nodes, and nodes that were ambiguous with respect to the event/action distinction, i.e., *the daughters cried, the daughters enjoyed themselves, the birdcatcher threw down the trap*. The latter nodes possess both a goal-driven and a cause-driven aspect. For example, the daughters may have intentionally cried in order to draw somebody's attention; alternatively, the cries may have been elicited involuntarily. In order to isolate and distinguish the Q/A procedures for actions versus events, we needed to focus on unambiguous statement nodes.

Path Specifications for Arc Search Procedures.   Each Q/A procedure contains an arc search procedure which specifies the categories of arcs that are followed when candidate nodes are generated. For most question catego-

TABLE 2.7
Actions and Events that were Analyzed

Events

The daughters forgot the time
The daughters stayed in the forest too long
The heroes heard the cries
The Czar heard about the rescue
The stream carried the ant away
The ant was about to drown
The leaf fell into the stream
The ant floated to shore
The ant saw the birdcatcher's plan
The noise made the bird fly away

Actions

The daughters went walking in the woods
The dragon kidnapped the daughters
The dragon dragged off the daughters
The heroes went to the dragon
The heroes rescued the daughters
The heroes fought the dragon
The heroes returned the daughters to the palace
The Czar rewarded the heroes
The ant went to the river
The dove plucked the leaf
The dove let the leaf fall
The ant climbed onto the leaf
The birdcatcher came
The birdcatcher laid a trap
The birdcatcher put the trap in the tree
The ant stung the birdcatcher

ries, there are several levels (or layers) of candidate answer nodes that radiate from the entry statement node. Moreover, most layers of candidate answer nodes involve paths that are computationally equivalent in different question categories. For example, the arc categories that are followed in *causal antecedent* paths are identical in all Q/A procedures that specify causal antecedent paths.

Table 2.8 defines the paths that are specified in the arc search procedures of the 14 question categories. There are nine types of paths, altogether. *Causal antecedent* paths include nodes that exist or occur prior to a specified node (e.g., the entry node), whereas *causal consequence* paths include nodes that exist or occur subsequent to a specified node. The causal consequence path is the inverse of the causal antecedent path. Paths of *superordinate* goals radiate from a goal node by way of forward Reason arcs ($\overrightarrow{R}$), whereas paths of *subordinate goals* radiate from a goal node by way of backward

TABLE 2.8
Path Specifications for Arc Search Procedures

Causal Antecedents

General candidate answer nodes that radiate from node X via paths of { $\overleftarrow{C}$ | $\overleftarrow{O}$ | $\overleftarrow{Im}$ | $\overrightarrow{Im}$ | $\overleftarrow{OI}$ } arcs.

Causal Consequences

Generate candidate answer nodes that radiate from node X via paths of { $\overrightarrow{C}$ | $\overrightarrow{O}$ | $\overrightarrow{Im}$ | $\overleftarrow{Im}$ | $\overrightarrow{IO}$ } arcs.

Superordinate Goals

Generate candidate answer nodes that radiate from Goal node X via paths of $\overrightarrow{R}$ arcs.

Subordinate Goals

Generate candidate answer nodes that radiate from Goal node X via paths of { $\overleftarrow{R}$ | $\overrightarrow{M}$ } arcs.

Subsequent Goal

Generate candidate answer node that is connected to node X via the $\overrightarrow{I}$ arc.

Goal Initiator

Generate candidate answer node that is connected to node X via the $\overleftarrow{I}$ arc.

Style Specification

Generate candidate answer nodes that radiate from node X via paths of $\overrightarrow{M}$ arcs.

Time Indices/Location Indices

Generate candidate answer nodes that radiate from node X via paths of $\overrightarrow{P}$ arcs.

Embellishment of Location Indices

Generate candidate answer nodes that radiate from node X via paths of { $\overrightarrow{Im}$ | $\overleftarrow{Im}$ | $\overrightarrow{P}$ | $\overleftarrow{P}$ } arcs.

Reason arcs ($\overleftarrow{R}$) and forward Manner arcs ($\overrightarrow{M}$). The other paths in Table 2.8 are *subsequent goal, goal initiator, style specification, time or location indices,* and *embellishment of location indices.* The last five paths in Table 2.8 are relatively short (often only one arc) compared to the first four paths.

The paths in Table 2.8 specify both the categories of arcs and the direction of the arcs. For example, the causal antecedent paths include all statement nodes that are encountered when traversing arcs and combinations of arcs in the following categories: backward Consequence ($\overleftarrow{C}$), backward Outcome ($\overleftarrow{O}$), backward Implies ($\overleftarrow{Im}$), forward Implies ($\overrightarrow{Im}$), and the $\overleftarrow{OI}$ arc combination (i.e., a backward Outcome arc and then a backward Initiate arc). Legitimate paths can contain any ordering of these directed arc categories. For example, the arc paths below are legitimate. (The candidate answer node would be positioned on the right in these paths, whereas the entry node would be on the left.)

$\overline{\text{CCCC}}$

$\overline{\text{CIm}}$ $\overrightarrow{\text{Im}}$ $\overline{\text{C}}$

$\overline{\text{COIC}}$ $\overrightarrow{\text{Im}}$

$\overrightarrow{\text{Im}}$ $\overleftarrow{\text{Im}}$

The Arc paths below would not be legal.

$\overleftarrow{\text{CC}}$ $\overleftarrow{\text{C}}$

$\overrightarrow{\text{P}}$ $\overleftarrow{\text{CC}}$

$\overline{\text{C}}$ $\overrightarrow{\text{Im}}$ $\overrightarrow{\text{I}}$ $\overrightarrow{\text{R}}$

$\overline{\text{C}}$ $\overrightarrow{\text{IO}}$

We should emphasize again that both the arc category and the arc direction must be considered when isolating legal paths.

Causal antecedent paths are incorporated in the arc search procedures of many question categories. The generated candidate answers include events, states, and actions that occur prior to (and at the same time as) a particular event. We should point out the temporal relationships for the arc categories in Table 2.2. According to the temporal relationships in Table 2.2, the directed arc categories of causal antecedent paths always generate nodes that are temporally prior to the designated event, but never subsequent to the designated event. All of the arcs of a causal antecedent path are in the backward direction, except for the Implies arc. Forward Implies arcs are legitimate because two nodes occur or exist at the same time if they are connected by an Implies arc.

Node Restrictions.   Each Q/A procedure has an arc search procedure that generates candidate answer nodes. Only a subset of these candidate answers are theoretical answers to a question. Many of the candidate answers are not theoretical answers because they fail to meet the node restrictions of the Q/A procedure.

Table 2.9 lists and describes the node restrictions that we identified when we analyzed the 14 question categories. As we mentioned earlier in this chapter, we discovered these node restrictions inductively. They appeared to be important for achieving a close match between obtained answers and theoretical answers to specific questions. We cannot strongly defend the validity of these node restrictions. They should be construed as potential restrictions that need to be verified and probably modified in future research.

Most of the node restrictions in Table 2.9 are self explanatory. According to node restriction A, the candidate answer node is a verbatim node. Accord-

TABLE 2.9
Node Restrictions

(A)	*Verbatim node.* The candidate answer node was explicitly mentioned in the passage.
(B)	*Argument overlap with entry node.* The candidate answer node has at least one argument that matches an argument in the entry node.
(C)	*Argument overlap with another candidate node.* The candidate answer node has at least one argument that matches an argument in another candidate node which is specified in the Q/A procedure.
(D)	*Predicate relevance.* The candidate answer node is relevant to the entry node.
(E)	*Event node.* The candidate answer node is an event.
(F)	*Node is not an ongoing state.* The candidate answer node is not an ongoing state that exists throughout the setting and plot.
(G)	*Node is a continuing state.* The candidate answer node is a state that continues to exist after the entry statement node is achieved in the story.
(H)	*Node is not an enabling state.* The candidate answer node is not a state that enables an event in the story.
(I)	*Node is not a general node.* The candidate answer node is not a general node.
(J)	*Meta node.* The candidate answer node is a meta node.
(K)	*Node is not a prior event.* If the candidate answer node is an event, it does not occur prior to the entry node in the story.
(L)	*Node occurs during story plot.* The candidate answer node occurred during the story plot rather than the setting.
(M)	*Time frame.* The candidate answer node is in the same time frame as the entry node.
(N)	*Time index.* The candidate answer node is a time index that marks the time when another event or action occurred.
(P)	*Location or direction index.* The candidate answer node is an index for the location or direction in which another node occurs or exists.
(Q)	*Important style node.* The candidate answer node is a style node which is important for the entry node to occur.
(S)	*Different concrete argument.* The candidate answer node contains a concrete argument which does not match any argument in the entry node.
(T)	*Node does not contradict entry node.* The candidate answer node does not contradict the entry node.
(U)	*Primary plot node.* The candidate answer node is a primary plot node.

ing to node restrictions B, C, and S, the answerer must evaluate whether a candidate answer has an argument that ovelaps an argument in some other specified node. Node restrictions E, I, and J involve the node category of the candidate answer node (see Table 2.1). The reader should be able to interpret node restrictions F, G, H, K, L, N, P, Q, and T by virtue of the definitions in Table 2.9.

A few of the node restrictions require some elaboration because they are important, but rather difficult to define. (For purposes of illustration, we will assume that the entry node is *daughters forgot the time* in the Czar story.). According to node restricton M, the candidate anser node must be in the same time frame as the entry node. Evaluating the candidate answer on the time frame dimension involves a number of steps. First, we analyzed the time span of the event or action conveyed in the entry node. This time frame includes (a) the beginning of the state change (e.g., what directly led to the daughters forgetting), (b) the process of the change (e.g., what happens during the forgetting process), and (c) the end of the state change (e.g., when forgetting is completed). Second, we anlyzed the time characteristics of the candidate answer. If the candidate answer is a State node and the state is not correct during the course of the entry node's time frame (e.g., *the daughters were in the palace*), the candidate answer node would be rejected. The candidate answer would be rejected if it is an event or action that did not occur during the time frame of the entry node. For example, *the Czar's wife gave birth to the daughters* is outside of the time span of the daughters forgetting the time (by several years!). The above criteria for evaluating time frame were satisfactory for our analyses, although we must acknowledge that the problem of temporality requires further exploration (see Allen, 1982; McDermott, 1982).

Evaluating answer nodes on predicate relevance is more subtle. The first step requires a semantic/conceptual analysis of the entry node predicate. "Agent forget X" is the predicate in our example. When testing a node on predicate relevance we were concerned with the following questions: (1) Was it necessary for the candidate answer node to occur or exist in order for the event to occur? and (2) was it important for the candidate node to occur or exist in order for the event to occur? If the answer to *both* of these questions is negative, then the candidate answer node would not pass the *predicate relevance* node restriction D. For example, the fact that the daughters were able to walk was neither necessary nor important for the event of the daughters forgetting the time.

According to node restriction U, the candidate answer node is a primary plot node. Primary plot nodes include central goals, actions, and events in the story plot. The primary plot nodes capture the essence of the plot and would probably be included in a story summary (see Lehnert, 1982; Omanson, 1982). Primary plot nodes include inferences in addition to the verbatim story statements. Some example primary plot nodes in the Czar story are *the dragon kidnapped the daughters, the daughters wanted to be saved, the heroes saved the daughters,* and *the Czar paid back the heroes.*

Symbolic Procedures for Questions About Events.   Table 2.10 presents the symbolic procedures for the seven question categories about events. The table specifies both the arc search procedure and the node restrictions for each question category. The node restrictions in Table 2.10 are presented in the form of Boolean expressions. The letter symbols in these expressions refer to the node restrictions in Table 2.9. Many of the question categories have several levels of nodes generated by the arc search procedure; separate node restrictions are specified for each of these levels. Table 2.10 specifies the predecessor node(s) from which each level of nodes radiates. The term "en-

TABLE 2.10
Symbolic Procedures for Questions About Events

Question Type		Arc Search Procedure	Predecessor Nodes	Distance Limitation	Node Restrictions	Number of Obtained Answers
WHY	(1)	Causal Antecedents	Entry	7	A or (B & D & M)	69
HOW	(1)	Causal Antecedents	Entry	7	A or (B & D & M)	57
	(2)	Style Specifications	Entry and level 1	none		12
ENABLE	(1)	Causal Antecedents	Entry	7	A or (B & D & M)	56
WHEN	(1)	Causal Antecedents	Entry	7	M & I & H	64
	(2)	Time Indices	Entry and level 1	none	N	3
CONS	(1)	Causal Antecedents	Entry	7	A or (B & D & M)	10
	(2)	Causal Consequences	Entry	7	C & F & I	13
	(3)	Subsequent Goal	Entry and level 2	none		2
	(4)	Superordinate and Subordinate Goals	level 3	none		12
	(5)	Causal Consequences	level 3,4	7	A	1
	(6)	Goal Initiators	level 3,4	none		0
	(7)	Causal Antecedents	level 2,5,6	7	A & K	6

SIG	(1)	Causal Antecedents	Entry	7	A or (B & M & F & U)	17
	(2)	Causal Consequences	Entry	7	A or (C & F & U)	11
	(3)	Subsequent Goals	Entry and level 2	none		2
	(4)	Superordinate and Subordinate Goals	level 3	none	A or U	10
	(5)	Goal Initiators	levels 3,4	none	F & M	0
	(6)	Causal Antecedents	levels 2,5	7	C & F & L	4
WHERE	(1)	Causal Antecedents	Entry	7	A or (I & T & S)	30
	(2)	Causal Consequences	Entry	7	A or (I & T & S)	4
	(3)	Location Indices	Entry and levels 1,2	none	P	18
	(4)	Embellishment of Location Indices	level 3	none	A or (I & T & S)	2

try" refers to the entry statement node, whereas the "levels" refer to nodes generated from previous levels (or layers) of the Q/A procedures in Table 2.10. The final column in Table 2.10 lists the number of obtained answers that subjects generated from each level in the Q/A procedure.

There is a "distance limitation" on some of the levels in the Q/A procedures. For example, when the path involves causal antecedents, the candidate answer node must be within seven arcs of an entry statement node. Our analyses of causal antecedents revealed that 97% of the obtained answers were within seven arcs of an entry statement node. This distance limitation (of seven arcs) eliminates answers that are too remote from the probed event. If these distance limitations were not imposed, then the final event in a story would generate a staggering number of causal antecedent nodes. In fact, a causal antecedent path can be followed all the way from the last event in each story to the first.

The symbolic procedures of the seven question categories vary in number of levels. The WHY and ENABLE questions have only one level, namely causal antecedent nodes. The HOW and WHEN questions have two levels, with the causal antecedent nodes comprising the first level. The second level includes information that dangles off the causal antecedent nodes; these dangling nodes involve short paths of Manner arcs (Style nodes for HOW) or Property arcs (time indices for WHEN). WHERE questions have four levels and also include causal antecedent nodes; additional nodes are (1) causal consequences, (2) location indices that dangle off antecedents and consequences via Property arcs, and (3) nodes that embellish location indices. The SIG and CONS questions have six or seven levels in their symbolic procedures. The procedures for the SIG and CONS questions are complex, but quite similar to each other.

We have provided an overview of the seven Q/A procedures for queried events and are now ready to turn to a more detailed discussion of each question category. Our discussion of WHY-event questions is comparatively lengthy because it is the first question category that is discussed.

WHY-event Questions.   Among the 10 events that were questioned, the mean number of unique answers per question was 7.0. Therefore, the subsequent analyses were based on 70 obtained answers when considering all 10 questions. The mean proportion of subjects that generated a specific answer to a specific question was .39 (roughly 3 out of 8 subjects).

According to Table 2.10, the Q/A procedure for WHY-event questions has only one level. This level consists of causal antecedents that are within seven arcs of the entry node. When the arc search procedure is applied to an average WHY-event question, 50 candidate answer nodes are generated. We reported earlier that each passage structure contained hundreds of statement nodes (401 in the Czar story and 427 in the Ant and Dove story). Although there are roughly 400 passage nodes, only 50 of these are accessed by the arc search procedure when a particular event is queried. Hence, the arc search procedure cuts the note space to 12% of the original passage structure. When the "seven arc distance limitation" is ignored, the arc search procedure generates 125 candidate answers (on the average), or 30% of the original passage structure.

The arc search procedure generates roughly 50 candidate answers, but only a subset of these nodes satisfies the node restrictions shown in Table 2.10. If a candidate answer is a verbatim passage statement, it is automatically considered a theoretically acceptable answer. However, if the candidate answer is an inference, then it must satisfy three constraints. First, the candidate node must possess at least one argument that overlaps an argument in the entry node. Second, the candidate node must be in the same time frame as the entry node. Third, the candidate node must be relevant to the semantic/conceptual features of the entry node's predicate. A candidate answer node must satisfy all three of these constraints (or else be verbatim) before it is scored as a theoretically generated node.

An example should help clarify the node restrictions. Listed below are a question and a subset of the candidate answer nodes.

Why did the daughters forget the time?

1. The daughters were enjoying themselves.
2. The daughters did not pay attention to the time.
3. It was getting dark.
4. Woods are the only place to walk.
5. The daughters were able to walk.
6. The daughters were in the palace.

Answer 1 would automatically be included as a theoretical answer because it was verbatim, that is, it was explicitly mentioned in the passage. Answer 2 is an inference and would be a theoretical answer because it satisfies all three node restrictions. First, it satisfies the *argument overlap* restriction; there are two common arguments (*daughters* and *time*) between answer 2 and the entry node. Second, answer 2 satisfies the *time frame* restriction; the daughters continued to not pay attention to the time while they were forgetting the time. Third, answer 2 satisfies the *predicate relevance* restriction; the semantic/conceptual properties of "A forgetting X" would embrace or imply that the agent was not paying attention to X.

The other four answers (3,4,5 and 6) would not be generated theoretically because they fail to satisfy one or more of the node restrictions and are not verbatim nodes. Answer 3 does not share any arguments with the entry node so it would be rejected. Answer 4 also fails the argument overlap restriction. Answer 4 fails the predicate relevance restriction; the fact that the woods are the only place to walk is entirely irrelevant to semantic/conceptual properties of forgetting. Answer 5 passes both the time frame and argument overlap restrictions, but fails the predicate relevance restriction; being able to walk is irrelevant to forgetting something. Answer 6 passes the argument overlap restriction, but fails both the predicate relevance and the time frame restrictions. The daughters were in the palace before they went walking in the woods; when the daughters forgot the time, they were no longer in the palace.

When node restrictions are imposed on the candidate answer nodes, many of the candidate answers are rejected as theoretical answers. We reported earlier that 50 candidate answers are generated (on the average) when the arc search procedure operates on the passage structure. Of these 50 candidate nodes, 24 answers (48%) pass the node restrictions in Table 2.10. Consequently, there are 24 theoretical answers for the average WHY-event question. Out of roughly 400 passage nodes (on the average), only 24 nodes (6%) are theoretical answers. According to our own intuitions, roughly 80% of the theoretical answers were reasonably good answers to the question, whereas very few of the nontheoretical answers were good answers (less than 1%).

The sufficiency of the WHY-event symbolic procedure in Table 2.10 was quite impressive. Of the 70 obtained answers, 69 were generated theoretically from the Q/A procedure in Table 2.10. Thus, the sufficiency score is 99%. The power of the Q/A procedure can be measured by computing the proportion of theoretical answers that were obtained. The power score was 28% in the Czar story and 29% in the Ant and Dove story. The power score may seem low in the sense that 100% is perfect. However, from other perspectives, the power is respectable. Although 71% of the theoretical answers were not obtained answers, most of the unobtained answers were plausible answers according to our intuitions. If more than eight subjects were run, we would expect the power to increase substantially. Moreover, in certain pragmatic contexts that call for more detailed answers, many of the unobtained theoretical answers should emerge.

Two issues need to be discussed regarding the articulation of the answer nodes. One issue involves the amalgamation rules. The action, causal, and set membership amalgamation rules may be applied to the theoretical nodes when answers are produced. The amalgamation rules are frequently, but not always, applied by subjects. A second issue involves connectives that are expressed in the answer protocols. When subjects are asked *Why did the daughters forget the time?* they usually insert the connective *because* before the answer node, e.g., *because the daughters were enjoying themselves.*

HOW-event Questions.   This Q/A procedure has two levels of candidate answer nodes. The first level generates causal antecedent nodes, whereas the second level generates style nodes that dangle off the candidate causal antecedent nodes. Level 1 of the HOW-event procedure is equivalent to the symbolic procedure of WHY-event questions; the arc search procedure, the seven arc distance limitation, and the node constraints are exactly the same. The difference between the WHY-event and HOW-event procedures lies exclusively in the style nodes of level 2. Level 2 generates style nodes that spin off the candidate nodes of level 1.

The 10 queried events produced a total of 72 obtained answers. Of these 72 obtained answers, 69 would be generated theoretically. This amounts to a 96% sufficiency score. Most of the 69 answers were generated from level 1. The power of the HOW-event procedure was comparable to that of the WHY-event procedure. The proportion of theoretical nodes that were obtained was the same (.27) for both stories, which amounts to a 27% power score.

When answers to HOW-event questions are articulated, the subjects often apply the action, causal, and set membership amalgamation rules. HOW-event and WHY-event questions are similar in this respect. However, the two question categories differ with regard to the connectives. The *because* connective often occurs in WHY-event protocols, but rarely occurs in *HOW-event protocols.*

ENABLE-event Questions. This procedure is exactly the same as the procedure for WHY-event questions. Consequently, the theoretical answers are the same for the two question categories.

The 10 queried events produced a total of 61 obtained answers. The sufficiency of the ENABLE-event procedure was high, although not quite as high as the previous two question categories. The sufficiency score was 92%, with 56 of the 61 obtained nodes being generated theoretically. The power score was 23%.

Like the previous two question categories, the three amalgamation rules are often applied when answers are articulated. The *because* connective is rarely used when ENABLE-event questions are answered.

WHEN-event Questions. The Q/A procedure has two levels. Level 1 includes causal antecedents of the entry node, whereas level 2 includes time indices that dangle off the entry node and causal antecedent nodes. Most of the answers came from level 1. The node restrictions of causal antecedent nodes are different for WHEN-event questions than for the previous question categories. Specifically, the verbatim, argument overlap, and predicate relevance constraints do not apply to WHEN-event questions. Instead, answers to WHEN-event questions have three node restrictions: (1) the answer must be in the same time frame as the entry node, (2) the answer cannot be a General node, and (3) the answer cannot be a state that enables an event or initiates an action, i.e., the answer must be an event or a state that is a result of an event or action in the plot. Regarding the level 2 answers, the answers must specify a time index (e.g., an event occurred *in the morning,* the agent did something *one day*).

The sufficiency of the WHEN-event procedure was fairly high (93%). Of the 73 obtained answers, 67 were generated theoretically. Of the 6 obtained answers that were not theoretically generated, 5 were causal antecedent nodes that exceeded the 7-arc limitation constraint of the search procedure. These 5 causal antecedent nodes were between 10 and 21 arcs from the entry statement node. The arc limitation constraint could perhaps be eliminated for WHEN-event questions. However, if we eliminated this constraint, the number of theoretical answers would increase substantially. The power of the WHEN-event procedure was moderate (19%).

The fact that WHEN-event questions produce causal antecedent nodes has at least one interesting implication. Subjects relate the entry node to prior actions, events, and states rather than to nodes that unfold in the future of the narrative. Subjects could have produced answers referring to subsequent events and actions, i.e., entry node occurred *before* a future event or action. However, 98% of the answers to WHEN-event questions referred to nodes that occurred before or during the entry node. Subjects apparently have a bias toward the past when they answer WHEN-event questions.

When the subjects articulate the causal antecedents, they often apply the three amalgamation rules. Regarding connectives, *when* and *after* are typically expressed in the Q/A protocols.

CONS-event Questions.   This procedure is much more complex than that of the first four question categories. There are seven levels of candidate nodes, whereas the previous procedures had only one or two levels. CONS-event questions do not seem to involve a simple, elegant symbolic procedure. Perhaps individuals do not have a well-defined symbolic procedure for these questions. For example, a subset of the obtained nodes includes causal antecedents to the entry node. These answers refer to information that exists or occurs prior to the probed event instead of after it! (Perhaps these antecedent nodes served as context answers that provided some justification or rationale for answers referring to subsequent actions and events.) Most of the answers do refer to events and actions that occur after the probed event. However, the subjects were not very discriminating about the paths of arcs that extend into the future.

What paths of arcs are pursued when answerers generate consequence nodes? For one, the subjects generate causal consequence nodes (level 2). Consequences involve much more, however. Subsequent Goal nodes (level 3) and Goal structures (level 4) are generated, as well as initiators (level 6) of these subsequent Goals. In addition, there are paths of second-generation causal antecedents (level 7) and causal consequences (level 5) that spin off from a variety of levels. CONS-event questions are hardly simple.

The 10 queried events produced a total of 46 obtained answers. The sufficiency score of the CONS-event procedure is very high (96%). Of the 46 obtained answers, 44 were generated theoretically. This outcome is not very impressive, however, because there are many theoretical answers and they radiate in several directions. The power score was embarrassingly low. Only 7% of the theoretical answers were obtained answers.

When answers to CONS-event questions were articulated, the subjects frequently applied the three amalgamation rules. The subjects did not usually articulate connectives.

SIG-event Questions.   This procedure has six levels and is very similar to the symbolic procedure for CONS-event questions. The arc search procedures for SIG and CONS questions are the same except that CONS-event has one additional level of candidate nodes (level 5, causal consequences to subsequent goals). There are more node restrictions for SIG-event questions than for CONS-event questions. Most of the answers to SIG-event questions tapped information subsequent to the entry node (61%) as opposed to information that is during or prior to the entry node. It appears that the significance of an event in a story depends on what the event leads to.

The 10 queried events produced 47 answers. Of the 47 obtained answers, 44 were generated theoretically, yielding a 94% sufficiency score. The power of the SIG-event question procedure was a modest 6%.

The articulation of SIG-event questions normally does not include connectives. However, the three amalgamation rules are frequently applied.

WHERE-event Questions.   This procedure has four levels. Level 1 consists of causal antecedent nodes, whereas level 2 consists of causal consequences. Level 3 includes location indices that dangle off the entry node and theoretical answers from level 1 and level 2. Sometimes location indices are embellished by nodes that radiate from them via Implies and Property arcs; these embellishing nodes come from level 4. Levels 1, 2, and 4 have the same node restrictions (see Table 2.10).

The sufficiency of the arc search procedure was very high (98%). Of the 55 obtained answers, 54 were theoretically generated answers.

The articulation of answers to WHERE-event questions is more complicated than the previous question categories. As with the previous question categories, the action, causal, and set membership amalgamation rules were frequently applied. The complexity lies in the connectives. For some answers, the entire answer node is articulated and the connective is *where*. For example, consider the question *Where did the daughters stay too long?* One theoretical answer is *daughters enjoyed themselves.* The answer would be articulated as *where the daughters were enjoying themselves.* More frequently, however, only an argument of the answer node is articulated, and the connective is a preposition (e.g., *near, at, in front of, by, in*). For example, one of the theoretical answers to the example question is *dragon was in forest.*

The *dragon* argument does not match any arguments in the entry node (see node restrictions). This answer node would be decomposed in order to isolate the nonmatching argument and the nonmatching argument would be the focus of the answer. The articulated answer would have a prepositional connective (e.g., *near the dragon;* alternatively, *where* could be the connective (e.g., *where the dragon was*). Among the 36 obtained answers generated from levels 1, 2, and 4, (a) 7 answers had a *where* connective with the entire node articulated; (b) 27 answers had a preposition connective with a focus on an argument of a decomposed answer node; and (c) 2 answers had a *where* connective with a focus on an argument of a decomposed node.

Most of the answers to WHERE-event questions relate the event spatially to a story character, object, or spatial region (e.g., forest). Among the 47 answers that did *not* make reference to an entire event or action node, 49% referred to a region, 18% referred to a character, and 33% referred to an object. Referring to a region normally had containment prepositions (e.g., *in, within*), whereas references to objects and characters normally had proximity prepositions (e.g., *near, by, above, under, in front of*).

The computation of power is problematic when answers involve decomposed answer nodes. Most answers to WHERE-event questions referred to an argument of a node rather than to the entire node. For example, one answer was *near the dragon*. This articulated answer could be derived from several answer nodes that contained *dragon* as an argument. There is no way of knowing which of these theoretical answer nodes produces the articulated answer. An estimate of the power score would be somewhere between 17% and 59%.

Summary of Symbolic Procedures of Event Questions.   Table 2.11 presents a summary of our analysis of event questions. Table 2.11 presents the number of obtained answers per question, the proportion of subjects who gave a specific answer to a specific question, the sufficiency score, the power score, the number of levels in the Q/A procedure, the number of candidate answers, and the number of theoretical answers for each question category. These data will permit us to compare the seven question categories on a number of dimensions.

The arc search procedures substantially reduced the set of passage nodes to a smaller set of candidate answer nodes. When an event is probed with a question, there are approximately 400 passage nodes from which answers could be extracted. After the arc search procedure is applied, the node space is reduced to an average of 72 candidate answers, or 18% of the passage nodes. The number of candidate answers varies among question categories. There are between 50 and 65 candidate nodes for WHY, HOW, ENABLE, WHEN, and WHERE questions, whereas SIG and CONS questions have between 90 and 140 candidate answers. The arc search procedures reduce the node space that is accessed for answers in two ways. First, the arc search pro-

TABLE 2.11
Summary of Questions about Events

	WHY	HOW	ENABLE	WHEN	CONS	SIG	WHERE
Number of obtained answers per question	7.0	7.2	6.1	7.3	4.6	4.7	5.5
Proportion of subjects that give a specific answer to a question	.39	.36	.36	.39	.29	.31	.43
Sufficiency score	99%	96%	92%	92%	96%	94%	98%
Power score	28%	27%	23%	19%	7%	12%	17–59%
Number of levels in Q/A procedure	1	2	1	2	7	6	4
Number of candidate answers from arc search procedure	50	52	50	57	140	90	—
Number of theoretical answers after node restrictions	24	26	24	35	59	36	—

cedure only pursues paths of arcs with specific categories of directed arcs. Second, there is a distance limitation of seven arcs when pursuing causal antecedent and causal consequence paths.

The node restrictions reduce the set of candidate answers to a subset of theoretical answers. The number of theoretical answers per question varied from 24 to 59, depending on the question category, with a mean of 34. Thus, only 47% of the candidate answers and 8% of the passage nodes were theoretical answers for a typical question.

The Q/A procedures in Table 2.10 were quite sufficient in the sense that they generated the obtained answers in the protocols. The sufficiency scores varied from 92% to 99% among question categories, with a mean of 95%. Thus, 95% of the obtained answers would be generated theoretically. The sufficiency scores among question categories were not significantly correlated with the other measures and indices listed in Table 2.11, e.g., power scores, number of candidate answers.

The fact that our Q/A procedures accounted for nearly all the obtained answers is encouraging, but does not in itself demonstrate the validity of the procedures. A Q/A procedure could be very sufficient but in an uninteresting way. If a Q/A procedure generates a very large set of theoretical answers, then the obtained answers are virtually assured of being produced. The power scores estimate the extent to which the Q/A procedure generates the obtained nodes and only the obtained nodes. The power scores were low for the CONS and SIG questions (7%–12%) compared to the WHY, HOW, ENABLE, and WHEN questions (19% to 28%). Interestingly, the CONS and SIG questions also had many more levels, more candidate answers, and more theoretical answers than the other question categories. Power is inversely related to (a) number of levels in the Q/A procedure, (b) number of theoretical answers, and (c) number of candidate answers.

The number of answers per question varied among the question categories. The number of answers varied from 4.6 to 7.2, with a mean of 6.1. Question categories with more levels, more theoretical answers, more candidate answers, and lower power scores (i.e., CONS and SIG) tended to have fewer distinct answers than the other categories. For CONS and SIG there were also fewer subjects that generated any given obtained answer (.29 and .31) compared to the other five categories (.36 to .43). These data suggest that a question category that has many theoretical answers and many levels imposes high sampling variability regarding what nodes are produced as answers. When there are many theoretical answers, (a) there is lower intersubject agreement on those answers that are obtained and (b) there are fewer answers that are common among the subjects' protocols.

Symbolic Procedures for Questions about Actions.   Actions differ from events in one very important way. Actions are always goal-driven whereas events are not. As we expected, the action/event distinction has a profound impact on the Q/A procedures. Indeed, the Q/A procedures for actions are quite different from those for events. Specifically, the Q/A procedures for queried actions tend to pursue Goal structures in the conceptual graph structures.

Table 2.12 presents the symbolic procedures of the seven question categories for actions. The seven Q/A procedures vary in number of levels. WHY and HOW questions both have three levels. However, WHY-action questions tap information that is superordinate to the queried action whereas HOW-action questions tap subordinate information. ENABLE- and WHEN-action questions have five levels, with four levels that are quite similar for these two question categories. ENABLE- and WHEN-action questions tap information that is both superordinate and subordinate to the queried action. The CONS- and SIG-action questions have six or seven levels with similar symbolic procedures that spread out in many directions through the conceptual graph structure. The WHERE-action question has seven levels; the last four levels were equivalent to the symbolic procedure of WHERE-event questions. The node restrictions for these action questions vary among question categories. However, the action questions as a group involve the same types of restrictions as those for event questions.

An action is an amalgamation of a Goal node and an outcome node that achieves the Goal. Therefore, we can distinguish between a goal entry node and an outcome entry node in the arc search procedures. Table 2.12 does not specify which entry node is relevant at each level of the arc search procedures, so we should clarify this matter before turning to the specific procedures. The entry node is the Goal node whenever the path involves superordinate goals, subordinate goals, and goal initiators. The style specification paths can emanate from either a Goal node or an outcome node. The entry node is the outcome node for the other types of paths.

WHY-action Questions. This procedure has three levels of answer nodes. The first level consists of superordinate Goal nodes, with no node restrictions. The second level includes goal initiators, that is, events and states that directly initiate the goals from level 1. There is a predicate relevance restriction on the goal initiators. The third level includes causal antecedents to the goal initiators from level 2. The causal antecedents have the same node restrictions as those for WHY-event questions. These restrictions include the verbatim, argument overlap, time frame, and predicate relevance constraints.

The 16 queried actions produced a total of 100 answers. The sufficiency of the WHY-action procedure was very high (97%). Of the 100 obtained answers, 97 were generated theoretically. The power of the WHY-action procedure was relatively high (27%).

TABLE 2.12
Symbolic Procedures for Questions About Actions

Question Type		Arc Search Procedure	Predecessor Nodes	Distance Limitation	Node Restriction	Number of Obtained Answers
WHY	(1)	Superordinate Goals	Entry	none		54
	(2)	Goal Initiators	Entry and level 1	none	D	29
	(3)	Causal Antecedents	level 2	7	A or (B & D & M)	14
HOW	(1)	Subordinate Goals	Entry	none		54
	(2)	Goal Initiators	Entry and level 1	none		38
	(3)	Location/Direction Indices	Entry and levels 1,2	none	P	8
ENABLE	(1)	Superordinate Goals	Entry	none		24
	(2)	Subordinate Goals	Entry	none		20
	(3)	Goal Initiators	Entry and levels 1,2	none		24
	(4)	Subordinate Style Specification	Entry and level 2	none	Q	2
	(5)	Causal Antecedents	level 3	7	A or (B & D & M)	29
WHEN	(1)	Superordinate Goals	Entry	none		14
	(2)	Subordinate Goals	Entry	none		18
	(3)	Goal Initiators	Entry and level 1	none	L	18

(4)	Causal Antecedents	level 3	7	M & I & H	42
(5)	Time Indices	Entry and level 1	none	N	9
CONS					
(1)	Superordinate Goals	Entry	none	A or (B & M & G)	22
(2)	Goal Initiators	Entry and level 1	none	A or (B & M & G)	4
(3)	Causal Antecedents	level 2	3	B & M & E	7
(4)	Causal Consequences	Entry and level 1	10	B	19
(5)	Superordinate and Subordinate Goals	level 1	none	B	3
(6)	Subsequent Goals	Entry and levels 1,4,5	none	B	8
(7)	Superordinate and Subordinate Goals	level 6	none	B	4
SIG					
(1)	Superordinate Goals	Entry	none	A or (B & M)	25
(2)	Goal Initiators	Entry and level 1	none	A or (B & M)	10
(3)	Causal Antecedents	level 2	3	A or (B & M)	11
(4)	Causal Consequences	Entry and level 1	10	B	8
(5)	Subsequent Goals	Entry and levels 1,4	none	A	1
(6)	Meta Nodes		none	J	3

TABLE 2.12 (continued)

Question Type		Arc Search Procedure	Predecessor Nodes	Distance Limitation	Node Restriction	Number of Obtained Answers
WHERE	(1)	Superordinate Goals	Entry	none		8
	(2)	Subordinate Goals	Entry	none		5
	(3)	Goal Initiators	Entry and levels 1,2	none	A or (I & T & S)	4
	(4)	Causal Antecedents	Entry and level 3	7	A or (I & T & S)	36
	(5)	Causal Consequences	Entry and levels 1,2	7	A or (I & T & S)	4
	(6)	Location Indices	Entry and levels 1-5	none	P	34
	(7)	Embellishment of Location Indices	level 6	7	A or (I & T & S)	5

The articulation of the WHY-action answers depends on the level from which a theoretical node was generated. For answers from levels 2 and 3, the three amalgamation rules are frequently applied and the typical connective is *because*. For example, one answer to *Why did the dragon drag off the daughters?* was *because the dragon was lonely.* This answer was a goal initiator. Answers from level 1 do not involve any of the amalgamation rules. There are four alternative ways of expressing the Goal nodes from level 1. These four ways are illustrated in the example below.

Why did the dragon drag off the daughters?

1. the dragon wanted to eat the daughters
2. because the dragon wanted to eat the daughters
3. in order to eat the daughters
4. so that the dragon could eat the daughters

The first answer is a direct articulation of the answer Goal node with no connective. The second answer is a direct articulation of the answer Goal node with the connective *because.* The third answer (a) has an *in order to* connective, (b) deletes the intention predicate (*want*) of the answer node, and (c) expresses the intended event/state in the present tense, e.g., (dragon) *eat daughters.* The fourth answer (a) has a *so that* connective, (e.g., *so (that)* . . . *could*), (b) deletes the intention predicate of the answer node, and (c) expresses the intended event/state in the present tense. The level 1 answers do not involve an action amalgamation rule, however. The action amalgamation rule would erroneously produce an action description in the past tense, e.g., *the dragon ate the daughters*, and would presuppose that the Goal is achieved.

HOW-action.   There are three levels of nodes in this procedure. Subordinate Goal nodes and Style nodes are generated from level 1. Initiators of the candidate goal answers are generated in level 2. Level 3 answers are nodes dangling from the level 1 and 2 candidate answers by Property arcs. There are no node restrictions on candidate answers from levels 1 and 2. However, candidate nodes from level 3 must specify a location (e.g., the agent did something *near the dragon*), or a direction (e.g., the agent did something *through the woods*).

The 16 queried actions produced 111 obtained answers. Of these obtained answers, 100 were generated theoretically, yielding a sufficiency score of 90%. Of the 11 violations, 6 answers were verbatim passage nodes. The 11 violations were superordinate goals, superordinate goal initiators, and causal consequences of achieved Goals. The power of the HOW-action procedure was very high (47%).

When articulating answers to HOW-action questions, all three amalgamation rules are frequently applied. Regarding the connectives, answers referring to a subordinate achieved goal either had (a) the action description with no connective or (b) the connective *by* with an action description as a gerund. The example below illustrates the two ways of expressing subordinate actions.

How did the dragon drag off the daughters?

> the dragon grabbed the daughters
> by grabbing the daughters

The answers from levels 2 and 3 included style nodes and location/directional indices. These nodes are usually articulated as prepositional phrases or adverbs. The protocols below illustrate these kinds of answers.

How did the dragon drag off the daughters?

> by the hair
> on the ground
> with his claws

ENABLE-action Questions.   There are five levels of nodes in this procedure. Level 1 generates superordinate goals, with no node restrictions. Level 2 generates subordinate goal nodes. Level 3 generates goal initiators for the entry node and the candidate answers from levels 1 and 2. Level 4 includes Style nodes that dangle from the achieved subordinate goals, provided that the Style is important for achieving the entry Goal node. Level 5 generates causal antecedents of goal initiators, with the same node restrictions as those for ENABLE-event questions. The ENABLE-action procedure has similarities to the WHY-action and HOW-action procedures combined.

The 16 queried actions produced 101 obtained answers. Of the 101 obtained answers, 99 were theoretical answers, yielding a high sufficiency score of 98%. The power of the ENABLE-action procedure was moderate (17%).

The format of articulating the answers depends on the level from which an answer is generated. The action amalgamation rule is not applied to superordinate goals in level 1 and there normally is no connective. The action amalgamation rule is applied to the subordinate goal answers in level 2 and again there is usually no connective. There usually are no connectives for level 4 and level 5 answers, but the three amalgamation rules are applied. Regarding the level 3 Style nodes, there is no connective and the entire answer node is expressed in the form of an action (e.g., *the heroes used a sword*). Alternatively, there is a prepositional phrase that is incorporated with an action that is superordinate to the Style node (e.g., the heroes fought *with a sword).*

WHEN-action Questions.   There are five levels in this procedure. Level 1 generates superordinate Goals whereas level 2 generates subordinate Goals. There are no node restrictions on the candidate answers from levels 1 and 2. Level 3 includes goal initiators of the entry goal node and superordinate goals. However, the goal initiators must be an event or a state that is created in the story plot. The level 4 candidate answers are causal antecedents to goal initiators, with the same node restrictions as those for WHEN-event questions (see Table 2.10). Level 5 generates time indices via Property arcs, with the same node restrictions as in WHEN-event questions.

There were 109 obtained answers generated from the 16 queried actions. The sufficiency of the WHEN-action procedure was high (93%). Of the 109 obtained answers, 101 were theoretical answers. The power of the WHEN-action procedure was modest (13%).

The articulation of answers to WHEN-actions is complex and varies from level to level. The articulation of the superordinate and subordinate goal nodes often has a *when* connective, with the action amalgamation rule being applied. For example, consider the question *When did the dragon drag off the daughters*? The answers below are articulated by a *when* connective and an action amalgamation rule.

1. When the dragon kidnapped the daughters
2. When the dragon grabbed the daughters

Answer 1 refers to a superordinate Goal whereas answer 2 refers to a subordinate Goal. The action amalgamation rule is sometimes not applied when a superordinate Goal is articulated, as shown below.

When the dragon wanted to kidnap the daughters

The action amalgamation rule must be applied when subordinate Goals are articulated. For example, the answer below is an awkward answer for *When did the dragon drag off the daughters*?

When the dragon wanted to grab the daughters

The connective *after* is sometimes used when subordinate goals are articulated, as shown below.

after the dragon grabbed the daughters

The connectives *when* or *after* are used when level 3 and 4 answers are articulated.

When did the dragon drag off the daughters?

> when the dragon was lonely
> after the dragon saw the daughters
> when the dragon saw the daughters

The time indices from level 5 are usually articulated by prepositional phrases (e.g., the agent did something *in the afternoon*).

CONS-action Questions.   There are seven levels in this procedure. Level 1 generates superordinate goals, with no node restrictions on these candidate answers. When considering the chronology of events over time, the achievement of these superordinate goals does occur subsequent to the probed action. Level 2 answers include goal initiators of the entry goal node and the superordinate goals generated from level 1. These goal initiators must satisfy certain node constraints. The goal initiator must either be verbatim or must (a) be a state that continues to exist after the entry goal is achieved, (b) have at least one argument that overlaps the entry goal node, and (c) be in the same time frame as the entry goal node. Level 3 nodes include those causal antecedents to the goal initiators (from level 2) that are within three arcs of the goal initiator. The node restrictions on level 2 goal initiators also apply to the causal antecedents of level 3. Although these goals initiators and causal antecedents existed in time prior to the entry goal node, these nodes are states that continue to exist after the entry goal node is achieved. Level 4 nodes include causal consequences of the entry goal node and those superordinate goal nodes that are achieved. According to the node restrictions, a causal consequence must be within 10 arcs of the achieved goal node. A causal consequence node also must (a) be an event as opposed to a state, (b) be in the same time frame as the entry goal node, and (c) have at least one argument that overlaps the entry goal node. Levels 5, 6, and 7 include goal nodes that are achieved after the entry goal node is achieved. Level 5 generates goals that are subordinate to the superordinate nodes from level 1. Level 6 nodes are second-generation goals that are initiated from the achieved entry goal node as well as nodes generated from levels 1, 4, and 5. Level 7 nodes are second-generation goal nodes that radiate from level 6 goal nodes. The goal nodes that are generated in levels 5, 6, and 7 must have an argument that overlaps the entry goal node. It should be obvious that CONS-action questions do not involve a simple, elegant procedure. The answers do involve events, states, and actions that exist or occur after the achieved entry goal node. However, the symbolic procedure pursues many paths of arcs in a relatively nondiscriminating fashion.

The 16 queried actions produced 69 obtained answers. Of the 69 obtained answers, 67 were theoretical, which amounts to a high sufficiency score (97%). The power score for this procedure was very low (8%).

When answers to CONS-action questions are articulated, there usually are no connectives. The action amalgamation rule is usually applied when the answer is a Goal node that is achieved. The action amalgamation rule is obviously not applied when the Goal node is not achieved.

SIG-action Questions.   The first five levels of this procedure have a direct correspondence to the first five levels of CONS-action questions, except for some slight differences in node restrictions. Level 6 includes "meta" nodes. Meta nodes include comments about the story instead of references to events, states, and actions in the story setting and plot. Example meta answers are *stories must have heroes* and *this action is part of the story plot.* There were very few obtained answers in this meta category so we will not specify the arc search procedure and the node restrictions for level 6.

There were 64 obtained answers generated from the 16 queried actions. Like the other question categories, the sufficiency of the SIG-action procedure was high (91%). However, the power of the SIG-action procedure was low (7%) and comparable to the power of CONS-action questions.

When answers to SIG-action questions are articulated, there usually are no connectives. The action amalgamation rule is not usually applied when level 1 nodes are articulated, but this rule is applied when level 5 nodes are articulated.

WHERE-action Questions.   There were seven levels in this procedure. Level 1 generates Goal nodes that are superordinate to the entry Goal node, whereas level 2 generates subordinate Goal nodes. There are no node restrictions on levels 1 and 2. Level 3 answers include goal initiators to the entry goal node and the goals generated from levels 1 and 2. Levels 4, 5, 6, and 7 are identical to the four levels in the symbolic procedure for WHERE-event questions.

There were 99 obtained answers generated from the 16 queried actions. The sufficiency of the WHERE-action procedure was very high (97%). Of the 99 obtained answers, 96 were generated theoretically. We pointed out in the earlier section on WHERE-event questions that power scores cannot be accurately estimated for WHERE questions. We will therefore not report a power score analysis for WHERE-action questions.

The articulation of WHERE-action questions is directly comparable to that of WHERE-event questions.

Summary of Symbolic Procedures of Action Questions.   Table 2.13 presents a summary of our analyses of questions about actions. These data permit us to compare the seven question categories.

The arc search procedures substantially reduced the set of passage nodes to a smaller set of candidate answer nodes. When an average action is probed

TABLE 2.13
Summary of Questions about Actions

	Questions							
	WHY	HOW	ENABLE	WHEN	CONS	SIG	WHERE
Number of obtained answers per question	6.3	6.9	6.3	6.8	4.3	4.0	6.2
Proportion of subjects that give a specific answer to a question	.38	.38	.33	.38	.32	.32	.42
Sufficiency score	97%	90%	98%	93%	91%	91%	97%
Power score	27%	47%	17%	13%	8%	7%	—
Number of levels in Q/A procedure	3	3	5	5	7	6	7
Number of candidate answers per question	62	14	86	78	76	54	—
Number of theoretical answers per question	22	13	37	49	54	49	—

with a question, there is an average of 413 passage nodes from which answers could be extracted. After the arc search procedure is applied, the node space is reduced to an average of 62 candidate answers or 15% of the passage nodes.

The node restrictions reduced the set of candidate answers to a subset of theoretical answers. The number of theoretical answers per question varied from 13 to 54 answers, depending on the question category, with a mean of 37 answers. Therefore, only 9% of the passage nodes and 60% of the candidate answer nodes were theoretical answers for a typical question. This 9% figure for actions is comparable to the 8% figure for events.

The Q/A procedures in Table 2.12 were quite sufficient because they generated nearly all of the obtained answers in the Q/A protocols. The sufficiency scores varied among question categories from 90% fo 98%, with a mean of 95%. The mean sufficiency score for events was also 95%. The sufficiency scores were not systematically related with other measures and indices list in Table 2.13; this outcome also held true for events (see Table 2.11).

The power scores in Table 2.13 varied among question categories from 7% to 47%, with a mean of 20%. Therefore, one out of five theoretical answers was empirically obtained in the Q/A protocols. The power scores were low for the CONS-action and SIG-action questions (7% to 8%), medium for the ENABLE-action and WHEN-action questions (13% to 17%), and relatively high for WHY-action and HOW-action questions (27% to 47%). We reported earlier that the power scores of the different event questions decreased with (a) the number of levels in the Q/A procedures and (b) the number of theoretical answers generated by the Q/A procedures. These trends also occurred for the action questions.

The number of distinct answers per question varied from 4.0 to 6.9, with a mean of 5.8. The corresponding mean for events was 6.1. As was the case for events, those action question categories with many levels, many theoretical answers, and low power scores tend to have fewer distinct answers. Therefore, question categories that have many theoretical answers and many levels in their Q/A procedures also have high sampling variability regarding what answers are actually produced as answers. Intersubject agreement was lower for CONS and SIG questions (which had many levels in their Q/A procedure) than for WHY and HOW questions (which had few levels), .32 versus .38, respectively. In summary, when there are many theoretical answers and levels in the Q/A procedure, (a) subjects collectively produce relatively fewer answers that are common in at least two subjects' protocols and (b) those answers that are common tend to have relatively lower production proportions. The fact that a Q/A procedure has many levels (and many theoretical answers) does not imply that there will be many obtained answers. Instead, there will be less intersubject agreement on those answers that are obtained.

VALIDITY OF THE PROPOSED Q/A PROCEDURES

In the last section we specified Q/A procedures for 14 different question categories. According to these analyses, 95% of the obtained answers would be generated when the Q/A procedures are applied to the conceptual graph structures for the passages. However, the Q/A procedures for specific question categories generated many more theoretical answers than were actually obtained in the subjects' Q/A protocols. On the average, only one out of five theoretical answers for a question category was obtained empirically. In other words, the sufficiency of our Q/A procedures was very high, but the power of these procedures was nothing to brag about.

The fact that 80% of the theoretical answers were not obtained answers is not necessarily a devastating blow to our research. Most of the unobtained, theoretical answers were reasonably good answers to the questions. Many of these answers would probably emerge in the Q/A protocols if we were to run more than eight subjects per question category. According to our informal estimates, approximately 60% of the unobtained, theoretical answers are fairly good answers; the other 40% would not be good answers according to our judgment. In contrast, less than 1% of the nontheoretical answers are good answers (in our judgment). If we used our own intuition as a criterion, the majority of our theoretical answers are plausible answers to any given question; virtually none of the nontheoretical answers are plausible answers. In short, we believe that we have uncovered most of the systematic properties of the question categories that we have investigated.

Aside from our intuition, we desired some independent criterion for assessing the validity of our Q/A procedures. An analysis of "overlap scores" provided one assessment. Consider the obtained answer distributions when a specific statement (e.g., *the heroes fought the dragon*) is queried with a WHY question versus a HOW question. Suppose that there were N obtained answers to the question *why did the heroes fight the dragon?* and M obtained answers to the question *how did the heroes fight the dragon?* Some of the answers in the two distributions may be the same, i.e., *common* answers between the two answer distributions. An overlap score would be computed as shown in formula 1.

$$\text{Overlap Score} = \frac{2 \times C}{M + N} \tag{1}$$

An overlap score computes the extent to which two answer distributions share common answers. An overlap score varies from 0 (no overlap in answers) to 1 (perfect overlap in answers).

A set of overlap scores was computed for each queried statement. Altogether, we computed 15 overlap scores (OS) per statement: OS (why, how),

OS (why, enable), OS (why, when), OS (why, cons), OS (why, sig), OS (how, enable), OS (how, when), OS (how, cons), OS (how, sig), OS (enable, when), OS (enable, cons), OS (enable, sig), OS (when, cons), OS (when, sig), and OS (cons, sig). We did not include WHERE questions in these analyses because a given answer to a WHERE question often cannot be uniquely associated with one and only one node in the conceptual graph structure. (This problem was discussed in the last section.) Except for the WHERE questions, we computed overlap scores for all possible pairs of question categories. Since there are 6 question categories, there are 15 ([6 × 5]/2 = 15) overlap scores to compute for each queried statement.

Table 2.14 shows the mean overlap scores for the pairs of question categories. We obviously segregated queried events from queried actions because the symbolic procedures are quite different for events and actions. Consequently, there are 30 overlap scores in Table 2.14, 15 for events and 15 for actions. The mean overlap scores varied from .03 to .59, with a mean of .21.

The critical question is whether our theoretical Q/A procedures can explain the overlap scores in Table 2.14. When two Q/A procedures are very similar, there should be a high overlap score for obtained answers; when two Q/A procedures are very different, there should be a low overlap score for obtained answers. The extent to which two Q/A procedures overlap should

TABLE 2.14
Mean Overlap Scores for Pairs of Answer Distributions

| Question Type | Queried Events | | | | |
	HOW	ENABLE	WHEN	CONS	SIG
WHY	.59	.49	.35	.06	.11
HOW		.47	.35	.06	.05
ENABLE			.25	.08	.06
WHEN				.10	.08
CONS					.26

| | Queried Actions | | | | |
	HOW	ENABLE	WHEN	CONS	SIG
WHY	.04	.36	.20	.30	.34
HOW		.18	.18	.06	.03
ENABLE			.28	.20	.26
WHEN				.16	.12
CONS					.23

predict the overlap scores of obtained answers. Therefore, we computed theoretical overlap scores for pairs of Q/A procedures.

The theoretical overlap scores were based on the levels when examining pairs of Q/A procedures (see Tables 2.10 and 2.12). Suppose there are N levels in one Q/A procedure, M levels in a second Q/A procedure, and C levels that are common between the two procedures. The theoretical overlap between the two procedures would be computed according to formula 1. When computing these theoretical overlap scores, we distinguished between completely common levels and partially common levels. A level is completely common when the sets of the theoretical answers are identical for the pair of Q/A procedures. For example, level 1 of the WHY-action procedure generates the same set of answers as level 1 of the ENABLE-action procedure. When there is a completely common level in a pair of Q/A procedures, the common level received full credit in the computation of the overlap scores. A level received only half credit when there was a partially common level in a pair of Q/A procedures. A level is partially common when some, but not all, of the theoretical answers are the same for the pair of Q/A procedures. A partially common level would have the same arc search procedure in both Q/A procedures, but would differ with respect to (a) node restrictions, (b) distance limitations, or (c) predecessor nodes. For example, level 1 of the WHY-event procedure has only a partial overlap with level 1 of the WHEN-event procedure because the node restrictions are somewhat different. We computed theoretical overlap scores for the 15 pairs of questions about events and the 15 pairs of questions about actions. These 30 theoretical overlap scores varied from .10 to 1.00, with a mean of .36.

We should emphasize one critical point regarding the relationship between the theoretical overlap scores and the overlap scores of obtained answer distributions. The fact that a pair of Q/A procedures has high theoretical overlap does not directly (or trivially) guarantee that there will be a high overlap score between the obtained answer distributions. The reason is because the power scores were generally modest (20%) for the question categories. For example, consider the WHY-event and ENABLE-event questions that had identical Q/A procedures and a 1.00 theoretical overlap score. The power scores were only 28% and 23% for WHY-event and ENABLE-event questions, respectively. Since only 25% of the theoretical answers were obtained answers for each of these two Q/A procedures, an entirely different set of obtained answers could have been produced in the WHY-event protocols than in the ENABLE-event protocols. Indeed, all 30 overlap scores in Table 2.14 could have potentially been 0 when considering the modest power scores of the Q/A procedures.

Figure 2.5 is a scatterplot that plots the 30 overlap scores for obtained answer distributions as a function of theoretical overlap scores of the Q/A procedures. The events are depicted by solid circles, whereas the actions are de-

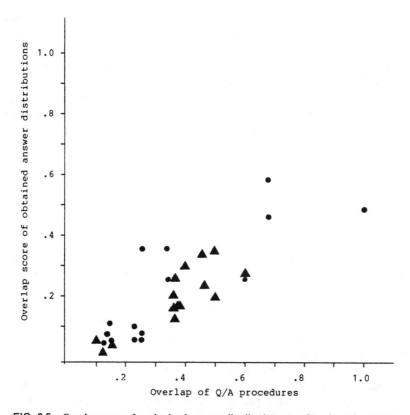

FIG. 2.5 Overlap scores for obtained answer distributions as a function of predicted overlap scores. An obtained overlap score estimates the similarity of the obtained answers when a passage statement is queried with two different types of questions (e.g., WHY and HOW). A theoretical overlap score estimates the similarity of the theoretical answers when two different Q/A procedures (e.g., for WHY versus HOW) are applied to a conceptual graph structure.

picted by triangles. According to the data in Fig. 2.5, the obtained overlap scores increase robustly as function of theoretical overlap. In order to verify this claim, we performed a multiple regression analysis which assessed the extent to which the obtained overlap scores can be predicted by (1) the theoretical overlap in Q/A procedures and (2) the action/event distinction. These two predictors together accounted for 69% of the variance (R^2) of the obtained overlap scores, $F(2, 27) = 30.5, p < .01$. The obtained overlap scores were not predicted by the event/action distinction, $F(1, 27) < 1.0, p > .50$, but were robustly predicted by the theoretical overlap scores, $F(1, 27) = 60.2, p < .01$. The predictive regression equation showed a .60 slope for the theoretical overlap predictor and a .04 intercept constant. The beta weight for the theoretical overlap predictor was .83. Therefore, the similarity of theoretical Q/A procedures robustly predicts overlap scores for pairs of obtained answer distributions. These data offer encouraging support for the validity of the Q/A procedures.

Our analysis of overlap scores obviously does not completely substantiate the validity of the Q/A procedures. Further research is needed to examine the proposed procedures in more detail. The chapter by Murachver, Murray, and Graesser in this book examines the extent to which our Q/A procedures can explain "goodness-of-answer" ratings. That chapter also describes a LISP program that simulates the candidate answer nodes for each of our questions. The program demonstrates that our arc search procedures are computationally sound.

FUTURE DIRECTIONS

In this chapter we have uncovered symbolic procedures for 14 question categories. However, our research in question answering is obviously far from finished. The purpose of this final section is to point out some potentially fruitful directions for future research.

One direction for future research addresses the problem of generalization. Do the proposed Q/A procedures generalize to other passages and statements? We have examined only two passages and both of them were in the narrative genre. To what extend do our Q/A procedures survive other narrative passages and other text genres, such as expository prose and persuasive prose? In addition, can our procedures explain question answering when generic schemas are probed?

A second research direction is to provide more rigorous tests of our Q/A procedures. Studies need to be conducted to test the specific arc search procedures, arc distance limitations, and node restrictions of each Q/A procedure. Such studies might involve the collection of goodness-of-answer ratings (see Murachver, Murray, & Graesser in this volume), or perhaps cleverly designed experiments that measure reaction time latencies. For the most part, we are happy with the arc search procedures of our 14 question categories. However, we strongly suspect that our node restrictions and arc distance limitations are not completely correct. More work is clearly needed to refine the appropriate node restrictions (and distance limitations) for each Q/A procedure. We would not be surprised if some of our node restrictions are unsatisfactory.

A third research direction addresses the pragmatics of question answering. Social context and pragmatic rules will undoubtedly influence our Q/A procedures. The question asker and question answerer are obviously affected by the amount of shared knowledge that they possess and by the social goals of the speech interchange (Cohen, Perrault, & Allen, 1982; Hobbs & Robinson, 1979; Miyake & Norman, 1979). But how do pragmatic variables influence the Q/A procedures? We suspect that the pragmatic goals will substantially influence the node restrictions of our Q/A procedures but will have a comparatively modest impact on the arc search procedures. However, research is needed to substantiate this speculation.

There are a number of ways to investigate pragmatic variables experimentally. One way is to vary the goals of the question-answer interchange through instructional manipulations and context manipulations. For example, in one condition the answerer would be told that the questioner knows some, but not all, of the story; in another condition the answerer would be told that the questioner knows the story by heart. A second method of studying pragmatic variables involves a comparison of rating scales when subjects judge a question-answer test item. For example, in addition to goodness-of-answer ratings, subjects could rate answers on an informativeness-of-answer scale, an adequacy-of-answer scale, versus a best-answer scale. There are still other ways to investigate the role of pragmatic variables in question answering.

A fourth research direction is to explore other question categories. We have examined WHY, HOW, ENABLE, WHEN, CONS, SIG, and WHERE questions for queried actions and events. What about queried states? What about other types of complex questions, such as *why not* and *what would happen if*? We have introduced a methodology for discovering the symbolic procedures of 14 complex questions. Our methods can be used to explore other question categories.

A fifth research direction addresses the working assumptions that we adopted in our explorations of question answering. Some of the working assumptions may ultimately be modified, if not abandoned altogether. We might need to revise our representational theory. For example, instead of adopting statement nodes as a basis unit of analysis, we might desire a slightly different theoretical unit in order to capture amalgamation rules and decomposition rules in a more systematic and elegant manner. Perhaps it is unreasonable to adopt the working assumption that comprehenders construct many inferences at comprehension. We might want to explore the alternative assumptions that (a) very few inferences are generated at comprehension and (b) the answerer accesses and consults a variety of relevant generic knowledge structures (schemas) when generating answers to a question. If the latter assumptions are adopted, we would need to specify how these schemas are accessed, how the information in these schemas are searched, and how the information in the schemas are symbolically integrated or compared to the available passage structure. Of course, we expect that the reported Q/A procedures will assist us in exploring mechanisms that have different Q/A architectures.

In closing, we are encouraged by the methods and analyses that we have reported in this chapter. It should be obvious by now that complex symbolic mechanisms are involved when individuals answer complex questions. We seriously doubt that simpler mechanisms will account for the intricate patterns of data. However, a complex explanation of a complex phenomenon does not imply that the phenomenon is unsystematic. Answering complex questions is indeed systematic. We have introduced a method and theoretical architecture for uncovering much of the systematicity.

REFERENCES

Abbot, V., & Black, J. B. *A comparison of the memory strength of alternative text relations.* Paper presented at the meeting of the American Educational Research Association, New York, 1982.

Abelson, R. P. The psychological status of the script concept. *American Psychologist,* 1981, *36,* 715–729.

Agar, M., & Hobbs, J. R. Interpreting discourse: Coherence and the analysis of ethnographic interviews. *Discourse Processes,* 1982, *5,* 1–32.

Allen, J. F. Modeling events, actions, and time. *Proceedings of the Fourth Annual Conference of the Cognitive Science Society,* Ann Arbor, 1982.

Anderson, J. R., & Bower, G. H. *Human associative memory.* Washington, DC: Winston, 1973.

Bach, K., & Harnish, R. M. *Linguistic communication and speech acts.* Cambridge, MA: MIT Press, 1979.

de Beaugrande, R. *Text, discourse, and process.* Norwood, NJ: Ablex, 1980.

Black, J. B., & Bern, H. Causal coherence and memory for events in narratives. *Journal of Verbal Learning and Verbal Behavior,* 1981, *20,* 267–275.

Black, J. B., & Bower, G. H. Story understanding as problem solving. *Poetics,* 1980, *9,* 223–250.

Bower, G. H., Black, J. B., & Turner, T. J. Scripts in memory for text. *Cognitive Psychology,* 1979, *11,* 177–220.

Bruce, B., & Newman, D. Interacting plans. *Cognitive Science,* 1978, *2,* 195–233.

Carbonell, J. G. Metaphor: An inescapable phenomenon in natural-language comprehension. In W. G. Lehnert & M. H. Ringle (Eds.), *Strategies for natural language processing.* Hillsdale, NJ: Lawrence Erlbaum Associates, 1982.

Chaffin, R. Knowledge of language and knowledge about the world: A reaction time study of invited and necessary inferences. *Cognitive Science,* 1979, *3,* 311–328.

Charniak, E. A framed PAINTING: The representation of a common sense knowledge fragment. *Cognitive Science,* 1977, *1,* 355–394.

Clark, H. H. Responding to indirect speech acts. *Cognitive Psychology,* 1979, *11,* 430–477.

Clark, H. H., & Clark, E. V. *Psychology and language.* New York: Harcourt Brace Jovanovich, 1977.

Cohen, P. R., Perrault, C. R., & Allen, J. F. Beyond question answering. In W. G. Lehnert & M. H. Ringle (Eds.), *Strategies for natural language processing.* Hillsdale, NJ: Lawrence Erlbaum Associates, 1982.

Collins, A. M. Processes in acquiring knowledge. In R. C. Anderson, R. J. Spiro, & W. E. Montague (Eds.), *Schooling and the acquisition of knowledge.* Hillsdale, NJ: Lawrence Erlbaum Associates, 1977.

Collins, A. M., & Loftus, E. F. A spreading activation theory of semantic processing. *Psychological Review,* 1975, *82,* 407–428.

Collins, A. M., & Quillian, M. R. Retrieval from semantic memory. *Journal of Verbal Learning and Verbal Behavior,* 1969, *8,* 240–247.

van Dijk, T. A. *Macrostructures: An interdisciplinary study of global structures in discourse, interaction, and cognition.* Hillsdale, NJ: Lawrence Erlbaum Associates, 1980.

Dunay, P. K., Balzer, R. H., & Yekovich, F. R. *Using memory schemata to comprehend scripted texts.* Paper presented at the annual meeting of the American Psychological Association, Los Angeles, 1981.

Dyer, M. G., & Lehnert, W. G. *Memory organization and search processes for narratives.* Technical Report #175, Department of Computer Science, Yale University, 1980.

Fetler, M. E. Methods for the analysis of two-party question and answer dialogues. *Discourse Processes,* 1979, *2,* 127–144.

Fillmore, C. J. The case for case. In E. Bach & R. T. Harms (Eds.), *Universals in linguistic theory.* New York: Holt, Rinehart & Winston, 1968.

Fine, J. Conversation, cohesion, and thematic patterning in children's dialogues. *Discourse Processes,* 1978, *1,* 247–266.

Fodor, J. A. *Representations: Philosophical essays on the foundations of cognitive science.* Cambridge, MA: MIT Press, 1981.

Freedle, R., & Duran, R. P. Sociological approaches to dialogue with suggested applications to cognitive science. In R. O. Freedle (Ed.), *New directions in discourse processing* (Vol. 2). Norwood, NJ: Ablex, 1979.

Galambos, J. A., & Black, J. B. Why do we do what we do? *Proceedings of the Third Annual Conference of the Cognitive Science Society,* Berkeley, 1981, 277–280.

Gamst, G. Memory for conversation: Toward a grammar of dyadic conversation. *Discourse Processes,* 1982, *5,* 33–51.

Gentner, D. Verb semantic structures in memory for sentences: Evidence for componential representation. *Cognitive Psychology,* 1981, *13,* 56–83.

Gordon, D., & Lakoff, G. Conversational postulates. *Papers from the seventh regional meeting, Chicago Linguistics Society,* 1971, *7,* 63–84.

Graesser, A. C. How to catch a fish: The representation and memory of common procedures. *Discourse Processes,* 1978, *1,* 72–89.

Graesser, A. C. *Prose comprehension beyond the word.* New York: Springer-Verlag, 1981. (a)

Graesser, A. C. A question answering method of exploring prose comprehension: An overview. *Proceedings of the Third Annual Conference of the Cognitive Science Society,* Berkeley, 1981, 268–269. (b)

Graesser, A. C., & Goodman, S. M. Implicit knowledge, question answering, and the representation of expository text. In B. Britton & J. B. Black (Eds.), *Understanding expository text.* Hillsdale, NJ: Lawrence Erlbaum Associates, in press. (a)

Graesser, A. C., & Goodman, S. M. Research Handbook: How to construct conceptual graph structures. In B. Britton & J. B. Black (Eds.), *Understanding expository text.* Hillsdale, NJ: Lawrence Erlbaum Associates, in press. (b)

Graesser, A. C., & Nakamura, G. V. The impact of a schema on comprehension and memory. In G. H. Bower (Ed.), *The psychology on learning and motivation* (Vol. 16). Hillsdale, NJ: Lawrence Erlbaum Associates, 1982.

Graesser, A. C., Robertson, S. P., & Anderson, P. A. Incorporating inferences in narrative representations: A study of how and why. *Cognitive Psychology,* 1981, *13,* 1–26.

Granger, R. H. Judgmental inferences: A theory of inferential decision-making during understanding. *Proceedings of the Fourth Annual Conference of the Cognitive Science Society,* Berkeley, 1982, 177–180.

Grice, H. P. Logic and conversation. In P. Cole & J. L. Morgan (Eds.), *Syntax and semantics (Vol. 3): Speech acts.* New York: Seminar Press, 1975.

Haberlandt, K., & Bingham, G. Verbs contribute to the coherence of brief narratives: Reading related and unrelated sentence triples. *Journal of Verbal Learning and Verbal Behavior,* 1978, *17,* 419–425.

Hobbs, J. R., & Robinson, J. J. Why ask? *Discourse Processes,* 1979, *2,* 311–318.

Kieras, D. E. Component processes in the comprehension of simple prose. *Journal of Verbal Learning and Verbal Behavior,* 1981, *20,* 1-23.

Kieras, D. E., & Bovair, S. *Strategies for abstracting main ideas from simple technical prose.* Technical Report #10, University of Arizona, 1982.

Kintsch, W. *The representation of meaning in memory.* Hillsdale, NJ: Lawrence Erlbaum Associates, 1974.

Kintsch, W., & van Dijk, T. A. Toward a model of text comprehension and production. *Psychological Review,* 1978, *85,* 363-394.

Lehnert, W. G. Human and computational question-answering. *Cognitive Science,* 1977, *1,* 47-73.

Lehnert, W. G. *The process of question answering.* Hillsdale, NJ: Lawrence Erlbaum Associates, 1978.

Lehnert, W. G. Plot units and narrative summarization. *Cognitive Science,* 1981, *4,* 293-331.

Lehnert, W. G. Plot units: A narrative summarization strategy. In W. G. Lehnert & M. H. Ringle (Eds.), *Strategies for natural language processing.* Hillsdale, NJ: Lawrence Erlbaum Associates, 1982.

Lehnert, W. G., Robertson, S. P., & Black, J. B. Memory interaction during question answering. In H. Mandl, N. L. Stein, & T. Trabasso (Eds.), *Learning and comprehension of text.* Hillsdale, NJ: Lawrence Erlbaum Associates, 1983.

Levin, J. A., & Moore, J. A. Dialogue-Games: Metacommunication structures for natural language interaction. *Cognitive Science,* 1977, *1,* 395-420.

Lewis, D. General semantics. In D. Donaldson & G. Harmon (Eds.), *Semantics in natural language.* Boston: Reidel, 1972.

Lichtenstein, E. H., & Brewer, W. F. Memory for goal-directed events. *Cognitive Psychology,* 1980, *12,* 412-445.

Loftus, E. F. *Eyewitness testimony.* Cambridge, MA: Harvard University Press, 1979.

Luria, M. Question answering: Two separate processes. *Proceedings of the Fourth Annual Conference of the Cognitive Science Society,* Berkley, 1982, 167-168.

Mandler, J. M. Representation. In J. H. Flavell & E. M. Markman (Eds.), *Cognitive development,* Vol. 2 of P. Mussen (Ed.), *Manual of child psychology.* New York: Wiley, 1983.

McCloskey, M., & Glucksberg, S. Decision processes in verifying category membership statements: Implications for models of semantic memory. *Cognitive Psychology,* 1979, *11,* 1-37.

McDermott, D. A. A temporal logic for reasoning about processes and plans. *Cognitive Science,* 1982, *6,* 101-155.

McKoon, G., & Ratcliff, R. The comprehension processes and memory structures involved in instrumental inference. *Journal of Verbal Learning and Verbal Behavior,* 1981, *20,* 671-682.

Meyer, B. J. F. *The organization of prose and its effects on memory.* New York: American Elsevier, 1975.

Miller, G. A., Galanter, E., & Pribram, K. H. *Plans and the structure of behavior.* New York: Holt, Rinehart & Winston, 1960.

Minsky, M. A framework for representing knowledge. In P. H. Winston (Ed.), *The psychology of computer vision.* New York: McGraw-Hill, 1975.

Miyake, N., & Norman, D. A. To ask a question, one must know enough to know what is not known. *Journal of Verbal Learning and Verbal Behavior,* 1979, *18,* 357-364.

Nelson, K., & Gruendel, J. M. At morning it's lunchtime: A scriptal view of children's dialogues. *Discourse Processes,* 1979, *2,* 73-94.

Newell, A., & Simon, H. A. *Human problem solving.* Englewood Cliffs, NJ: Prentice-Hall, 1972.

Nicholas, D. W., & Trabasso, T. Towards a taxonomy of inferences. In F. Wilkening, J. Becker, & T. Trabasso (Eds.), *Information integration by children.* Hillsdale, NJ: Lawrence Erlbaum Associates, 1980.

Nix, D. H. Links: A teaching approach to developmental progress in children's reading comprehension and meta-comprehension. In J. Fine & R. O. Freedle (Eds.), *New directions in discourse processing*. Norwood, NJ: Ablex, 1983.

Norman, D. A., & Rumelhart, D. E. *Explorations in cognition*. San Francisco: Freeman, 1975.

Olson, G. M., Mack, R., & Duffy, S. *Strategies for story understanding*. Paper presented at the meetings of the Cognitive Science Society, Yale University, New Haven, CT, 1980.

Omanson, B. C. An analysis of narratives: Identifying central, supportive, and distracting content. *Discourse Processes*, 1982.

Reder, L. M. Plausibility judgments versus fact retrieval: Alternate strategies for sentence verification. *Psychological Review*, 1982, *89*, 250-280.

Reiser, B. J., & Black, J. B. Processing and structural models of comprehension. *Text*, 1983.

Robertson, S. P., Black, J. B., & Johnson, P. N. Intention and topic in conversation. *Cognition and Brain Theory*, 1981, *4*, 303-326.

Robertson, S. P., Lehnert, W. G., & Black, J. B. *Alterations in memory for text by leading questions*. Paper presented at the Annual Meeting of the American Educational Research Association, New York, March 1982.

Rumelhart, D. E. Understanding and summarizing brief stories. In D. LaBerge & S. J. Samuels (Eds.), *Basic processes in reading: Perception and comprehension*. Hillsdale, NJ: Lawrence Erlbaum Associates, 1977.

Rumelhart, D. E., & Ortony, A. The representation of knowledge in memory. In R. C. Anderson, R. J. Spiro, & W. E. Montague (Eds.), *Schooling and the acquisition of knowledge*. Hillsdale, NJ: Lawrence Erlbaum Associates.

Sadock, J. M. *Toward a linguistic theory of speech acts*. New York: Academic Press, 1974.

Schank, R. C. Conceptual dependency: A theory of natural language understanding. *Cognitive Psychology*, 1972, *3*, 552-631.

Schank, R. C. Identification of conceptualizations underlying natural language. In R. C. Schank & K. M. Colby (Eds.), *Computer models of thought and language*. San Francisco: Freeman, 1973.

Schank, R. C., & Abelson, R. *Scripts, plans, goals, and understanding*. Hillsdale, NJ: Lawrence Erlbaum Associates, 1977.

Schank, R. C., Goldman, N., Rieger, C., & Riesbeck, C. MARGIE: Memory, analysis, response generation and inference on English. *Proceedings of the Third International Joint Conference on Artificial Intelligence*, Stanford, August, 1973, 255-261.

Schmidt, C. F., Sridharan, N. S., & Goodson, J. L. The plan recognition problem: An intersection of psychology and artificial intelligence. *Artificial Intelligence*, 1978, *11*, 45-83.

Scragg, G. W. Answering questions about processes. In D. A. Norman & D. E. Rumehlart *Explorations in Cognition*. San Francisco: Freeman, 1975.

Searle, J. R. *Speech acts*. London: Cambridge University Press, 1969.

Seifert, C. M., Robertson, S. P., & Black, J. B. On-line processing of pragmatic inferences. *Proceedings of the Fourth Annual Conference on the Cognitive Science Society*, Ann Arbor, MI, 1982.

Singer, M. The role of case-filling inferences in the coherence of brief passages. *Discourse Processes*, 1980, *3*, 185-201.

Smith, E. E., & Medin, D. L. *Categories and concepts*. Cambridge, MA: Harvard University Press, 1981.

Smith, E. E., Shoben, E. J., & Rips, L. J. Structure and process in semantic memory: A feature model for semantic decisions. *Psychological Review*, 1974, *81*, 214-241.

Stefik, M. Planning with constraints (MOLGEN: Part 1). *Artificial Intelligence*, 1981, *16*, 111-141.

Stein, N. L., & Glenn, G. G. An analysis of story comprehension in elementary school children. In R. O. Freedle (Ed.), *New directions in discourse processing* (Vol. 2). Norwood, NJ: Ablex, 1979.

Taylor, S. E., & Crocker, J. Schematic bases of social information processing. In E. T. Higgins,

P. Herman, & M. P. Zanna (Eds.), *The Ontario symposium on personality and social psychology*. Hillsdale, NJ: Lawrence Erlbaum Associates, 1981.

Trabasso, T. D., Secco, T., & van den Broek, P. Causal cohesion and story coherence. In H. Mandl, N. L. Stein, & T. Trabasso (Eds.), *Learning and comprehension of text*. Hillsdale, NJ: Lawrence Erlbaum Associates, 1983.

Trabasso, T. D., & Stein, N. L. Children's knowledge of events: A causal analysis of story structure. In B. H. Bower (Ed.), *The psychology of learning and motivation* (Vol. 15). New York: Academic Press, 1981.

Warren, W. H., Nicholas, D. W., & Trabasso, T. Event chains and inferences in understanding narratives. In R. O. Freedle (Ed.), *New directions in discourse processing* (Vol. 2). Norwood, NJ: Ablex, 1979.

Wilensky, R. Why John married Mary: Understanding stories involving recurring goals. *Cognitive Science,* 1978, *1,* 235–266.

Wilensky, R. *Planning and understanding.* Cambridge, MA: Addison Wesley, 1983.

3 Answering Some Questions About a Model of Question Answering

Tamar Murachver
University of California, San Diego

Kelly E. Murray
University of Massachusetts, Amherst

Arthur C. Graesser
California State University, Fullerton

A model of question answering was presented in the Graesser and Murachver chapter. The model was designed to explain how an individual arrives at answers to complex questions, such as WHY, HOW, WHEN, WHAT ENABLED. The strongest evidence for the model consisted of an analysis of overlap scores. Specifically, question answering (Q/A) procedures with high overlap have corresponding subject-generated answers with a high degree of overlap (see Fig. 2.5 in the Graesser and Murachver chapter). As an initial test of our model these data were quite compelling. However, a more detailed evaluation of the model is obviously needed.

We should begin by briefly summarizing the nature of the Q/A procedures. Upon hearing or reading a passage, a comprehender is assumed to have formed a representation of the passage content. This representation can be described by conceptual graph structures. Conceptual graph structures are comprised of categorized statement nodes that are interconnected by relational arcs. Suppose the comprehender is asked a question about an event or goal occurring in the passage. This queried event or goal is located in the conceptual graph structure and is called the *entry node*. Depending on the type of question asked (e.g., WHY, HOW), specific paths of arcs are searched to locate an answer to the question. These paths are called *arc search procedures*. Some arc search procedures have *distance limitations*. In these cases, only nodes within a specified number of arcs can be accessed. The set of nodes accessed through the arc search procedure and passing the distance limitations are called *candidate nodes*. Not all of these candidate nodes are good answers to the question. *Node restrictions* are applied to the candidate nodes in order to derive a final set of appropriate answers. This final set of nodes consists of *theoretical answers*. Theoretical answers must pass the arc search procedure, the distance limitations, and the node restrictions.

How psychologically plausible is this model of question answering? In this chapter we examine psychological evidence for the model. We begin by providing evidence for the reliability and validity of our representational system. Second, we report a study that collected goodness-of-answer ratings in order to assess the plausibility of the arc search procedures, distance limitations, and node restrictions of our model. Third, we briefly describe a computer simulation of our question-answering procedures. This computer simulation demonstrated that our arc search procedures are computationally sufficient.

EVIDENCE FOR THE REPRESENTATIONAL SYSTEM

A representational system can be evaluated in terms of its reliability and validity. A reliable system generates similar representational structures for a knowledge domain across various scorers and subjects. A valid system receives support when it helps explain data in different tasks. For example, in this section we consider recall, summarization, and truth verification tasks.

Are Conceptual Graph Structures Reliable?

To assess the reliability of our representational system, we compared the representational structures (conceptual graph structures) of two stories constructed at three different time periods. These two stories are *The Czar and his Daughters* and *The Ant and the Dove*. The first conceptual graph structures were constructed according to the representational system described in Graesser, Robertson, and Anderson (1981). A second set of conceptual graph structures was prepared according to the representational system in Graesser (1981); these structures were based on the protocols of a different group of subjects. The third set of conceptual graph structures was constructed following the revised representational system reported in the Graesser and Murachver chapter. These structures were based on protocols of a third group of subjects.

Although there have been substantial refinements of Graesser's representational system over the years, there is enough similarity that direct comparisons are still possible. The above three sets of conceptual graph structures were based on different subjects, so these structures did not have exactly the same sets of nodes. Nonetheless, roughly 25% of the nodes were identical between any two representations of a passage. It is possible to perform analyses on subsets of nodes that are common from structure to structure. In particular, we correlated the number of arcs radiating from these common nodes. Number of radiating arcs have been found to be critical predictors of recall, summarization, and inference verification, as we discuss later. Correlations were performed among the three combinations of the conceptual graph structures, i.e., versions 1 and 2, 1 and 3, and 2 and 3. For the Czar story, the correlations ranged from .67 to .84. The correlations ranged from .49 to .61 for the Ant and the Dove story. These correlations for number of radiating arcs (sometimes called structural centrality) are quite high considering that there were different sets of nodes in each structure, the nodes were generated by different groups of subjects, and the representational system underwent substantial revisions during the time these structures were constructed.

The second, and more interesting question, addresses the validity of the representational system. If conceptual graph structures correspond to individuals' organized knowledge of a passage, they should be able to explain psychological data in a variety of tasks (see Graesser, 1981; Reiser & Black, 1982).

Two structural dimensions of conceptual graph structures have been considered in predicting psychological data. The first is structural centrality. This dimension served as the basis for our reliability assessment above. The second structural dimension is the relative position of a statement node within a goal hierarchy. The goals of a single protagonist are often represented in hierarchical form. In a hierarchy, subordinate goals are pursued in order to achieve a superordinate goal. Consider Fig. 3.1, for example. The highest-level goal is *Heroes wanted the daughters to be safe.* A number of subordinate goals are performed in order to achieve the superordinate goal. In this example, the heroes set off toward the dragon in order to fight the dragon. This was done in order to free the daughters from the dragon's clutches, which in turn would save the daughters. The position of a statement within a goal hierarchy is expected to be a good predictor of recall and summarization, with superordinate goals being more accessible and important than subordinate goals. Each of these characteristics of conceptual graph structures, structural centrality and position in a goal hierarchy, is now examined in more detail.

Can Conceptual Graph Structures Explain Recall and Summarization?

Recall for actions in narratives can be predicted by the position of the action statement in a goal hierarchy involving a single agent. Graesser (Graesser, 1978, 1981; Graesser, Robertson, & Anderson, 1981; Graesser, Robertson,

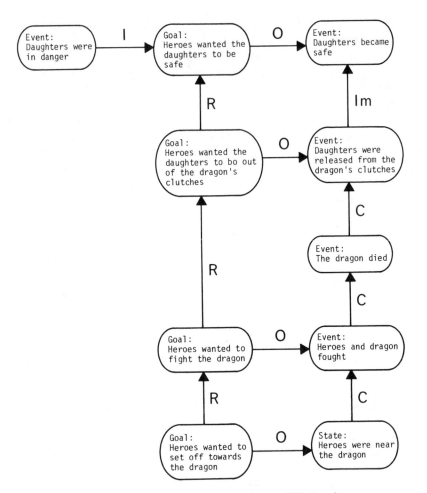

FIG. 3.1   A goal hierarchy from *The Czar and His Daughters*.

Lovelace, & Swinehart, 1980) has reported that superordinate actions and goals of a goal hierarchy have a higher probability of being recalled than more subordinate goals. Similar results have been reported by Black and Bower (1980) and by Omanson (1982). Kemper (1982) has reported a preference for restoring missing superordinate actions in narrative passages. Subordinate information can usually be inferred from the superordinate information, but not vice versa. Therefore, it is less critical for subjects to include subordinate information when recalling or summarizing a passage (Graesser, 1981; Johnson & Mandler, 1980; Rumelhart, 1977).

Structural centrality is another important predictor of passage recall and summarization (Graesser, 1978, 1981; Graesser et al., 1980; Graesser et al., 1981; Omanson, 1982; Trabasso, Secco, & van den Broek, 1984). These researchers have reported that the probability of recalling a statement increases with the number of other statements directly related to it (i.e., the number of relational arcs radiating from the statement node).

An alternative method of predicting story recall has been quite popular with story grammar researchers (Mandler & Johnson, 1977; Stein & Glenn, 1979). According to these investigators, story statements can be parsed into categories such as initiating event, attempt, consequence, internal response, and reaction. Certain categories, such as initiating events and consequences, are more likely to be recalled than the remaining categories. Omanson (1982) has suggested that the story grammar categories most often recalled also tend to have the largest proportion of central statements. Although structural centrality and story grammar categories are correlated, centrality appears to predict recall independently of story grammar category (Trabasso et al., 1984).

Can Conceptual Graph Structures Explain Verification Ratings?

Graesser et al., (1981) reported a robust effect of structural centrality on truth ratings for passage inferences. Subjects first read the passages and later rated inferences on a 4-point truth scale. Inference nodes with more radiating arcs tended to have higher truth ratings than those with few radiating arcs. Of course, there is the pressing question of whether some extraneous third variable is actually responsible for this correlation.

In a recent study, we collected verification ratings for 285 inferences in the Czar passage and 472 inferences in the Ant and Dove passage. These inferences had been generated systematically. Subjects generated the inferences by answering WHY, HOW, and WHAT-HAPPENED-NEXT questions on passage material. They were provided with either no context, partial-story context, or full-story context. Subjects in the no-context condition did not hear the story prior to the Q/A task, whereas subjects in the full-story-context condition read the entire story before they generated inferences. Subjects in the partial-story-context condition read only the portion of the story occurring before the statement they were questioned on.

In the inference verification task, the inferences were presented to 24 subjects who had just finished listening to the taped passages. These subjects then rated the inferences on the following 4-point scale: 1 = false, 2 = possibly true, 3 = probably true, and 4 = definitely true. The inferences were presented in canonical order to eliminate ambiguities in interpretation.

We performed multiple regression analyses in order to assess a large number of possible predictors of truth ratings. These predictors are listed below. *Amount of context* provided during the inference generation (Q/A) task might predict truth ratings. Some of the inferences had been generated by subjects in all three context conditions, whereas other inferences were generated only in the full-story context condition. We wondered whether differences in context would predict the truth ratings.

Serial position of the story statement eliciting the inference might also have an impact on truth ratings.

The number and type of schemas from which an inference was generated might also be a useful predictor of truth ratings. The content of schemas relevant to the two passages had been empirically extracted from subjects prior to this study. There were roughly 30-35 schemas identified in each passage. Eighty percent of the story inferences were identical or analogous to at least one node in these story-relevant schemas. We wondered whether an inference would receive higher truth ratings if it matched a node in a large number of schemas related to the story. The schemas were also categorized into two types, micro and macro. Micro schemas were explicitly referenced in the passages. Examples of micro schemas from the *Czar and his Daughters* are DAUGHTERS, KIDNAPPING, and FIGHTING. Macro schemas, on the other hand, were not directly referenced in a passage. Instead, they were inferable from a set of passage statements. BEING FRIGHTENED is an example of a macro schema from the Czar story. Fright is never mentioned in the story but is inferred from the knowledge that the daughters were kidnapped by a dragon and subsequently began to cry.

Generation frequency was scored as the number of subjects that mentioned the inference in the generation task. Some inferences were generated by many subjects, but others were generated by only a few subjects. The obvious expectation is that inferences generated by many subjects would receive higher truth ratings than inferences generated by a small number of subjects.

Converging evidence was measured as the number of queried story statements that elicited a particular inference during the generation task. Perhaps an inference will be rated as truer if it had been activated by several story statements.

Type of question that elicited the inference was another variable included in the analyses. Inferences were elicited from subjects by asking WHY, HOW, or WHAT-HAPPENED-NEXT questions.

Statement node category is another potential predictor of truth ratings. In our representational system, some statements were classified as goals/actions, some as events, and others as states. We were curious whether truth ratings would differ among these statement categories. One possibility is that states would receive lower truth ratings than either goals, actions, or events. States are less memorable than actions (Graesser et al., 1980; Seifert, Robertson, & Black, 1982) and are more readily modified by misleading questions (Lehnert, Robertson, & Black, 1984).

Structural centrality was expected to be a critical predictor of truth ratings. The most central nodes in a conceptual graph structure have many relational arcs directly radiating from them (in either the forward or backward direction).

Multiple regression analyses were performed on the truth ratings for the inferences. A separate multiple regression analysis was performed on each story. Three predictors performed so poorly in these analyses that they were removed. The eliminated predictors were converging evidence, type of question eliciting the inference, and type and number of schemas containing the inference. With these three variables removed, regressions were again performed. This time, however, the variables coding for statement category (using dummy coding) were entered in the analysis first. The remaining variables were entered in the regression on the second step. We adopted this procedure in order to examine the predictive strength of structural centrality on ratings after first partialling out the predictive ability of statement category. Since Lehnert et al. (1984) found a strong effect of statement category in their research, it seemed important to perform this hierarchical regression.

The total set of predictors together accounted for 30% of the variance in the *Ant and the Dove* passage, and 28% of the variance in the *Czar and his Daughters* passage. The strongest predictor of truth ratings was structural centrality, judging from the magnitude of the Beta weights and the semipartial correlations. Even after controlling for possible confounding variables, structural centrality had the most significant impact on truth ratings. As expected, the more central inferences received higher truth ratings than less central inferences.

Most of the remaining predictor variables were not very impressive. The statement category variables did not significantly predict truth ratings, even when entered into the regression before all other variables. Serial position was a significant, but modest, predictor of truth ratings in both stories. Inferences generated from statements occurring later in a passage received higher truth ratings than inferences generated from statements occurring early in the passage. The "amount of context" predictor was significant in only one of the two stories.

A counterintuitive outcome in our regression analyses involved the generation frequency variable. Graesser (1981) reported that for expository text, inferences generated by many subjects were rated as truer than those generated by few subjects. For narratives, however, generation frequency did not predict truth ratings. We replicated this negative outcome for narrative passages. Generation frequency was not significant in any of our regression analyses.

To summarize, the best predictor of the inference truth ratings resided in structural aspects of a story's conceptual graph structure. Statement nodes with higher structural centrality (nodes at busy intersections) were considered to be more true than nodes that had lower structural centrality (dead-end nodes). In contrast, some serious alternative predictors of truth did not fare as well. First, truth ratings could not be predicted by predictor variables associated with the dynamic process of constructing conceptual graph structures during comprehension (i.e., number of story statements activating an inference, number of schemas activating an inference, amount of context activating an inference). Second, truth ratings were not substantially predicted by individual differences and serial position effects. Third, truth ratings were not predicted by node category (goal/action, event versus state).

The structural properties of our representational system have been able to account for a variety of psychological data. We have presented evidence for our representational system (and other similar systems) in such tasks as recall, summarization, and verification ratings. We are now ready to discuss the research that has tested our question-answering procedures that operate on the conceptual graph structures.

VALIDATION OF THE QUESTION-ANSWERING PROCEDURES

The question-answering procedures in the Graesser and Murachver chapter are sufficient in that they generate most of the answers obtained from subject question-answering protocols. However, many answers that are theoretically generated by these procedures were never articulated by subjects. Are these theoretical but not articulated answers actually good answers? This section presents a study in which goodness-of-answer ratings were collected in order to test our question-answering procedures. These data provided a more fine-grained test of the arc search procedures, the distance limitations, and the node restrictions specified in the question-answering procedures.

Goodness-of-Answer Ratings

The process of determining the adequacy of an answer to a question is not quite the same as the process of generating an answer to a question. Nonetheless, there should be a high correspondence between the answers generated in a question-answering task and the "good" answers in a goodness-of-answer rating task.

In the goodness-of-answer rating task, subjects first read a story and then rated the adequacy of possible answers to questions from the story. Some of these answers were generated by subjects who answered questions about the story. Other answers were theoretically generated following the question-answering procedures described in the Graesser and Murachver chapter. However, some answers would not be generated theoretically and in fact were not elicited by the question in the Q/A task (they were elicited by a different question). For our evaluation purposes, four basic types of answers can be identified:

1. *Arc search violations.* These answers were not generated by the arc search procedures.

2. *Preliminary answers.*   These answers were generated by the arc search procedure. They may or may not have passed the arc distance limitation and the node restrictions.
3. *Candidate answers.*   These answers were generated by the arc search procedure and passed the distance limitation. They may or may not have passed the node restrictions.
4. *Theoretical answers.*   These answers were generated by the arc search procedure and passed both the distance limitation and the node restrictions.

We should point out that answers in category 1 are never in categories 2, 3, or 4. However, there is an overlap in answers with the last three categories. Category 4 answers are a subset of category 3 answers, and 3 is a subset of 2. These answer categories involve progressively more constraints as one goes from the arc search violations to the theoretical answers. It is predicted that goodness-of-answer ratings will increase as the number of constraints placed upon the answers increases. In other words, theoretical answers should receive the highest ratings, and arc search violations should receive the lowest ratings. The ratings for preliminary answers and candidate answers should fall somewhere between the two.

Methods

The queried statements were explicitly mentioned in the *Czar and his Daughters* and the *Ant and the Dove* stories. All explicit actions and events were tested except for (1) the first and last action and event in each passage and (2) statements that were ambiguous with respect to the action/event distinction (e.g., *the daughters cried*). Each queried statement was queried with six separate types of questions. For example, the queried statement *The heroes fought the dragon* would be questioned by the following six question types:

Why did the heroes fight the dragon?
How did the heroes fight the dragon?
What enabled the heroes to fight the dragon?
When did the heroes fight the dragon?
What were the consequences of the heroes fighting the dragon?
What was the significance of the heroes fighting the dragon?

The set of answers to be rated for each queried statement was sampled systematically. First, we randomly selected two empirically generated answers from each of the six question types for the particular queried statement. This produced 12 answer items (2 sampled items from 6 question categories). Second, six answers were randomly selected from the previous statement node in the passage, one answer from each question type. Third, six answers were randomly selected from the subsequent statement node in the passage. Again, one answer was chosen for each of the six question types. For example, suppose that the queried statement was the fourth statement node in the passage. There would be 12 answers from node 4, 6 answers from node 3, and 6 answers from node 5. Following this procedure, answers were selected for 6 queried event statements and 6 queried action statements in the *Ant and the Dove* passage. Likewise, answers were selected for 4 queried event statements and 6 queried statements in the *Czar and his Daughters* passage. It should be noted that the set of answers to a queried statement posed as a WHY question, for example, were identical to answers to the queried statement posed as a HOW question. In fact, for all six question types, the set of answers to a queried statement remained constant. The set of answers to be rated varied only between the queried statements.

Booklets were constructed with the appropriately articulated question at the top of each page, followed by the list of 24 answers. As mentioned in the Graesser and Murachver chapter, articulation of answers differs depending on the type of question posed. The articulation of answers in the booklets corresponded to the rules specified in Graesser and Murachver. For example, the question *Why did the dragon kidnap the daughters* might have an answer articulated as *because the daughters were lovely*. The same answer to the question *What was the significance of the dragon kidnapping the daughters* would be articulated as *the daughters were lovely* (without the connective *because*). We followed these articulation rules to ensure that the answers would appear as natural as possible.

There were separate booklets for queried actions and queried events. The pages of the booklets were ordered so that the order of queried statements matched their sequence of occurrence in the story read by the subjects. The six question types were also counterbalanced so that each subject rated answers to a different type of question for each queried statement. Thus, each subject rated answers to a WHY question, a HOW question, an ENABLE question, and so on.

A total of 72 college students read a passage and then rated the questions in a booklet. Half of the subjects rated answers to queried actions and the other half rated answers to queried events. Subjects rated each answer on the following 4-point scale: 1 = bad answer to the question, 2 = possibly an acceptable answer to the question, 3 = fairly good answer to the question, and 4 = very good answer to the question. Subjects were then given the second passage to read and subsequently rated answers to the second passage. Of course, the ordering of passages was counterbalanced across subjects.

Interpretation of Goodness-of-Answer Ratings

The mean goodness-of-answer rating was computed for each answer. Thus, for each queried statement, mean ratings were obtained for the 24 answers to the WHY-question type, the HOW-question type, the ENABLE-question type, and so forth. We segregated queried events from queried actions because the question answering procedures are quite different for events and actions.

Consider first the event questions. We computed mean goodness-of-answer ratings for each of the four answer categories that we defined earlier: arc search violations, preliminary answers, candidate answers, and theoretical answers. As predicted, arc search violations were rated as the poorest answers, with a mean rating of 1.53. Moreover, theoretical answers received the highest ratings, with a mean of 2.67. The mean ratings for preliminary answers and candidate answers were 2.41 and 2.45, respectively. Clearly, these means follow the expected trend. The goodness-of-answer ratings increased with increasing number of constraints.

In order to show the relative contributions of the arc search procedures, the distance limitations, and the node restrictions, mean ratings for the question categories are displayed in a bar graph in Fig. 3.2. Note how powerful the arc search procedure is for each question type (e.g., HOW, WHY). For answers to each question type, the arc search procedure had a substantial, positive influence on answer ratings. In fact, if our model only specified arc search procedures (i.e, if it did not specify distance limitations and node restrictions), we could still discriminate good answers from poor answers quite well. The addition of the distance limitation did not seem to greatly increase the answer ratings, but it did lead to a small increase in the ratings for each of the question types. Node restrictions consistently further increased the answer ratings a moderate amount.

An observant reader may have noticed the two bars for the CONS and SIG questions. The first bar for each question shows the mean ratings that are based upon the arc search procedures as specified in the Graesser and Murachver chapter. When these procedures were introduced, we were somewhat surprised that subjects pursued the causal antecedent path to generate answers to CONS and SIG questions. Subjects appeared to be providing context by following this path. When asked *what was the consequence of the heroes rescuing the daughters,* a typical answer might be, for example:

because the heroes risked their lives when they fought the dragon, the Czar was impressed. He wanted to show his appreciation, so he gave the heroes a reward.

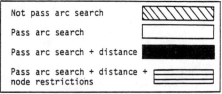

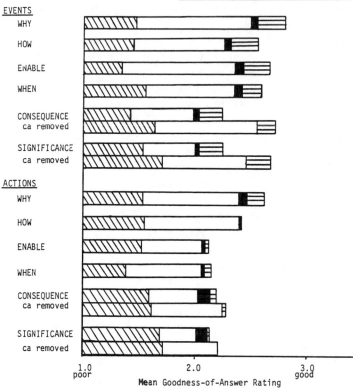

FIG. 3.2   Mean goodness-of-answer ratings for event and action question-answering procedures.

The statement *Heroes fought the dragon* is given as part of the answer, yet it is not a *consequence* of the heroes rescuing the daughters; it is accessed via the causal antecedent path. Because it was mentioned by a subject, this statement would be coded as an obtained answer. The arc search procedures were developed to account for obtained answers so the causal antecedent paths were included as steps in the arc search procedures for CONS and SIG questions. We believed, however, that the answer nodes from causal antecedent paths did not really generate good answers to CONS and SIG questions. The goodness-of-answer data confirmed this suspicion. As can be seen from Fig.

3.2, when the causal antecedent path is eliminated from the arc search procedures of CONS and SIG questions, goodness-of-answer ratings increase substantially (see the second bar in the CONS and SIG portions of Fig. 3.2).

Consider now the action questions. Of the four answer categories, theoretical answers were rated the highest, with a mean of 2.30. The second highest category was candidate statements, with a mean of 2.25. Preliminary answers received ratings slightly lower than candidate answers, with a mean of 2.23. Finally, arc search violations were rated the poorest, with a mean rating of 1.56. As with event questions, distance limitations do not generally lead to substantially better answer ratings for action questions. This can most clearly be seen on the bar graph in Fig. 3.2. Figure 3.2 also reveals that answer ratings appear to be less influenced by the node restrictions for the actions than for the events. As with events, ratings were higher for CONS and SIG questions when the causal antecedent path was removed from the arc search procedure.

An important question to consider is whether our theoretical answers are rated as high as the obtained answers generated by the subjects who participated in the question-answering task reported in the Graesser and Murachver chapter. Table 3.1 presents the mean ratings for the following categories of answers:

1. Answers to a specific question that were not generated theoretically and were not obtained (by that specific question in the Q/A task).
2. Answers to a specific question that were generated theoretically, but were not obtained (by that specific question in the Q/A task).
3. Answers to a specific question that were generated theoretically and were obtained (by that specific question in the Q/A task).

For events, the mean difference between categories 2 and 3 was .10, while the mean difference between categories 1 and 2 was .91. For actions, the mean difference between categories 2 and 3 was .33, whereas the mean difference between categories 1 and 2 was .55. Furthermore, all of the mean ratings for the theoretical answers were above 2.00, while none of the mean ratings of the non-theoretical answers were above 2.00. These data indicate that there was virtually no difference between theoretical answers and obtained answers for event questions, and the difference was very small for queried actions.

In the remaining section of this chapter we examine the adequacy of our question-answering procedures in more detail and then offer some modifications.

Up to now we have been considering our question-answering procedures as a whole. In actuality, many arc search procedures contain several paths. In subsequent analyses, the procedures were broken down into distinct paths. In

TABLE 3.1
Mean Goodness-of-Answer Ratings for Theoretical
and Obtained Answers

	Not Obtained		Obtained
	Not Theory	Theory	
Events			
WHY	1.67	2.59	2.82
HOW	1.68	2.34	2.67
ENABLE	1.54	2.63	2.66
WHEN	1.61	2.41	2.69
*CONS	1.66	2.59	2.63
SIG	1.77	2.70	2.39
Actions			
WHY	1.58	2.41	2.91
HOW	1.55	2.18	2.47
ENABLE	1.61	2.03	2.28
WHEN	1.50	2.08	2.32
CONS	1.70	2.21	2.38
SIG	1.74	2.08	2.60

*Theoretical answer ratings for consequence and significance
questions were computed without the causal antecedent path for
these ratings.

some analyses, we compared question types when they pursued the same
paths.

The majority of answers sampled for the ratings came from the following
paths:

causal antecedent
causal consequence
goal initiator
subordinate goal
superordinate goal

These paths are defined in Table 2.8 of the Graesser and Murachver chapter.
Only 28% of answers to queried events and 20% of answers to queried actions came from paths other than these five paths. In discussing the answer
paths, we refer to the five basic paths listed above as first-generation paths.

All other paths will be referred to as second-generation paths. We chose to separate the first-generation paths from the second-genration paths for two reasons. First, the number of answers generated by second-generation paths was relatively low. Second, these second-generation paths were much more complex and were implemented only after pursuing a first-generation path. Their adequacy was therefore highly dependent upon the adequacy of the first-generation paths.

Fine-Grain Analysis of the Arc Search Procedures

Figure 3.3 presents the mean ratings for answers to event and action questions, categorized by type of path. Consider first the event questions. The procedures for WHY, HOW, ENABLE, and WHEN questions specify the causal antecedent path but not the causal consequence path (see Table 2.10 in the Graesser & Murachver chapter). Therefore, answers on the causal antecedent paths should have much higher ratings than answers on the causal consequence path. Figure 3.3 clearly depicts this difference in ratings. The mean rating for causal antecedent answers fell well above "possibly an acceptable answer" on our scale (i.e., 2.0). Ratings for causal consequences, on the other hand, lay below this criterion.

The procedures for CONS and SIG questions previously allowed both the causal antecedent and causal consequence paths. As we have already shown, causal antecedent answers are not very good. In fact, we consider these to be arc search violations in the remainder of this chapter. Therefore, only causal consequence answers are acceptable for CONS and SIG questions. The mean ratings for answers on the causal consequence paths were clearly beyond the "possibly acceptable" criterion for these two questions.

Event questions only have two possible first-generation paths in their procedures. Action questions, however, have five first-generation paths. Consider WHY-action questions. Permissible paths include the causal antecedent, goal initiator, and superordinate goal paths (see Table 2.12 in the Graesser & Murachver chapter). Answers obtained by following these three paths received high ratings. The remaining paths (causal consequences and subordinate goals) were not theoretically permissible for WHY-action questions. These answers should receive low ratings according to the model and in fact did receive low ratings.

The HOW-action procedure specified only two paths, goal initiators and subordinate goals. These answers should therefore receive high ratings and the other three paths should include answers with low ratings. As expected, answers from the two permissible paths received much higher ratings than answers generated from the three unacceptable paths.

The procedure for ENABLE-action questions specified all paths except the causal consequence path. As can be seen from Fig. 3.3, answers obtained via

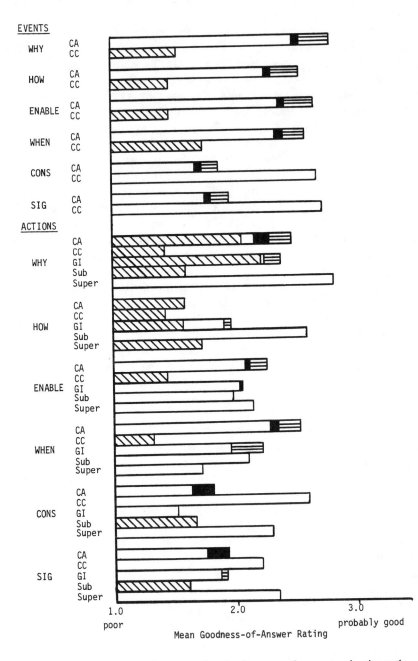

FIG. 3.3 Mean goodness-of-answer ratings for first generation event and action paths.

the causal consequence path received much lower ratings than answers from the remaining four paths. As with WHY and HOW questions, the procedure for ENABLE-action questions is able to distinguish relatively good answers from poor answers.

The WHEN-action procedure is similar to the ENABLE-action procedure in the sense that it includes all paths except the causal consequences. Again, answers from the causal consequence path received the lowest ratings. However, there is one difficulty with the WHEN-action procedure. Specifically, superordinate goals were predicted to be good answers. The mean rating for these answers, however, was 1.72. Thus, these did not even reach the criterion "possibly good." It appears that the superordinate goal path should be eliminated from the WHEN-action procedure.

Consider next the CONS-action procedure. As predicted by our model, answers generated from causal consequence paths and superordinate goal paths were rated as acceptable answers. Answers from the subordinate goal paths and causal antecedent paths were predicted to be poor answers, and in fact had mean ratings below the "possibly good" criterion. There was one unexpected quirk in these data for the CONS-action procedure. The goal initiator path should generate good answers according to our model. Subjects in the rating task did not seem to agree with us, however. The goal initiator path produced answers receiving the lowest ratings. Obviously, this path needs to be reconsidered.

The SIG-action was the final procedure we examined. The first generation path specifications for this procedure are identical to those of the CONS-action procedure. Not surprisingly then, the goodness-of-answer ratings for the SIG-action paths were also quite similar to the ratings for the CONS-action paths. As predicted, answers derived from causal consequence paths and superordinate goal paths received much higher ratings than answers derived from the theoretically unacceptable subordinate goal paths and causal antecedent paths. As with the CONS-action question, the goal initiator path posed a problem for the SIG-action question. Although specified in the model, the goal initiator path produced answers with relatively poor ratings.

In summary, the goodness-of-answer data have supported the majority of the arc search procedures as specified in our model. In fact, out of the 42 individual paths we examined, 39 were supportive of our model (if we assume that a 2.0 rating segregates bad answers from good answers). There were only 3 paths in which ratings were contrary to the predictions of our model. In these cases, either revisions or elimination of the paths are necessary.

Fine-Grain Analysis of Distance Limitations

Our question-answering model also makes predictions about the effect of distance between the entry node and the answer node. Some paths of a question-answering procedure have distance limitations. For example, the causal antecedent path in the WHY-event procedure has a seven-arc distance limitation. Only those nodes within seven arcs of the entry node would be considered as candidate answers. Thus, a node that is eight arcs away from the entry node would be eliminated as a possible answer.

If the distance limitations are psychologically plausible, answer ratings should vary as a function of distance between the answer node and the entry node. In order to examine the plausibility of the distance limitations, we plotted mean answer ratings as a function of the number of arcs between the answer node and the entry node. These data are presented in Fig. 3.4 for the causal antecedents and causal consequences of queried events.

A seven-arc distance limitation was specified in the causal antecedent path for WHY-, HOW-, ENABLE-, and WHEN-event questions. A distinct linear trend can be seen for the causal antecedent paths in Fig. 3.4. As distance from the entry node increased, answer ratings steadily decreased. In fact, by the time a node was nine arcs away from the entry node, its mean rating was below the "possible good" (2.0) criterion. Answers to CONS- and SIG-event questions also showed a distance effect, but these answers were not theoretically generated and had much lower ratings.

A very different trend is obvious for the causal consequence paths. The two event questions containing distance limitations for causal consequence paths were CONS and SIG. Both questions had a seven-arc distance limitation. These paths showed a definite curvilinear relationship between distance and goodness-of-answer ratings. Apparently there is an optimal distance from the entry node where the preferred answers are chosen. Perhaps there is some basic or natural level that subjects chose for their answer selection. This notion is reminiscent of the basic level categories investigated by Rosch (Rosch, 1975; Rosch, Mervis, Gray, Johnson, & Boyes-Braem, 1976). Although this curvilinear trend was not anticipated, the seven-arc distance limitation is still applicable. The answer ratings for the causal consequence paths began a steep decline after a distance of eight arcs was reached. The remaining four causal consequence paths (WHY, HOW, ENABLE, and WHEN) were not theoretically permissible and therefore did not have distance limitations.

Figure 3.5 shows similar plots for answers to queried actions. We segregated causal antecedent, causal consequence, and superordinate goal paths. According to the theoretical Q/A procedures, the causal antecedent paths have a seven-arc distance limitation for WHY, ENABLE, and WHEN questions. The effect of distance on answer ratings is not entirely clear for these causal antecedent answers. A slight downward trend was present, with ratings decreasing as distance increased. However, this trend is quite noisy, perhaps because many of the data points are based on a small sample size.

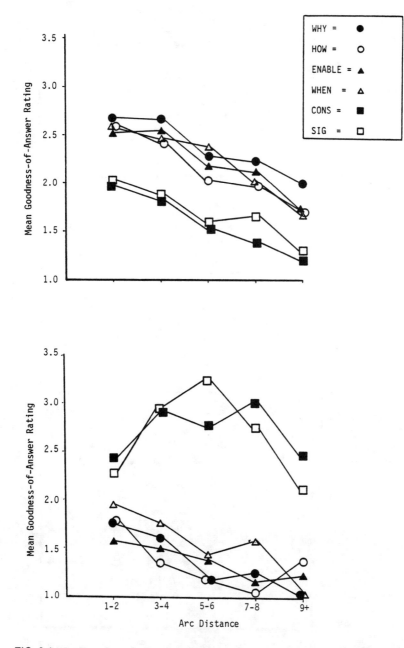

FIG. 3.4 Impact of arc distance on goodness-of-answer ratings for causal antecedent and causal consequence paths. Note: Upper graph portrays the causal antecedent path; the causal consequence path is displayed in the lower graph.

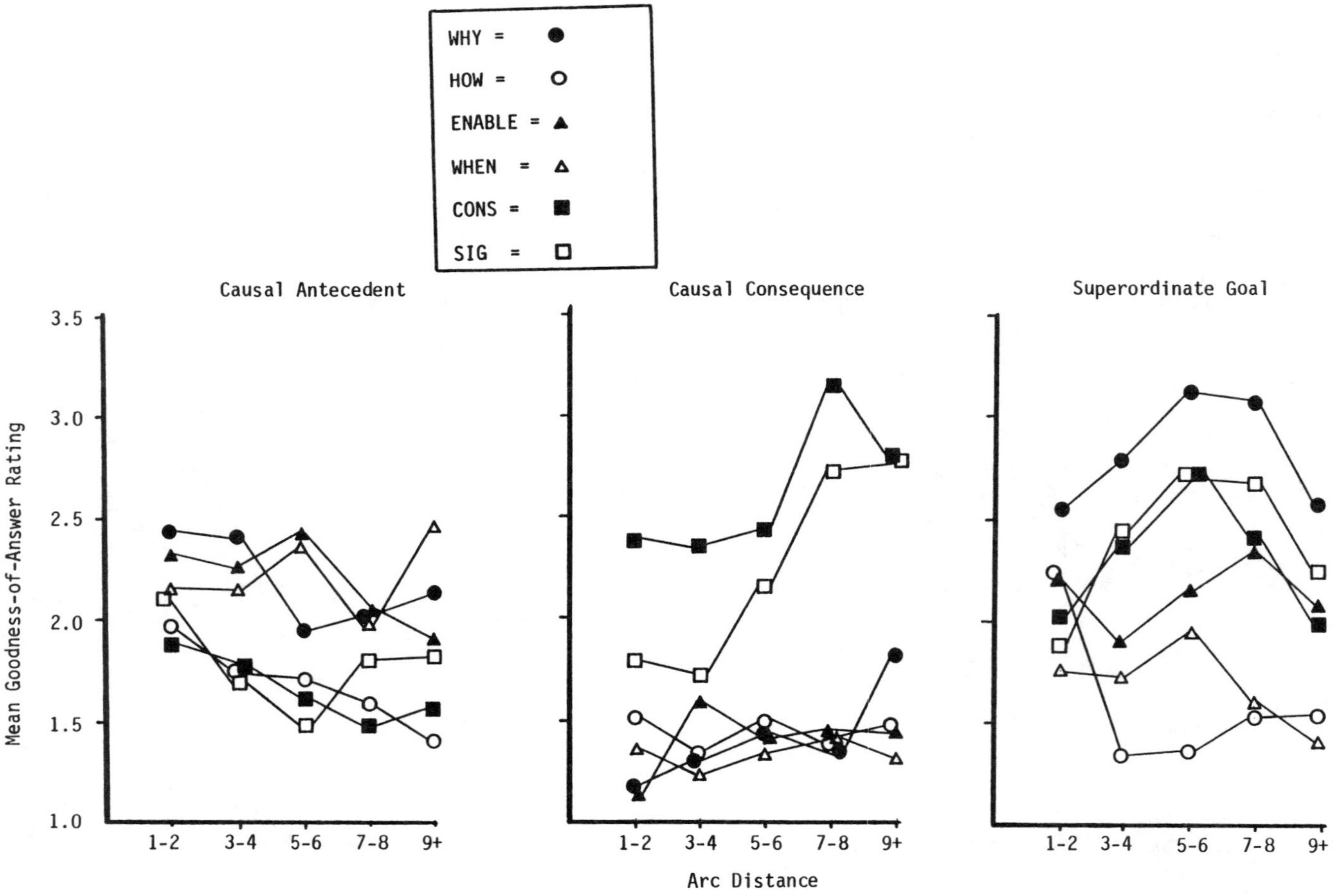

FIG. 3.5 Impact of arc distance on goodness-of-answer ratings for causal antecedent, causal consequence, and superordinate goal paths.

The relationship between distance and answer ratings was more apparent for action causal consequence paths. Both CONS and SIG questions showed a curvilinear trend, with answer ratings peaking at a distance of 7–8 arcs. It is interesting to note that our theoretical distance limitations for these causal consequence paths was 10 arcs. This larger distance limitation seems justified considering that the answer ratings do not begin to decline much until after a distance of 9 arcs is reached.

Superordinate goal paths do not have distance limitations. However, when we plotted the mean answer ratings against distance from the entry node, we found a distinct curvilinear relationship. Ratings for the theoretically acceptable superordinate goal paths increased with arc distance up to an intermediate distance. After this point they began to decline with increasing distance.

Subordinate goal paths, like superordinate goal paths, do not have distance limitations. We did not provide a graph for the subordinate goal path because it was quite noisy without any obvious trends.

Overall, these data suggest that the distance an answer is from the entry node has differential effects on answer ratings. The nature of the relationship depends upon the question type and path. It is appropriate, therefore, to apply our distance limitations selectively, rather than blindly, to all paths within a procedure. We believe that distance limitations are a worthwhile component of our question-answering model. However, we are not completely satisfied with the present specifications and expect refinements in the future.

There is an issue we have not addressed concerning the plausibility of the distance limitations. Up to now we have dealt with brief passages. How feasible are the distance limitations in the case of lengthy text? Our current distance limitations (such as seven arcs) would seem severe. A solution to this potential problem would be to vary the distance limitation specification according to the length of the text. A more plausible solution would involve two steps. First, a summary structure would be abstracted from the more detailed passage representation. Second, the distance limitations would be applied to this summary structure. A model of summarization has been proposed by Lehnert (1982) based on the analysis of plot units. A model similar to Lehnert's might be incorporated into our Q/A procedures.

Fine-Grain Analysis of Node Restrictions

According to Fig. 3.2, the node restrictions specified in the Graesser and Murachver chapter (see Table 2.9 in Graesser & Murachver) contribute to the prediction of good answers, but the impact is rather modest. Of course, the restrictions are only applied to answers passing both the arc search procedures and distance limitations; they affect a smaller range of answers, namely those receiving higher goodness-of-answer ratings to begin with. Therefore, we needed a more sensitive means of assessing these node restrictions. In this section we present a more fine-grain analysis of the node restrictions. Our goal is to discover which node restrictions are predictive of goodness-of-answer ratings.

Multiple regressions were performed on the goodness-of-answer ratings for candidate answers. Again, candidate answers are answers generated by the arc search procedure that also pass the distance limitations. As in the previous set of analyses, we included those answers that were in the first generation.

We began by entering all conceivable node restrictions into the regression analyses. Two predictors were included in addition to the node restrictions listed in Table 2.9 of the Graesser and Murachver chapter. They were arc distance and intentionality. Arc distance was simply the number of arcs traversed between the entry node and the answer node. Intentionality differentiated answers that were motivated by a goal (i.e., outcomes of a goal) from those that were not.

Multiple regressions were performed for all acceptable paths within each question-answering procedure. The goal of these regressions was to reduce the large set of node restrictions to a more manageable number. Following these initial regressions, decisions were made on which restrictions to keep for further investigation. Node restrictions were retained if (1) they were significant in a majority of the regression analyses, or (2) they were theoretically predicted and had significant Beta weights in at least two regression runs. The retained node restrictions are listed below:

1. *Verbatim node.*   This restriction indicated whether a candidate answer was explicitly stated in the passage. If it was verbatim, it was said to pass this restriction.

2. *Arc distance.*   This was the added predictor that specified the number of arcs between the entry node and the candidate answer node.

3. *Predicate phrase relevance.*   This restriction was very similar to the predicate relevance restriction in Graesser and Murachver. We did not determine whether the predicate per se of the candidate answer was relevant to the entry node. Rather, we determined whether the predicate in combination with the object(s) and/or prepositional phrases following the predicate was relevant to the entry node. For example, suppose the entry node was *The heroes rescued the daughters* and the candidate answer was *The heroes carried the daughters home.* We would ask whether carrying the daughters home is relevant to rescuing them. Had we only been interested in predicate relevance, we would have asked whether carrying is relevant to rescuing.

4. *Intentionality.*   This predictor was not specified in the Graesser and Murachver chapter. As previously mentioned, it specifies whether an answer node existed because of some intentional act.

5. *Primary plot node.*   This restriction indicated whether a candidate answer was primary to the story plot. For example, *the heroes saved the daughters* is primary to the plot in the Czar story. *The dragon went to the daughters,* however, would not be primary to the plot.

6. *Time frame.*   This restriction indicated whether the candidate answer occurred within the same time frame as the entry node. For example, *The daughters cried* occurs within the same time frame as *The dragon dragged off the daughters. The heroes received the reward* does not occur within the *dragging off* time frame.

7. *Not-ongoing-state.*   Some states existed throughout the setting and plot of the story. These were ongoing states. Examples of ongoing states are *the daughters were lovely,* and *the heroes were able to hear.* Candidate answers passed this restriction if they were *not* ongoing states.

It is encouraging to note that this set of retained node restrictions happens to contain the most heavily relied upon restrictions within our model.

Before going on, it is interesting to consider some of the node restrictions that were not retained. A discussion of all the eliminated restrictions would be quite lengthy. Therefore, we will point out only a few of the more interesting eliminated restrictions.

The *argument overlap* node restriction required that a theoretical answer contain at least one argument in common with the entry node. This restriction was specified in a large number of the question-answering procedures. Argument overlap, or repetition, has been utilized by Kintsch (Kintsch, 1974; Kintsch & van Dijk, 1978) to describe text structure and predict recall protocols. Contrary to our model, it did not fare well in the regression analyses. The argument overlap restriction was therefore discarded as a plausible restriction.

The *general node* restriction was eliminated as well. It was not very powerful in discriminating between good and poor answers. There are two possible explanations for its poor performance. The general node restriction may actually be an implausible restriction. On the other hand, it may be psychologically plausible. Since general nodes occurred so infrequently, this restriction may not have received a fair test in our regression analyses. A larger number of passages will have to be examined before the general node restriction can be adequately tested.

We are now ready to assess the contributions of the retained node restrictions on the goodness-of-answer ratings. We performed a second series of multiple regressions. One technical point needs to be mentioned about these analyses. According to the model in the Graesser and Murachver chapter, verbatim nodes have a different status than the remaining candidate nodes. In most cases, node restrictions did not apply to verbatim nodes. Consider the causal antecedent path in the WHY-event procedure, for example. If a candidate answer from this procedure were verbatim it would automatically be a theoretical answer. Candidate answers that were not verbatim would have to pass the argument overlap, time frame, and predicate relevance restrictions in order to be a theoretical answer. In order to preserve some semblance of the special status given to verbatim nodes, hierarchical regressions were performed. Specifically, the verbatim restriction was always entered in the regression first. It was therefore evaluated without partialling out the effects of the other restrictions. The remaining variables were entered together in the second step of the regression.

Multiple regressions were conducted on the ratings of candidate answers. As before, a separate regression was performed on the theoretically acceptable paths for each question-answering procedure. Of course in this second set of regressions, the number of node restrictions entering the equation was much smaller.

The results of these regressions are summarized in Table 3.2. The positive and negative signs in Table 3.2 indicate the direction of the relationship between the node restriction and the goodness-of-answer ratings. Circled signs indicate a significant Beta weight at the .10 level. For clarity, we consider separately the performance of each node restriction.

Table 3.2 reveals that the verbatim node restriction is quite plausible. The Beta weights for the verbatim node restriction were consistently positive. In other words, verbatim nodes received higher ratings than non-verbatim nodes. In fact, out of 19 regressions, the Beta weight for the verbatim restriction was positive in 18 instances. Furthermore, it was significant in 9 of these. The verbatim restriction was significant in half of the paths specifying its occurrence. Moreover, this restriction added to the prediction of answer ratings in four paths that were not originally expected. The verbatim node restriction was more powerful than we had imagined.

The arc distance predictor was not an actual node restriction, but it was important to include this variable in our analyses. As previously discussed, arc distance had a differential effect on answer ratings depending on the path examined. The arc distance predictor was significant in six of the regressions. Only one of these six instances occurred in a path that did not have specified distance limitations. The Beta weights for the distance predictor was consistent with our earlier findings. Causal antecedent paths for queried events showed a negative relationship between goodness-of-answer ratings and arc distance, just as our graphs in Fig. 3.2 had. The curvilinear trends for causal consequence paths, on the other hand, were reflected by positive Beta weights. This is because ratings tended to peak close to our distance limitation cut-off points. Again, we should point out that only the nodes passing both the arc search procedure and distance limitations were included in the multiple regression analyses. Thus, only a portion of the curvilinear trend seen in the graphs was actually represented in the regressions.

The next restriction to be examined is predicate phrase relevance. This was an extremely powerful predictor, significant in 10 out of 19 regressions. Furthermore, it was significant in every path predicted by the model. Of course, in all these instances, the trend was for answers with relevant predicate phrases to also receive high answer ratings. Even in the instances where the Beta weight for predicate phrase relevance was not significant, it was still positive in all but one occasion. Clearly, predicate phrase relevance is a node restriction we will want to retain in our model.

The primary plot node restriction was theoretically expected in only one of the examined paths. Although it received a positive Beta weight for this path, the weight was not significant. The primary plot node restriction proved to be a useful predictor in other paths. Not only was it significant in six action procedure paths, but it had a positive Beta weight in every possible regression analysis. These data indicate that this restriction may be beneficial in many more procedures than are presently specified in the model.

Intentionality was a predictor added after the Graesser and Murachver model was developed. Therefore, we have no predictions for the relationship between this variable and goodness-of-answer ratings. An interesting trend occurred in our analyses with this variable. The Beta weight for intentionality was positive in all of the procedures for queried events. In other words, answer nodes motivated by goals received higher ratings than answer nodes not motivated by goals. An opposite trend was evident for the procedures of queried actions; these Beta weights were negative in six out of eight instances. Actions, by our definition, are intentional; yet our subjects preferred to explain actions using non-intentional answers. Conversely, our events were non-intentional. Subjects chose intentional answers to explain these non-intentional events.

The time frame node restriction matched our predictions quite closely for the event procedures. In the four cases where a positive Beta weight was predicted, it was obtained. Moreover, in three of these four cases, time frame was a significant predictor of answer ratings. The time frame node restriction was not theoretically expected in two of the event procedures. In both these cases, the Beta weights were nonsignificant.

The time frame node restriction did not receive much support in the regressions on the action procedures. It was theoretically expected in four procedure paths for queried actions, yet was significant in none. In addition, it was positively related to answer ratings in two of these paths and negatively related to answer ratings in the remaining two paths. The role of the time frame node restriction in the procedures for queried actions obviously needs to be reconsidered.

TABLE 3.2
Node Restrictions for First Generation Event and Action Procedures

EVENTS	Ver	Arcs	Rel	Prim	Int	TF	NOS	R^2
WHY								
C Antecedent	⊕	⊖	⊕	+	+	+	−	.30*
HOW								
C Antecedent	+	⊖	⊕	+	⊕	⊕	+	.37*
ENABLE								
C Antecedent	⊕	−	⊕	+	+	⊕	+	.30*
WHEN								
C Antecedent	⊕	−	⊕	+	⊕	⊕	⊕	.37*
CONSEQUENCE								
C Consequence	+	+	+	+	+	−	−	.29
SIGNIFICANCE								
C Consequence	+	⊕	+	+	+	−	−	.41*
ACTIONS								
WHY								
C Antecedent	⊕	+	⊕	⊕	−	+	+	.20
Super Goal	⊕	+	⊕	⊕	C**	+	−	.42*
HOW								
Sub Goal	+	−	+	C	+	C	⊖	.22
ENABLE								
C Antecedent	+	−	⊕	+	⊖	−	⊕	.23*
Sub Goal	⊕	⊕	+	C	−	C	+	.21
Super Goal	+	−	+	⊕	C	−	⊖	.35*
Actions								
WHEN								
C Antecedent	+	+	−	+	−	+	⊕	.37*
Sub Goal	−	−	+	C	−	C	−	.05
Super Goal	⊕	−	+	⊕	C	+	+	.24
CONSEQUENCE								
C Consequence	⊕	⊕	⊕	+	−	−	−	.37*
Super Goal	+	+	⊕	⊕	C	−	+	.45*

114

TABLE 3.2 *(continued)*

EVENTS	Ver	Arcs	Rel	Prim	Int	TF	NOS	R^2
SIGNIFICANCE								
C Consequence	+	+	+	+	+	−	−	.40*
Super Goal	+	⊕	⊕	⊕	C	−	−	.48*

Note: Ver = Verbatim, Arcs = Arc Distance, Rel = Predicate Phrase Relevance, Prim = Primary Plot Node, Int = Intentionality, TF = Time Frame, NOS = Not-Ongoing-State, C = Constant
*$p < .05$

The final node restriction was not-ongoing-state. The interpretation of its performance is almost as awkward as its name. The not-ongoing-state restriction was specified in three paths for event procedures. It followed our predictions in one of these event paths, the causal antecedent path for WHEN-event questions. In the remaining two event paths, it was both nonsignificant and negative. The not-ongoing-state restriction was specified in one action procedure path. As predicated, this restriction was significant. The not-ongoing-state node restriction was a significant predictor of answer ratings in three additional action procedure paths. However, in two of these paths, the relationship was negative between answer ratings and answers that were not-ongoing-states.

Taken as a set, these restrictions were significant predictors of goodness-of-answer ratings in 5 out of 6 event procedure paths and 8 out of 13 action procedure paths. More importantly, these analyses have pointed out the strengths and weaknesses in the original choice of node restrictions. They have allowed us to access our model of question answering. Based on the outcome of these analyses, a revised model is proposed in the following section.

Before discussing proposed revisions, a few points need to be mentioned. These regressions were based on goodness-of-answer ratings, not on answer articulation data. We do not suggest that rating answers and generating answers are the same processes. The revisions we suggest will be tentative, and must be further tested on answer generation data. In addition, some of our restrictions could not be adequately tested by multiple regression. A few restrictions, such as the general node restriction, have infrequent violations. Even the primary plot node and not-ongoing-state restrictions are skewed in their distribution of violations. For these reasons, we do not view the regression analyses as the final word on our selection of node restrictions. Rather, we see the multiple regressions as a helpful tool in directing us in further modifications of our model.

PROPOSED MODEL REFINEMENTS

We have covered a lot of ground in this section. Where has it gotten us? We began with a model of question answering described in the Graesser and Murachver chapter. Through a series of tests on this model we have seen its predictive power on goodness-of-answer ratings. We have also seen the need for modifications.

We are generally pleased with the arc search procedures as specified in the Graesser and Murachver chapter. Based on the analyses presented in this chapter, we have chosen to eliminate the causal antecedent path for all CONS and SIG procedures. We also realize that our understanding of the goal initiator paths for action procedures is incomplete. Finally, we prescribe the elimination of the superordinate goal paths in the WHEN-action procedure.

The distance limitations were not particularly powerful in most of the question-answering procedures; they did not add much to the prediction of good answers. On the other hand, our analyses did not reveal any blatant discrepancies between the distance limitations described in the model and the goodness-of-answer rating data. Therefore, we do not propose major alterations of the distance limitations until they have undergone further examination.

We do propose major changes in our node restrictions. Many restrictions, such as argument overlap, will be completely eliminated. Other node restrictions, such as primary plot node and intentionality, will be added to some of the Q/A procedures.

The process of evaluating such model refinements is especially time consuming using our current methodology. There is hope, however, that this problem will be solved in the near future by computer simulations of the model. In the following section we present an initial program to do just this.

SIMULATION OF QUESTION ANSWERING PROCEDURES

The goal of any computer simulation is to translate the theoretical ideas of a model into a working, testable computer program. If the model can be implemented on the computer and the computer output closely matches human output, then the model is computationally sufficient. Ideally, all aspects of the model would be incorporated into the program. In practice, however, the program usually ends up being a simplification of the theory or model. In the present simulation, our initial goal was to implement only the arc search procedures and arc distance limitations. Therefore, the program is capable of generating the candidate answers for questions. We are not ready yet to simulate all of the node restrictions.

The utility of computer simulation as a research tool is generally acknowledged. However, we would like to point out some practical reasons for developing the simulation. An obvious practical reason is that it substantially reduces the time and effort needed to generate candidate answers to a question. Previous work has involved tracing through the knowledge structure by hand. Considering the fact that the structures contain hundreds of nodes and arcs, the process is extremely tedious and time consuming without the aid of a computer.

The computer simulations allow relatively easy modification of the Q/A procedures. Because the simulation eliminates the difficult and time-consuming process of generating answers by hand, any modifications to the procedures can be evaluated almost immediately. Thus, time can be spent refining the model, testing out new steps and procedures, and working towards a closer match between the computer output and output generated by human subjects.

The program was written in University of Texas LISP at California State University, Fullerton. A detailed description of the program can be found in Murray and Graesser (1983). The knowledge structure used in the simulation is from the narrative passage, *The Czar and His Daughters*. However, the simulation is not restricted to any specific passage. Any conceptual graph structure can be accommodated by the program once a list of nodes and the relations between them has been constructed.

To implement the arc search procedures, two arc search functions are used. The first function searches either causal consequence or causal antecedent paths, with a specification of the maximum arc distance to search. The second function searches any combination of forward and backward arc types, with no distance limitation. Consequently, the arc search procedures for each question type consist of these two functions. In this way, the Q/A procedures can be easily modified. To change a procedure, any number or combination of arc types can be added or deleted with a minimal amount of effort.

Given the large number of possible candidates in a knowledge structure, the arc search procedures are fairly powerful in that they greatly reduce the number of possible answers to a question. The candidate answers generated from the arc search procedures are usually good answers. However, a number of candidate answers are highly suspect. The node restrictions in the Q/A models provide a way of discarding these implausible and irrelevant answers.

While the arc search procedures have been relatively easy to implement, the node restrictions have been more elusive. Some of the node restrictions can be implemented by making a priori judgments and including this information in the nodes. Verbatim and primary plot nodes could contain flags indicating their status. The time restrictions could be implemented using the system advocated by Allen (1982), where each node would have both a starting index and an ending index. Using this system, overlapping and embedded duration could be derived. Taken to the extreme, the relevancy restriction could be implemented in a similar way. Each node could contain pointers to nodes that are relevant to it. With the exception of the verbatim restriction and possibly the primary plot node restriction, however, this scheme is clearly not a viable solution. The use of a priori judgments merely postpones the problem.

Any solution to the node restriction problems would require a much more sophisticated and intelligent program. How could a program contain this intelligence? Clearly it would no longer be possible to represent node statements as simple character strings. A conceptual dependency-like representation (Schank, 1975) would seem to be appropriate. But this would not be enough by itself. Human decisions of relevancy and time frame duration have been cumbersome to model, even in rather intelligent systems (Hobbs, 1982; McDermott, 1982). A possible solution would be to have schemas of major concepts in the story included in the program. These schemas could be consulted when relevancy and time frame decisions must be made. Regarding relevance judgments, candidate answers could be checked to see if they were included in the schema representations of each argument and predicate in the entry node. The schemas would include information about the typical duration of the events and actions; so the schemas could also be used to check for time frame constraints.

We still have some distance to cover before we are completely satisfied with our model. Up to now we have laboriously assessed our model by hand. This presents many limitations, including time and researcher fatigue. As we have shown, our procedures have been recently implemented on a computer system. This presents opportunities that beforehand seemed overwhelming, such as systematically altering a path in a procedure and examining the outcome.

FINAL COMMENTS

This chapter began with a discussion of our representational system. Our evaluations have found it to be both reliable and psychologically valid. We then went on to discuss the Q/A procedures that operate on the representational structures (conceptual graph structures). The Q/A procedures can be thought of as having three components: arc search procedures, distance limitations, and node restrictions. With minimal modifications, the arc search procedures have passed our evaluations with flying colors. They can predict goodness-of-answer ratings. They are computationally sound. The distance limitations have unobtrusively avoided much criticism. Like an average student, they are neither problematic nor outstanding. The node restrictions, on the other hand, need taming. They bear the brunt of our proposed refinements and will be the subject of extensive study in our future research.

REFERENCES

Allen, J. F. Modeling events, actions, and time. *Proceedings of the Fourth Annual Conference of the Cognitive Science Society*, Ann Arbor, 1982.

Black, J. B., & Bower, G. H. Story understanding as problem solving. *Poetics*, 1980, *9*, 223–250.

van Dijk, T. A. Relevance assignment in discourse comprehension. *Discourse Processes*, 1979, *2*, 113–126.

Graesser, A. C. How to catch a fish: The representation and memory of common procedures. *Discourse Processes*, 1978, *1*, 72–89.

Graesser, A. C. *Prose comprehension beyond the word*. New York: Springer-Verlag, 1981.

Graesser, A. C., Robertson, S. P., & Anderson, P. A. Incorporating inferences in narrative representations: A study of how and why. *Cognitive Psychology*, 1981, *13*, 1–26.

Graesser, A. C., Robertson, S. P., Lovelace, E., & Swinehart, D. Answers to why-questions expose the organization of story plot and predict recall of actions. *Journal of Verbal Learning and Verbal Behavior*, 1980, *19*, 110–119.

Hobbs, J. R. Cohesion in text. In W. G. Lehnert & M. H. Ringle (Eds.), *Strategies for natural language processing*. Hillsdale, NJ: Lawrence Erlbaum Associates, 1982.

Johnson, N. S., & Mandler, J. M. A tale of two structures: Underlying and surface forms in stories. *Poetics*, 1980, *9*, 51–86.

Kemper, S. Filling in the missing links. *Journal of Verbal Learning and Verbal Behavior*, 1982, *21*, 99–107.

Kintsch, W. *The representation of meaning in memory*. Hillsdale, NJ: Lawrence Erlbaum Associates, 1974.

Kintsch, W., & van Dijk, T. A. Toward a model of text comprehension and production. *Psychological Review*, 1978, *85*, 363–394.

Lehnert, W. G. Plot units: a narrative summarization strategy. In W. G. Lehnert & M. H. Ringle (Eds.), *Strategies for natural language processing*. Hillsdale, NJ: Lawrence Erlbaum Associates, 1982.

Lehnert, W. G., Robertson, S. P., & Black, J. B. Memory interaction during question answering. In H. Mandl, N. L. Stein, & T. Trabasso (Eds.), *Learning and comprehension of text*. Hillsdale, NJ: Lawrence Erlbaum Associates, 1984.

Mandler, J. M., & Johnson, N. S. Remembrance of things parsed: Story structure and recall. *Cognitive Psychology*, 1977, *9*, 111–151.

McDermott, D. A temporal logic for reasoning about processes and plans. *Cognitive Science*, 1982, *6*, 101–155.

Murray, K. E., & Graesser, A. C. *SQUEEKY: A simulation of the symbolic procedures of question answering*. Cognitive Research Group Technical Report 1, California State University, Fullerton, 1983.

Omanson, R. C. The relation between centrality and story category variation. *Journal of Verbal Learning and Verbal Behavior*, 1982, *21*, 326–337.

Reiser, B. J., & Black, J. B. Processing and structural models of comprehension. *Text*, 1982, *2*, 225–252.

Rosch, E. Cognitive representations of semantic categories. *Journal of Experimental Psychology: General*, 1975, *104*, 192–233.

Rosch, E., Mervis, C. B., Gray, W. D., Johnson, D. M., & Bayes-Broem, P. Basic objects in natural categories. *Cognitive Psychology*, 1976, *8*, 382–439.

Rumelhart, D. E. Understanding and summarizing brief stories. In D. LaBerge & J. Samuels (Eds.), *Basic processes in reading: Perception and comprehension.* Hillsdale, NJ: Lawrence Erlbaum Associates, 1977.

Schank, R. C. The structure of episodes in memory. In D. Bobrow & A. Collins (Eds.), *Representation and understanding: Studies in cognitive science.* New York: Academic Press, 1975.

Seifert, C. M., Robertson, S. P., & Black, J. B. On-line processing of pragmatic inferences. *Proceedings of the Fourth Annual Conference of the Cognitive Science Society,* Ann Arbor, MI, 1982.

Stein, N. L., & Glenn, C. G. An analysis of story comprehension in elementary school children. In R. O. Freedle (Ed.), *New directions in discourse processing* (Vol. 2). Norwood, NJ: Ablex, 1979.

Trabasso, T., Secco, T., & van den Broek, P. Causal cohesion and story coherence. In H. Mandl, N. L. Stein, & T. Trabasso (Eds.), *Learning and comprehension of text.* Hillsdale, NJ: Lawrence Erlbaum Associates, 1984.

4 Mental Processes of Question Answering

Murray Singer
University of Manitoba

The goal of this chapter is to describe and evaluate an additive stage process model that identifies some of the mental operations of question answering. The model is called VAIL, because it was originally developed to address the "*v*erification of the *a*ssertions and *i*mplications of *l*anguage" (Singer, 1981).

Surprisingly little research to date has been designed to study the component mental processes of question answering. However, several detailed models of sentence verification have been proposed (Carpenter & Just, 1975; Clark & Chase, 1972; Trabasso, Rollins, & Shaughnessy, 1971). These sentence verification models are relevant to the present concerns because sentence verification and question answering are similar in many respects. For example, Clark and Clark (1977, p. 101) have argued that if we are told that *the artist swept the floor,* it makes little difference whether we then verify the truth of a test sentence like *the floor was swept by an artist,* or answer the question, *was the floor swept by an artist?*

In order to make progress in the examination of sentence verification, researchers have frequently studied people's performance on relatively artificial tasks. Clark and Chase (1972), for example, asked their subjects to judge the truth of sentences like *the star is not below the plus* in relation to an accompanying picture like $\overset{*}{+}$. In the present project, however, an attempt has been made to address a variety of issues particularly related to realistic question answering. The following issues were considered: (1) How does a person answer questions about a realistic message that has been encountered? (2) How do people answer questions about the implications of a message? (3) What are the processes that permit a person to correctly use answers like "I don't know" or "probably" in addition to the usual "yes" and "no"? (4) Are the processes of answering questions about passages similar to those that contribute to answering questions about single sentences?

The first section of this chapter describes additive stage process models in general, and the assumptions and processing stages of VAIL in particular. VAIL is then evaluated with respect to some experiments conducted in my laboratory. These experiments examined the verification of sentences about the assertions and implications of a message, the anwering of yes-no questions, the answering of wh- questions, and the answering of questions about brief passages. The last section of this chapter examines certain issues of question anwering that are not directly addressed by VAIL.

VAIL: A MODEL OF QUESTION ANSWERING

Additive Stage Process Models of Sentence Verification

VAIL is an additive stage process model. It generates predictions concerning the time people need to judge the truth of sentences. The crucial assumption of VAIL is that response latency reflects the execution of a sequence of processing stages whose durations are additive (Sternberg, 1969).

Two familiar methods are commonly used to examine models like VAIL. First, the *subtraction method* (Donders, 1868, cited by Sternberg, 1969) involves the comparison of two tasks, the more complex of which requires all of the mental operations of the simpler, plus one. The difference between the mean response latencies of the two tasks is interpreted as corresponding to the duration of the extra stage of the more complex task.

The subtraction method has certain shortcomings (Sternberg, 1969). First, it is often difficult to find two tasks that differ precisely by the stage that the investigator wishes to study. Second, even when two such tasks can be identified, it is questionable whether the "extra" stage can avoid having an impact on the duration of the other stages.

Because of these weaknesses of the subtraction method, Sternberg (1969) proposed a method of studying additive stage models, called the *additive factor method*. According to Sternberg, the additivity of two hypothetical stages, A and B, can be established as follows. First it is necessary to identify two experimental variables or factors, F and G, that can be argued to influence stages A and B, respectively. For example, the factor "intact versus degraded stimulus" might be argued to influence a stage of visual encoding, but not some other stage. Second, an experiment is conducted to examine variables F and G. Sternberg argues that the absence of an $F \times G$ interaction in this experiment supports the addivity of stages A and B.

Recent models of sentence verification have used both the additive factor method and the subtraction method (Chase & Clark, 1972, p. 206). VAIL is likewise shown to use both methods.

The Component Stages of VAIL

VAIL consists of a sequence of hypothetical mental operations. There is some variation in the precise form of the model from one task to another. For example, the structure of the component operations is influenced by the particular response options (*yes, no, don't know, probably*) available to the subject. This is in keeping with the proposals of Clark and Chase (1972), who presented different forms of their model to address sentence-first and picture-first versions of their sentence-picture comparison task. Despite this variation, most of the components and assumptions of VAIL are common to all versions of the model.

The model is explained with reference to Fig. 4.1, which combines two versions of VAIL, which will be called VAIL-A and VAIL-B. All of the components of VAIL-A can be discussed with reference to the following task. Suppose that the subject reads either sentence (1a), (1b), or (1c), followed by question (1d). The answers to (1d) after (1a) and (1b) are *yes* and *no,* respectively. After (1c), it would be reasonable to answer *don't know* to (1d), since there is no way of knowing who drank the coffee.

(1) a. The salesman drank the coffee from the cup. (Yes antecedent)
   b. The actor drank the coffee from the cup. (No antecedent)
   c. The coffee was drunk from the cup. (Don't Know antecedent)
   d. Was the coffee drunk by a salesman? (Question)

1. Question Encoding.   The VAIL model directly addresses mental activities beginning with the encoding of the question. The model adopts principles of language encoding presented by Kintsch (1974) and Clark and Clark (1977).

Following Kintsch (1974), it is assumed that questions are encoded as one or more propositions, with each proposition consisting of a predicate plus one or more arguments. The predicate usually corresponds to the main verbal element in a clause, such as a verb or an adjective. The arguments correspond to nouns in the clause. Each noun is identified as playing a particular role in relation to the predicate of the proposition. Fillmore (1968) has enumerated many important roles or "cases" of this sort. For example, the agent case refers to the concept (usually a person) that has performed the action mentioned in the predicate, and the patient case refers to the concept to which the action has been applied. The propositional notation for *was the coffee drunk by a salesman* is (DRINK, AGENT:SALESMAN, PATIENT:COFFEE).

Clark and Clark (1977) have pointed out that yes-no questions typically interrogate one particular concept. In the current example, the interrogated concept is *salesman*. To reveal this, the encoded form of the question must distinguish between the given and new information conveyed by the question (Haviland & Clark, 1974). The given information is that someone drank the coffee. The new information is a request to know whether that someone was a salesman. Clark and Clark (1977, p. 101) propose that this question be represented in terms of two propositions: (1) Given: X drank the coffee. (2) New: X = salesman? Using Kintsch's notation, this might be shown as (DRINK, AGENT:SALESMAN? PATIENT:COFFEE).

2. Accessing the Appropriate Information.   In stage, 2, the given information of the question is matched with a corresponding proposition in memory. This results in the retrieval from memory of the relevant antecedent. Clark and Clark (1977) argue that it is relatively safe to assume that a match can be found for the given information, since it would be "uncooperative" to ask someone *was the coffee drunk by a salesman* if the answerer knew nothing about the coffee. Retrieval via the new information (*salesman*) would not constitute a reliable procedure, since the very nature of the question makes it uncertain whether the salesman was the drinker at all.

It might be argued that stage 2 should take the form of a test rather than an action. This test would ask, "can the given element be matched with a proposition in memory?" If one were asked *was the coffee drunk by a salesman* in relation to a 500-page novel, for example, one might not remember anything about the coffee even if it had been discussed. For the tasks used in the present project, however, it was assumed that stage 2 would seldom fail. Therefore, it is shown as an action.

3. Case Interrogation.   The model proposes that, once a "given" match has been achieved, a test is executed at stage 3. This test asks whether the representation of the antecedent message includes any information in the case of the new information. In question (1d), for example, the new information, *salesman,* is in the agent case. Thus, stage 3 would ask whether or not the antecedent message included an agent. Antecedents (1a) and (1b) include agents, but (1c) does not.

The inclusion of stage 3 has been motivated by observations that one often can easily decide that something is not known. Lindsay and Norman (1977, p. 370), for example, point out how quickly one can judge that one doesn't know "Hemingway's phone number." Several important predictions of VAIL depend on the inclusion of stage 3.

4. Comparison.   At stage 4, the new element of the question is compared with the corresponding case information, if stage 3 has shown that this information is present in the antecedent representation. A match results in the response *yes,* and mismatches lead to the response, *no.* Stage 4 is similar but not identical to Carpenter and Just's (1975) operation for "finding and comparing" a pair of propositional constituents. The lack of identity is due to the fact that Carpenter and Just's "constituents" are themselves complete propositions. VAIL, on the other hand, posits the comparison of propositional arguments rather than propositions. Carpenter and Just's subjects were able to compare complete propositions, like (RED, DOTS), since their tasks used highly redundant materials (see Singer, 1981, p. 56). Since all of their pictures showed red or black dots, the DOTS argument of (RED, DOTS) could not influence the subject's decision.

4'. Response Index Change.   An important assumption of previous sentence verification models (Carpenter & Just, 1975; Clark & Chase, 1972) has been that the reader maintains an internal response index. All things being equal, it is assumed that the response index is initialized as *true* or *yes.* The discovery of one or more mismatches results in the change of this index to *false (no)* and possibly back again.

The response index assumption is included in VAIL, with several changes and qualifications. First, it is assumed that the response index can have values like *don't know* and *probably* as well as *yes* and *no.* Second, it is assumed that all response index changes take the same amount of time, regardless of the initial and final values. Third, it is proposed that under certain circumstances, the response index may receive an initialization other than *yes,* or even not be initialized at all. Fourth, it is noted that Carpenter and Just (1975) and Clark and Chase (1972) were particularly interested in the verification of negative sentences. Carpenter and Just's subjects, for example, had to compare sentences like *the dots are not red* with a picture of black dots. This comparison results in the discovery of two mismatches. Therefore, the response index must be changed from true to *false,* and then back to the final correct answer, *true.* Since the present research did not examine negative questions, no more than one response index change was ever required on a given trial.

5. Response.   Stage 5 refers to the output of the response. The exact form of the response depends on the way in which subjects are asked to register it. However, Clark and Chase (1972) have argued that because all of the component operations of the response are executed after a decision has been made, it is not essential to further analyze the response stage in verification models.

3'. Retrieval of Information from Long-Term Memory.   Figure 4.1 shows another operation, stage 3', which is not relevant to the yes-no-don't know task already discussed. However, it comes into play in closely related tasks. Suppose a subject reads a sentence like, *the tailor swept the floor,* and then is asked, *did the tailor use a broom*? It is determined at stage 3 that the antecedent did not include an instrument. We can judge, however, that *probably* is a better answer to this question than *don't know*. To decide that *probably* is a reasonable response, it is necessary for the subject to search long-term memory (LTM) to determine whether there is a particular instrument that is usually used to sweep floors. If the memory search produces the instrument "broom," then the subject may answer *probably*.

VERIFYING SENTENCES IN RELATION TO REALISTIC ANTECEDENTS

The VAIL model was first evaluated with respect to data from several sentence verification experiments. It will be shown later that sentence verification and yes-no question-answering tasks yield highly similar results. For this reason, it is argued that the results presented in this section are pertinent to question answering.

The Task

Most of the experiments described in this chapter used the following procedure. Sessions were conducted with groups of one to four individuals. Each subject sat in a separate room. The sentence materials were viewed on computer-controlled television screens, and responses were registered using two or more labeled switches in a response panel.

On each trial, a fixation point appeared on the screen for 3 sec followed by the antecedent sentence for either 2.5 or 3.0 sec. Then the subject had up to 4.0 sec to register a response to the test item, after which the item disappeared. There was a 5-sec intertrial interval.

In all experiments, each sentence set (like set 1, above) appeared in different response conditions (*yes, no, don't know*) in different lists. The test sentence of a sentence set was always the same, so the crucial comparisons in these experiments were always made with reference to precisely the same verbal test items. It was the antecedent sentence of a set that varied among the different conditions. The experiments were conducted with between 24 and 54 sentence sets, which were always divided equally among the three semantic cases: agent, patient, and instrument (Braine & Wells, 1978). Between 10 and 16 subjects viewed each of the lists in each experiment.

Verifying Assertions and Implications

The first experiment to be discussed examined the verification of the assertions and implications of sentences (Singer, 1979, 1981). The task can be explained with reference to the following sentences. Sentences (2a) and (2b) were possible antecedents while (2c) and (2d) were possible tests. Antecedent-test sequences 2a-2c, 2a-2d, 2b-2c, and 2b-2d represent the experimental conditions, explicit true, explicit false, implicit true, and implicit false, respectively. For example, we can judge (2d), *the butcher used a pan,* to be false in relation to (2b), *the butcher tied the package for the customer,* but only if we infer that the package was probably tied with string.

(2) a. The butcher tied the package with the string.
    b. The butcher tied the package for the customer.
    c. The butcher used some string.
    d. The butcher used a pan.

Sentence set (2) was based on the pragmatic implication that tying a package frequently involves string (Singer, 1979, p. 197). In set (2), string fills the instrument case. The experimental materials included equal numbers of sentence sets which probed implications about the agent, patient, and instrument cases. Table 4.1 shows one set for each case.

The model that addresses the present verification task is VAIL-B, shown in Fig. 4.1. The operation sequences for explicit true (1-2-3-4-5) and explicit false (1-2-3-4-4'-5), are quite straightforward. The implicit sequences are also tractable. Consider a sentence and corresponding question in the implicit true condition, *the butcher tied the package for the customer, the butcher*

TABLE 4.1
Sample Sentence Sets Used in the Study of the Verification of
Assertions and Implications

Case	Sentence Role[a]	Sentence
Agent	Explicit antecedent	The judge[b] sentenced the prisoner in the court.
	Implicit antecedent	The prisoner was sentenced in the court.
	True test	A judge sentenced the prisoner.
	Falst test	A batter sentence the prisoner.
Patient	Explicit antecedent	The cowboy rode the horse[b] to town for help.
	Implicit antecedent	The cowboy rode to town for help.
	True test	The cowboy rode a horse.
	False test	The cowboy rode a train.
Instrument	Explicit antecedent	The worker drove the nail with the hammer[b].
	Implicit antecedent	The worker drove the nail.
	True test	The worker used a hammer.
	False test	The worker used a hose.

[a]See text.
[b]Crucial element.

used some string. At stage 3, it is determined that the antecedent includes no information in the case (instrument) of the new test element, string. Control then flows to the LTM search process, stage 3′. For the materials of this experiment, it was considered that this search could almost always be successful. For the present example, the search would result in the retrieval of the concept "string," since packages are usually tied with string.

Before a response could be registered, it would be necessary at stage 4 to compare the new element, *string,* with the information retrieved from memory. For the present example, this would result in a match, *string-string.* Control could then flow to stage 5, at which a *true* response would be registered. The complete sequence for implicit true items would then be 1-2-3-3′-4-5. Similarly, VAIL-B specifies an operation sequence of 1-2-3-3′-4-4′-5 for implicit false items, like 2b-2d.

Based on this analysis, VAIL-B generates a number of predictions. First, VAIL-B predicts that correct response latencies to false items will be longer than for trues. Second, implicit items will have longer latencies than explicit items. Third, there will be no *truth* × *explicit-implicit* interaction.

The results, shown in Table 4.2, were consistent with these predictions. Mean correct response latencies of 1926, 2302, 2167, 2480 msec were measured for the explicit true, explicit false, implicit true, and implicit false conditions, respectively. Analysis of variance, alternately treating subjects and sentences as the random variable, revealed significant effects of truth, explicit-implicit, and also of case. The *truth* × *case* interaction was significant, reflecting the fact that the effect of truth was smaller for the instrument case than for the agent or patient cases. As predicted by VAIL-B, the *truth* × *explicit-implicit* interaction did not approach significance.

VAIL-B makes use of both the additive factor and subtraction methods. With respect to the former, explicit-implicit and truth are analogous to the hypothetical factors, *F* and *G,* discussed earlier. Explicit-implicit is hypothe-

TABLE 4.2
Verifying Assertions and Implications: Mean Response Latencies (msec) as a
Function of Test Status, Truth, and Case

	True		False	
Case	Explicit	Implicit	Explicit	Implicit
Agent	1948	2225	2433	2648
Patient	1979	2147	2349	2606
Instrument	1850	2130	2126	2187
Mean	1926	2167	2302	2480

sized to influence stage 3, and truth is hypothesized to influence stage 4. The absence of an *explicit-implicit* × *truth* interaction supports the additivity of stages 3 and 4.

With respect to the subtraction method, there are several pairs of conditions that are posited to differ by exactly one processing stage. For example, explicit false and implicit false differ by stage 3', LTM retrieval.

In this experiment, subjects committed errors on 4, 8, 15, and 17% of trials in the explicit true, explicit false, implicit true, and implicit false conditions, respectively. Across these four conditions, there was a correlation of .74 between the error rates and response latencies. Other investigators have likewise detected large positive correlations between these two measures (Carpenter & Just, 1975; Clark & Chase, 1972). The interpretation of error rates is considered in detail in the next experiment.

Three-Option Verification: True-False-Don't Know

Since the main goal of this project has been to examine the mechanisms of realistic sentence verification and question answering, VAIL was next extended to address a person's ability to express uncertainty in a sentence verification task (Singer, 1981). As discussed earlier, having read *the coffee was drunk from the cup,* it is reasonable to respond *don't know* when verifying the test sentence, *the coffee was drunk by a salesman.* The materials used in this experiment are exemplified by sentence set (1), considered earlier, and three additional sets shown in Table 4.3.

Latency predictions for this task are generated by VAIL-A (Fig. 4.1). Consider first the *true* item 1a-1d, *the salesman drank the coffee from the cup, the coffee was drunk by a salesman.* At stage 1, the test item is encoded propositionally, with *coffee* and *salesman* designated as the given and new nouns, respectively. At stage 2, a match is established between *coffee* and the corresponding term in the antecedent representation. At stage 3, it is determined that the antecedent includes information in the crucial case, the agent. This results in a match, *salesman-salesman,* at stage 4. The *true* response is then registered at stage 5. The complete sequence is 1-2-3-4-5.

For the *false* sequence, 1b-1d, the only difference is that a mismatch at stage 4 results in a change of the response index at stage 4'. For the *don't know* sequence, 1c-1d, stage 3 reveals that the antecedent includes no information in the agent case. The response index may be immediately changed to *don't know,* and a response registered. VAIL-A specifies the sequences 1-2-3-4-4'-5 and 1-2-3-4'-5 for the *false* and *don't know* conditions, respectively. The crucial prediction was that *false* latencies would be longer than *don't knows,* because of the extra match, stage 4. It might also be predicted that *trues* will be faster than *false* responses. The *trues,* however, also had the confounding ad-

TABLE 4.3
Sample Sentence Sets Used in the Three-Option Verification Experiment

Case	Sentence Type	Sentence
Agent	True antecedent	The plumber kicked the stone in the field.
	False antecedent	The librarian kicked the stone in the field.
	Don't know antecedent	The stone was kicked in the field.
	Test	A plumber kicked the stone.
Patient	True antecedent	The doctor ate the stew in the yard.
	False antecedent	The doctor ate the fish in the yard.
	Don't know antecedent	The doctor ate in the yard.
	Test	The doctor ate some stew.
Instrument	True antecedent	The janitor cleaned the bottle with the cloth.
	False antecedent	The janitor cleaned the bottle with the brush.
	Don't know antecedent	The janitor cleaned the bottle.
	Test	The janitor used a cloth.

vantage of an extra content word in common with their antecedents (the crucial element, *salesman*) as compared with the other response conditions.

Latencies.   The results, shown in the top part of Table 4.4, revealed faster *don't know* than *false* latencies for all three semantic cases (Singer, 1981). Response was the only significant effect, with means of 2087, 2392, and 2101 msec for *true, false,* and *don't know* items, respectively. Thus, a version of VAIL, similar to the one relevant to the verification of assertions and implications, was shown to generate accurate predictions concerning the use of three realistic responses.

Errors.   The subjects could commit errors by failing to respond before the 4-sec limit, or by pressing the incorrect response key. The overall error rate was 10.6%, based on rates of 3.5, 18.4, and 10.0% for the *true, false,* and *don't know* conditions, respectively. Across the three response conditions, the error rates were correlated .917 with response latencies.

How can the pattern of error rates be explained? Carpenter and Just (1975) have stated that the error rate for a particular verification condition increases with the number of processing stages contributing to that condition. This observation is consistent with the data of the present experiment, in that the *false* condition had both the largest number of hypothetical processing stages, and the highest error rate.

An alternate interpretation, however, is that subjects made the greatest number of errors on *false* trials because they were somewhat uncertain of what they were supposed to answer. Consider the *false* item, *the actor drank the coffee from the cup, the coffee was drunk by a salesman.* The subjects might have reasoned that a salesman, as well as an actor, had drunk some coffee. Such reasoning might result in the registration of a response other than *false.* Furthermore, this interpretation of the error rates provides an alternate explanation of the response latency pattern. It states that the long *false* latencies are due to the subjects' uncertainty rather than the extra processing stage.

To further examine the possibility that the response latency pattern might simply be a result of subjects' uncertainty on *false* trials, another latency

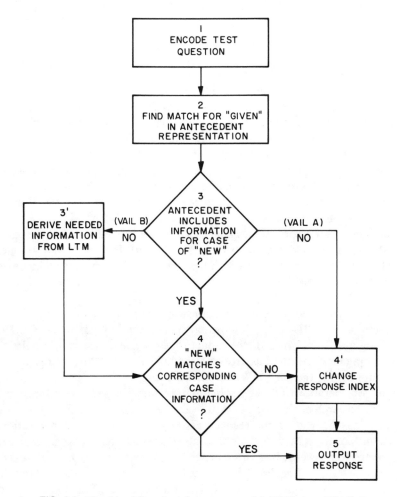

FIG. 4.1   Combined flowchart for process models VAIL-A and VAIL-B.

TABLE 4.4
Mean Response Latencies (msec) for the Three-Response Task:
Sentence Verification and Yes-No Question Answering

Task	Case	True/Yes	False/No	Don't Know
Verification	Agent	2079	2373	2209
(Singer, 1981)	Patient	1971	2384	2066
	Instrument	2210	2417	2028
	Mean	2087	2392	2101
Answering	Agent	2372	2558	2397
(Singer, 1984)	Patient	2097	2297	2154
	Instrument	2128	2374	2141
	Mean	2199	2410	2231

analysis was performed. First, an identification was made of experimental sentence sets that had almost the same number of errors in the *false* and *don't know* conditions. Of the 27 sets, 14 met this criterion. Then, the mean response latencies of these 14 sets were computed. These "equal-error" sets had mean latencies of 1978, 2404, and 2174 msec and error rates of 4.6, 6.2, and 7.5% in the *true, false,* and *don't know* conditions, respectively. Since the *false* latencies still exceed the *don't knows* by 230 msec, it is possible to reject the proposal that the long *false* latencies are entirely due to subjects' uncertainty in the *no* condition.

Similar "equal-error" latency analyses were performed for all of the yes-no question-answering experiments (see next section). However, they are mentioned only in the one case in which they yielded a latency pattern inconsistent with the overall results.

Discussion.   The pattern of response latencies was consistent with the predictions of VAIL-A. It is important to keep in mind that VAIL-A differs only slightly from VAIL-B, the model that generated accurate predictions concerning verification of assertions and implications. Thus, the results provide support for the general VAIL formulation.

The consideration of the errors in this experiment raises some important issues for research of this sort. First, the answer to an antecedent-question sequence may depend on the reader's assumptions about the conversational postulates of the task. For example, subjects in the present experiment were instructed to answer *false* to a sequence like *the actor drank the coffee from the cup, was the coffee drunk by a salesman.* The subjects were told to think of this test sentence as contradicting its antecedent. In this vein, if a child's story described an actor drinking some coffee, and a subsequent test sentence stated that a salesman drank it, it would be reasonable to demand that the child answer *false*.

Glucksberg and McCloskey (1981), in contrast, instructed their subjects to answer *don't know* to sequences of this sort. They invoked the rationale described earlier, that a salesman as well as an actor might have drunk some coffee. Thus, neither *false* nor *don't know* is the definitive answer to the sequence under discussion. However, for the purpose of studying question answering, sentence verification, and fact retrieval it will be necessary to focus on specific interpretations of *the actor drank the coffee from the cup, the coffee was drunk by a salesman.*

A second issue raised by the consideration of the error rates, and a corollary of the previous point, is that experiments like the present one require that the subjects receive clear instructions about the meaning of each response option. Furthermore, the experimental materials must be chosen so as to avoid confusing the subject. For example, a subject can more confidently answer *don't know* to *the aunt made the purchase, the aunt purchased some flowers,* than to *the boy broke the window, the boy used a stone.* The present experiment chose *don't know* sequences of the former type.

Third, it is likely that a subject's uncertainty about the correct answer to a question will result in a longer answer latency. For this reason, an effort should be made to keep error rates (a possible reflection of uncertainty) approximately equal across experimental conditions. However, this is likely to be quite difficult to achieve.

Fourth, in a speeded task like that of the present experiment, it is possible for subjects to "trade off" speed and accuracy (Wickelgren, 1979). In such circumstances, the experimental conditions with the highest error rates will have the shortest latencies, and vice versa. In the present study, the high positive correlation between error rate and latency seems to rule out the possibility of a serious speed-accuracy trade-off.

Finally, Singer (1981, p. 52) presented a version of VAIL that generates accurate predictions concerning the task in which Glucksberg and McCloskey (1981) asked their subjects to respond *don't know* to test items like the present *no* responses. I believe that this indicates that VAIL is a flexible and versatile model, capable of addressing many facets of sentence verification.

ANSWERING YES-NO QUESTIONS

Comparing Sentence Verification and Yes-No Questions

Clark and Clark (1977, p. 101), as discussed earlier, have pointed out that sentence verification is very similar to answering yes-no questions. At the next stage of the project, it was considered useful to shift attention to yes-no questions. The rationale was simply that it is more usual for a person to have to answer yes-no questions in relation to a message than to verify sentences. Despite Clark and Clark's analysis, it was deemed necesssary to replicate the true-false-don't know experiment just discussed, rephrasing the test sentences as yes-no questions. Thus, instead of verifying *the coffee was drunk by a salesman,* subjects answered *was the coffee drunk by a salesman*?

The application of VAIL to this task results in precisely the same analysis that was described for the three-option verification task (see Singer, 1984). Thus VAIL-A (Fig. 4.1) is the version of VAIL that addresses this task.

The overall error rate was 7.6%, reflecting rates of 5.8, 13.7, and 3.4% for the *yes, no,* and *don't know* conditions, respectively. Most importantly, the effect of response was significant, with mean latencies of 2199, 2410, and 2231 msec for *yes, no,* and *don't know* items, respectively. *No* responses took longer than *don't know* for all three semantic cases (Table 4.4, bottom).

The data analysis also revealed a main effect of case, with agent latencies being longer than the others. This was almost certainly due to the fact that only the agent questions were phrased in the passive voice, like *was the book read by a chemist*? They were so phrased so that the new or interrogated element, *chemist,* would appear at the end of the question (cf. Clark & Clark, 1977, p. 79). For the patient and instrument cases, the interrogated element occurred at the end of the questions when the active voice was used, like *did the janitor use a cloth*?

In contrast, in the three-option verification experiment discussed earlier, the agent test items were phrased not in the passive but in the active. In that experiment, the case main effect was not significant. This supports the conclusion that the present case effect was due to the use of the passive voice for agent.

The results were viewed as reasonably replicating the three-response verification experiment. This outcome was considered to support the assertion of Clark and Clark (1977) of a close similarity of sentence verification and the answering of yes-no questions.

Response Index Bookkeeping

The assumption that a person maintains an internal response index during sentence verification has received support from the considerable success of investigations such as those of Carpenter and Just (1975) and Clark and Chase (1972). It was considered important to make a more direct test of this assumption. Toward this end, it was observed that people can be instructed to change their strategy in sentence verification tasks (Clark & Chase, 1972; Mathews, Hunt, & MacLeod, 1980). It was reasoned that if subjects could be induced to initialize their response index at some value other than *true* or *yes,* this would result in a change in the response latency pattern.

The aim of the procedure was to encourage subjects who were performing the yes-no-don't know answering task to initialize the response index with the value *don't know*. This manipulation would add a response index change to the *yes* operation sequence and remove one from the *don't know* sequence, resulting in predicted sequences of 1-2-3-4-4'-5, 1-2-3-4-4'-5, and 1-2-3-5 for *yes, no,* and *don't know* conditions, respectively (see VAIL-A, Fig. 4.1). This would appear to predict, among other things, faster *don't know* than *yes* latencies. It should be remembered, however, that *yes* questions have an encoding facilitation advantage. This is because they share one more word in common with their antecedents than do the questions in the other conditions. Thus, the main prediction was that the difference between *yes* and *don't know,* measured in the usual three-response task, would diminish with a *don't-know* response index initialization.

In order to test this hypothesis, it was necessary to compare the response latencies in the "don't know-initialization" task with the latencies of the usual yes-no-don't know task conducted with the same materials. A new set of materials was constructed in which every antecedent had a total of two nouns from the semantic cases, agent, patient, and instrument (Singer, 1984).

The regular version of the task was carried out as before. In the *don't know*-initialization task, the subjects were told that on any given trial, they should expect the correct answer to be *don't know*. In order that the materials conform with this expectation, nine filler *don't know* sequences were randomly interspersed in lists. This resulted in *yes, no,* and *don't know* sequences in the proportions of .25, .25, and .50 of the total, respectively.

The two tasks were examined in different experiments and were initially analyzed separately. The mean correct response latencies, collapsing across case, are shown in Table 4.5. The mean error rate for each condition is shown in parentheses. In the "regular" task, the mean *no* latency was 118 msec slower than for *don't know,* and *don't know* was 147 msec slower than *yes*. Both of these differences were significant. In the don't know-initialization task, *no* responses took a significant 222 msec longer than *don't know*. *Don't know,* however, was only 14 msec slower than *yes,* a difference that was not

TABLE 4.5
Mean Correct Response Latencies for the Three-Response Yes-No Question Answering Task: "Regular" Procedure Versus Don't Know Initialization

| Task | *Response* | | |
	Yes	No	Don't Know
Regular	2296(.069)[a]	2561(.199)	2443(.079)
Don't know initialization	2622(.089)	2858(.180)	2636(.074)

[a]Proportion of errors.

significant. Thus, the difference between *don't know* and *yes,* was, as predicted, smaller in the don't know-initialization than the regular task.

The results of these two experiments were more systematically compared using regression analysis. The regression model consisted of three dummy variables relevant to the response conditions of the two studies. Two of these variables referred to whether or not a response condition required a comparison at stage 4, and an index change at stage 4'. The third variable, however, did not refer to an operation in VAIL; but rather, to the encoding facilitation accruing to the yes sequences. Singer (1984) has argued that the inclusion of this factor is not gratuitous, since partial physical identity between test items and their antecedents has been shown to have a large impact on response times and other measures in tasks like these (Hayes-Roth & Hayes-Roth, 1977; Kintsch & Bates, 1977).

Table 4.6 shows the factor loadings for each of the six conditions. The overall mean latency in the don't know-initialization task was 271 msec longer than that of the regular task. For this reason, it was decided to subtract the constant, 271 msec, from the condition means of the don't know-initialization task that were entered into the regression.

The regression analysis revealed that comparison, index change, and encoding facilitation all accounted for significant proportions of the variance, receiving estimates of 135, 67, and 215 msec, respectively. The model accounted for 99.4% of the variance among the means.

It was concluded that the data of these experiments lend more direct support to the response index assumption than has previously been provided. Furthermore, it was shown that in certain circumstances (e.g., if there are enough distinct experimental conditions), regression analysis can be used in

TABLE 4.6
Factor Loadings for Regression Analysis Examining Assumptions about
Response Index Initialization

	Response	Base	Compare	Index Change	Encoding Facilitation
Regular	Yes	t_0	+c		
	No	t_0	+c	+i	+e
	Don't know	t_0		+i	+e
Don't know initialization	Yes	t_0	+c	+i	
	No	t_0	+c	+i	+e
	Don't know	t_0			+e

the evaluation of VAIL. The regression analysis yielded sensible estimates of the duration of some of the operations posited by VAIL. For reasons that are discussed later, however, parameter estimates like this need to be treated cautiously.

Four Response Options: Yes, No, Don't Know, and Probably

With the intention of examining tasks that closely resemble natural question answering, the major goal of the next experiment was to expand the subjects' response options to include *probably*. The subjects were instructed to make this response for sequences like, *the brother dried the dishes, did the brother use a towel*. The *probably* sequences were exactly like the implicit-true sequences previously used in the study of verification of assertions and implications (see sequence 2b-2c).

In the experiments about yes-no questions already discussed, VAIL has accounted for the relative speed of *don't know* responses by showing that the control of processing flows directly from stage 3 to stage 4' for *don't know* questions. The analysis of the present four-option task revealed that an additional mental operation is interposed between stage 3 and stage 4' for *don't know* questions. Accordingly, a second major goal of this experiment was to test the prediction that the previously measured difference between the *don't know* and *no* conditions would be eliminated or even reversed.

The version of VAIL appropriate to this task, VAIL-C, is shown in Fig. 4.2. VAIL-C combines features of VAIL-A and VAIL-B. Consider first the *probably* sequence, *the brother dried the dishes, did the brother use a towel*. As usual, the response index is assumed to be initialized *yes*. At stage 3, it is discovered that the antecedent includes no information in the case (instrument) of the new question element. As in VAIL-B, the subject next derives the needed information from LTM at stage 3'. For the present example, this results in the retrieval of the information that dishes are, in fact, usually dried with towels.

Because successful LTM searches occur only on Probably trials, the response index can next be changed to *probably* at stage 4'. The response is then registered at stage 5.

The *yes* and *no* operation sequences for VAIL-C are identical to those derived from VAIL-A, namely 1-2-3-4-5 and 1-2-3-4-4'-5, respectively. However, the *don't know* sequence differs from that specified by VAIL-A. Consider the *don't know* item, *the doctor ate with the fork, did the doctor eat some fish*. The new question element, *fish*, is in the patient case. When it is discovered, at stage 3, that the antecedent does not include any information in the patient case, control cannot flow directly to the index change at stage 4'. The reason for this is that at stage 3, the subject has no way of knowing whether the current sequence is in the *don't know* or *probably* condition. For this reason, a LTM search must be executed at stage 3'. For *don't know* items, this search fails. Then, the response index is changed to *don't know* at stage 4', and a response is registered at stage 5. The complete operation sequence is 1-2-3-3'-4'-5, the same as for the *probably* condition.

The VAIL-C analysis is summarized in Table 4.7. Several predictions are derived from this analysis. First, *yes* latencies are predicted to be the fastest. Second, there is no reason to predict faster latencies for *don't know* than for

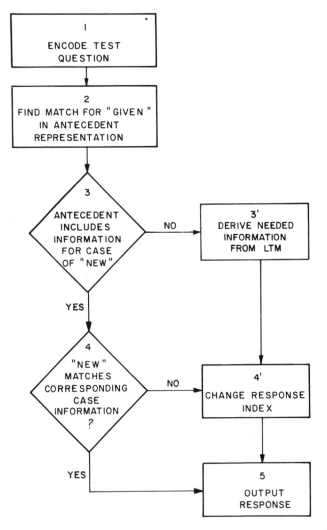

FIG. 4.2   Flowchart of the model for the four-response yes-no question answering task (VAIL-C).

TABLE 4.7
Analysis of the Four-Response Yes-No Answering Task

Response	Base $(1,2,3,5)^{a,b}$	LTM Search (3')	Compare (4)	Index Change (4')
Yes	t_0		+c	
No	t_0		+c	+i
Don't know	t_0	+r		+i
Probably	t_0	+r		+i

[a]Numbers in parentheses refer to stage numbers in Fig. 4.2
[b]The "base" factor refers to all stages common to all of the response conditions.

no trials. This is important, in that it stands in clear contrast with the three-option task. VAIL-C specified that both *no* and *don't know* trials require six operations. Since we do not know the duration of stages 3' and 4, we cannot predict the relative duration of *no* and *don't know* trials. Nevertheless, there is reason to believe that the previous advantage of *don't know's* will disappear.

A third prediction concerns the comparison of the *don't know* and *probably* latencies. Since both of these conditions require the sequence 1-2-3-3'-4'-5, it would seem apparent that VAIL-C predicts equal *don't know* and *probably* latencies. However, there is a complication. Suppose that the LTM search operation at stage 3' were "self-terminating"; that is, that it terminated upon the successful derivation of the needed information (see Sternberg, 1966). According to this view, the search would quickly succeed in the *probably* condition. For *don't know* items, the search might continue until some self-imposed time limit was exceeded (Anderson, 1976, p. 268). This would result in longer latencies in the *don't know* condition than in the *probably* condition.

Thus, VAIL-C was viewed as being equivocal with regard to the comparison of the *don't know* and *probably* conditions. Nevertheless, the experiment was considered to be a valuable one in that it tested the strong prediction that the introduction of *probably* sequences would abolish the previously measured latency advantage of *don't know* versus *no* items. Furthermore, the examination of the *probably* latencies was expected to clarify the nature of the search of LTM at stage 3'.

Method. The verbal materials consisted of three lists of sentence-question sequences. The sequences were constructed from 54 sentence sets. Of these, 27 *probably* sets could be passed through the response conditions *yes, no,* and *probably.* For example, sequences 3a-3d, 3b-3d, and 3c-3d constituted *yes, no,* and *probably* items respectively.

(3) a. The cowboy rode the horse to town for help.
    b. The cowboy rode the train to town for help.
    c. The cowboy rode to town for help.
    d. Did the cowboy ride a horse?

A reexamination of Table 4.1 reveals that the *probably* sets were derived from the materials used in the study of the verification of assertions and implications. The *probably* sets interrogated concepts (e.g., *horse*) that were agreed upon by an average of 82.9% of subjects in a norming study of inference (Singer, 1979, p. 197).

The other 27 sets were *don't know* sets, and were passed through the response conditions *yes, no,* and *don't know* across the three lists. These sets were the same as those used in the three-option verification study described earlier. Three of these sets were shown in Table 4.3.

Detailed instructions were written for this experiment, to ensure that the subjects would understand the meaning of the four responses. The subjects held the index and middle fingers of both hands in contact with a total of four labeled switches, and responded by pressing the correct switch.

Results.   The effect of case was significant in this experiment, again reflecting the use of the passive voice for the agent questions. For simplicity, and because case did not interact with response, Table 4.8 shows the mean latencies collapsed across case. The results are shown separately for the *don't know* and *probably* sentence sets. The subjects made errors on 9.4, 18.8, 17.7, and 15.2% of *yes, no, don't know,* and *probably* trails, respectively.

The Bonferroni *t* statistic was used to evaluate the crucial predictions. First, the *yes* latencies were significantly faster than the others. Second, *don't know* latencies were 67 msec *slower* than corresponding *no's*. While this dif-

TABLE 4.8
Mean Response Latencies (msec) in the Four Response Yes-No Question Answering
Task Collapsing across Case

Analysis	Type of Sentence Set	Response		
		Yes	No	Don't Know/ Probably
All sets	Don't Know	2282	2537	2604
	Probably	2228	2468	2363
Equal-error sets	Don't Know	2150	2412	2472
	Probably	2298	2397	2485

ference was not significant, it represents a clear reversal of the pattern measured in the three-reponse tasks; and thus supports the model VAIL-C.

Third, *probably* latencies were significantly faster than *don't knows*. This outcome is consistent with the suggestion that the LTM search operation at stage 3' is self-terminating.

The mean response latencies of those sentence sets that had approximately equal error rates across response conditions are also shown in Table 4.8. There were 10 *don't know* sets in this category and 11 *probably* sets. Consistent with the pattern for all sets, *don't know* latencies exceeded corresponding *no's*, with values of 2472 and 2412 msec, respectively. However, unlike the overall pattern the mean *probably* latency, 2485 msec, was approximately equal to the mean *don't know* latency, 2472 msec.

Discussion.   Several points need to be made about this experiment. The most important feature of the results is that, as predicted, *don't know* latencies were not faster than *no* latencies. It is argued that the inclusion of *probably* items introduced the LTM search operation at stage 3'. This lengthened the overall *don't know* latencies. This outcome is viewed as supporting the general VAIL model.

On the other hand, the data were equivocal with regard to the *probably* response, in that the latency pattern for the equal-error sets was inconsistent with the overall pattern. Further experimentation is therefore needed to clarify the nature of the *probably* response in the four-option task.

It should be pointed out that VAIL-C is a "shortcut" model (see Smith, Adams, & Schorr, 1978, Footnote 8). The shortcut refers to the fact that the subjects could deduce from the success of the LTM search at stage 3' that the current answer was *probably*. This is because only *probably's* involved successful LTM searches. In future studies, it would be preferable to eliminate this shortcut, which might be achieved by adding the response condition *probably not*.

Finally, it might seem that the proposal of a variable duration LTM search at stage 3' violates the principles of additive-stage models. Sternberg (1969), however, states that the duration of a stage can be influenced by relevant factors. In this vein, the present experimental variable response might influence the duration of stage 3' in VAIL-C.

Conclusion

In a series of four experiments, the VAIL model was brought to bear on the answering of yes-no questions. The accuracy of many of the predictions derived from the model indicates that the application of VAIL to question answering is a useful endeavour.

ANSWERING WH- QUESTIONS

Upon first consideration, the application of VAIL to wh- questions seems surprisingly simple. Consider the sentences in set (4). When question (4c) follows antecedent (4a), one can readily answer "salesman." When (4c) follows (4b), however, one would have to say that one doesn't know who drank the coffee.

(4) a. The salesman drank the coffee.
    b. The coffee was drunk from the cup.
    c. Who drank the coffee?

A relevant version of VAIL, VAIL-D, is shown in Fig. 4.3. The encoding of the question achieved at stage 1 might be represented as (DRINK, AGENT:X? PATIENT:COFFEE). The given element, *coffee,* is matched with the antecedent representation at stage 2. For a sequence like 4a-4c, which will be called a "Word" sequence, test 3 succeeds, and the requested information is retrieved at stage 4.

Stage 4' concerns the response index, and it requires special consideration. For yes-no questions, the response index is restricted to a small set of values, like *yes, no,* and *don't know.* For wh- questions, in contrast, the correct answer can be any word or words that have appeared in the antecedent message. Two proposals are made: First, stage 4' refers to the same mental operation as stage 4' of the previous versions of the model. Second, the response index is not initialized in wh- question answering.

The rationale for the second proposal is that having read an antecedent like *the nurse cleaned the desk with the cloth,* the reader has no way of knowing which element of the sentence will be asked about. Because of this, there is no value with which it would be especially efficient to initialize the response index. Because the response index has not been initialized, it cannot be "changed" at stage 4', but rather must be "set" (see Fig. 4.3).

Let us return to sequence 4a-4c. After the retrieval of the requested information at stage 4, the response index is *set* at the appropriate value, *salesman,* at stage 4'. The answer is finally registered at stage 5.

In contrast, the test at stage 3 fails for the *don't know* sequence, 3b-3c. The subject should be able to immediately set the response index to *don't know* at stage 4', and respond. This analysis yields predicted sequences of 1-2-3-4-4'-5 and 1-2-3-4'-5 for *word* and *don't know* responses respectively. Furthermore, it is important to note that the word condition does *not* have an encoding facilitation advantage in this task: Neither the *word* nor the *don't know* questions mention the crucial element, *salesman.* For this reason, VAIL-D clearly predicts faster don't know than word latencies.

The evaluation of this model, however, required decisions concerning several issues. The first problem was that subjects could no longer register their responses using two or three convenient response switches, since each *word* question had a different answer. One solution to this problem is to have subjects respond vocally, uttering the appropriate word, or "don't know." The dependent measure of interest then becomes vocal onset latency (see Sasson, 1982).

There is, however, another solution to this problem. It is possible for subjects to register their responses to the questions using response switches in the following way. The subject is instructed to read the antecedent and the question, and then to press a yes button if the antecedent includes the answer to the question, and no if it does not. This technique has the advantage of mak-

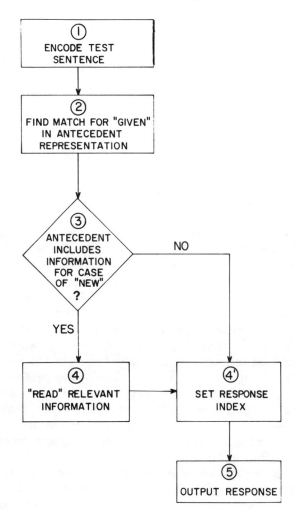

FIG. 4.3   Flowchart for the vocal wh- question answering task (VAIL-D).

ing it possible to conduct the sessions with up to four subjects. Due to equipment restrictions, vocal latencies could be measured for only one subject at a time.

A reexamination of VAIL-D (Fig. 4.3) resulted in the somewhat surprising conclusion that the correct analysis of the button press task may be different than that derived for vocal onset latencies. First, with buttons labeled "yes" and "no," it again becomes plausible to posit a *yes* initialization of the response index. In this case, *yes* items would no longer require a response index change. As a result, there would be no basis for predicting faster *no* than *yes* responses.

Second, for the button press task, it is conceivable that the retrieval stage, number 4, might be bypassed for *word (yes)* questions. The reason for this is that the success of stage 3 is enough to determine that the correct answer is *yes*. The logic of this observation, in fact, is similar to that which permits an immediate response index change to *don't know* upon the *failure* of stage 3. These alternatives made it difficult to generate any convincing predictions for the button press task.

It was decided, therefore, to conduct both a vocal latency and a button press version of this experiment. A comparison of the results of the two would indicate how closely the button press task approximated the more straightforward vocal onset latency task.

Method

Sequence 4a-4c, discussed earlier, was a *word* item for the vocal latency task and a *yes* item for the button press task. Analogously, sequence 4b-4c functioned alternately as a *don't know* and a *no* sequence.

The materials for both experiments included 10 catch trials. Consider first the vocal latency experiment. On each catch trial, the antecedent sentence was not followed by a question. Instead it was followed either by a content noun from the antecedent sentence or the phrase "don't know." The subjects were told that in these events, they should simply say what was on the screen. The purpose of the catch trials was to provide a more direct test of the assumptions about response index initialization for wh- question answering. For example, if the response index was initialized *don't know* in the vocal latency task, then responses should be faster on *don't know* catch trials than *word* catch trials. Similarly, for the button press task, the questions on catch trials were replaced by either "yes" or "no." The subjects were instructed to press the corresponding button.

Excluding catch trials, there were 10 sentence sets for each of the agent, patient, and instrument cases. Table 4.9 shows one set for each case. Agent and patient questions were signaled by the interrogative adjectives *who* and *what,*

TABLE 4.9
Sample Sentence Sets Used in the Study of Answering
Wh- Questions about Sentences

Case	Role of Sentence or Question	Sentence or Question
Agent	Word antecedent	The chemist[a] read the book.
	Don't know antecedent	The book was read near the lamp.
	Question	Who read the book?
Patient	Word antecedent	The pilot painted the fence[a].
	Don't know antecedent	The pilot painted with the brush.
	Question	What did the pilot paint?
Instrument	Word antecedent	The computer was destroyed with the torch[a].
	Don't know antecedent	The teller destroyed the computer.
	Question	How was the computer destroyed?

[a]Crucial element.

respectively. Instrument questions, however, could begin with either *how* (*how was the coffee stirred*) or *what* (*what did the salesman use*).

Results

The mean correct response latencies for the vocal latency and the button press experiments are shown in Figs. 4.4 and 4.5, respectively. The results of the two experiments were very similar. First, there was a main effect of response. Counter to prediction, however, *don't know* (*no*) latencies were 273 msec longer than *word* (*yes*) latencies in the vocal task, and 137 msec longer in the button press task. Second, there was a main effect of case, with agent (who) questions being answered considerably faster than the others. Third, there was a *response* × *case* interaction: In both experiments, there was little difference between the latencies for the two responses for the instrument questions only. Fourth, neither experiment revealed a significant difference between the latencies, for *word* (*yes*) and *don't know* (*no*) catch trials.

Given the similarity of the results of the two tasks, it was decided to apply analysis of covariance to the combined vocal and button press sentence means. There were two covariates: the number of words in the antecedent sentence, and the number of words in the question. Only the latter covariate was significant. The pattern of the adjusted means was similar to that of the original means. In particular, mean values of 2035 and 2235 msecs were measured for the *word* and *don't know* conditions, respectively. Response

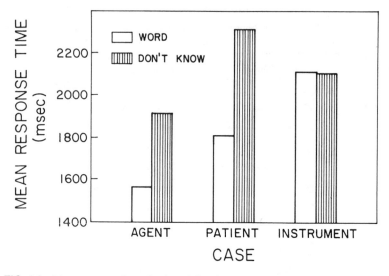

FIG. 4.4   Mean response latencies (msec) for the vocal wh- question answering task.

and case once again were significant. The *response* × *case* interaction was only marginally significant.

One possible explanation of the latency advantage of *word* over *don't know* responses in the vocal latency task is that the possible answers in the *word* condition (i.e., the content nouns of the antecedent sentence) reside in short-term memory at the time the question is encountered, while the phrase *don't know* does not. Although this possibility is inconsistent with the catch trial results, an experiment was conducted in which an attempt was made to displace the antecedent sentence from short-term memory.

To accomplish this, simple sentences expressing category relations were inserted between the antecedent and the question of each experimental item. On each trial, the subject had 2 sec to answer a question like *is a pig a dwelling* immediately after reading the antecedents. The question referring to the antecedent then appeared, as in the other two experiments. Since the explanation under consideration referred primarily to the vocal latency task, this experiment used only vocal onset latency as the dependent measure.

The mean correct latencies in this experiment are shown in Fig. 4.6. *Don't know* latencies were 288 msec longer than *word* latencies, a significant difference. This difference is very close to that of 273 msec measured in the original vocal task. The case effect was significant, again primarily reflecting the fact that the agent questions were answered faster than the others. The *response* × *case* interaction failed to reach significance, but an examination of Fig. 4.6 reveals that the *word* versus *don't know* difference was smaller for the instrument questions than for agents and patients. In sum, the similarity of these results to those obtained in the original vocal task is inconsistent with the hypothesis that the *word-don't know* difference is simply due to the presence of the antecedent sentence in short-term memory (STM).

Discussion

In all three experiments examining wh- questions, response latencies were longer for the conditions in which subjects did not know the answer than for those in which they did. This contradicts what seemed to be a clear prediction derived from model VAIL-D, particularly for the vocal task. Two explanations of this result may be offered. The first explanation states that the failure of the test at stage 3 (see Fig. 4.3) always results in a search of LTM in wh-question answering. This explanation is consistent with the analysis and results of the yes-no-don't know-probably experiment. In that experiment, it was predicted and found that *don't know* latencies would *not* be faster than *no* latencies if the subject had to execute a search of LTM (stage 3′, Fig. 4.2) upon the failure of test 3. Perhaps, therefore, it is simply the nature of an-

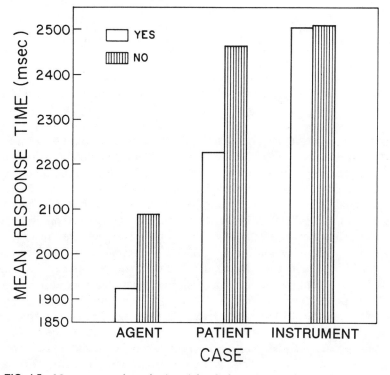

FIG. 4.5   Mean response latencies (msec) for the button press wh- question answering task.

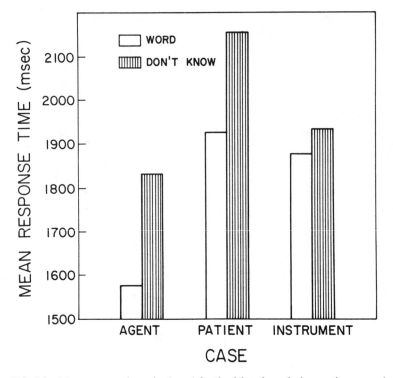

FIG. 4.6   Mean response latencies (msec) for the delayed vocal wh- question answering task.

swering wh- questions that one strives, if necessary, to retrieve the requested information from LTM. This explanation is not completely satisfactory, however, because of its ad hoc nature, and because it is unparsimonious vis à vis the analysis and results of the three-option yes-no task. It should also be remembered that both intuition (Lindsay & Norman, 1977, p. 370) and data (Glucksberg & McCloskey, 1981) point to fast *don't know* responses in tasks in which the subject can be highly confident of his or her ignorance.

A second explanation of the slow *don't know* responses is that subjects in this task take advantage of the simplicity of the materials, and arrive at their decisions by executing a serial scan of the antecedent sentence as it resides in STM. Suppose this scan were self-terminating. This would lead to the prediction of monotonically increasing latencies, from agent to patient to instrument, for "positive" (i.e., word or yes) items. It also results in the prediction of approximately equal positive instrument and negative instrument latencies. Both of these predictions are consistent with the data. There are, however, several other explanations for the speed of the agent latencies, such as the simplicity of the agent questions, discussed later in this chapter. Such confounding factors make it difficult to evaluate the serial scan hypothesis with reference to the present data.

A worrisome feature of the STM scan explanation is that if it were correct, then it would simply show that the present tasks are very open to strategic choices on the part of the subject. This would suggest that these tasks are not appropriate for the study of wh- questions. That is, while it might be interesting to find that subjects perform the immediate wh- answering task by serially scanning their memories of the antecedent, it is not likely that this would tell us much about answering wh- questions in relation to realistic messages.

Clearly, it would be wise to avoid drawing strong conclusions from the results of the wh- question experiments. It is proposed that the most fruitful way to pursue these results will be to study the answering of wh- questions in relation to more extensive prose messages. This would remove unusual strategies that might be available for the tasks used here.

Two other features of the results of the wh- question experiments deserve comment. First, several factors are presumed to have contributed to the fast agent latencies. (1) The agent questions were the shortest in average length, always four words long (e.g., *who drank the coffee*). (2) Since the interrogative adjective *what* could signal both patient and instrument questions, *what* questions would require extra processing to determine which case was being interrogated. This might increase the average patient and instrument latency. (3) The agent cases were always phrased in the active voice, while the others sometimes used the passive. (4) People can make judgments about agents more quickly than about other cases (Segalowitz, 1982). Second, the absence of significant differences between the catch trials in both experiments suggests that in neither task is the response index initialized. This is useful information about the answering of wh- questions, and also constitutes another piece of evidence that the button press task approximates the vocal latency task.

ANSWERING QUESTIONS ABOUT TEXTS

The ultimate goal of the present work is to achieve an understanding of how people answer questions about complex messages. In all of the experiments that have been described, however, the subjects answered questions about immediately preceding single sentences. The single sentence paradigm was adopted because it permitted the present work to be compared directly with previous investigations of sentence verification. Nevertheless, it is clear that one must ask whether the present results carry implications concerning answering questions about more extensive messages.

There are, in fact, several particular reasons that some of the results reported here might not generalize to text antecedents. When one reads a text, the component ideas are not stored in memory with equal probability (Kintsch & Van Dijk, 1978). Furthermore, it is reasonable to expect that the reader will forget parts of the message. Some of the predictions of the VAIL model, however, were predicated on the assumption that no forgetting would have occurred by the time the test item was encountered. Given the fallibility of the reader's memory, it is conceivable that some of the findings reported here might not be obtained with text antecedents.

A closely related issue concerns the impact of metacognitive factors upon the question answerer's decision processes. Reconsider the experiments that examined response latencies in the yes-no-don't know task. It was argued that for an item like *the aunt made the purchase with the money, did the aunt purchase some flowers,* the subjects would not initiate a search of LTM because they would be highly confident that the antecedent had not specified what was purchased. Suppose, however, that the antecedent had appeared as part of a longer text. In that case, the initial failure to retrieve an answer might result in the reader's initiation of a more systematic search of LTM. This would occur because readers may be aware of their imperfect memory for text. Readers would not feel nearly as confident that the message had not supplied the requested information. It was argued earlier, in fact, that readers carry out just such a search for *don't know* questions in the yes-no-don't know-probably task.

I attempted to address such concerns by replicating two of the experiments described earlier. In each replication, the single sentence antecedents of the previous studies were replaced with passages that were three sentences in length (see Singer, 1982).

The first of these experiments replicated the experiment that studied the verification of assertions and implications. The passage-test sequences fell into the conditions explicit true, explicit false, implicit true, and implicit false. The results were consistent with the corresponding single sentence experiment. Both the explicit-implicit and the truth main effects were significant, but there was no *explicit-implicit × truth* interaction.

The second experiment replicated the three-option yes-no question answering study described earlier. The subjects read brief passages, followed by test sentences that could be answered *yes, no,* and *don't know.* The response main effect was significant. As predicted, *no* latencies exceeded *don't know* latencies. However, unlike the single sentence experiment, there was also a significant *response × case* interaction. The interaction reflected the fact that *no* latencies exceeded *don't know's* for the patient and instrument cases but not the agent case.

Thus, experiments that have used brief passages as the antecedent messages have reasonably replicated the corresponding single sentence antecedent studies. However, the measurement of the *response × case* interaction in the yes-no-don't know experiment suggests that VAIL might need to be modified before it adequately addresses question answering about texts. Certainly, given the brevity of the texts examined, these experiments can be viewed as only a preliminary step in the inspection of question answering about lengthy messages.

MEMORY SEARCH IN QUESTION ANSWERING

In order to achieve some progress in identifying the mental operations of question answering, it has been necessary to use tasks that examine only certain facets of this capacity. Of the component operations of the VAIL models, the one that will demand the most attention in further investigations is the one referred to as stage 3', "derive the needed information from LTM memory." While it is possible to refer to the activities of memory search and retrieval with a simple phrase like this, to do so does not require much understanding of the nature of these activities. The aim of this section is to identify some factors that bear on the processes of memory search in question answering. The implications of these issues for VAIL will be considered.

Organization of Text Representation

Several investigators have closely examined the relationship between question answering and the organization of the representation of text. Lehnert, for example, has discussed text representation in terms of causal chains (Lehnert, 1977) and a variety of more complex types of knowledge structure (Lehnert, Dyer, Johnson, Yang, & Harley, 1981). Lehnert's (1977) proposals concerning the answering of yes-no and wh- questions bear considerable similarity to some aspects of the VAIL model (see Singer, 1981, p. 58). More pertinent to the present issues are Lehnert's analyses of certain complex question types, including questions about how someone accomplished a particular action, or what caused a certain event. Suppose one is asked a question like, "why didn't John have any money?" The retrieval of the requested information, according to Lehnert (1977), requires a complex search of the appropriate text representation. There are a variety of factors that probably influence the success and/or duration of this search. These factors include the importance of the fact being interrogated ("John didn't have any money"), and the distance, in the causal chain, between the interrogated fact and the requested information.

Graesser and his colleagues (Graesser, Robertson, & Anderson, 1981; Graesser, Robertson, Lovelace, & Swinehart, 1980) assigned text facts to categories like "physical event" and "goal." From their text analysis, it is possible to determine (1) the "level" of each fact in a hierarchically organized representation, and (2) the number of other facts to which a fact is closely connected ("relational density"). Using this framework, the investigators propose that the nature of answers to questions about a fact are influenced by the values of the fact on these dimensions. Suppose, for example, that "saving the princess" is a high-level goal in the representation of a story, while "finding the dragon's cave" is a low-level goal. Graesser and his colleagues predicted and found that there are a greater number of *different* answers available to "why" questions about low-level goals than high-level goals. For example, reasonable answers to "why did the knight look for the cave" might include: "he wanted to find the cave"; "he wanted to find the dragon"; "he wanted to kill the dragon"; and "he wanted to save the princess."

It is interesting that both Lehnert and Graesser use readers' answers to deduce the content and organization of the internal representation of texts. Conversely, a major goal of the present project is to use our knowledge of text representation to deduce the nature of question answering. The extension of the present research to the examination of complex questions like "why" or "how" will demand that considerably more attention be paid to the nature of text representation than has been necessary to this point.

The Role of Spreading Activation

Anderson (1975, 1976) has presented extensive evidence in support of his proposal that the spread of neural activation plays an important role in fact retrieval. His work is relevant to the concerns of this chapter, in that there are many similarities between fact retrieval and question answering. However, the fact retrieval paradigm addresses only a person's ability to decide whether a test fact belongs to an earlier learned set of facts. It does not account for a person's ability to judge an implied fact to be true in the context of an antecedent message.

In a recent study, Sasson (1982) applied Anderson's (1976) ACT model to the study of answering wh- questions about prose. He created materials that permitted the testing of numerous predictions derived from ACT. In different versions of his stories, for example, he presented either one or three facts about certain concepts. This permitted an examination of Anderson's "fan" principle, which states that the more facts that one knows about a concept, the longer it will take to retrieve one of those facts. Sasson also tested Anderson's (1976, Ch. 8) size effect. The size effect states that the time needed to retrieve a fact increases as a function of the number of concepts (nouns) in the fact (factoring out the total number of words). Sasson tested the size effect by varying the number of content words in his questions.

Interestingly, Sasson independently developed a task similar to one of those used in the present project for the study of wh- questions. His subjects were instructed to answer a question positively if the story included the answer to the question, and negatively otherwise. His results provided only equivocal support for the predictions he derived from the ACT model. While he detected a fan effect, he rejected the appearance of a size effect (Sasson, 1982, p. 26).

One difficulty with Sasson's approach may concern the version of ACT that he proposes to address question answering. Consider the fact "the dog ate the cereal in the kitchen." According to Sasson, the representation of this fact includes a node for each underlying concept, including dog, eat, cereal, and kitchen. These nodes are linked by labeled pathways to a superordinate node that represents the fact as a whole. The labels of the pathways identify the relations between the concepts and the fact. For example, the pathway from "dog" to the superordinate node might be labeled "agent" (Sasson calls this the "subject").

Having learned the above fact, suppose one is now asked *what ate the cereal.* According to Sasson, activation spreads simultaneously from concepts "cereal" and "eat" until an intersection of activation occurs at the superordinate node. Activation may now emanate from the superordinate node, resulting in the activation of other nodes in the fact. For example, the node "kitchen" might be activated. To determine whether "kitchen" is the answer to the question, the label of its pathway to the superordinate node would be checked. Since "kitchen" is not the agent of the fact, it would be rejected as the correct answer. Only if and when "dog" was activated could an answer be registered.

An alternate adaptation of ACT seems to address question answering more effectively. This adaptation specifies a focused or guided search for the answer, rather than Sasson's random spread of activation. According to this position, a wh- question initiates a search for information that plays a specified role in relation to a fact. The question, *what ate the cereal,* initiates a search for the agent. Anderson (1976, p. 477) proposes a mechanism to achieve this. He suggests that the above question might result in the activation of the network called "speaker wants to know the agent." An intersection between this network and the cereal-eat link results in the retrieval of the requested information, "dog."

The focused search proposal has several advantages over Sasson's formulation. First, it eliminates the need to test pathway labels, a mechanism that goes well beyond the use of those labels proposed by Anderson (1976). Second, both intuition and data suggest that one should be able to carry out focused searches. The intuition refers simply to the feeling that the question *what ate the cereal* does not result in the retrieval of "kitchen." More relevant are the results of a study of McCloskey and Bigler (1980). These investigators asked subjects to learn sets of facts about "people" who were identified by their professions. For example, the subjects might have learned that the "dentist" liked the country Holland plus five types of animals. When later asked whether the dentist liked a particular country, the subjects acted as though they knew only one rather than six facts about the dentist. In other words, "dentist," for this question, had a fan of one, rather than six. The authors concluded that people can execute memory searches that focus upon a specific category (e.g., "countries"). While an inferential leap is required, it is speculated that if people can execute searches focusing upon semantic categories, the same is true if that category happens to be a semantic case, like the agent or instrument.

It is concluded that spreading activation will be shown to contribute significantly to memory retrieval in question answering. That role, however, is quite vague at the present time.

CONCLUSIONS

The present chapter examined a process model of question answering, VAIL. The model met with considerable success in addressing how people make use of a variety of realistic responses in answering yes-no questions, and in specifying the mental operations contributing to people's judgments about the implications of simple messages. With respect to wh- questions, on the other hand, it was found that contrary to VAIL's prediction, people needed more time to correctly answer *don't know* than to correctly answer with a specific word. A possible explanation of the latter outcome is that when a person cannot immediately retrieve the answer to a wh- question, an extensive search of LTM is conducted. Future research will need to examine question answering in relation to extended prose passages, in order to resolve this issue.

Finally, Carpenter and Just (1976, p. 320) have suggested that a framework like that of VAIL can be valuable even if it occasionally generates inaccurate predictions. First, by specifying the processing stages of question answering, VAIL helps to identify useful lines of research about this topic. Then, in the event of unconfirmed predictions, experimental results can still be used to induce the nature of the underlying processing. This induction is not completely post hoc, in that it is founded upon a model whose principles and component stages have been shown to be consistent from one task to another.

ACKNOWLEDGMENTS

The research was supported by grant A9800 from the Natural Sciences and Engineering Research Council of Canada, and grants from the University of Manitoba Research Board. I am grateful to Alice Healy, Walter Kintsch, and Wendy Lehnert for their suggestions concerning the interpretation of the results of the wh- question experiments.

REFERENCES

Anderson, J. R. Item-specific and relation-specific interference in sentence memory. *Journal of Experimental Psychology: Human Learning and Memory,* 1975, *1,* 249–260.

Anderson, J. R. *Language, memory, and thought.* Hillsdale, NJ: Lawrence Erlbaum Associates, 1976.

Braine, M. D. S., & Wells, R. S. Case-like categories in children: The actor and some related categories. *Cognitive Psychology,* 1978, *10,* 100–122.

Carpenter, P. A., & Just, M. A. Sentence comprehension: A psycholinguistic model of verification. *Psychological Review,* 1975, *82,* 45–73.

Carpenter, P. A., & Just, M. A. Models of sentence verification and linguistic comprehension. *Psychological Review,* 1976, *83,* 318–322.

Chase, W. G., & Clark, H. H. Mental operations in the comparison of sentences and pictures. In L. Gregg (Ed.), *Cognition in learning and memory.* New York: Wiley, 1972.

Clark, H. H., & Chase, W. G. On the process of comparing sentences against pictures. *Cognitive Psychology,* 1972, *3,* 472–517.

Clark, H. H., & Clark, E. V. *Psychology and language.* New York: Harcourt Brace Jovanovich, 1977.

Fillmore, C. The case for case. In E. Bach & R. Harms (Eds.), *Universals in linguistic theory.* New York: Holt, Rinehart & Winston, 1968.

Glucksberg, S., & McCloskey, M. Decisions about ignorance: Knowing that you don't know. *Journal of Experimental Psychology: Human Learning and Memory,* 1981, *7,* 311–325.

Graesser, A. C., Robertson, S. P., & Anderson, P. A. Incorporating inferences in narrative representations: A study of how and why. *Cognitive Psychology,* 1981, *13,* 1–26.

Graesser, A. C., Robertson, S. P., Lovelace, E. R., & Swinehart, D. M. Answers to why-questions expose the organization of story plot and predict recall of actions. *Journal of Verbal Learning and Verbal Behavior,* 1980, *19,* 110–119.

Haviland, S. E., & Clark, H. H. What's new? Acquiring new information as a process in comprehension. *Journal of Verbal Learning and Verbal Behavior,* 1974, *13,* 512–521.

Hayes-Roth, B., & Hayes-Roth, F. The prominence of lexical information in memory representations of meaning. *Journal of Verbal Learning and Verbal Behavior,* 1977, *16,* 119–136.

Kintsch, W. *The representation of meaning in memory.* Hillsdale, NJ: Lawrence Erlbaum Associates, 1974.

Kintsch, W., & Bates, E. Recognition memory for statements from a classroom lecture. *Journal of Experimental Psychology: Human Learning and Memory,* 1977, *3,* 150–159.

Kintsch, W., & van Dijk, T. A. Toward a model of text comprehension and production. *Psychological Review,* 1978, *85,* 363–394.

Lehnert, W. Human computational question answering. *Cognitive Science,* 1977, *1,* 47–73.

Lehnert, W., Dyer, M. G., Johnson, P. N., Yang, C. J., & Harley, S. *Boris—An experiment in in-depth understanding of narratives.* Research report no. 188, Department of Computer Science, Yale University, 1981.

Lindsay, P. H., & Norman, D. A. *Human information processing* (2nd ed.) New York: Academic Press, 1977.

Mathews, N. N., Hunt, E. B., & MacLeod, C. M. Strategy choice and strategy training in sentence-picture comparison. *Journal of Verbal Learning and Verbal Behavior,* 1980, *19,* 531–548.

McCloskey, M., & Bigler, K. Focused memory search in fact retrieval. *Memory and Cognition,* 1980, *8,* 253–264.

Sasson, R. Y. Search processes in answering questions about stories: A possible model and a puzzling finding. Manuscript submitted for publication, 1982.

Segalowitz, N. S. The perception of semantic relations in pictures. *Memory and Cognition,* 1982, *10,* 381–388.

Singer, M. Processes of inference in sentence encoding. *Memory and Cognition,* 1979, *7,* 192–200.

Singer, M. Verifying the assertions and implications of language. *Journal of Verbal Learning and Verbal Behavior,* 1981, *20,* 46–60.

Singer, M. Answering questions from text: A process model. In A. Flammer & W. Kintsch (Eds.), *Discourse processing.* Amsterdam: North-Holland, 1982.

Singer, M. Toward a model of question answering: Yes-no questions. *Journal of Experimental Psychology: Learning, Memory and Cognition,* 1984, *10,* 285–297.

Smith, E. E., Adams, N., & Schorr, D. Fact retrieval and the paradox of interference. *Cognitive Psychology,* 1978, *10,* 438–464.

Sternberg, S. High speed scanning in human memory. *Science,* 1966, *153,* 652–654.

Sternberg, S. The discovery of processing stages: Extensions of Donders' method. In W. Koster (Ed.), *Attention and performance II. Acta Psychologica,* 1969, *30,* 412–431.

Trabasso, T., Rollins, H., & Shaughnessy, E. Storage and verification stages in processing concepts. *Cognitive Psychology,* 1971, *2,* 239–289.

Wickelgren, W. A. *Cognitive psychology.* Englewood Cliffs, NJ: Prentice-Hall, 1979.

5 Using Knowledge of Activities to Understand and Answer Questions

James A. Galambos
John B. Black
Yale University

> *It appears to me that in Ethics, as in all other philosophical studies, the difficulties and disagreements, of which history is full, are mainly due to a very simple cause: namely to the attempt to answer questions, without first discovering precisely* what *question it is which you desire to answer.*
> — *G. E. Moore,* Principia Ethica, *1903*

Moore's comment, which presages much of philosophical analysis in the twentieth century, is also relevant to examining question-answering behavior in more mundane situations. The understanding of even commonplace questions is crucial when attempting to answer them. Moore implies that misunderstanding a question leads to inappropriate answers that, for one reason or another, miss the target. For philosophical questions, this can result from misinterpreting the question in ways that are irrelevant or tangential to the point of the question.

Everyday questions can also be misinterpreted. For example, the answer to the following question varies depending on how the question is understood.

Why did Sam eat dinner at the Copper Beech Restaurant?

If we understand that the question is about Sam's *motivation for eating,* we might reply that he ate there "because he was hungry." If we understand that the question is about why Sam *chose that particular restaurant,* we might answer that "He had heard that this was a good restaurant and he wanted to try it." If we understand that the question is about Sam's going to a *restaurant instead of eating at home,* we would respond that "Sam's wife is out of town and he can't cook." These various answers do not begin to exhaust the range of possibilities. However, Moore's comment and these examples indicate that, in general, the interpretation of a question is directly tied to the type of knowledge and reasoning that is used to answer it. In this paper, we examine the influence of different knowledge structures on how simple questions are understood and answered. Specifically, we show how different types of answers indicate the differences in the knowledge structures used in understanding why-questions.

Consider the natural context of question answering. Questions typically occur in a situation with two people exchanging information. Given the potential for ambiguity in any question and the wide range of potentially appropriate answers, it is almost miraculous that question answering works at all. However, it does work because the participants share much pragmatic knowledge. From the perspective of the question *answerer,* this shared knowledge must be used to correctly understand the question and to access the information relevant to the speaker's request. The answerer must determine what the speaker knows already and thus what information needs to be provided. It is necessary to integrate various aspects of the context of the discussion (including what the participants know about each other, the topic of the discussion, the specific context of the question in terms of the last few sentences of the discussion, etc.) in order for the answerer to access an appropriate response. In this paper we examine some of the types of knowledge that must be integrated and how that integration occurs.

Question Answering as Question Understanding

Our perspective is that understanding a question, and responding to it, are intimately fused. The processes involved in comprehending a question fundamentally influence the generation of the answer by appropriately contextualizing the question in a knowledge representation that contains the information for the answer. Questions (and most other linguistic and conceptual entities) are encountered in a context. The interpretation of a question will be strongly influenced by the nature of its context of occurrence. This is even true for cases like "What is two plus two?" because in the normal base 10 context the answer is "4," but if the context was base 3 then the answer would be "11." As we said earlier, a question that occurs in a normal conversation will be contextualized by a memory representation that incorporates many sorts of knowledge, because a comprehended situation is represented in memory as an integration of the relevant knowledge structures used to comprehend it. This representation determines the way in which questions (and anything else) will be understood.

Our integrated perspective on question answering is motivated by the work of Lehnert and Dyer on the BORIS (Better Organized Remembering and Inferencing System) computer model of text understanding (Dyer, 1983; Lehnert, Dyer, Johnson, Yang, & Harley, 1983). In particular, Lehnert and Dyer found that BORIS worked better if the comprehension processes were integrated with the memory processes so that at any given point the current memory representation of the text was used to help understand the next statement. Thus integrated comprehension worked better than having separate comprehension and memory processes. Furthermore, they found that the superiority of integrated systems extended to answering questions. In particular, BORIS could answer questions better if the memory representation of the text was used to help understand questions than if the question was first comprehended and then matched to the memory representation in search of the answer (as in Lehnert's earlier QUALM model; Lehnert, 1978).

This integrated approach to comprehending and answering questions has an interesting side-effect. On encountering a question, the comprehension process adds the information in the question to the memory representation being queried. This changes the representation in ways that depend partly on the prior state of the representation and partly on the nature of the question. It is important to notice that the question-answer process involves more than merely surgically probing the representation for the answer but leaving no trace of the question information. Rather, the question adds information to the memory representation. Research on misleading questions indicates that answering questions caan indeed alter memory (Lehnert, Robertson, & Black, 1983; Loftus, 1975; Robertson & Black, this volume).

Understanding a question could involve the activation of knowledge that had not previously been connected to the memory representation being queried. In this case, the question (and the new information that was involved in understanding it) is integrated with the representation at a point in the "vicinity" of the answer to the question. Determining this point of integration is a function of the processing expectations that are active when the question is encountered. Thus, much of the "search" for an answer to a question is accomplished by the correct understanding of the question. Our perspective, therefore, differs from those that consider question answering as first specifying search descriptors and then conducting a brute-force search through a large data-base. Rather, we maintain that question understanding is the key to question answering.

We do not intend to imply that question answering is always simple and fast. Frequently, answering questions is a long, laborious task—for instance, when trying to remember specific events from one's life. However, what we do claim is that in such laborious question-answering situations, the time and effort is devoted to re-understanding the question in a number of different ways until an answer is found. For example, if asked "Have you ever been frustrated in a restaurant?" people re-understood the question by adding to the question a context likely to contain the sought experience—e.g., re-understanding the question as "Have I ever been frustrated in a crowded restaurant?" (Reiser, 1983; Reiser, Black, & Abelson, in press).

Knowledge Structures

In order to restrict the scope of the discussion, we examine only the types of knowledge structures that embody our knowledge about simple familiar activities. These knowledge structures represent information about the component parts of an activity (among which are the actions done when the activity is performed) and about the relations connecting those components to each other and to the concept of the activity. Here we are using the term *activity* to refer to a self-contained series of actions performed to attain a goal in a particular situation, and we are using the term *action* to refer to the component actions of the activity. There are other types of knowledge structures and much more complex contexts in which why-questions appear. For example, why-questions concerning the behavior of characters in a story will often elicit responses that explain the behavior in terms of the motivations and psychological states of the characters. It may be that different types of knowledge structures will be actively involved in representing information about affective states, person stereotypes, and the roles and themes that influence a character's behavior. These structures will influence the process of generating reasons insofar as they are involved in the representation of the context of the question. For example, if asked why a policeman chased a crook, one would not have to search for a motivating action because chasing crooks is something that policemen do. Thus knowledge about the role of policemen provides the information needed to answer the question. In order to begin to understand the involvement of knowledge structures in the process of question answering, we have focused on questions that tap script-like knowledge structures, since at present, these are the most well understood (Abelson, in press; Bower, Black, & Turner, 1979; Graesser, 1981; Schank & Abelson, 1977).

There are many cases where the response to a question about one action is a reason that mentions another action. For example, a reason for doing the action *Get the Shampoo* when performing the activity of *Washing your Hair* may involve mention of a subsequent action, such as, To Put Shampoo in your Hair. The frequency of this sort of answer supports our view that the knowledge structures used to comprehend the question contain the information for the response. The bases for many of these responses are the causal linkages that connect different component actions in the activities (Black & Bern, 1981). Having such causal connections is a characteristic of the representation of activities that provides the basis for answering many of the why-questions we asked our subjects.

These knowledge structures have some other features. In a number of memory retrieval experiments (Galambos, 1983; Galambos & Black, 1982; Galambos & Rips, 1982; Reiser, Galambos, & Black, 1982), four other features of the representations have been shown to influence the time to answer questions about activities. These features are the *distinctiveness, centrality,* and *standardness* of actions vis-à-vis the activity in which they occur and the *sequence* in which the actions occur in the activity.

We will describe these different features briefly here; Galambos (1983) provides a more detailed discussion. The *distinctiveness* of an action is a measure of whether the action occurs in one or many different activities. Thus the action *See Head Waiter* is distinctive to the *Going to Restaurants* activity because it appears in few if any other activities. *Eat the Meal* or *Stand in Line* are low in distinctiveness because they occur in a large number of activities. The *centrality* of an action is a measure of how important an action is to its activity. Thus *Eat the Meal* is central to the *restaurant* activity because it is one of the main reasons for doing the activity in the first place. In contrast, *See Head Waiter* is low in centrality because it is not as important to that activity. The *standardness* of an action is a measure of the frequency with which an action is performed when doing the activity of which it is a component. For example, when *Starting a Car,* the action *Turn the Key* is always done, but the action *Fasten Seat Belts* is done less frequently. The former action is high in standardness and the latter low. Finally, the *sequential position* of the actions in the course of performing the activities is objectively rated (i.e., the action *Put on Apron* occurs early in the sequence of actions involved in the activity *Doing the Dishes,* and the action *Wash the Pans* occurs later).

In the next section, we use these features to determine what kinds of actions yield what kinds of answers to why-questions. In other words, we determine the influence of knowledge structure features on the generation of answers to why-questions.

A STUDY OF THE REASONS FOR ACTIONS IN ROUTINE ACTIVITIES

In this study we examined a number of issues concerning question-answering behavior. Our primary goal is to account for the regularities we observed in the answers to the questions we asked our subjects. Prerequisite to this goal, however, was determining the regularities, and we did this by developing a classification scheme that allowed us to examine different characteristics of the answers our subjects gave to the simple questions we asked them. Our claim is that the basis for the regularities derives from common knowledge structures being involved in the processing of the questions. We gave support to this view by examining how the component parts of these structures are interrelated by classifying the parts they play in the performance of the common activities. Thus, a major portion of this paper is devoted to (a) the classification of the parts the actions play in the activities and (b) the influence of the kind of action on the type of response that a question about it elicits. From these analyses we outline a theory of question answering that focuses on the characteristics of the knowledge structures and their integration during question comprehension.

We examined responses to why-questions in a situation where the nature of the request is clear — namely, requests concerning the reasons for doing actions that are commonly performed in routine activities. Subjects were encouraged to be factual, informative, and brief in their responses, so that variation due to differences in intended conversational impact would be reduced. With the exception of a few "clever" responses, the reasons given are clear and to the point. Subjects seemed to understand the request being made by our why-questions (i.e., that the questions were requests for factual information as opposed to requests about motivations or opinions) and they appeared to intend their responses to be direct and factual. Thus, we were able to hold the request type constant, as well as the conversational intent of the response. We are classifying and explaining the variation in the straightforward responses that are appropriate replies to direct factual questions.

Why-Question Procedure

We examined the answers to questions about the component actions in 30 familiar common activities (e.g., *Shopping for Groceries, Changing a Flat, Cashing a Check*). These activities have been examined in a number of other studies that demonstrated features of the organization of this type of knowledge (Galambos, 1983; Galambos & Black, 1982; Galambos & Rips, 1982).

Subjects in this experiment were presented with an activity and one of its component actions and then asked to give one or two reasons for doing that action during the activity. So, subjects saw:

Cashing a Check — Write your Signature _____

and were instructed to write down why they perform the component action of *writing their signature* when they are doing the general activity of *cashing a check*. Each subject saw the activity/action pairs in unique random order on a computer-generated printout with the question frame:

When you are _____, *why do you* _____?

at the top of each page.

The data set collected in this experiment is quite extensive. There are 12 component actions in each of the 30 activities examined. Because 10 subjects gave reasons for doing each action (and because a subject could give more than one reason for the action), more than 4000 answers to why-questions were analyzed. The analyses attempted to group similar responses together and to determine how the type of action influenced the type of reasons given for it. Thus, we describe two types of categories — action categories and reason categories. These two types of coding were done independently so that we could examine the relationship between the type of action and the type of reason it elicits from our subjects. When reading the following, it is important to keep track of the distinction between actions (the items about which the why-questions were asked) and reasons (the responses to the why-questions).

The Action Categories

One simple formulation represents knowledge about an activity as a causal chain of actions that are performed in the course of accomplishing the activity. While this sort of representation provides a useful organization of information about the activity, it has become clear that not all actions have equal status in the representation of the activity. For example, actions embodying the main goals of an activity (like *Eat the Meal* in the *Restaurant* script) have a higher prominence in the knowledge structure. Thus actions play various parts in activities, and this variety is reflected in their representation in the knowledge structures for the activities. If these knowledge structures are utilized by question-answering processes, then different kinds of actions should be given different kinds of reasons. Relating the types of actions to the types of reasons that our subjects gave for them allow us to examine the organization of the knowledge structures and their use in question answering. The first step, however, is to categorize the actions.

Two raters provided independent categorizations of the actions in terms of six different parts that an action can play in an activity. The classification of the actions was done without reference to any of the four representational features of the actions that we discussed earlier (centrality, distinctiveness, standardness, and sequential position). The six action categories are:

1. Preparatory Decisions
2. Test Actions
3. Main Goals
4. Cautionary Actions
5. Concluding Actions
6. Enablement Actions

These are six general parts that actions play in activities. Most activities have a preparatory phase in which actions are performed to prepare for the main part of the activity and a concluding phase to "clean up" after it. The specific things that are done in these phases will differ depending on the activity, but some instantiation of these categories is present in almost all activities. The main goal and enablement categories include those actions that are fundamental to the activity. The test and cautionary categories include actions that influence the manner in which the activity is performed (i.e., smoothly, efficiently, or safely).

Preparatory decisions are mental actions that involve choosing from among a number of alternatives for the way to do the activity. Some examples are *Decide on Place* when in the activity *Going on Vacation, Check the Newspaper* when *Going to Movies,* and *Determine How Much* when *Brewing some Tea. Test actions* are those which are done to determine whether one portion of the activity is finished or to determine whether conditions are appropriate for beginning a new phase of the activity. Some examples are *Check if Done* when *Barbecuing a Steak, Count the Money* when *Cashing a Check, Look for Sediment* when *Serving good Wine,* and *Take Test Drive* when *Buying a Car. Main goals* are the actions that constitute the primary accomplishment of the activity. Examples of main goals are *Eat the Meal* when *Going to Restaurants, Brush the Wall* when *Painting a Room,* and *Sew Pieces Together* when *Making New Clothes. Cautionary actions* are done in order to ease the efficiency, increase safety, or avoid problems when doing the activity, or avoid problems in other activities that are related to the present activity. Some examples are *Stop the Newspaper* when *Going on Vacation, Get it Insured* when *Sending a Gift, Lock Seat Belts* when *Starting a Car,* and *Move out Furniture* when *Painting a Room. Concluding actions* finish the activity. Examples of this type of action are *Climb Exit Stairs* when *Taking the Subway, Pick up Bag* when *Shopping for Groceries, Shake Opponent's Hand* when *Playing some Tennis,* and *Put away Jack* when *Changing a Flat.* The final group of actions are those not classified into any of the above categories. We call them *enablement actions* because they are done to allow subsequent actions and goals. Enablement is a weak relation between components of an activity. An enablement action conventionally precedes or establishes the preconditions for some subsequent action. Some examples of this category are *Take off Hubcap* when *Changing a Flat, Buy the Tickets* when *Going to Movies, Go to Gate* when *Catching a Plane,* and *Order a Meal* when *Going to Restaurants.*

Before we turn to classifying the reasons given for the different types of actions, it is useful to examine the profiles of the actions in each of the six categories in terms of their centrality, distinctiveness, standardness, and sequential position. We argue that the different parts played by the actions will be reflected in differing value patterns of these four features. For example, main goal and enablement actions should be relatively high in standardness, since those actions are the fundamental parts of the activity and should therefore occur with high frequency across instances of the activity. Table 5.1 gives the number of actions in each category and the mean ratings on these four fea-

TABLE 5.1
Characteristics of Different Types of Actions in Activities

Action Type	(n)	Sequence	Centrality	Standardness	Distinctiveness
Preparatory Decision	(27)	2.75	7.80	7.13	3.13
Test	(24)	7.80	6.42	6.80	4.18
Main Goal	(41)	8.48	8.33	7.66	5.10
Cautionary	(32)	6.76	4.72	5.49	4.43
Concluding	(48)	9.92	4.61	7.09	4.70
Enablement	(196)	5.64	6.67	7.29	4.53
Overall	(360)	6.50	6.50	7.12	4.49

tures. Also listed are the overall means for all actions on each feature from Galambos (1983). Subjects in the Galambos studies rank ordered the 12 actions in each activity according to the centrality of the action to the activity and the sequential order of the actions in the activity. Thus the rank for any action on these two features can vary between 1 and 12 with the mean rank being 6.5. A low number in the sequence indicates that an action is early in the activity sequence, and a low number in centrality indicates that it is peripheral for the activity. The standardness and distinctiveness features were measured by having subjects rate the actions on a 0 to 9 scale, where 9 meant highly standard or highly distinctive.

The results in Table 5.1 show that preparatory decisions do indeed occur early in the course of performing the activity. They are somewhat higher than average in centrality, but they are lower than average in distinctiveness. Test actions are relatively low in standardness, which would indicate that they may not always be performed. Main goals tend to occur later in the activity and are high in centrality and distinctiveness. Cautionary actions are fairly low in centrality and standardness. Concluding actions are low in centrality and occur late in the activity. Finally, the enablement actions are essentially at the mean on all the dimensions.

These results indicate how the different categories of actions are represented differently in the knowledge structures for these activities. Actions that are high in centrality tend to be important to the goals of the activity. Actions that are low in standardness and distinctiveness are not as tightly bound up in the activity structure as other actions. That is, if an action is not frequently done in the activity and is done in a number of other activities, its relation to the first activity may not be as strong. These distinctions influence the way questions about the action are understood, as seen in the sort of answers that subjects gave to the questions. In the next section, we describe the classification of the reasons the subjects gave as answers and again use the four features in Table 5.1 to help us interpret these categories. Following that, we describe the relationships between the action categories and the reason categories on the basis of our observations.

The Reason Categories

It was a challenging intellectual endeavor to develop a classification scheme for the 4000 reasons produced as answers to why-questions in the experiment. Any simple system with a small number of discrete categories quickly breaks down in the face of many responses that cross category boundaries. In order to solve this problem we isolated three distinct characteristics of reasons, classifying them: (a) the *source*—what knowledge structures subjects use in generating their responses; (b) the *result*—what relationships the subjects see between the questioned action and the reasons; and (c) *optionality*—what was implied about the relation of the action to its activity, in particular, whether the action in question is necessary to the performance of the activity or merely a conventional or desirable part of the activity. This classification system allows us to compare the answers to questions about the different kinds of actions. Thus, we can account for how the kind of action influences the specific type of reasons given for it.

The Sources of Reasons. The source is the type of knowledge structure from which the reason is selected. Under the constraints of this experiment, most reasons mentioned other parts of the activity, but some reasons did mention things that are not really part of the activity per se. The first kind of source is *internal*. An example of a reason with an internal source would be "in order to unscrew the lugs" when asked why one would *Take off Hubcap* when *Changing a Flat*. This reason is internal because it mentions an action that is in the same activity as the action in question. The second kind of the source is *intermediate* because the answer is related to the overall purpose of the activity but not an action internal to that activity. An example of an intermediate source is "to make sure it fits well" when asked why one would *Try on Garment* when *Making new Clothes*. One does the activity of making clothes in order to have clothes that look nice and the clothes must fit well in order for them to look nice. Thus this source of the answer is external to the activity but the answer is related to the purpose of the activity. The third type of source is *external* to the activity and fairly unrelated to it. An example of an external source is "to keep my checkbook balanced" when asked why one would *Record the Amount* when *Cashing a Check*. The external source answers are relatively rarer than the other two sources in our data because the experimental context of the question led subjects to mention internal or intermediate sources in their reasons.

Action Results Given in Reasons. The second characteristic of reasons is the sorts of results they specify. Three kinds of results capture differences in the nature of the force, or impact, mentioned in the reason. The different kinds of results reflect differing relationships that subjects see among the actions of an activity. The result characteristic captures how the actions are organized in a plan structure to accomplish goals and sub-goals. The plan structure is a hierarchy in which lower-level actions are done in the service of higher-level sub-goals, and the sub-goals are done to accomplish the main goals of the activity. The differences among the results given in reasons are primarily differences in level in a plan-goal hierarchy.

The first type of result mentions satisfaction of a *high-level goal,* which is generally the main goal of the activity. An example is "to get money" when asked why one would *Go to Bank* when *Cashing a Check.* The second type of result involves the mention of a *sub-goal* that is implicated in the accomplishment of a higher-level goal. An example of a sub-goal result is the response "to hand the check to the teller" when asked why you would *Go to Teller* when *Cashing a Check.* The final type of result involves reasons that do not directly mention subsequent actions or goals in the plan of the activity. An example of this type is the response "to prove my identity" when asked why you would *Show your Identification* when *Cashing a Check.* This is a *non-plan* type of result.

The distinctions between the various results are subtle, but the rationale for distinguishing these different kinds of result can be made clear by considering four possible reasons for the action *Show your Identification* in the activity *Cashing a Check.* One reason might involve mentioning the main goal of the activity "to get the money," and another might be "so the teller would accept the check." The acceptance of the check is a sub-goal in service of the main goal of getting the money. A result like "to prove my identity" differs from these other possibilities by not directly mentioning subsequent occurrences in the plan of the activity. Similar differences in hierarchical level have played an important role in Graesser's earlier work on the reasons for actions in activities (Graesser, 1978).

Action Optionality Given in Reasons. This characteristic of reasons is concerned with the degree of optionality or choice that is specified in the reason. At one end of the optionality continuum, the reasons for actions can emphasize the necessity of doing the action in order to continue the activity. At the other extreme, the reason may indicate that the action is merely desirable in the performance of the activity. We distinguish three levels of optionality. The first is the indication that the action is *necessary* in order to continue the activity. An example is the reason "to get to the sheets underneath" when asked why one would *Remove the Blankets* when *Changing the Linens.* This sort of non-optionality is based on the notion that the causal or logical constraints imposed by the activity force the subsequent actions mentioned in the reason. The next level of optionality is the mention of a slightly weaker sort of necessity, i.e., *conventional* necessity. Reasons of this type mention the conventions satisfied by the action. For instance, a response of this type is "to greet the person" when asked why one would *Put on Salutation* when *Writing a Letter.* The third type of optionality involves indicating the *desirability* of doing the action in question. An example of this type is "to cook both sides evenly" when asked why one would *Turn it Over* when *Barbecuing a Steak.*

Classification of the Observed Reasons. Having described the three kinds of reasons and the subcategories within each of the three kinds, we are now ready to discuss our findings using this classification scheme. For reference, the column on the left side of Table 5.2 summarizes the reason categories. The first analysis involves examining the reason categories in terms of the four representational features we discussed earlier. Table 5.2 contains the mean sequence, centrality, standardness, and distinctiveness of the actions whose reasons were assigned to the different categories. The means in this table were obtained by first determining which reason was given most frequently for each of the 360 presented actions. This most frequent reason was then classified according to which subcategory of each of the three reason categories it represented. For example, a given reason could be classified as being *external* in source, *high-goal* in result, and *necessary* in optionality. It is

TABLE 5.2
Characteristics of Different Types of Reasons for Actions

Reason Type Level	(n)	Sequence	Centrality	Standardness	Distinctiveness
Source					
Internal	191	5.70	6.94	7.44	4.61
Intermediate	109	8.28	6.00	6.86	4.42
External	60	5.82	5.97	6.59	4.21
Result					
High-goal	123	7.00	7.24	7.53	4.67
Sub-goal	168	6.11	6.28	7.15	4.46
Non-plan	69	6.59	5.73	6.31	4.22
Optionality					
Necessary	223	6.48	6.75	7.42	4.61
Conventional	40	6.54	5.97	6.72	4.44
Desirable	97	6.55	6.13	6.60	4.22
Overall	360	6.50	6.50	7.12	4.49

important to note that each reason is evaluated in order to assign to it a level on each of the three reason categories. Finally, the *actions* that elicited reasons of the same category and subcategory were grouped together. The columns in the table represent the mean of the four ratings of the representational features of these groups of actions.

The first thing to notice about this table is the distribution of the reasons in the column marked *n*. More than half of the reasons are classified as internal source. The results are a little more evenly distributed with the sub-goal level being the most frequent. Looking at optionality, reasons are far more frequently classified as necessary than as conventional or desirable. These patterns indicate that subjects are indeed relying on the relevant knowledge structures to generate their answers to the why-questions. The source of the reasons seems to be within the activity structure; the activity sub-goals and high goals were the most frequent indicating that the relation of the action in question to the plan structure of the activity is frequently the basis for the reasons. Finally, our subjects specified the necessity of the action in their phrasing of the reasons.

There are some marginally significant differences among the mean ratings of sequence, centrality, standardness, and distinctiveness in Table 5.2. The standard errors of the means ranged from .09 to .52, with the mean of these standard errors being .22. So, as a rough guide, a difference of approximately .45 units between a pair of means was usually a significant difference. There are some consistent patterns among the means which reflect the relationship between the representation of the action and the type of reason given for it. As we discuss these patterns, keep in mind that centrality, standardness, and distinctiveness are different measures of the ways in which an action is represented as part of the knowledge structure of the activity. Thus, in general, an action is more likely to be represented in the knowledge structure for an activity (as well as being a more salient aspect of that structure) when its centrality, standardness, and distinctiveness values are high. In other words, if an action is high in centrality, standardness, and/or distinctiveness, then it is a component of the knowledge structure for the activity. The results in Table 5.2 support our view that these knowledge structures and their components are implicated in the generation of answers to why-questions. In order to show this we will discuss the relevant patterns for each kind of reason, starting with the source.

Those actions that were given reasons involving internal sources tended to be higher in centrality and standardness than other actions. There also is a smaller trend in the distinctiveness means where the greater the internality of the source of the reason, the greater the distinctiveness. This finding indicates that actions tend to receive reasons that focus on the internal characteristics of the activity when the actions are: (1) important to the activity (high in centrality); (2) frequently performed when doing the activity (high in standardness); and (3) performed exclusively in the activity under consideration (high in distinctiveness). Conversely, actions that are not as intimately bound up in the representation of the activity receive reasons arising from other knowledge structures, for example, generalized scenes or lexical structures.

The patterns in the data for the results given in the reasons underscore and extend this conclusion. The centrality means, for the different levels of results, indicate that reasons are influenced by the hierarchical plan structure of the activity. The actions that received high-level goals as reasons were higher in importance (i.e., centrality) in the activity than actions receiving reasons that were sub-goals. These latter actions were, however, higher in centrality than were non-plan reasons. Centrality is correlated with the hierarchical level of the action in the goal–plan structure of the activity. Thus, more central actions are performed in the service of plans to accomplish these main actions. This sort of plan structure organizes the actions in the activity, and the mental representation of these activities reflects the goal–plan relationships. Our data, on the results given in reasons, show that this plan structure is used by subjects in their generation of reasons for the actions. Furthermore, the actions getting non-plan reasons were lower in standardness, indicating that actions done infrequently do not receive reasons that are related to the plan structure of the activity.

The pattern of optionality data mirrors that for the sources. Actions high in centrality and distinctiveness were given reasons indicating that the actions are a necessary part of doing the activity. The conclusion to be drawn from these data is that the knowledge structures for these activities guide the generation of reasons for the actions they represent. The data show that when an action is strongly associated to a knowledge structure, the reasons given it tend to: (1) mention other actions in that knowledge structure; (2) reflect the hierarchical plan structure of the activity; and (3) specify that the action is necessary to the accomplishment of the activity.

While these findings fit our predictions, it is important to show that the reasons for actions also reflect more subtle features of the knowledge structures for these activities. This will be the task of the next section where we examine how actions that serve different functions in their activities receive reasons that are sensitive to those functions. In the first part of the section, we present the findings obtained by considering the three reason categories in isolation from each other. Recall, however, that each reason has a level in *each* of the three categories. Thus, different combinations of levels can show how the different kinds of actions are reflected in the reasons given for them.

The Relations Between Actions and Reasons

In this section we relate the reason categories to the types of actions that elicited them. Here again we deal only with the most frequent reason given for each action. Tables 5.3, 5.4, and 5.5 contain the distribution of the reason categories in the answers over the actions in the six action categories.

The Source of the Reasons.   Table 5.3 contains the percentages of the different sources that each action type received. The bottom row in the table shows the overall distribution of sources.

As an example in reading this table let us take the decision actions (in the first row). Of the decision type of actions, 33% received reasons that were categorized as having an internal source. Compare this with the percentage of all reasons that received this same kind of source (in the last row of the table), which is 53%. A considerably smaller proportion of the decision actions received reasons classed as mentioning characteristics that were part of (or internal to) the activity. Similarly 30% of the decision actions received reasons that were classified as being intermediate in source, which equals the overall mean for this kind of source. Finally, 37% of the decision actions were given reasons that mentioned information that was external to the activity (as compared with 17% overall). Thus, although the distribution of reasons for preparatory-decision actions is quite uniform across the three kinds of source, this pattern is actually skewed toward external source when compared with the overall pattern. Subjects relied less strongly on the activity knowledge structures when giving reasons for preparatory decision actions compared to the other types of actions. This accords with the lower distinctiveness of preparatory-decision actions that we saw in Table 5.1, because low distinctive actions are connected to other knowledge structures that can serve as the sources for reasons.

The actions classed as tests received a much higher than average percentage of intermediate source reasons (75% vs. 30% overall). Indeed, almost all

TABLE 5.3
Reason Source for each Type of Action

Action Type	Internal	Intermediate	External
		Source	
Decision	33	30	37
Test	17	75	8
Main Goal	63	20	17
Cautionary	3	38	59
Concluding	25	67	8
Enablement	71	17	12
Overall	53	30	17

these actions received reasons that did not specify other actions of the activity. Rather, the reasons were focused on the manner in which the activities were performed. The reasons for the main goal actions were more or less distributed as the overall source means, with the possible exception that there is a somewhat higher percentage of internal reasons. Cautionary actions, like decisions, have a much higher than average percentage of external reasons, but they differ from decisions in that they almost never receive internal reasons. Concluding actions primarily get intermediate reasons with lower than average percentages of external and internal reasons. Finally, subjects show a strong bias toward giving internal reasons for the enablement actions.

These patterns can be cast in terms of how the types of actions relate to the activity knowledge structure. Main goal and enablement actions form the backbone of the activity representation, so they receive reasons that have a source internal to the activity representation. Subjects are using the components of the activity structure as reasons for these types of actions. In contrast, the other actions are not as intimately organized in the activity knowledge structure. They may be represented by somewhat specialized knowledge structures that are integrated in varying ways with the activity knowledge structure during comprehension. Thus, decisions and cautionary actions get reasons that specify external information. This is appropriate in that decisions and cautionary actions tend to be performed with a specific purpose that is basically the same across instances of those actions. The general form of preliminary decision actions is "decide among alternatives." The reasons given for making such preliminary decisions are quite similar regardless of the particular activity in which they occur. One does a cautionary action in order to prevent problems from cropping up. This is a very general function that is served in different ways in different situations. Nonetheless, actions of this type serve the same end in whatever their manifestation, and it is this end that provides their reason.

These results indicate that the knowledge structures involved in generating the reasons for decision and cautionary actions may be different from activities. There are knowledge structures that contain information (in a general, abstract, and somewhat content-less form) specifying what decisions and cautionary actions are and why they are performed. Schank (1982) calls these structures *generalized scenes*. One of the touchstones for determining the existence of generalized scenes is that they encode information that is abstracted from particular instances and that serves the same function in a variety of situations. In the process of understanding some situation, these generalized scene structures are instantiated (or colored) by the particular characteristics of the specific situation. This is one form of integration of different knowledge structures. For example, the general decision scene is colored by the contents of the *grocery shopping* activity to understand the specific action *Make a List* in the context of this activity. The data in Table 5.3

indicate that the reasons given for decision and cautionary actions depend on knowledge external to the activity, and generalized scenes are the most likely source.

In contrast, the overall tendency is to give reasons that mention information that is internal to the activity. Enablement actions show a stronger than average bias in favor of choosing reasons that are internal. Thus, information from within the activity structure is seen as the most relevant in the generation of reasons for this type of action.

The test actions are interesting in that they primarily receive reasons that have intermediate sources. The generalized test scene does not provide reason information that is sufficiently invariant across specific instances. The general reason for performing a test is to become aware of the state of some process in order to modify subsequent actions in light of that awareness. Subjects generate reasons for the tests that specify the relation of the test to the purpose for doing the activity in the first place. This result was somewhat unexpected, since it might have been that the reason for the test would involve mentioning that the test was done in order to get to the next action in the sequence (i.e., there would have been a greater number of internal reasons). However, the observed pattern is quite interpretable in terms of the function of a test as a more general guide to the successful performance of the entire activity. The test structure is integrated with the particulars of the activity, but the reason for the test still arises from the generalized structure.

At a more general level, the data in Table 5.3 indicate that the distinctions between different types of actions and between different sources of reasons do permit generalizations about the relations of why-question answers to knowledge structures. This is a very encouraging result that hints at ways to manipulate these factors in more precise tests of these relationships. The utility of these analyses is further underscored by the results of the other reason categories.

Results Given in Reasons.   Table 5.4 shows a breakdown of the reasons for the different action categories in terms of the kinds of results. As in Table 5.3, the numbers are percentages indicating the proportion of the actions of a given type that received reasons with each kind of result. Recall that the result characteristic of reasons attempts to capture the basic impact of the action in question (as indicated in the reason given). Once again, the overall distribution of the reasons is in the last row of the table.

There are a number of individual action types that deviate markedly from the overall distribution. For example, main goal actions get reasons that specify high goals. Since the main goal actions are themselves fairly high in the plan to accomplish the activity, the reasons given for them must be at even higher levels. This would involve giving the reason for doing the activity as the reason for doing the main goal action.

TABLE 5.4
Reason Result for Each Type of Action

Action Type	Result		
	High-goal	Sub-goal	Non-plan
Decision	26	37	37
Test	33	38	29
Main Goal	68	22	10
Cautionary	3	38	59
Concluding	27	52	21
Enablement	35	53	12
Overall	34	47	19

Results in reasons reflect relationships among the actions and other components in an activity. Thus, the choice of a reason for an action tells us something about the representation of the action in the activity knowledge structure. Our general assumption is that actions that are detailed parts of an activity will tend to be explained in a similarly detailed way. For example, if asked why one closed his fingers around a knife (in the context of *Going to Restaurants*) it seems likely that the response would mention something about the need to grasp it, the desire to pick it up, or the relevance of the action to the cutting of food. Clearly this detailed action is also done in the service of a plan to satisfy a high-level goal (to stay alive by providing nutrients to the body). There are a large number of potential reasons for this action that fall in between these two extremes. Various circumstances in which the question is asked can influence the choice of level for the reason. Nonetheless, it appears that there is a strong tendency to match the level of detail in the question when selecting an answer. The data seem to show this effect quite strongly. Compare the patterns of reasons for the main goal actions to those for the enablement actions (which are more detailed, and lower-level actions in the activity). The enablement actions receive high-goal reasons with much less frequency than the main goal actions. Later, we return to this issue of the match in level of detail between the action and the reason.

The pattern of responses is again similar for the decisions and cautionary actions. Table 5.4 shows that they both have much higher than average percentages of non-plan reasons. This accords with, and extends, the analysis of these actions given earlier. Since the actions may be represented in generalized scene structures that are external to the activity, there is a tendency to mention characteristics of those scenes rather than features of the activity plan. Nonetheless these data do show the effects of integration of these scenes with the activity structures; 41% of cautionary actions and 63% of the decision actions have reasons that are either sub-goal or high-goal results. These two types of actions differ in the extent to which the reasons mention high goals; about a quarter of the decision actions receive high-goal reasons compared with almost none of the cautionary actions. This indicates that decision actions are much more likely (than the cautionary actions) to be integrated with the performance of the high-level goals of the actions. Thus, decisions receive reasons that mention the influence of the action on whether or not to perform the activity (as well as within the plan of the activity). Cautionary actions, when integrated with the activity structure during comprehension, are integrated at a more specific site within the plans (i.e., they receive sub-goal reasons) but not with the high-level goals.

Test actions receive reasons that are fairly evenly distributed over the various kinds of results. The pattern for concluding actions does not differ markedly from that of the overall distribution. The overall means indicate that more than 80% of the reasons reflect the impact of the action on the performance of the activity (i.e., reflect the activity's goals). This alone argues that the activity is the context within which the actions are interpreted.

Action Optionality Given in Reasons.   The distribution of reasons in terms of optionality is given in Table 5.5. The overall pattern is that reasons specify the necessity of doing the actions rather than their mere conventionality or desirability. This is expected since most of the actions are fairly important parts of the performance of the activities. However, there are some interesting deviations from this overall trend that confirm our interpretations of the data for the other two reason categories. Specifically, decisions, tests and cautionary actions differ from the others in that many of them receive rea-

TABLE 5.5
Reason Optionality for Each Type of Action

| Action Type | Optionality | | |
	Necessary	Conventional	Desirable
Decision	30	4	67
Test	33	21	46
Main Goal	85	2	12
Cautionary	9	34	56
Concluding	65	10	25
Enablement	72	9	18
Overall	62	11	27

sons that indicate that doing those actions is merely desirable. Some decisions and tests are thought to be necessary to the activity (30% and 33%, respectively). However, in contrast, main goal, concluding, and enablement actions all receive a much higher percentage of reasons indicating the necessity of doing the action in question. These patterns are quite consistent with the analyses presented so far. The observed pattern indicates that those actions that are not as closely bound up in the activity representation receive reasons that stress the desirability rather than the necessity of those actions. Subjects respond that they do a cautionary action "because it is a good idea" or "because you're supposed to," rather than "because you have to do it" in order to accomplish the activity.

Combinations of the Three Reason Categories

Let us move from the discussion of the reason categories individually to consider their combinations. The three categories are not completely orthogonal to each other. The complete 27-cell classification array (3 source × 3 result × 3 optionality levels) has 3 empty cells. It is still rather striking that fully 24 of the different combinations were observed, so the classification into these three categories permits the differentiation of 24 different types of reasons to simple questions about common activities. Of course, some of these combinations had low frequencies in our data, and 14 of the 24 combinations accounted for 94% of the responses. While this non-orthogonality is partly a result of the particular classification criteria, it is nevertheless instructive to examine which categories seem to go together.

Table 5.6 gives the most frequent combinations of reason categories given by the subjects. The clusterings reflected in the most frequent combinations in Table 5.6 are indicative of more general patterns running throughout the

TABLE 5.6
Most Frequent Combinations of Reason Categories

Category			Percentage of Reasons
Source	Result	Optionality	
Internal	Sub-Goal	Necessary	26
Internal	High-Goal	Necessary	23
Intermediate	Non-plan	Desirable	8
Intermediate	High-Goal	Necessary	6
Intermediate	Sub-Goal	Necessary	6
External	Non-plan	Desirable	6

reason array. For example, when a reason is internal in source it is likely to be necessary also. Similarly, if it is non-plan it is likely to be merely desirable in optionality.

The percentages in the last column of this table are computed by dividing the frequency of reasons, with the particular combination specified by the row, by the total number of reasons (again, using only the most frequent reason for each action). The most salient finding here is that almost half of the actions received (as their most frequent response) a reason that had an internal source and was necessary to the performance of the activity. This is fairly strong support for the idea that the activity knowledge structure serves as the basis for generating reasons for the component actions it contains. Therefore, the most typical response to a question about why one would do an action involves saying that it was necessary in order to accomplish some other action. There was some variation in terms of the reason result when the reason was internal and necessary. This is merely a function of what kind of action or goal is given in the reason. Thus, if the reason for some action is that it is required to accomplish the main goal action in the activity, then this reason falls into the high-goal result. If, instead, the reason is that the action is necessary to accomplish some low-level subsequent action, then this reason is classified as a sub-goal result.

While these overall percentages are important, the classification system permits a more detailed analysis of patterns of reasons given in response to the different types of actions. Although internal and necessary reasons are the most frequent response overall, they are not the most frequent response for each type of action. The way the reason combinations are distributed across the different action types can be seen in Table 5.7, which shows the most frequent combinations for reasons given to the various action types.

The percentages in the last column of Table 5.7 were computed by dividing the number of reasons with the subcategory combinations given in the row by the total number of actions of that action type. For example, 19% of the decision actions received reasons that were internal, sub-goal, and necessary. The findings in this table will provide the basis for claims about the relation of the action type to the nature of the reason given. Furthermore, we will examine the evidence for the degree of integration of the different actions in the activity knowledge structure. The basic pattern is that main goal and enablement actions are most highly integrated, followed by some decision actions. Concluding actions are somewhat more integrated than test actions and some cautionary actions. Finally, some of the decision and cautionary actions are the least well integrated. Before going into these claims, we want to note two general points about this table and the analyses that went into its construction.

First, it is interesting that our classification scheme based on the reason characteristics makes it possible to distinguish fairly well between the action

TABLE 5.7
Distribution of Reason Categories over Different Action Types

Action Type	Category			Percentage of Reasons for Action Type
	Source	Result	Optionality	
Decision	Internal	Sub-Goal	Necessary	19
Test	Intermediate	Sub-Goal	Desirable	21
	Intermediate	Non-plan	Desirable	21
Main Goal	Internal	High-Goal	Necessary	46
Cautionary	Intermediate	Non-plan	Desirable	19
Concluding	Intermediate	Sub-Goal	Necessary	21
	Intermediate	High-Goal	Necessary	21
Enablement	Internal	Sub-Goal	Necessary	38

types in terms of the reasons they receive. Each type of action, with the exception of decision and enablement action types, receives reasons with a unique combination of reason categories. This ability to distinguish the actions in terms of the reasons they receive supports our analysis of the actions into types based on the parts they play in the activities. Furthermore, it allows us to generate hypotheses concerning the relation of those action types to the sorts of reasons given for them. Having done these analyses, we can test such hypotheses more directly and in a more controlled fashion than would have been possible without them.

The second point is that there is a high degree of agreement within each action type on the combination of reason categories. Since, a priori, there are 27 possible combinations of the various levels of the reason categories, it is somewhat remarkable that as many as 46% of the reasons for the actions in one action type have the same combination. Thus, it is clear that there are some fairly marked regularities across subjects in the relationships between the type of action and the type of reason that is given for it.

Main Goal and Enablement Actions. Let us now interpret the results in Table 5.7. Main goal and enablement actions are very much part of their activities. The enablement actions (although a somewhat heterogeneous class at the present state of taxonomic sophistication) are those that must be done in order to get the activity done. The main goal actions constitute the *point* of doing the activity or the central focus of the performance of the activity. In the terms of Schank and Abelson (1977), these main goal actions are the Main Conceptualizations of the script. For these types of actions, subjects give reasons that indicate the function of these actions to the performance of the activity. The reasons have an internal source and indicate the necessity of the action in accomplishing the activity. The reasons for these two types of action differ in result category, but this is primarily a matter of the level of detail that is appropriate for the response (more on this later). If we ignore the differences in results, then fully 61% of the reasons for main goal actions, and 67% of the responses for enablements, are internal and necessary.

Decision Actions. The most frequent combination of reasons for decision actions was the same as for enablement actions. However, for decision actions there was lower agreement on this most frequent reason type (19% vs. 38% for enablement actions). There was a bimodal distribution of the reasons for decision actions. The most frequent reason for a decision action indicated the necessity of the decision to the performance of a sub-goal in the activity, and that the action was internal to that activity. As seen in Table 5.6 this was the most frequent reason type in the dataset. However, as we saw in Table 5.3, the decision action also had a much higher than average percentage of external source reasons. Thus, the second most frequent reason type for decision actions was external, non-plan, and desirable. These reasons stressed the optionality of the decision, i.e., that it was often desirable to make these sorts of decisions but with the implication that in many cases the activity could go on without them. Furthermore, these reasons tended not to include mention of the specific impact of the decision on other actions in the plan to accomplish the activity.

Thus, it appears that decision actions serve two functions in activities. Some of these actions are highly integrated with the activity and serve a fairly specific function in the plan structure of the activity. These decision actions function as enablement actions in terms of the reasons given by subjects. The other group of decision actions are external to the activity, and the activity knowledge structure appears not to be strongly implicated in the reason generation process.

Cautionary Actions. Cautionary actions also did not receive any one combination of reasons with a high frequency. The most frequent combination was intermediate, non-plan, and desirable. This combination was also one of the most frequent responses to the test actions. The source characteristic is the basis for distinguishing these two types of actions (see Table 5.3). Seventy-five percent of the reasons for test actions were intermediate in source, whereas the reasons for cautionary actions were more frequently classed as external. Reasons for cautionary actions are distributed fairly evenly across the combinations with external source and either non-plan or sub-goal results (reasons of these types accounted for 56% of the responses to cautionary actions). So, for these actions, the modal response somewhat misrepresents the distribution. The most frequent reason type does, however, capture the other major feature of the distribution — namely, having intermediate and non-plan reasons. Thus, cautionary actions also seem to serve two functions in the activities.

Our interpretation of this pattern of reasons for cautionary actions is based on the different ways in which these actions are integrated with the activity knowledge structures. The majority of the cautionary actions are only weakly integrated, in that the reasons appear not to mention specifics of the activity, but rather of the nature of the cautionary action in general (i.e., the goal the action serves in whatever context it appears). The other frequent reason for cautionary actions is intermediate in source (while still non-plan and desirable). The difference here is that this type of reason represents a greater degree of integration of the more general features of cautionary actions with the specifics of the particular activity. This intermediate level of source is difficult to capture, but in the case of cautionary actions, the reasons tend to specify what particular type of protection is afforded when the cautionary action is performed in the context of the particular activity. For example, protecting something by covering it prior to its exposure to a noxious substance is a general characterization of a type of cautionary plan. An example of this plan is the cautionary action *Cover the Floor* in the activity *Painting a Room*. Subjects unanimously gave the reason "so you don't get paint on it." This is intermediate in source as contrasted to the possible response, "to protect it," which doesn't mention paint as the particular substance protected against. This difference in phrasing indicates that the action is more integrated with the specific activity. That is, subjects agree on this slightly longer and more specific form when a shorter and more general response would seem an equally adequate reason. Specifying the impact of the action in terms of the characteristics of the activity implies that the knowledge structure for the cautionary action was instantiated by these particulars of the activity. This is a major mechanism for integration of knowledge structures. We return to this question of integration of different knowledge structures later.

Test Actions.   For test actions, the salient characteristic is an intermediate source. Reasons for test actions vary according to whether the result is non-plan or sub-goal, but the majority of the responses have an intermediate source. Test actions also seem to have something of an independent representation outside of their activity instantiations. Like some of the cautionary actions, many tests receive reasons that have an intermediate source. However, very few of the reasons for test actions have external sources. In general, test actions are more integrated with the activity than cautionary actions, but not as fully integrated as main goal or enablement actions.

Another difference between test and cautionary actions is that the result of the actions can be indicated more specifically. Thus, while cautionary actions seem to affect conditions that hold over sizable chunks of the activity (such as protecting the floor during painting), test actions are performed at specific points. Although the sub-goal and non-plan results (with intermediate sources) were the most frequent combinations for the test actions, the result characteristics for this action type are fairly evenly distributed (see Table 5.4). The distribution of reasons for test actions with intermediate sources shows many more answers that are classed as sub-goal and high-goal results as compared to the reasons for cautionary actions with intermediate sources. Thus test actions are more fully integrated than cautionary actions. Not only are reasons for test actions almost never external, but subjects reported the impact of the test on other parts of the activity (i.e., these test actions are more integrated with the plan structure of the activity than the cautionary actions).

Concluding Actions.   Concluding actions receive reasons that have intermediate sources and necessary optionality. There is some variation in terms of the result characteristic of reasons for this category of actions: sub-goal and high-goal results were the most frequent. This pattern indicates that concluding actions are more integrated into the representation of the activity than cautionary, test, and the external decision actions. Subjects mentioned the impact of the action on the activity in their reasons. Subjects also indicated the necessity of the action rather than the desirability indicated in the reasons for cautionary and test actions. Concluding actions have an interesting status that arises from their position in the temporal sequence of actions in the activity. These actions occur after the main goals of the activity have been accomplished (see Table 5.1). Thus, their relation to the major plan path is ambiguous. It is possible to consider them as part of a more general "cleanup" or "finish-off" knowledge structure which might serve a similar function in many different activities. Nevertheless, this general structure typically is instantiated by characteristics of the particular activity as evidenced by the high frequency of occurrences of the intermediate source level. There also seems to be an interesting "looping" pattern in the responses to concluding actions. Thus, although the reasons indicate a necessary optionality, this sort of necessity may be more related to the ability to perform the activity *the next time* than necessity in the present occurrence. The reasons given specify the necessity to cleanup so that the next run through the activity "loop" will be normal.

Summary.   In summary, the combinations of the different reason characteristics have allowed us to profile the differences in the action types. The result characteristics distinguish between main goal and enablement actions, both of which have internal sources and necessary optionality. Decision actions get two types of reasons, either the same pattern as the enablement actions or external, non-plan, and desirable. Thus, on the basis of the reason classifications, some of the decision actions are well integrated with the activity and others seem quite non-integrated. The only other actions that receive many external reasons are the cautionary actions. Here again, the result categories distinguish between these external decision and cautionary actions. The external cautionary actions have more sub-goal reasons than the external decision actions. Another group of responses to cautionary actions were classified as intermediate in source. Test and concluding actions also received intermediate source reasons. Distinctions among these actions can be made by examining result and optionality. The reason classifications indicate that the cautionary actions are less integrated into the structure than the test actions, and the concluding actions are more integrated than either of these.

Our interpretation of these findings is that the type of reason given for an action reflects the part the action plays in the activity. The nature of the reason for an action can tell us what sorts of knowledge structures are integrated. In general, the more integrated the action in the activity, the more likely its reason will have an internal source and necessary optionality. Similarly, for actions with intermediate sources the nature of the result indicates the way in which the action is integrated. Our reason classification system allows us to support our claims concerning the differences among the parts that actions play in the performance of common activities. In the next section we use our findings to motivate a model of how reasons are generated. We also discuss two important issues that have been mentioned previously: the detail match effect and the integration of knowledge structures.

CONCLUSIONS FROM REASONS STUDY

The main issue that this experiment was designed to investigate is how knowledge structures (like activities) function in answering why questions. We have just begun to scratch the surface of this issue, but the classification schemes developed here can at least point the way to further investigation. More specifically, it appears that the basic plan sequence of actions in the representation of the activity is the primary source of information for the generation of reasons.

A Simple Algorithm for Reason Generation

Based on these findings, it is possible to give an overview of how a reason generation process would work. If asked why one does some action in a given activity, the most frequently used algorithm is to respond with a subsequent action on the same plan path. If action x is done to allow the performance of action y, then the reason given for x is "in order to do y." The fact that internal necessary reasons were so common supports this sort of algorithm. The process specified in the algorithm is facilitated if the following assumption is correct:

Processing the question in the first place involves accessing the appropriate knowledge structure and instantiating the action in the question.

Thus, the question answerer will be conceptually "located" (i.e., in the correct place in the context given by the activity) to follow the plan path to the next action. If the next action on the plan path is at the same level or higher in the hierarchical organization of the plan for performing the activity, then that action can be generated as the reason for the action in question.

An example of the question-answering process might go as follows. If asked why one would *Get the Matches* in the activity *Making a Campfire,* the first step would be to comprehend the question (determining the meaning of the action in this context) by locating the action in the plan associated with the activity, *Making a Campfire.* Once having understood what the question means, the algorithm computes an answer by going to the next action in the plan, in this case the action of *lighting the tinder.* This action is placed in a stock answer frame (e.g., "in order to ...," or "so I could ...") and the response "in order to light the tinder" is generated.

The same algorithm also applies to knowledge structures other than the script. Recall that some of the decision and cautionary actions received external reasons. Our interpretation of this is that these actions might be represented in generalized scenes, independent of the activity script. The reasons for these actions seem to have arisen from a similar algorithm applied to this type of knowledge structure. In this case, the algorithm yields the goal of the action. Comprehension of the question involves the scene structure and the action in question is located in that scene. The algorithm follows the plan path, which, for these simple structures, encounters the goal of the structure.

There are cases where this simple model is insufficient. For instance, not just any action that happens to follow the action in question will be an acceptable reason. Returning to our example above, what if the subsequent action in the campfire activity (following the action of *Get the Matches*) is *Get the Tinder*? This is not a good response to a question about why one does the action *Get the Matches*. In order to find an action that is an appropriate reason for the action in question, there needs to be an additional assumption. This is that the structural characteristics of the representation of the plan reflect the dominance relations among its components, that is, actions that accomplish higher-level goals need to be represented as superordinate to prior actions that lead up to them. This assumption has been reasonably well supported by previous psychological research (Galambos & Rips, 1982; Graesser, 1981; Lichtenstein & Brewer, 1980) into the structure of the information in activities and is basic to the organization of this type of knowledge in many computer simulations (e.g., Wilensky, 1983). The search of the activity structure for the appropriate response can take advantage of this hierarchical structure by following those paths that lead to the actions dominating the action in question. The avoidance of the response *Get the Tinder* when asked why one would *Get the Matches* would be accomplished by a representation where both of these actions are related to the sub-goal of lighting the tinder, but not to each other. Thus since they are not directly related to each other independently of their having the same sub-goal, the response algorithm working on the reason for the *Get the Matches* action will not erroneously find the *Get the Tinder* action.

The Detail Match Effect

Although this algorithm accounts for the majority of the answers in our study, it needs modification on two counts. First, the algorithm will not yield unique responses. Thus, it would give (at least) the following reasons to the question about why one would *Remove the Hubcap* when in the activity of *Changing a Flat:* (a) to get at the lugs; (b) to be able to put the wrench on the lugs; (c) to unscrew the lugs; (d) to be able to take the tire off; (e) to replace the flat; (f) to change the tire; (g) to be able to drive the car; and (h) to get where one was going. This is not a fatal flaw because all of these are good reasons for the action in question. The problem is that the algorithm does not account for the consistency in the subjects' responses; in fact, most subjects say either "to get at the lugs" or "to unscrew the lugs" in answer to this question. It will probably not do (as a general solution) to say that those particular concepts just happen to be the next things in the representation of that activity. Clearly, the knowledge structures are sufficiently rich to incorporate any of the list of aforementioned reasons. This can be demonstrated by asking the question in slightly different ways or by probing subjects to give more detail in their answers.

The second (and more general) issue is how to modify the model to account for the choice of the appropriate *level* in the hierarchy at which to make the answers. The result categories in the classification scheme address this to some extent. The observation that main goal actions get reasons that are at a high level in the hierarchy provides general support for the algorithm. Also, the finding that enablement actions get more reasons that come from a lower level in the hierarchy gives some evidence that the nature of the action in question influences the selection of the level of the reason. These two types of actions are important to this issue because they are both strongly internal in source. The data show a tendency to choose a level of detail for the reason that matches the implied level of detail in the question. This can be called the *Detail Match Effect*. Thus, in the aforementioned example, the action *Take off Hubcap* is a fairly specific detail in the *Changing a Flat* activity, and the most frequent response is similarly detailed, i.e., "to get at the lugs." Also Table 5.4 shows that the main goal actions (which are high in the hierarchy) predominately receive reasons that specify high goals.

In order to account for the detail match effect, it will be necessary to complicate the notion of how the activity structure is used in the generation of reasons. In order to do this in a motivated way, it will be important to analyze the enablement class of actions further in terms of the result categories. A classification of the enablement actions needs to be worked out that is sensitive to their level of detail. The enablement actions are the largest class of actions and they tend to be quite typical activity components (as compared with the other types of actions which are, for one reason or another, somewhat "special cases"). Thus, reanalysis of this group is likely to yield information that is the most relevant to the issue of differing levels of detail in the actions. The actions at different levels in this new classification could then be compared with the result levels of the reasons given for them. A cursory analysis of this sort gives support to the claim that the detail implied in the question influences the level of result detail in the answer.

If this is borne out by more complete analyses, then there are two options for the modification of our reason generation model. One is to complicate the algorithm by having some sort of "level-of-detail determination" which applies both during the comprehension stage and during the response generation stage. A more parsimonious solution would be to change the notion that the activity has an immutable structural representation of invariant relationships among its components. This proposal would continue to have the activity structure acting as a scaffold to aid the comprehension and "location-finding" portion in the process of understanding the question. However, the representation of the action in question would not be a matter of merely finding the right slot in the activity structure, but would involve a dynamic interaction between the question and the activity in order to provide a representation that contextualizes the question in terms of its level of detail as well. This representation would be primarily a function of the characteristics of the knowledge structure into which the action is parsed. The difference is that the relationships between the particular instance of the action in the question and other concepts in the activity would be tailored to fit (among other things) the level of detail specified in the question. Hence, a detailed action in the question would lead to a more detailed representation of its relation to other components. The advantage of having the activity structure as the locus of both the comprehension of the question and the generation of the response is maintained in this revised model. The only difference is that the internal characteristics and relationships among concepts in the activity are "changed" or modified slightly from their default values. Thus, a very detailed question will be represented in such a way that the most relevant detail levels in the hierarchy are most available for the generation of the response. This "representation tuning" notion has been adopted elsewhere, in varying forms, to describe the process of using scripts to understand text and experiences in general (Schank, 1982). Thus it appears likely that a further specification of the process (based on the additional analyses of the enablement actions) will support a theory that conceives of response generation in question answering as a special case of inference and expectation generation in the more general domains of understanding.

Integration of Different Knowledge Structures

The other problem with the simple model is that it does not account for responses to many of the action categories in Table 5.7. The data show that many of the reasons given do not come from an internal source and would not be generated from the algorithm as stated. The algorithm would fail to apply because the decision and cautionary actions have reasons with external sources. Similarly, test and cautionary actions are non-plan. Concluding actions, because they are at the end of the knowledge structure, do not have subsequent actions to be encountered by the algorithm. Nonetheless, these actions show a good deal of agreement in the reasons given by subjects for any particular action, as well as good agreement among the reasons for the action in each class in terms of their combinations of reason categories.

The explanation for these regularities invoked knowledge structures described earlier that are more generalized and serve essentially the same function in many contexts. For example, preparatory scenes and concluding scenes are involved in many different activities. It is more efficient to organize information that is common to a number of different contexts concisely in a single knowledge structure rather than redundantly with each activity. Thus, insofar as questions about this type of knowledge structure can be answered without reference to the particulars specified in the activity, the answers will not mention those particulars. Rather, subjects seemed to be applying the algorithm to these generalized knowledge structures when determining their answers. This would follow if these knowledge structures are the ones used to comprehend the questions about these actions.

There are two types of knowledge structures that are involved in the explanation of the non-internal reasons in Table 5.7. (There are however a host of different types of structures that can be probed by questions, see Dyer, 1983). One of these is the generalized scene mentioned earlier. For example, the preparation scene involves a representation of the knowledge that at the beginning of an activity, a number of actions involved with getting equipment and fulfilling other preconditions is necessary for any activity to proceed smoothly. A generalized conclusion scene involves the information that actions must be done to clean up or close off situations left open by actions in the earlier portions of the activity. The goal here is generally to return things to their normal state. These structures are small plans representing a certain type of action and the goal it serves.

The second sort of knowledge structure (other than the activity) that figures into these findings is the lexical structure. Certain actions will almost always serve the same function in whatever context they appear. In these cases the goal of the action can be considered part of the definition of the action. The reason for doing the action need not refer to the particular context because that context provides little relevant information other than that provided by the action itself. For example, in answer to the question of why one would do the cautionary action *Put on Apron* when *Washing the Dishes* the most frequent reason was "to keep my clothes dry (or clean)." This is an external, non-plan, desirable reason. The action is parsed into a knowledge structure that represents the action of putting on an apron. Part of the definition of an apron is the goal it serves, i.e., covering a person to avoid contact with some undesirable substance. The algorithm applies directly to this structure to generate the answer. Note that even these lexical structures may be instantiated by information from the particular activity; the response to the aforementioned question could have been "to keep my clothes from getting *dishwater* spilled on them." This response, however, did not occur, so we conclude that it was unnecessary to instantiate the lexical structure with the specifics of the dishwashing activity in order to generate an appropriate answer.

While there are a number of external, non-plan reasons that may not require activity information in order to generate an appropriate response, they appear to be the exception rather than the rule. Only 17% of all answers had an external source. Even among non-internal types of actions, there are a sizeable number of reasons that reflect a certain amount of integration of the external knowledge structures with the characteristics specific to the activity. Intermediate sources contain many instances of this sort of integration. Schank (1982), Dyer (1983) and Graesser and Clark (in press) discuss a number of theoretical issues concerning integration of knowledge structures such as, when the integration occurs, how the integration takes place, how the characteristics of the knowledge structures to be integrated influence the resulting integrated representation, and what impact this representation has on the process of question answering and, more generally, understanding text.

We have seen examples where some sort of integration of knowledge structures seems to have occurred in the generation of a reason for an action. These were cases in which an action received a reason that while mentioning characteristics of the activity, nevertheless seemed to go with that action in whatever activity it might appear. The mechanism to account for this type of answer involves the comprehension of the question. It is during the comprehension process that the internal representation is formed that reflects the integration of multiple knowledge structures. Thus, if the question can be understood by utilizing only a single knowledge structure (the activity in the majority of cases in these data), then there need not be any additional knowledge structures implicated in the reason given for the action. If, however, understanding the question involves determining the relation of a non-activity knowledge structure to the particular activity, then the internal representation will include information that was originally stored in the two different structures. Because it is this resulting representation to which the answer generation algorithm applies, the reasons given for actions of this sort will reflect some mix of information from the two structures. In order to examine issues of integration it is necessary to reanalyze the reasons with intermediate sources. One interesting issue here would be to examine the different sites of integration for different types of actions. Information relevant to this would be obtained by examining the result categories, since reasons at different result levels indicate the impact in the activity of the action in the question. Integration of another knowledge structure with the script can occur at the high-goal level (as was the case with some concluding actions) and at the subgoal level (test actions). This kind of analysis might pin down, to some extent, the range of variability in the types of integration.

We have outlined a general process model of question answering, and we have described two areas where that model needs to be extended by further analysis of the data. Throughout, we have attempted to develop the model in such a way that the process of question answering shares many of the attributes of information processing in more general domains such as text and discourse understanding. Since question understanding is so fundamental to the process of question answering, it is not surprising that the knowledge structures that are used to process the questions leave their mark on the answers. We have gone a step further in our analyses by demonstrating how different sorts of knowledge structures are integrated during question understanding. It is our view that the theory of question answering is a special case of the much broader theory of language comprehension. This special case however provides an important research opportunity.

Knowledge structure integration is an extremely complex phenomenon. Our approach to the study of this phenomenon has been to collect and analyse responses to questions about very familiar activities. This technique allows us to examine integration where the number of structures that potentially can be integrated is quite constrained. In future experiments, it may be possible to manipulate the knowledge structures that are integrated by careful selection of question type. If so, we may have an important tool with which to examine various types of knowledge structure integration, one of the key issues in any theory of language comprehension.

ACKNOWLEDGMENTS

We would like to thank Arthur Graesser for comments on an earlier version of this paper. We would also like to thank William Ressler and Steven Read for their help in coding and analyzing these data and for their helpful comments. The writing of this report was supported by a grant from the System Development Foundation.

REFERENCES

Abelson, R. P. The psychological status of the script concept. *American Psychologist,* 1981, *36,* 715–729.

Black, J. E., & Bern, H. Causal coherence and memory for events in narratives. *Journal of Verbal Learning and Verbal Behavior,* 1981, *20,* 267–275.

Bower, G. H., Black, J. B., & Turner, T. J. Scripts in memory for text. *Cognitive Psychology,* 1979, *11,* 177–220.

Dyer, M. G. In-depth understanding: A computer model of integrated processing for narrative comprehension. Cambridge, MA: MIT Press, 1983.

Galambos, J. A. Normative studies of six characteristics of our knowledge of common activities. *Behavioral Methods and Instrumentation,* 1983, *15,* 327–340.

Galambos, J. A., & Black, J. B. Getting and using context: Functional constraints on the organization of knowledge. *Proceedings of the Fourth Conference of the Cognitive Science Society.* Ann Arbor, Michigan, 1982.

Galambos, J. A., & Rips, L. J. Memory for routines. *Journal of Verbal Learning and Verbal Behavior,* 1982, *21,* 260–281.

Graesser, A. C. How to catch a fish: The representation and memory of common procedures. *Discourse Processes,* 1978, *1,* 72–89.

Graesser, A. C. *Prose comprehension beyond the word.* New York: Springer-Verlag, 1981.

Graesser, A. C., & Clark, L. F. *The structures and procedures of implicit knowledge.* Norwood, NJ: Ablex, in press.

Lehnert, W. G. *The process of answering questions.* Hillsdale, NJ: Lawrence Erlbaum Associates, 1978.

Lehnert, W. G., Dyer, M. G., Johnson, P. N., Yang, C. J., & Harley, S. BORIS — An in-depth understander of narratives. *Artificial Intelligence,* 1983, *20,* 15–62.

Lehnert, W. G., Robertson, S. P., & Black, J. B. Memory interactions during question answering. In H. Mandl, N. L. Stein, & T. Trabasso (Eds.), *Learning from text.* Hillsdale, NJ: Lawrence Erlbaum Associates, 1983.

Lichtenstein, E. H., & Brewer, W. F. Memory for goal-directed events. *Cognitive Psychology,* 1980, *12,* 412–445.

Loftus, E. F. Leading questions and the eyewitness report. *Cognitive Psychology,* 1975, *7,* 560–572.

Reiser, B. J. *Contexts and indices in autobiographical memory.* Ph.D. dissertation, Yale University, 1983.

Reiser, B. J., Black, J. B., & Abelson, R. P. Knowledge structures in the organization and retrieval of autobiographical memories. *Cognitive Psychology,* in press.

Reiser, B. J., Galambos, J. A., & Black, J. B. *Retrieval from semantic and autobiographical memory.* Paper presented at the Twenty-third Annual Meeting of the Psychonomic Society, 1982.

Schank, R. C. *Dynamic memory: A theory of reminding in people and computers.* New York: Cambridge University Press, 1982.

Schank, R. C., & Abelson, R. P. *Scripts, plans, goals and understanding.* Hillsdale, NJ: Lawrence Erlbaum Associates, 1983.

Wilensky, R. *Planning and understanding.* Reading, MA: Addison-Wesley, 1983.

6

Misleading Question Effects as Evidence for Integrated Question Understanding and Memory Search

Scott P. Robertson[1]
John B. Black
Wendy G. Lehnert[2]
Yale University

ABSTRACT

Questions containing misleading presuppositions can alter memory, either by replacing old information or by introducing new information. In this chapter we turn to an analysis of this phenomenon in the context of narrative comprehension and representation. We argue first that question comprehension and information retrieval are not separate stages of processing, but rather two facets of the same integrated mechanism. We suggest that memory modification is an integral part of normal comprehension because it is always necessary to correct erroneous inferences and otherwise alter unfulfilled expectations that are generated during understanding. Next we present experimental results that explore the modifiability of representationally different kinds of information, actions versus states, and that show memory modification by inferential processes. Because of their central role in narrative representations, actions were shown to be harder to modify than states. However, because inferential processes operate primarily among connected actions, modification of actions by inference was more likely than modification of states. Finally, we suggest a new way to approach the issue of memory modification by detailing some representational issues revealed by a few

[1]Now in the Psychology Department at The Catholic University of America, Washington, D.C.

[2]Now in the Department of Computer and Information Sciences at the University of Massachusetts, Amherst.

items used in our experiments. In this last section we will specify some general computational difficulties that are encountered when detailed representations are being considered.

1.   INTRODUCTION

Most questions contain at least two parts. One part indicates the type of question that is being asked and the other part specifies what is being asked about. Consider the question *Why are Scott, John, and Wendy writing a chapter for the question book?* In this question, the word "Why" signifies to the answerer that he or she will be required to search memory for a goal or motivation. The rest of the question asserts that three specific people are writing a chapter for a particular book. This assertion contains the information required for directing the memory search. This information is referred to as the question *presupposition* because the answerer can presuppose that it is true. When questions are asked in a cooperative manner, the information used to direct memory search is presumed, by the question asker, to be present in the memory of the other person.

Memory can be affected by information contained in the presuppositions of questions. Loftus (1979) has conducted a number of studies demonstrating the effects of misleading question presuppositions on memory for traffic accidents and other incidents with legal consequences. She and her colleagues have demonstrated that when a question presupposes an event or state of the world that is new or that contradicts an event already witnessed, the novel information may later be found in memory for the witnessed event. For example, in one study Loftus (1975) showed subjects a short film depicting a traffic accident at an intersection. Later, she asked subjects the question "How fast was [the car] going when it ran the stop sign?" Among other things, this question presupposes that there was a stop sign at the intersection. In fact, for some of Loftus' subjects there was no stop sign shown in the film. After answering this question, however, many of the subjects in the no-sign condition said that they remembered seeing a stop sign in the slide sequence. The misleading question presupposition had introduced new information into their memories.

There has been considerable discussion regarding how to interpret Loftus' findings. Much attention has been paid, for example, to the question of whether new information introduced into prior memory representations alters old information in some way or simply "coexists" with it and is more retrievable (Greene, Flynn, & Loftus, 1982). We would like to turn our attention, however, to the broader implications of Loftus' findings for computationally based models of question answering. Specifically, we think that memory modification by misleading questions derives naturally from a model of question answering that *integrates* understanding processes and memory search procedures. In this paper we develop this view and report some experiments we have done to test it.

We first present the *integrated processing* view in the context of story comprehension and sentence understanding. In this view, memory is very active during sentence understanding and it is assumed that many false expectations and inferences are generated while a sentence is being understood. Erroneous information generated in this way must be quickly discarded, *on-line,* in light of new incoming information. Memory modification during understanding is thus seen as a natural component of integrated processing.

After introducing the integrated processing view in the context of sentence understanding, we address some additional issues involved in question understanding. We argue that the same interactions that occur with memory during sentence understanding, plus new interactions necessitated by question-answering procedures, occur during question understanding. Again, this claim implies that memory modification is a natural component of the question-answering process.

After this initial theoretical treatment, we report some experiments on memory modification that we believe demonstrate the integrated nature of question parsing and memory search. One experimentally interesting avenue of research in this area examines the question of what kind of information is easy to modify and what kind is difficult to modify. Predictions about this issue derive from the representational characteristics of different kinds of information and how we feel that question-answering procedures operate on different kinds of representations. The results of the experiments depend on processes of inference and memory interaction during question understanding.

Finally, we face the issue of conceptual representations in more detail by exploring some of the computational mechanisms involved in memory modification. Our last section is a collection of case studies on some of the experimental items. These analyses assume that the representations being modified are in a canonical form like that specified by conceptual dependency theory (Schank, 1975), and that they are isolated from other knowledge structures that may be present.

2.   FROM MODULAR SYSTEMS TO INTEGRATED PROCESSING

2.1. Computational Models of Story Understanding

Many computer models of story comprehension involve separate stages for sentence parsing and memory integration (Cullingford, 1978; Marcus, 1980;

Riesbeck & Schank, 1978; Wilks, 1973; Winograd, 1972; Woods, Kaplan, & Nash-Webber, 1972). In such systems, a natural language sentence undergoes an initial transformation into a grammatical form or canonical case frame. These structures, in turn, are used as input to a separate module in which conceptual or semantic interpretation occurs. This approach involves a "double parsing" (DeJong, 1979) in which a second, concept module interprets the output of a primary, syntactic parser. Even in models where some conceptual analysis is allowed during initial parsing, conceptual mechanisms are typically called in when help is needed to produce parts of the syntactic representation (Marcus, 1980; Winograd, 1972).

Other comprehension models favor a more *integrated* approach in which conceptual structures become involved in the understanding process as soon as possible and syntactic analysis is deemphasized (DeJong, 1979; Lebowitz, 1980; Schank & Birnbaum, in press). Such models introduce predictive components in which knowledge frames produce expectations about the nature of future input. Instead of pre-parsed syntactic structures or canonical information being input to conceptual analyzers, in many of these comprehension models an initial conceptual analysis produces canonical forms that can be used to incorporate incoming information. Canonical representations now become the *product* of conceptual analysis, not the input.

In conceptually driven systems, in which predictive knowledge structures guide parsing, the story understander's job becomes to match input to expectations. Expectation generation actually narrows the field of possible interpretations, so expectation-based parsers actually save computational work compared to more *bottom-up* approaches. Interestingly, once expectations are matched to input, much of the work of conceptual inferencing and causal connection is completed as well. The distinction between parsing and conceptual analysis becomes blurred, if not altogether misleading. The most important aspect of the integrated approach in this context, however, is the fact that generic knowledge structures and episodic information in memory are activated by sentence understanding procedures *during reading*.

2.2. Psychological Evidence for Integrated Processing

Several experimental studies have supported the conceptually driven approach to sentence understanding, particularly by demonstrating that episodic memory traces are activated during reading. When a sentence in a story is read, it provides the reader both with *new* information that will enhance the reader's representation of the story, and with *old* information that provides directions for how to integrate the new embellishments into the existing representation. Reading time experiments have established that when old information is encountered, the time to read a sentence increases (Clark & Haviland, 1977). This increase is due to integration processes involving the establishment of referents and the generation of inferences necessary to establish coherent bridges between textual information and old information in memory. Reading time increases have also been shown for pronouns, other nouns with prior antecedents, and sentence presuppositions.

The exact concepts that are activated by referential components of sentences have been studied using priming techniques (Ratcliff & McKoon, 1978). A priming methodology allows measurement of concept activation during reading. In the typical paradigm, reading times of critical sentences or concepts are measured in contexts where the information in the sentences is predicted to be active or not active. Activated concepts can be recognized and understood in a shorter amount of time than unactivated concepts. The results of priming studies confirm that the understanding of anaphoric reference involves activation of antecedents in memory and the activation of information conceptually related to antecedents (McKoon & Ratcliff, 1980). Also, priming studies have demonstrated the activation of inferential material in memory, including instrument inferences (McKoon & Ratcliff, 1981). Current work along these lines is investigating the on-line activation of inferences about goals and even thematic knowledge structures (Seifert, Robertson, & Black, 1982).

There is considerable experimental evidence from other methodologies that inferences about goals, plans, and causally related actions are activated during reading (Graesser, 1981; Seifert et al., 1982; Warren, Nicholas, & Trabasso, 1979). Such inferences operate to connect story elements both by backward chaining and by expectation generation. Seifert et al., for example, measured the reading times of sentences in several stories. Their subjects took longer to read statements about actions when the motivating goals for the actions were not stated. They demonstrated the same effect for unstated plans. Their findings suggest that inferences about the goals and plans of characters are being generated while subjects are reading about the characters' actions.

2.3. The Additional Components of Question Understanding

Many models of question answering divide processing into separate stages for question parsing and information retrieval (Lehnert, 1978; Winograd, 1972; Woods, 1978). A modular approach to question answering seems quite reasonable at first because understanding a question and looking for an answer seem intuitively to be different kinds of processes. We quite naturally think of memory as a data base in which information about past experience resides and consider questions to be search keys that are applied to that data base. From this perspective, it seems important to have as complete a search key as possible *before entering* the data base. The construction of a good search key out of a natural language question thus becomes a separate matter from search heuristics.

Many artificial intelligence researchers and others working in the area of story comprehension, however, have suggested that memory and comprehension processes are highly interrelated (DeJong, 1979; Gershman, 1979; Granger, 1980; Schank & Birnbaum, in press; Schank, Lebowitz, & Birnbaum, 1980). Since we know that there is considerable conceptual analysis of sentences during understanding, there is every reason to believe that similar conceptual analysis would be going on while questions are being understood. We suggest that this conceptual analysis is exploited by question-*answering* processes during understanding as well (Dyer, 1982; Dyer & Lehnert, 1980, 1982; Lehnert, Dyer, Johnson, Yang, & Harley, 1983; Lehnert, Robertson, & Black, 1983). That is, to understand the meaning of a question, appropriate generic knowledge structures and episodic information must be activated. This information is also useful in directing memory search procedures and should be utilized *during understanding.*

The additional component of *question* understanding (as opposed to sentence understanding) is the determination of a question category (Lehnert, 1978) and thereby the activation of specific memory search procedures. Expectations about the category of a question can usually be generated early on in question understanding. Often the first word is enough to narrow the possibilities considerably. For example, a question that starts off with the word "Why" is most likely a *causal antecedent,* or *goal orientation* question. A question that starts with "How many" is surely a *quantification* question. "Did" signals a *verification* question, and so on. Knowledge of the question category allows the use of specific search strategies that can be applied to whatever portion of a conceptual representation is activated by the rest of the question. For example, when a *why* question is being asked, an integrated question answerer can be ready to search causal links and reason links even before the event or action being asked about is known. This gives the question-answering process a head start and allows search of knowledge structures activated by incoming information during understanding. In a more modular system, these knowledge structures would have to be kept active until the entire question was asked, or pointers to them would have to be set up, or memory would have to be searched again after initial understanding in order to reactivate them.

A further advantage of integrated question processes is that criteria for what kind of information will constitute a good answer can be determined early. This is important because if relevant information is activated during understanding it can be caught immediately by question-answering procedures. In this view, *answer demons* are activated as soon as possible and can be applied to the information activated by understanding processes. This increases efficiency and decreases the time for derivation of an answer.

As an example, consider the question "Why did Mary marry John?" When the word "Why" is read, procedures can be activated that will select motivation links in the memory representation for search. To answer a question of the form "Why-action," one strategy is to follow any motivation links from the specified action (Graesser, 1981; Lehnert, 1978). "Did" signifies that the action is about to be specified. When "Mary" is read, it may be possible to initiate search strategies immediately. We know from experiments on sentence understanding that the concept **Mary** is activated *when the name is read*. Thus, the portion of the memory representation relevant to the episode being questioned may be activated at this time. If the memory representation contains only one action with Mary as the actor (i.e., that she got married), then a search can be made for motivation links and appropriate answers to the question can be activated at this point during understanding. Alternatively, when the verb "marry" is read, the action is sufficiently specific to allow a search for motivation links (assuming there was only one marriage in the memory representation). By the time "John" is read, memory search may be complete and an answer could be ready (Dyer & Lehnert, 1982).

Memory is therefore extremely active during question processing, with both understanding and answer-search processes at work. Given this level of activity, it is not surprising that questions containing misleading presuppositions affect memory. However, this effect is an instance of a more general phenomenon involving the interaction of incoming information with information already in memory. Not all concepts activated or generated by comprehension processes will be useful or even appropriate, however. Predictive understanding mechanisms require that many dead-end concepts be activated during comprehension, and because of this, memory modification is a natural part of comprehension. We turn next to the issue of memory modification.

3.   THE EFFECT OF UNDERSTANDING PROCESSES ON MEMORY

3.1. Memory Modification in Normal Comprehension

The price that a predictive understanding mechanism pays for faster, on-line comprehension is the probable generation of erroneous inferences. Erroneous inferences are simply predictive components of activated knowledge structures that turn out to be unnecessary for connecting propositions or that incorrectly connect propositions. For example, the sentence "He hit the nail on the head" may give rise to the inference that a hammer was swung at the nail. This inference serves to connect the isolated action in a longer chain of events and foregrounds concepts like *hammer* that may be useful in future comprehension processes. Other inferences may be made as well, such as *there was wood, something was being built, the nail went into wood,* and so forth. The next sentence, however, might be "The rock split as the nail bent on the chrome surface." This sentence nullifies the validity of the instrument inference about a hammer and all of the inferences about wood.

In an experiment aimed at discovering the inferences available at different points during reading (Graesser, Robertson, & Clark, 1983) it was estimated that, on the average, 31% of the potential inferences about goals in a story and 47% of the potential inferences about upcoming actions will prove to be erroneous. Erroneous inferences may never connect to anything else and therefore fade away, they may be contradicted by later information, or they may remain in the representation as invalid inferences. Whatever happens to them, it is clear that much of the time, especially during comprehension, memory will contain not only incomplete information, but *incorrect* information as well.

While many such inferences can be blocked from generation at the time of reading (Rieger, 1975), many will have to be taken care of at a later time when new information becomes available (Graesser, 1981; Granger, 1980). A considerable amount of processing must be devoted to recognizing and cleaning up unnecessary conceptual information generated by inference processes during understanding. Therefore, it is a characteristic of an integrated processing mechanism that information in memory, no matter what its source, must be modifiable.

3.2. Memory Modification During Question Understanding

The same comprehension processes that are used to understand statements are used to understand questions. Questions may contain presuppositions and pronouns with prior referents, present new information, cause inferences to be generated, and disconfirm erroneous inferences. Often, concepts already in memory must be accessed to understand a question correctly. This interaction with memory can cause modifications to information already in memory.

As an example, consider the following story and set of questions (from Lehnert et al., 1983):

John and Bill went to a restaurant to discuss a business deal. When the meal was over, John left a very large tip, and apologized to Bill for wasting his time. Bill encouraged John to look for another investor, and they went their separate ways.

Question 1: Was the meal a success?
Question 2: Why did he leave a big tip?
Question 3: Why did John apologize to Bill after lunch?

The first question has two interpretations, *Was the meal good?* and *Did the business deal succeed?* In a modular approach to question comprehension and memory search, the version of the question to use as a search key for an answer would have to be determined before memory search began. Alternatively, both interpretations would have to be used in different searches and a decision would have to be made later about which answer was appropriate. However, the context of the story determines which version of the question is relevant. Therefore, the memory representation for the story must be accessed in order to understand the question. We believe that, for most people, the question is never understood in more than one way because of constraints put on the understanding process by the relevant knowledge in the story. Indeed, for verification questions like Question 1, the understanding of a question amounts to the same thing as searching for an answer, since when the information necessary to understand the question is retrieved, the answer is retrieved as well (Dyer, 1982).

Similarly, the pronoun in Question 2 requires that the story representation be consulted in order that the referent be understood. Since there are two individuals mentioned in the story that could technically serve as antecedents to the pronoun *he,* interactions with memory must be complex in order to resolve the referent correctly. When the word *leave* is read, referential processes activated by the earlier pronoun can now successfully disambiguate it.

Unlike verification questions, further processing will be required in order to find or generate an answer to the *why* component of Question 2. But this further processing is not a separate stage of question analysis. Instead, it is a continuation of ongoing processing involving the story representation that started at the word *Why.* In a predictive understander, search mechanisms for reason links to goals and actions would be activated by the word *Why,* and expectations would be generated for an upcoming description of an event or action. When the word *leave* is encountered, the only action in the story involving a leaving episode with one actor is John's leaving of the tip. Reason links to those goal nodes that are connected to the episode involving the tip could be traversed immediately upon designation of the episode. This would begin even before the question was completely read.

Our final example question, Question 3, includes information that was not presented in the story, specifically that the meal was *lunch.* Presumably, there is some portion of the story representation that includes information about a meal, and at some point an inference about the kind of meal John and Bill were having may have been generated. If such an inference was *not* made during reading, the new information in the question provides this information explicitly and we would expect the meal specification to be incorporated into the representation during understanding of the question. It is as if subjects had read an additional statement like *The meal John and Bill had was lunch.*

If an inference *was* made about the kind of meal John and Bill had, two very different understanding processes will be set in motion depending on whether the inference was right or wrong. If it was right, then the inferred concept (i.e., lunch), would be activated during comprehension of the question as part of a simple referential process (again, indicating that the story representation was being accessed during question comprehension). If it was wrong, as many inferences naturally are, then the new information should overwrite the erroneous inference. This is what we would expect when a sentence is read that contains new information contradicting erroneous prior inferences (Graesser, 1981; Granger, 1980). A similar mechanism employed during question answering would not be surprising.

Memory modification by misleading question presuppositions, or other incorrect information in questions, seems to be no different than modification, activation, or updating of memory by other means. The fact that questions produce the same kinds of effects on memory as sentences containing new, more specific, or contradictory information is evidence for an integrated understanding and memory search mechanism for questions.

4. WHAT KIND OF INFORMATION CAN BE MODIFIED?

Research on effects of misleading or inconsistent information on memory has been devoted primarily to demonstrating that misleading does occur (Loftus, 1979) and to differentiating between a "coexistence" and an "alteration" model of memory modification (Greene et al., 1982). The coexistence model suggests that inconsistent information introduced into an existing memory representation coexists with the old information but is somehow more retrievable. The alteration model holds that old information is replaced by new information. Because we believe that memory is modified as part of normal processing, we think that the alteration model is more accurate. In either case, we feel that an interesting avenue of research would be to show different degrees of modification depending on the representational nature of the material being modified. If understanding a question is very much like understanding a sentence in a story, then we should find story comprehension processes (such as inference generation) operating not only during sentence understanding but also when questions are asked.

In most prior studies of memory modification, target episodes that were relatively easy to modify were selected for study. However, the issue of why some episodes or items are easier to modify than others has not typically been addressed. The reasons that some kinds of information are easier to modify than others must be found in the representational details of the concepts being modified. In particular, some kinds of representations are structurally more central than others, and this should make them harder to modify.

4.1. The Representational Distinction Between States and Actions

One representational distinction that has received considerable attention in the literature on story understanding is the distinction between actions and states. An *action* is a behavior by an animate actor that is directed toward a goal. Actions are connected to other information in memory in causal and motivational networks that are very central to narrative structures. When a why question is asked about an action, for example, a reason or goal state is typically given as the answer. One goal may dominate a number of subordinate actions in a hierarchical fashion, and long goal-subgoal chains are often found in story structures (Abbott & Black, 1982; Galambos, 1982a; Graesser, 1981). *States,* on the other hand, are descriptions of environmental, emotional, locational, or other physical or psychological conditions. States are typically connected to other information in memory as modifiers specifying the manner or style in which more important events occurred. When a why question is asked about a state, a set of antecedent conditions that lead causally to the state is typically given as an answer (Graesser, 1981; Lehnert, 1978).

Both actions and states appear in stories. In narratives, however, actions are more central than states. Most theorists agree that the backbone of narrative representations is a hierarchy or network containing connected actions and their associated goals (Abbott & Black, 1982; Galambos, 1982a; Galambos & Rips, 1982; Graesser, 1981). States are included in such representations, but not as centrally as actions. Experimental data consistently support this view, with actions being recalled much more frequently and accurately than states (Black, 1980; Graesser, Robertson, Lovelace & Swinehart, 1980; Seifert et al., 1982) and with actions being rated as more important and central (Galambos, 1982b). It has also been shown that unmentioned actions are more likely to be inferred on the basis of activated plans and scripts than are unmentioned states (Seifert et al., 1982).

If actions play a more central role in narrative representations than states, then it should be harder to modify actions using misleading question presuppositions. The modification of an action would be more likely to disrupt the structure of highly central goal hierarchies and chains of inferences. The modification of a state, on the other hand, might not affect any other information in a representation. This prediction stems from the hypothesis that the representation of a story is being accessed by question-answering procedures *during question comprehension*. It also depends on the argument that the nature of the internal representations of states and actions determines the effects on memory of misleading questions about those items.

4.2. The Spread of Misleading Information Along Conceptual Links

Information introduced by misleading questions should act the same way as information introduced by normal reading. In particular, *inferences* should be generated by misleading information. Of course, such inferences would themselves be incorrect.

Smith & McMahon (1970) conducted a study showing that inferences are sometimes required in order to answer a question. They presented subjects with sentence-question pairs like the following:

- John is preceding Dick. Who is ahead?
- Dick is following John. Who is ahead?

Subjects took longer to read the question in the second pair than the question in the first pair. In the first pair, the proposition stated in the question matches the proposition stated in the sentence. In the second pair, however, the subject and object of the first sentence are reversed, and an inference is presumably required to change the sentence proposition so that it matches the question. Other experiments have replicated this finding using different types of questions (Clark, 1969, 1972; Clark, Carpenter, & Just, 1978; Olson, 1972; Wright, 1969).

These results show that inferences are made when they are required for answering a question. We feel that inferences can be generated simply as a byproduct of comprehension. In this study, we ask if a misleading question presupposition can cause modification to other, inferentially related material in memory.

There is one study (Loftus & Palmer, 1974) that suggests that the effects of misleading questions are not restricted to memory for the exact proposition misled. In that study, subjects were asked questions about an automobile accident using verbs that implied different degrees of severity (i.e., "smashed" versus "hit"). The different verbs resulted in different estimates of the speed of the cars involved. The more severe the description, the higher the speed estimate. This suggests that different inferences about the speed of the car were available from the different verb implications. Furthermore, one week later subjects who had been asked the question with the more severe verb were more likely to say that they had seen broken glass after the accident. This "new memory" was a product of inferential processes.

To go a step further, we tested the effects of misleading question presuppositions on explicit, conceptually linked propositions in memory. Again, because it is known that actions are representationally different from states, and since unmentioned actions are more likely to be generated inferentially than unmentioned states (Seifert et al., 1982), we hoped to show that inferences about actions would be more affected by misleading information than inferences about states.

4.3. Experiment 1

In one experiment directed at these issues (Lehnert et al., 1983), we asked subjects to read five short narratives. The narratives contained a number of states and actions, but each narrative contained one target state and one target action. The target states involved ownership of an object, locations of two actions (room location and inside or outside), position of an object (high or low), and weight of a person. The target actions involved opening a window, letting a dog in, smearing mascara on an object, turning down the volume of a car radio, and checking hair in the window of a car.

For each of the target items in the stories, there was a conceptually connected target-inference item. For the target states, the conceptually connected inference-items were actions. For example, one target state described an object (photographer's lamps) as being too high, and the connected action described someone lowering the object. For the target actions, the conceptually connected inference-items were states. For example, one target action described turning the volume down on a radio; the connected state described the prior loudness of the music as being too high.

After subjects read the five stories containing target states and actions and their connected inference items, they answered several questions about the stories. Each subject answered a question about both of the target items in every story, but there were no questions about the inference items. One of the target item questions for each story contained a misleading presupposition; the other target item question contained a neutral presupposition. For example, a subject might have been asked "Was it on the first or second day that Shelly noticed her lamps were too low?" or "Was it on the first or second day that Shelly noticed her lamps were wrong?" In the first case, the question presupposes that the lamps were too low, which is misleading. In the second case, the question presupposes that the lamps were wrongly positioned, which is neutral because it is correct whether they were too high or too low. Half of the subjects were misled about states only, and half were misled about actions only.

After about 10 minutes during which the subjects participated in unrelated experimental tasks, they answered a second set of questions. Some of these questions were designed to test memory for the target information that was asked about in the first question set. Others were designed to test memory for the conceptually related information. Answers to these questions were judged *misled* if they conformed to the misleading question presuppositions, *confused* if they were wrong (inconsistent with the story) or answered by "I don't know," and *correct* if they were answered correctly. A *misleading difference score* for target items was the proportion of answers judged *misled* when a misleading question presupposition was present in the initial questions minus the proportion of answers judged *misled* when the initial question presupposition was neutral. A *confusion difference score* was the same measure for answers judged *confused*.

As Table 6.1 shows, state items were much more susceptible to the effects of misleading question presuppositions than action items. This was the case as measured both by misleading difference scores and by confusion difference scores. In fact, although the state scores differed significantly from zero for both measures, $t (11) = 3.46, p < .01$ for misleading difference scores and $t (11) = 2.63, p < .05$ for confusion difference scores, the action scores did not. This suggests that on the average, actions were not modified at all.

Overall, the connected state inference-items showed no effects of the misleading question manipulation. However, the mean confusion difference score for connected action inference-items proved to be different from zero, $t (11) = 2.17, p < .05$, and different from the lower, mean confusion difference score for connected state inference-items, $F (1,20) = 7.62, p < .05$. The bad showing for connected action items is not surprising, however, since there was so little effect of the misleading questions on initial states. Table 6.2 shows the proportions of conceptually connected inference item answers judged misled and correct in cases where their initial target item answers were

TABLE 6.1
Mean Misleading Difference Scores and
Confusion Difference Scores for State and
Action items in Experiment 1 (from
Lehnert, Robertson, & Black, 1983)

	Dependent Measure	
Item Type	Misleading Difference Score	Confusion Difference Score
State	.19	.14
Action	.05	.03

TABLE 6.2
Proportions of Conceptually Connected Items That Were
Modified and Not Modified When Initial States and Actions
Were Modified or Not Modified in Experiment 1

Type of Initial Items	Category of Initial Items	Category of Connected Items	
		Modified	Not Modified
States	Modified	.73	.27
	Not Modified	.00	1.00
Actions	Modified	.50	.50
	Not Modified	.02	.98

Items connected to initial states were actions, items connected to initial actions were states (from Lehnert, Robertson, & Black, 1983).

judged misled and correct. This table shows that there was indeed a tendency for misleading information to spread from target states to their connected actions and from target actions to their connected states. Still, however, misleading by inferential processes seemed to be stronger to connected actions than to connected states.

4.4. Experiments 2a and 2b

The data from Experiment 1 prompted us to conduct a second, more thorough experiment. In the second experiment, we wanted to study in more detail the state-action distinction and provide stronger evidence for the spreading of incorrect information by inferential processes to conceptually related material. The study was replicated and we report both sets of findings as Experiments 2a and 2b. In Experiment 2b, the items were redistributed throughout the conditions so that analyses over items could be performed. In both studies, 24 Yale undergraduates participated for credit in an Introductory Psychology course.

4.4.1. Materials and Procedure.   In Experiment 2 we decided to use a large number of state and action items. A long (3300 word) narrative was constructed containing 12 target states and 12 target actions. For each target state and target action there were two conceptually related items, one related state and one related action. Thus, the items really were triads, 12 of which consisted of an initial target state, a conceptually related state, and a conceptually related action, and 12 of which consisted of an initial target action, a conceptually related state, and a conceptually related action. Examples of a state triad and an action triad appear in Table 6.3.

TABLE 6.3
Example State and Action Triads from Experiment 2

STATE TRIAD

Initial State:

The notes were lying (under/next to) a pile of other papers
on the floor.

Connected Action:

She (lifted up/pushed aside) the papers, however, and found
the notes after a while.

Connected State:

The notes (weren't/were) visible (and/but) Shelly overlooked
them at first.

ACTION TRIAD

Initial Action:

As the car passed (over/under) one of the many small streets
that intersect the highway, John dreamed up an idea.

Connected Action:

He looked (down/up) at the cars and wondered how many of the
people in them were doing what they liked.

Connected State:

The cars (below/above) provided a convenient focal point for
his concentration

The modified concepts are indicated in parentheses with different
versions on either side of a slash "/".

After reading the story and participating in an unrelated experimental task
for 15-20 minutes, the subjects answered a set of 75 written questions about
episodes in the story. Included in this question set were 24 critical questions
that contained presuppositions about one part of each of the 24 item triads,
12 for the initial state triads and 12 for initial action triads. For every subject,
half of the 24 critical questions contained *misleading* presuppositions, six
from the state triads and six from the action triads. The other half contained
neutral presuppositions. For any one subject, the six questions in each condition (initial state, misleading presupposition; initial state, neutral presupposition; initial action, misleading presupposition; and initial action, neutral
presupposition) consisted of two questions about the initial item, two questions about the connected action, and two questions about the connected
state. The misleading question manipulation was counterbalanced in such a
way that across 24 subjects, every part of every item triad was misled twice
and not misled twice.

After answering these questions, the subjects worked 30–35 minutes on other tasks. Finally, they were given a long recognition test containing 112 items. They were instructed to rate each item on a 1–7 confidence scale where 1 = "Very confident that the item WAS NOT in the story," 7 = "Very confident that the item WAS in the story," and 4 = "unsure." There was a recognition item for each of the 3 parts of the 24 item triads. Half of the recognition items were true (with respect to the story) and half were false (with respect to the story). The false versions were consistent with the misleading presuppositions of questions about those items. All three items from a particular triad were always of the same validity (i.e., all true or all false). Each subject received true recognition items about half of the state triads and half of the action triads and false recognition items about the other halves.

Because of the design of the recognition materials in Experiment 2a, the comparison of misled versus not-misled items was between-subjects, and analyses of scores based on a combination of misled and not-misled items were not possible over subjects. This did not preclude analyses over items, however, and we will discuss primarily item analyses for Experiment 2a. In Experiment 2b this was modified so that analyses could be performed both over subjects and over items.

4.4.2. Dependent Measure and Predictions.

The dependent measure of greatest interest is the mean recognition score for items when they were not-misled minus the mean recognition score for items when they were misled. This *recognition difference score* corrects for baseline differences in the memorability of items. When looking at true items, a large, positive recognition difference score indicates misleading. When looking at false items, a large, negative recognition difference score indicates misleading. In Experiment 2b, each subject provided recognition difference scores for true and false recognition items for initial states, initial actions, and their connected states and actions (12 scores in all). In both Experiment 2a and 2b, each item also provided recognition difference scores (combined over subjects) on all of its three parts.

The most straightforward prediction was that the mean recognition difference score for initial states would be different from the mean recognition difference score for initial actions. Specifically, the mean recognition difference score for initial states should be higher when looking at true recognition items and lower when looking at false recognition items. Also, the state recognition difference scores should differ significantly from zero, since zero indicates no increase in recognition as the result of misleading information.

To test for the spread of misleading information to conceptually connected nodes, correlations between the mean recognition difference scores for initial items and the mean recognition difference scores for their connected states and actions were examined (of course, the recognition difference score for a connected item is calculated from its mean recognition scores in cases when its initial item was not-misled minus when its initial item was misled). This analysis should prove to be maximally sensitive, since it is conditional on the modifiability of the initial item. For this discussion, we restrict ourselves to analysis of data in the cases where misleading questions were asked about the initial items only.

4.4.3. Results on Initial States and Actions. Table 6.4 shows the mean recognition difference scores from both experiments for initial state items and initial action items based on true and false recognition scores. Analysis of recognition difference scores indicate that they were not different from zero in Experiment 2a for actions as measured by either true or false items. For states, on the other hand, subjects were more likely to say that they had seen false items when misled and were possibly less confident about true items, t (11) = -1.97, $p < .05$ and t (11) = 1.52, $p < .10$, respectively.

In Experiment 2b, where analysis over subjects was possible, the results were similar, although subjects now seemed to be less confident about true actions that were misled, t (23) = 2.5, $p < .01$ over subjects and t (11) = 1.7, $p < .10$ over items. The results again marginally indicated less confidence about true state items, t (23) = 2.1, $p < .05$ over subjects, not significant over items. There was again strong evidence for increased confi-

TABLE 6.4
Mean Recognition Difference Scores for Initial States and
Actions in Experiments 2a and 2b

Recognition Item Type	Type of Item Misled	Experiment	
		2a	2b
True	State	1.00 [i+]	.71 [s*]
	Action	.17	1.00 [s**, i+]
False	State	−.83 [i*]	−1.33 [s**, i*]
	Action	.33	−.42

High positive values indicate misleading for true recognition items; high negative values indicate misleading for false recognition items. Tests are one-tailed t-tests for differences from zero.

[s] analysis over subjects, df = 23.
[i] analysis over items, df = 11.
[+] $p < .10$
[*] $p < .05$
[**] $p < .01$

dence about false state items, t (23) = -2.5, $p<.01$, and over items, t (11) = -1.98, $p<.05$. Tests between mean recognition difference scores for states and mean recognition difference scores for actions failed to show a difference on true items in either experiment. Tests between state and action mean recognition difference scores for false items showed states to be lower than actions when tested over subjects in Experiment 2b only, t (23) = -1.71, $p<.05$.

Taken together, these results suggest that state items were affected more by misleading question presuppositions than action items. There was also some evidence for reductions in confidence about true recognition items and very consistent increases in confidence about false recognition items. However, there was some suggestion in Experiment 2b that confidence was reduced on true action items as well. These results are consistent with the results of Experiment 1 and suggest that different processing mechanisms are active when questions about states are being understood than when questions about actions are being understood.

4.4.4. Results on Connected States and Actions.   What happens to information that is conceptually connected to misled information? If the modifications in initial items are associated with modifications in their associated states and actions, then the correlations of recognition difference scores between the initial items and connected items should be positive. Table 6.5 shows these correlations between all initial and connected items for both experiments. In Experiment 2b, these correlations were computed over subjects as well as items.

Most of the relationships between misled items and their connected states and actions were positive, but few reached significance. The table shows evidence that changes in the recognition confidence of true state items were associated with changes in the recognition confidence of connected true action items in Experiment 2a, r (10) = .61, $p<.05$. Also, changes in the recognition confidence of false state items were associated marginally with changes in the recognition confidence of connected false states, r (10) = .52, $p<.10$; and more definitely with the recognition confidence of connected false actions, r (10) = .79, $p<.05$. It is interesting to note that all significant correlations involved connected actions. These correlations failed to hold up in Experiment 2b, with the exception of the marginal relationship between misled states and their connected actions. This relationship remained marginal over items, r (10) = .48, $p<.10$, but disappeared over subjects.

These data indicate that the spread of misleading information to conceptually connected items is weak, but that it occurs to connected actions mainly from initial states and also possibly from initial actions. Interestingly, this reiterates the finding in Experiment 1 that modification via inferential mechanisms is more likely *to* connected actions than *to* connected states.

TABLE 6.5
Correlation Coefficients between Initial State and Action Recognition Difference
Scores and Connected State and Action Recognition Difference Scores in Experiment 2

Recognition Item Type	Initial Item Type	Connected Item Type	Experiment		
			2a [i]	2b [i]	2b [s]
True	State	State	.41	.42	.18
		Action	.61*	−.02	.30
	Action	State	.41	−.03	−.32
		Action	.39	.03	.16
False	State	State	−.42	.17	.10
		Action	.52[+]	.48[+]	.10
	Action	State	.39	−.40	.13
		Action	.79*	−.01	−.30

[s] analysis over subjects, df = 22.
[i] analysis over items, df = 10.
[+] $p < .10$
* $p < .05$

These data are very consistent with the view that inferences about actions are more likely in narrative comprehension than inferences about states (Seifert et al., 1982), but they suggest that actions and states are equally likely *sources* of inference material. This phenomenon deserves further experimental treatment.

5. DETAILS OF THREE ITEMS IN ISOLATION

We have argued that the reason states are easier to modify than actions is that the two types of information are represented differently in memory. Similarly, it appears that inferential processes activated during question understanding primarily involve connections to actions, regardless of their source. This too can be explained by structural differences in the relationships of actions and states to other parts of a representation. In particular, actions are more central, they provide many more inference paths than states, and *motivational* and *causal* links in a narrative representation will lead to more informative and useful material than *manner* or other modification links. Question-answering processes should thus tend to favor links among actions over links to states. (This suggests that biasing inferential mechanisms to favor manner links, by asking primarily manner and style questions, for example, would increase the likelihood of inferential modification of states.)

What are some of these representational differences between actions and states that explain the effects in these experiments? In this section, we discuss the nature of modifications to several different kinds of informational structures in memory. The analysis is guided by details from proposed conceptual dependency representations of three of the items used in Experiment 2 (Schank, 1975).

Conceptual dependency representations consist of one or more *action primitives* and related concepts that modify these primitives. A conceptual primitive is a single abstract concept that captures the essential meaning of several different actions. Thus, PTRANS is the name of a primitive for physical movement. Conceptual dependency theory asserts that all actions involving physical movements will be parsed into the PTRANS concept in memory. Conceptual primitives have related *slots* which are filled either by stated information or default inferences. For example, all actions have an actor slot. Many actions have an object slot as well. Primitives like PTRANS have *slots* for the origin and destination of the object that was moved. The specifics of the conceptual dependency representations presented for our experimental items are not as important as the general idea that sentences and inferences are represented in memory as conceptually decomposed units containing primitives, associated slots, and conceptual links.

Naturally, not all of the items in Experiment 2 behaved as predicted. In fact, some of the actions were modified considerably while some of the states remained untouched. A post hoc analysis of the representational details of each item revealed that the items differed in many more ways than just being actions and states.

5.1. Representational Details

One of the most striking differences among items was the difference in the number of important dependencies within a representation that determine how much will change. Consider the following triad:

- Shelly immediately dropped her lipstick on the cover page.
- It left a red smear.
- She put the makeup on her lips where it belonged.

A conceptual dependency representation of these statements is shown in Fig. 6.1.

In the experiment, we attempted to change the representation of these statements by suggesting in a question presupposition that mascara was dropped instead of lipstick. Such a change would imply that the color of the

FIG. 6.1   Conceptual Dependency representation of the first triad in Section 5.1.

smear was not black, and that Shelly finally put the makeup on her eyes. Later recognition results for this item did not show such modifications. But the complexity of the changes is much greater than three simple token switches: (i.e, *lipstick to mascara, red to black,* and *lips to eyes*).

When considering the conceptual dependency representation in Fig. 6.1, the change of the lipstick token alone involves four slot modifications: the object slot of GRASP, the actor and object slots of the first PTRANS, and the object slot of the second PTRANS (recall that PTRANS is a conceptual primitive used to represent any physical transfer of an object from one location to another). If we now consider likely inferences that will be included in the representation, the task becomes even larger. For example, it is probable that the goal inference *Shelly wants to put lipstick on* will be generated and connected by a *reason* link to GRASP (Graesser, 1981; Seifert, et al., 1982; Warren et al., 1979). The failure of GRASP spells temporary failure of the goal as well. However, when the act of putting on lipstick is mentioned later, it will be tagged as a successful achievement of the failed goal (Lehnert, 1981). This goal-fate structure will again contain slots filled by the token for lipstick. Thus, the decomposition of actions into a number of primitives and the generation of inferences from actions both serve to multiply the number of tokens of a particular type in an internal representation.

For contrast, consider now the following triad which was easily modified:

- The car slid up to the stop sign and halted.
- The two stared at the stop sign through the front window for a full minute.
- The car had come to rest just before the crosswalk.

The conceptual dependency representation of these statements might look something like Fig. 6.2.

An attempt to modify the action from sliding *up* to the stop sign to sliding *through* the stop sign was highly successful with this item, but in fact, no *action* was changed at all. The action is still a physical movement through space. What is changed is the destination slot of the PTRANS, from *stop sign* to *intersection* maybe, or a slot in a consequent LOCATION specification. This change is much simpler than the slot modification in the first example triad. Even though they were changes in the same experimental category, changes of an "action," a processing mechanism for change in one case is much different than in the other.

Another deceptively complex change involves switching of symmetrical tokens. For example, in the case of a PTRANS, there are symmetrical tokens specifying the original and final locations of the object PTRANSed. In the case just discussed, the final location was changed (from stop sign to intersec-

```
                        +->stop-sign
      Shelly<=>PTRANS<-Car-|
              |                +--offramp
              |
              |consq.
              v
            LOCATION(Car, in-front-of, stop-sign)



      John                    +->stop-sign
      Shelly<=>ATTEND<-eyes-|
              |                +--
              |
              |manner
              v
      through front window
```

FIG. 6.2   Conceptual Dependency representation of the second triad in Section 5.1.

tion) and the original location (offramp) remained unaffected. Consider the following case, however:

- The psychologist went to the door to let the dog in.
- The dog jumped off of the porch step.
- His little feet made a thud on the carpet.

This triad is shown in Fig. 6.3. We tried to suggest in a question presuppostion that the psychologist actually let the dog *out,* thereby implying that the dog jumped *onto* the porch step and that its feet made a thud on *cement* or *bricks.* While this seems at first to be another simple case of a single token change, when we consider the representational difference between letting the dog in or out we see that it involves a swap of two symmetrical tokens. The *house* and *porch* tokens must be swapped in order to change *let in* to *let out.* Our data indicate that such token swapping is difficult for subjects. In particular, it is much more difficult than changing a single value.

5.2. Sources of Computational Difficulty

When the specifics of representations are taken into account, there are many more distinctions to worry about in predicting the difficulty of modifying memory than just actions versus states. An important factor is the proliferation of tokens in a representation as the result of decomposition of verbs into canonical forms, inferential processes, and slot filling. A single statement in a story may require a number of predicates with repeated arguments to specify it completely in a mental representation. The more times an argument is repeated in the decomposition of a statement, the harder it will be to modify that argument.

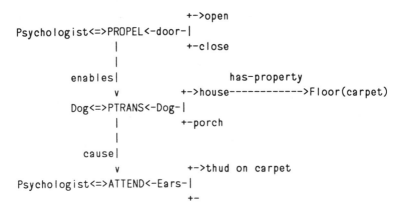

```
                               +->open
        Psychologist<=>PROPEL<-door-|
                      |                +-close
                      |
               enables|                     has-property
                      v               +->house----------->Floor(carpet)
                 Dog<=>PTRANS<-Dog-|
                      |               +-porch
                      |
                 cause|
                      v               +->thud on carpet
        Psychologist<=>ATTEND<-Ears-|
                                    +-
```

FIG. 6.3   Conceptual Dependency representation of the third triad in Section 5.1

The distinction between actions and states may, in fact, be found in this decompositional factor. What we have typically referred to as modification of an *action* is modification of a number of slots that are associated with the canonical form or primitive representing that action. The primitive was *never* actually modified in many of our materials. To modify a primitive, which is a canonical form that summarizes several actions of the same type, the action would have to be changed fundamentally. "Drove" might be changed to "thought," for example, and this would indeed be difficult! What we have referred to as modification of a *state,* on the other hand, typically involves a single modifying proposition or a single slot.

Another source of computational difficulty is the proliferation of tokens that arises from inference generation. This issue takes many forms, from the generation of intermediate linking inferences in a causal chain to the imputation of goals. Each new structure generated by inference will share tokens with its source proposition, and if one of these tokens is presupposed in a question, the difficulty of modification rises with the number of repetitions of the token or with the importance of inferred structures containing the token. For example, if a very central goal state is inferred on the basis of a concept modified by some less important state, the less important state might wind up conceptually connected to the goal and thereby be hard to modify.

Another issue involves verbs that imply the fillers of symmetrical slots in primitives like PTRANS. Modification of such verbs involves token switching, and this appears to be more difficult than replacement of single tokens.

Finally, an issue we have not addressed much, but which is very important, is the likelihood of activation of concepts that are connected to presupposed items by different kinds of links. For example, we suggested that causal and motivational links might be favored by understanding mechanisms, since they are more likely to lead somewhere important (e.g., goals) than modifying links. But this conjecture is surely dependent on the type of question being asked (Dyer, 1982; Graesser, 1981; Lehnert, 1978; Warren et al., 1979). An interesting empirical question remains about the modifiability of concepts along conceptual links that are searched preferentially when different types of questions are asked.

6. SUMMARY

To summarize, we have argued in general that question answering and sentence understanding utilize the same comprehension processes, and in particular that question parsing and memory search are not separable processes. Many psychological experiments and results of AI research on story comprehension indicate that normal comprehension includes continual interaction of the new information in sentences with old information in memory. Since the same issues arise in question comprehension, memory search is as much a part of question understanding as question answering. Since memory must remain open to constant updating and editing procedures, memory modification using misleading question presuppositions becomes an instance of normal understanding.

To demonstrate this, we conducted two experiments that investigate the modifiability of representationally different kinds of information—states and actions. It was found that actions, which are more central to narrative representations than states, were harder to modify using misleading question presuppositions. However, when information of either type was modified, changes spread by inferential mechanisms preferentially to conceptually connected actions. This supports a view of memory and question answering in which links among actions and their associated goals play an important role in memory access procedures.

More detailed examples of memory modifications were presented with an emphasis on representational issues and computational procedures. It was suggested that the difficulty of modification is related primarily to the proliferation of tokens through a representation by inferential processes or to details of the canonical forms of the items being modified. Finally, it was suggested that other major factors in the behavior of memory when misleading question presuppositions are encountered are the form of the misleading question and the conceptual links that are traversed when different kinds of questions are asked.

ACKNOWLEDGMENTS

This reseach was supported by grants from the Alfred P. Sloan Foundation and the System Development Foundation. We wish to thank Larry Hunter and Antoinette Daniello for their help with the experiments. Mara Miller and Arthur Graesser made valuable comments on the manuscript.

REFERENCES

Abbott, V., & Black, J. B. *A comparison of the memory strength of alternative text relations.* Paper presented at the Annual Meeting of the American Educational Research Association, New York, 1982.

Black, J. B. *Memory for state and action information in narratives.* Paper presented at the Twenty-First Annual Meeting of the Psychonomic Society, St. Louis, MO, 1980.

Clark, H. H. Linguistic processes in deductive reasoning. *Psychological Review,* 1969, *76,* 387–404.

Clark, H. H. Difficulties people have in answering the question "Where is it?" *Journal of Verbal Learning and Verbal Behavior,* 1972, *11,* 265–277.

Clark, H. H., & Carpenter, P. A., & Just, M. A. On the meaning of semantics and perception. In W. G. Chase (Ed.), *Visual information processing*. New York: Academic Press, 1978.

Clark, H. H., & Haviland, S. E. Comprehension and the given-new contract. In R. O. Freedle (Ed.), *Discourse production and comprehension*. Norwood, NJ: Ablex, 1977.

Cullingford, R. *Script application: Computer understanding of newspaper stories*. Technical Report #116, Department of Computer Science, Yale University, 1978.

DeJong, G. F. *Skimming stories in real time: An experiment in integrated understanding*. Technical Report #158, Department of Computer Science, Yale University, 1979.

Dyer, M. G. *In-depth understanding: A computer model of integrated processing for narrative comprehension*. Technical Report #219, Department of Computer Science, Yale University, 1982.

Dyer, M. G., & Lehnert, W. G. *Memory organization and search processes for narratives*. Technical Report #175, Department of Computer Science, Yale University, 1980.

Dyer, M. G., & Lehnert, W. G. Question answering for narrative memory. In J. F. Le Ny & W. Kintsch (Eds.), *Language and comprehension*. Amsterdam: North Holland, 1982.

Galambos, J. A. *Question answering and the plan structure of routine activities*. Paper presented at the annual meeting of the American Educational Research Association, New York, 1982. (a)

Galambos, J. A. *Normative studies of six characteristics of our knowledge of common activities*. Technical Report #14, Cognitive Science Program, Yale University, 1982. (b)

Galambos, J. A., & Ripps, L. J. Memory for routines. *Journal of Verbal Learning and Verbal Behavior*, 1982, *21*, 260–281.

Gershman, A. V. *Knowledge-based parsing*. Technical Report #156, Department of Computer Science, Yale University, 1979.

Graesser, A. C. *Prose comprehension beyond the word*. New York: Springer-Verlag, 1981.

Graesser, A. C., Robertson, S. P., & Clark, L. F. Question answering: A method for exploring the on-line construction of prose representations. In J. Fine & R. O. Freedle (Eds.), *New directions in discourse processing*. Norwood, NJ: Ablex, 1983.

Graesser, A. C., Robertson, S. P., Lovelace, E. R., & Swinehart, D. M. Answers to why-questions expose the organization of story plot and predict recall of actions. *Journal of Verbal Learning and Verbal Behavior*, 1980, *19*, 110–119.

Granger, R. H. *Adaptive understanding: Correcting erroneous inferences*. Technical Report #171, Department of Computer Science, Yale University, 1980.

Greene, E., Flynn, M. S., & Loftus, E. O. Inducing resistance to misleading information. *Journal of Verbal Learning and Verbal Behavior*, 1982, *21*, 207–219.

Lebowitz, M. *Generalization and memory in an integrated understanding system*. Technical Report #186, Department of Computer Science, Yale University, 1980.

Lehnert, W. G. *The process of question answering*. Hillsdale, NJ: Lawrence Erlbaum Associates, 1978.

Lehnert, W. G. Plot units and narrative summarization. *Cognitive Science*, 1981, *5*, 293–331.

Lehnert, W. G., Dyer, M. G., Johnson, P. N., Yang, C. J., & Harley, S. BORIS — An in-depth understander of narratives. *Artificial Intelligence*, 1983, *20*, 15–62.

Lehnert, W. G., Robertson, S. P., & Black, J. B. Memory interactions during question answering. In H. Mandl, N. L. Stein, & T. Trabasso (Eds.), *Learning and comprehension of text*. Hillsdale, NJ: Erlbaum, 1983.

Loftus, E. F. Leading questions and the eyewitness report. *Cognitive Psychology*, 1975, *7*, 560–572.

Loftus, E. F. *Eyewitness testimony*. Cambridge, MA: Harvard University Press, 1979.

Loftus, E. F., & Palmer, J. C. Reconstruction of automobile destruction: An example of the interaction between language and memory. *Journal of Verbal Learning and Verbal Behavior*, 1974, *13*, 585–589.

Marcus, M. *A theory of syntactic recognition for natural language.* Cambridge, MA: MIT Press, 1980.

McKoon, G., & Ratcliff, R. The comprehension processes and memory structures involved in anaphoric reference. *Journal of Verbal Learning and Verbal Behavior,* 1980, *19,* 668–682.

McKoon, G., & Ratcliff, R. The comprehension processes and memory structures involved in instrumental reference. *Journal of Verbal Learning and Verbal Behavior,* 1981, *20,* 671–682.

Olson, D. R. Language use for communicating, instructing, and thinking. In R. O. Freedle & J. B. Carroll (Eds.), *Language comprehension and the acquisition of knowledge.* Washington, DC: Winston, 1972.

Ratcliff, R., & McKoon, G. Priming in item recognition: Evidence for the propositional structure of sentences. *Journal of Verbal Learning and Verbal Behavior,* 1978, *17,* 403–417.

Rieger, C. Conceptual memory. In R. C. Schank (Ed.), *Conceptual information processing.* Amsterdam: North-Holland, 1975.

Riesbeck, C. K., & Schank, R. C. Comprehension by computer: Expectation-based analysis of sentences in context. In W. J. M. Levelt, & G. B. Flores d'Arcais (Eds.), *Studies in the perception of language.* New York: Wiley, 1978.

Schank, R. C. *Conceptual information processing.* Amsterdam: North-Holland/American Elsevier, 1975.

Schank, R. C., & Birnbaum, L. Memory, meaning and syntax. In T. Bever, J. Carroll, & L. Miller (Eds.), *Talking minds: Cognitive philosophical computational foundations of language.* Cambridge, MA: MIT Press, in press.

Schank, R. C., Lebowitz, M., & Birnbaum, L. An integrated understander. *American Journal of Computational Linguistics,* 1980, *6,* 13–30.

Seifert, C. M., Robertson, S. P., & Black, J. B. *On-line processing of pragmatic inferences.* Cognitive Science Technical Report #15, Yale University, 1982.

Smith, K. H., & McMahon, L. E. Understanding order information in sentences. Some recent work at Bell Laboratories. In G. Flores d'Arcais & W. J. M. Levelt (Eds.), *Advances in psycholinguistics.* Amsterdam: North-Holland, 1970.

Warren, W. H., Nicholas, D. W., & Trabasso, R. Event chains and inferences in understanding narratives. In R. O. Freedle (Ed.), *New directions in discourse processing,* (Vol. 2). Norwood, NJ: Ablex, 1979.

Wilks, Y. An artificial intelligence approach to machine translation. In R. C. Schank, & K. Colby (Eds.), *Computer models of thought and language.* San Francisco: W. H. Freeman & Co., 1973.

Winograd, T. *Understanding natural language.* New York: Academic Press, 1972.

Woods, W. A. Semantics and quantification in natural language question answering. *Advances in Computers,* 1978, *17.*

Woods, W. A., Kaplan, R., & Nash-Webber, B. *The LUNAR sciences natural language information system: Final report.* Technical Report #2378. Boston: Bolt Beranek & Newman, 1972.

Wright, P. Transformations and the understanding of sentences. *Language and Speech,* 1969, *12,* 156–166.

7 Question-Asking as a Component of Text Comprehension

Gary M. Olson
University of Michigan

Susan A. Duffy
University of Massachusetts

Robert L. Mack
IBM T. J. Watson Research Center

In its primary mode of use, a question is a device for seeking new information that is to be related to an existing knowledge structure. When to ask a question, and exactly what to ask, are both symptomatic of the status of the knowledge structure at issue, as well as, no doubt, the general intelligence of the asker. We have all encountered individuals (often ourselves!) who indicated they did not know enough about a topic to ask a question about it. Thus, intuitively, there is a link between one's knowledge or understanding of a topic and the ability to ask a question about it (e.g., see Miyake & Norman, 1979).

There is another connection between questions and comprehension. Educators and researchers have long suspected that approaching the comprehension of text with either general or specific questions in mind might facilitate understanding. There is a sizable research literature on this role of questions in understanding text (e.g., Anderson & Biddle, 1975; Frase, 1975). Questions of this type focus the reader's attention on exactly those pieces of information that are needed to understand what the text is about. Since one of the problems faced by the reader is selecting the most relevant or important information from a text, appropriate questions can serve as a guide for this process.

These two uses of questions in relation to understanding have an important relationship. Questions asked about a text are both an indication of having understood what has been read and a guide to the further understanding of what is about to be read. This suggested to us that questions asked by a reader while reading a text might be an especially informative kind of data for monitoring the reader's understanding of the text.

We have carried out a program of research aimed at finding what kinds of higher-level cognitive processes readers engage in while reading simple texts. We felt one simple strategy for obtaining this kind of information would be to have readers think out loud while reading. We were motivated by a belief that intelligent reading has many affinities with problem solving, a domain in which thinking-out-loud protocols have proved to be a useful research tool. A series of studies using this method have revealed a number of important phenomena about reading (Olson, Duffy, & Mack, 1980, 1984; Olson, Mack, & Duffy, 1981). One especially important finding has been that characteristics of the thinking-out-loud protocols correlate with silent reading time (see details in Olson et al., 1981, 1984), suggesting that the information obtained from this method is relevant to understanding the nature of text comprehension.

One of the things we noticed subjects doing while thinking out loud during reading was asking questions. The kinds of questions people asked and the places in the text they asked them seemed to us indicative of important comprehension processes. This led us to conduct a specific study on the relationship between on-line question asking and comprehension. In this chapter we report a few highlights of this study. A more complete report of it will appear in Olson, Duffy, Eaton, Vincent and Mack (in preparation).

Let us summarize the general rationale for this study. The kinds of considerations we have sketched led us to believe that questions asked by subjects during the reading of a simple text would be diagnostic of important comprehension processes. It seemed plausible to assume that each sentence encountered in a text raises certain questions in a reader's mind and answers other questions raised by earlier sentences. We wanted to explore this supposition in more detail by collecting data on the kinds of questions readers ask following each sentence in simple stories.

This study used four tasks. The primary task was one in which readers asked questions after reading each sentence in the story. In another task a different group of subjects read the same stories silently while we timed their reading. These same subjects later recalled the stories. Finally, another group of subjects rated the importance of the constituents of the story. Four short simple stories (maximum length was 41 sentences) were used as texts. They were all children's stories or simple folktales, and all were well formed.

To better understand the results, a somewhat more detailed description of the four tasks is necessary:

Question Asking.   All four stories were presented to nine subjects. Each sentence in the story was typed on a card, and the subject worked his or her way through the deck of cards, asking questions that were raised in his or her mind as a result of having read that particular sentence. The subject was told to imagine that the story's author was present, and that the author was willing to answer any questions the reader had about the story at that point, except for the obvious question of what happens next. The subject was allowed to spend as much time on any sentence as he or she desired, but was asked not to reread any previous sentences or to look ahead. The questions were tape-recorded and later transcribed. The number of questions asked for each sentence was tallied and pooled over subjects. In addition, the questions were classified in various ways.

Reading Times.   Sentence-by-sentence reading times were collected from 20 subjects. At the end of each story subjects wrote a brief (three to five sentences) summary of the story.

Recall.   The same 20 subjects were asked to recall the stories they had just read. They were presented with a brief descriptive title for each story and were given unlimited time to try to recall as much as they could. They were asked to recall exact words, but were encouraged to guess if they could not remember exact words. Recall was scored by first doing a propositional analysis of each story and then matching the subject's recall against this, using a gist criterion.

Importance.   Seventeen subjects read each story and crossed out the 50% of the words, phrases, or sentences in the story they felt were least important. For each sentence in each story the proportion of words left in averaged over subjects provided a measure of the relative importance of that sentence.

It is useful to have a better picture of what the question-asking data look like. Table 7.1 shows typical questions for the first sentence of one of the stories. These questions are grouped into those asked by two or more subjects and those that are idiosyncratic to one subject. Of course, we were also interested in the sentence-by-sentence variation in the questions asked. Figure 7.1 shows the total number of questions asked for each sentence in each of the four stories. With the possible exception of EMERALD, there is noteworthy variation in the number of questions asked from sentence to sentence. In EMERALD, there were a large number of questions at the beginning and then a fairly flat distribution of questions thereafter. Keep this difference in mind, because EMERALD does not follow the pattern of other stories in some of our later analyses.

TABLE 7.1
Sample Questions from *The Selling of the Cow*

Sentence 1: "Once there was a man named Cromer who lived on a farm that was way up on the side of a hill."

Questions asked by 2 or more subjects:	*# Subjects*
1. Who is Cromer?	2
2. What is Cromer like?	3
3. Did Cromer live alone?	5
4. When did this story take place?	5
5. Where was the farm?	4
6. Where was the hill?	4
7. Why was the farm on a hill?	2
8. How far up the hill was the farm?	2
9. How high was the hill?	3
10. What kind of farm was it?	4
11. What will happen to Cromer?	2

Idiosyncratic questions asked by only 1 subject:

1. Does the fact that he lives on a farm have any significance?
2. Does he farm for a living?
3. Does he have another vocation?
4. Is Cromer married?
5. How old is Cromer?
6. How far away were Cromer's nearest neighbors?
7. Why did Cromer like to live on a farm?
8. Are they going to roll something down the hill?
9. Did a lot of the dirt wash off the side of the hill so that Cromer couldn't have his crops?
10. What was Cromer's first name?
11. Was that Cromer's first name?
12. Then what was Cromer's last name?
13. Did Cromer have more than one name?
14. What kind of name is Cromer?
15. What does Cromer mean?
16. What nationality is Cromer?

The first issue we addressed was whether the question-asking task is related to the reading times. We examined this by looking at the relationship between the total number of questions asked for each sentence in a story and the average reading time for each sentence for those subjects who were reading silently. The expectation was that sentences that elicited a lot of questions would be especially salient during real-time processing, and therefore would be read more slowly by subjects who were reading silently. This hypothesis was confirmed. We conducted multiple regressions in which the average reading time per sentence was the dependent variable, and the predictor variables were sentence length, total number of questions, serial position, and importance. Only sentence length and number of questions emerged as significant predictors of reading time. In this analysis all four stories were entered, with story as a variable. There are two types of questions that occur: those that are asked by several subjects, and those that are idiosyncratic. We next asked whether these two types of questions contributed differentially to this outcome. The answer was no. A multiple regression with number of questions asked by two or more persons and idiosyncratic questions entered separately showed that both emerged as significant predictors. Table 7.2 shows the details of these analyses.

When we carried out multiple regression analyses for each story individually, the results mirrored the overall analysis. In these regressions we included as predictors idiosyncratic questions and questions asked by two or more persons as well as total number of questions asked. For three of the four stories,

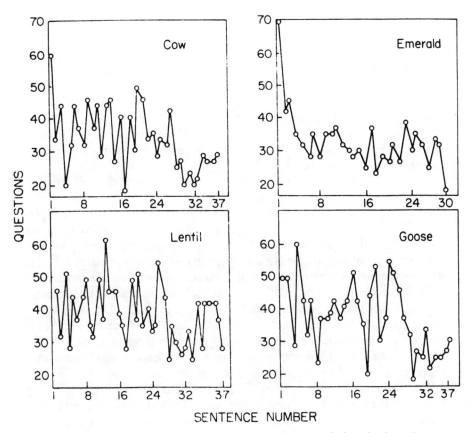

FIG. 7.1   Total number of questions asked for each sentence in four simple stories.

TABLE 7.2
Multiple Regression Analyses of Reading Time in Question-Asking Experiment

	Regression Coefficient	Significance Level	Cumulative R^2
1. *Predictors selected:*			
Sentence length	130.22	.0001	.589
Total number of questions asked	26.44	.0001	.640
Predictors not selected:			
Serial position of sentence			
Importance			
2. *Predictors selected:*			
Sentence length	130.81	.0001	.589
Idiosyncratic questions	40.27	.0004	.626
Number of questions asked by two			
or more subjects	87.42	.0015	.652
Predictors not selected:			
Serial position of sentence			
Importance			

Note: Forward stepwise regression, dependent variable = mean reading time per sentence.

at least one of these question counts emerged as a significant predictor of reading time (in addition to number of syllables). The exception was EMERALD, for which the question data provided no significant predictor. As mentioned earlier, EMERALD was the story that showed little variation in number of questions asked across sentences.

Number of questions asked accounts for a significant portion of the variance in sentence-by-sentence reading times. We next asked what relationship the question-asking task has with recall. And the answer was very simple: none. Table 7.3 shows the outcome of a multiple regression carried out on recall scores, and reveals that rated importance and serial position emerged as significant predictors of recall, while number of questions asked did not. This pattern is similar to other data that indicate that importance predicts recall (Kintsch, 1974; Meyer, 1975). Importance is not necessarily immediately perceived, but may result from having most or all of the final memory representation of the text. We conclude from this that the information being revealed by the question-asking task is more closely associated with the activities that occur during comprehension than with the form of the final memory representation constructed as a result of comprehension.

This basic result confirms our initial supposition that the question-asking task would tap an aspect of what is going on in the skilled reader's mind while reading. The obvious question, of course, is what is it tapping? It is unlikely that a reader who is reading silently is actually asking questions while reading. Rather, we believe that the question-asking task taps the kinds of informational needs a reader encounters while proceeding through a text. As each sentence is understood and added to a growing representation of the story, the reader revises and elaborates the set of information still needed to have the developing story make sense. These informational needs interact with what is presented in the next sentence to generate a new set of informational needs — or, if you will, a new set of questions — that guide the reader's comprehension through the succeeding parts of the text.

We have conducted a number of other analyses of these data that are discussed in Olson et al., (in preparation). We have categorized the questions to see if certain types are more important than others. So far, the categories we have examined have not shown any differences. We have also looked to see whether or not questions asked are later answered by the story, and there are interesting relationships here. Many questions *are* in fact answered, though it varies somewhat by type. However, the number of questions *answered* by a particular sentence does *not* predict reading time or recall. We have looked at the information tapped in the question and find that questions that are derived from new information contained in the current sentence are especially important in predicting reading times. These and other details of these data are interesting and important and will be reported on fully in Olson et al. (in preparation).

The main findings of this study strongly suggest that the question-asking task is a useful indicator of processes that may be an important part of comprehension. The number of questions asked by subjects as they read through a story correlates with the amount of time spent on that sentence by other readers reading silently. Keep in mind that this result is with the obvious effect of sentence length removed. But number of questions does not correlate with recall. Thus, question asking seems more closely related to the real-time

TABLE 7.3
Multiple Regression Analyses of Recall in Question-Asking Experiment

	Regression Coefficient	Significance Level	Cumulative R^2
Predictors selected:			
Importance	341.12	.0001	.235
Serial position of sentence	− 2.94	.0024	.283
Predictors not selected:			
Sentence length			
Total number of questions asked			

Note: Forward stepwise regressions, dependent variable = proportion propositions recalled per sentence.

processes that occur during reading than to the final product of comprehension that remains when reading is completed.

How general are these findings? We do not yet know. Clearly, we can only confine our conclusions to the reading of simple stories by reasonably sophisticated readers. Other types of stories, other types of texts, and other types of readers might yield quite different outcomes. But these initial results are promising enough to warrant the extension of this paradigm to these other situations.

ACKNOWLEDGMENTS

This research has been supported by a research grant from the National Institute of Education (NIE G-79-0133) and by a Research Career Development Award from NICHD (HD 00169) awarded to the first author.

REFERENCES

Anderson, R. C., & Biddle, W. B. On asking people questions about what they are reading. In G. Bower (Ed.), *The psychology of learning and motivation* (Vol. 9). New York: Academic Press, 1975.

Frase, L. T. Prose processing. In G. Bower (Ed.), *The psychology of learning and motivation* (Vol. 9). New York: Academic Press, 1975.

Kintsch, W. *The representation of meaning in memory.* Hillsdale, NJ: Lawrence Erlbaum Associates, 1974.

Meyer, B. *The organization of prose and its effect on memory.* Amsterdam: North-Holland, 1975.

Miyake, N., & Norman, D. To ask a question, one must know enough to know what is not known. *Journal of Verbal Learning and Verbal Behavior* 1979, *18,* 357–364.

Olson, G. M., Duffy, S. A., Eaton, M. E., Vincent, P., & Mack, R. L. *On-line question-asking as a component of story comprehension.* Manuscript in preparation.

Olson, G. M., Duffy, S. A., & Mack, R. L. Applying knowledge of writing conventions to prose comprehension and composition. In W. E. McKeachie (Ed.), *Learning, cognition, and college teaching.* San Francisco: Jossey-Bass, 1980.

Olson, G. M., Duffy, S. A., & Mack, R. L. Thinking-out-loud as a method for studying real-time comprehension processes. In D. E. Kieras & M. A. Just (Eds.), *New methods in reading comprehension research.* Hillsdale, NJ: Lawrence Erlbaum Associates, 1984.

Olson, G. M., Mack, R. L., & Duffy, S. A. Cognitive aspects of genre. *Poetics,* 1981, *10,* 283–315.

8 Questions of Facts and Questions of Inferences

Susan Kemper
Robert Estill
Nelson Otalvaro
Margaret Schadler
University of Kansas

We have exploited a distinction between factual and inferential questions to examine how the causes and consequences of characters' actions are understood. Causal inferences are an essential component of text comprehension processes (Graesser, 1981; Kemper, 1982a, 1983a; Omanson, Warren, & Trabasso, 1978; Warren, Nicholas, & Trabasso, 1979). Texts may be decomposed into chains of causally connected actions, physical states, and mental states. Actions include both the observable actions of human or other animate agents and the actions of natural or social processes. Physical states are enduring and observable properties of agents, objects, places, and events. Mental states are enduring but unobservable properties of sentient beings; they include emotions, cognitions, and dispositions. Actions, physical states, and mental states form the basic links in the chain of causally connected events underlying a text (Kemper, 1982a, 1983b). Since not all of the causal links in the chain of events may be stated in a text, inferences are required to determine the unstated causes and consequences of characters' actions. General information about the causes and consequences of characters' actions, knowledge of scripted actions, and cultural schema about appropriate and inappropriate behavior can be used to make such inferences about characters' actions and to answer factual and inferential questions.

Consider vignette 1. There is a gap in the sequence of events between Jean's walking toward the bus stop and entering the bar. In order to bridge this gap, the reader must infer an explanation for Jean's unexpected action. Based on general knowledge of causation, a motivating mental state is a likely explanation for the action; Jean enters the bar because she wants a drink. A more specific explanation can be derived from other types of background knowledge. Cues in the text can trigger such inferences by activating the necessary background knowledge. For example, different, specific motivating mental states are inferred in 1b and 1c. In 1b, the reader must infer that Jean was going to do her unwinding in the bar and in 1c, infer that Jean was going to get some change in the bar.

1. (a) Jean put in a long day at the office. As she was walking toward her bus stop, she detoured into her favorite bar.
   (b) Jean put in a long day at the office. She decided to unwind a bit before fighting the crowds to get home. As she was walking toward her bus stop, she detoured into her favorite bar.
   (c) Jean put in a long day at the office. To top it all off, she had used her last bus token in the morning and didn't have any change. As she was walking toward her bus stop, she detoured into her favorite bar.

Our assumption is that similar causal inferences are required during immediate comprehension and during question answering. Thus, the readers of 1a-c must infer motivating mental states to answer the question "why did Jean detour into the bar?" Both immediate text comprehension and question answering depend on an interaction of information from the text with information from memory. Contextual cues can facilitate both comprehension and question answering by activating appropriate causal explanations for the sequence of events. Our research examines how background knowledge, knowledge of scripted activities, and culture stereotypes can facilitate inferring answers to questions about characters' actions.

THE EVENT CHAIN ANALYSIS OF TEXTS

A three-step process for parsing texts has been developed (Kemper, 1982b). Texts are decomposed into linear sequences of actions, physical states, and mental states. Using a taxonomy of possible causal events, the event chain underlying the text is recovered and the inferred causal links are identified.

A text is initially divided into syntactically determined clauses. Two general types of clauses are recognized: tensed clauses which contain verbs inflected for tense and untensed clauses which contain imperative or infinitive verbs that are not inflected. Four tense markers can be used to identify tensed verbs: the -ed that is characteristic of past tense verbs, the -s that marks third-person, singular present tense verbs, the has that signals perfective tense verbs, and the -ing of progressive verbs. Irregular verbs are those that are not inflected by these markers.

Tensed and untensed verbs may be found in simple, coordinate, or complex sentences. A complex sentence consists of a main or matrix clause with one or more embedded clauses. Six types of complex sentences are recognized: sentences containing infinitive phrases, gerundive phrases, noun phrase complements, relative clauses, participal adjectives, and subordinate clauses. A text is parsed into clauses by first locating the verbs in each simple or coordinate sentence or in each matrix or embedded clause of a complex sentence.

In the second step of the analysis of texts as event chains, each clause is classified as an action, a physical state, or a mental state. As in the first step, syntactic criteria and procedures are used to classify the clauses. Actions are distinguished from states on the basis of three criteria: (1) actions can be expressed with verbs in the "progressive" aspect; (2) actions can answer questions such as "What happened?" or "What's happening?" (3) actions can be used in imperative constructions. Actions include processes involving the change of state or condition of objects and the activities of agents.

States include both observable physical states and unobservable mental states. Physical states include states of possession, attribution, and specification. Mental states include emotions, cognitions, and intentions. Such states represent enduring, although not permanent, properties or characteristics of agents, objects, and locations.

A taxonomy of possible causal connections is used to construct the event chain underlying a text. The taxonomy assumes that there are four types of causal connections: (1) one event may cause a new physical state — a resulting causal link; (2) one event may cause a new mental state — an initiation link; (3) one event may cause a new action by enabling the action to occur, or (4) by providing a psychological motive or reason for the action. These four types of causation are constrained so than an action cannot cause a new action, a physical state cannot lead to a new physical state, and a mental state cannot cause new mental or physical states.

Not all the causal links in the event chain underlying a text are explicitly stated. Some must be inferred. In general, action-action, physical state-physical state, mental state-mental state, and mental state-physical state sequences in a text require obligatorily inferred actions or states. These inferences are required in order to repair apparent violations of the causal taxonomy.

Thus the analysis of texts as causal event chains uses the causal taxonomy to establish connections between the actions and states described in the text. When necessary, actions and states are inferred to repair violations of this taxonomy. An example text and its underlying event chain is presented in Table 8.1.

This event chain analysis of texts does not provide an exhaustive inventory of inferences that readers may draw from a text. Rather, the event chain analysis identifies critical inferences that readers must make if they are to answer basic questions about what happened (resultants and initiations) and why

TABLE 8.1
The Event Chain Analysis of a Sample Passage from the McCall and Crabbs
Standard Test Lessons in Reading (1979)

A Mystery Spot

/There is a "mystery spot" near Santa Cruz, California. PS1/ All trees in this mystery spot lean in one direction, A2/ but redwoods a short distance from it grow straight and tall. A3/ People have great difficulty PS4/ walking in the mystery area. A5/ Their feet feel like lead. PS6/ It is almost necessary PS7/ to drag themselves along the trail A8/ by holding onto a handrail. A9/ Many are unable MS10/ to step over a low doorsill and into a cabin. A11/ They enter A12/ by sitting on the doorsill A13/ and swinging their feet over it. A14/ When standing in the cabin, PS15/ they lean in the same direction as the trees. A16/ They feel MS17/ as though they are standing as usual, PS18/ but actually they are leaning at such an angle A19/ that they look ludicrous to people PS20/ watching them. A21/

/Two concrete slabs lie about six inches apart. PS22/ One is inside the mystery spot PS23/ and the other outside it. PS24/ When a person five feet tall PS25/ stands on the mystery-spot slab A26/ he looks taller than a person PS27/ six feet tall PS28/ standing on the other slab, PS29/ although the two slabs are really on the same level. PS30/ It is the guess of Einstein and many other scientists PS31/ that gravity is pulling harder at that spot. A32/

```
PS1--->A2 & A3
PS1--->A5---PS4 & PS6
A5--->PS7--->A8
PS4--->MS10--->A11
MS10--->A13--->PS--->A14
A14--->PS--->A12
A12--->PS15--->A16 & MS17
PS18--->MS17
PS15--->A19--->PS20
A21--->PS20
PS1--->A--->PS22 & PS24--->A26
PS25--->A26--->PS27
PS28 & PS29--->A--->PS27
PS30--->A--->PS27
PS32--->PS1--->A--->PS31
```

Slash marks segment the text into clauses. Each clause is labeled as an action (A), a physical state (PS), or a mental state (MS). Clauses are serially numbered. Following the passage, the underlying event chain is schematically presented. Inferred actions and states are indicated by the unnumbered nodes.

this occurred (enablements and motivations). These causal inferences are assumed to occur during immediate text comprehension as readers attempt to understand the chain of events.

Noncausal inferences may also be generated as a consequence of reading a text. Noncausal inferences about the referents of anaphors, the time or location of an event, or the reader's evaluation of the text are included in the taxonomies of, e.g., Graesser (1981), Nicholas and Trabasso (1980), and Omanson and Formosa (1982).

QUESTIONS ABOUT FACTS AND INFERENCES

In order to investigate the role of causal inferences in text comprehension and question answering, we have examined sentence reading times and question-answering latencies. Our research strategy is to compare sentence reading times and question-answering latencies for different versions of texts. In order to determine whether causal inferences are made during immediate comprehension or not, we prepare versions of the texts in which key causal connections are explicitly stated and versions in which these causal connections are omitted. We assess the effects of this manipulation on the time to read sentences describing direct causal consequences of these key connections and the latency to answer questions about causal consequences of the key connection.

Two conditions were compared in the first experiment. In the first condition, target sentences were preceded by their immediate causes; in the second condition, the immediate causes of each target sentences were removed so that gaps in the causal structure of the texts occurred. This alteration of the causal structure of the text was predicted to have two effects: First, the causal connections between the target sentences and the texts were explicit in the first condition but not in the second. In the second condition, consequently, the readers must infer the causal connections. These inferences should take time and increase the time required to read the target sentences. Second, gaps in the causal structure of the texts will reduce the overall causal organization of the texts. Consequently, in the second condition, it was predicted that the readers would be required to infer missing causal connections in order to answer questions about the texts. These inference processes during question-answering should increase the latencies to read questions about the texts and to formulate answers. Thus, factual questions about explicitly stated causal connections should be more rapid and, perhaps, more accurate than inferential questions about missing causal connections (Camp, Lachman, & Lachman, 1980).

In order to test these hypotheses, eight passages were selected from the Spargo and Williston (1980) reading series. Half were designated for tenth-grade readers (easy passages) and half were designed for college-level readers (hard passages). Two versions were created. Common to each version were eight target sentences. The two versions of each passage differed in the intactness of the underlying causal chains. In the intact version, the direct cause of each target sentence was explicitly stated and immediately preceded the target sentence. In the abridged version, the direct cause was removed from the text so that the underlying causal chain was abridged. Across all easy and hard passages, the target sentences were matched for word length; pilot testing demonstrated that the target sentences were read equally rapidly in isolation.

For each passage, eight questions were prepared. Half asked for explicitly stated facts and half asked for inferences from the passage. The sets of factual and inferential questions were matched in word length and were read equally rapidly in pilot testing. An excerpt from one passage and example questions are presented in Table 8.2.

The passages were presented sentence by sentence using a computer-controlled system for self-paced reading. The subjects regulated the rate of sentence presentation. After reading each passage, each subject was presented with the eight questions about it. The subject was instructed to read each question and to formulate an appropriate answer. When the answer had been formulated, the subject was instructed to press a control key. An answer prompt appeared and the subject typed in the answer. The system automatically recorded sentence reading times, the question-answering latencies, and the subjects' answers. The question-answering latencies reflected the time to read the question and formulate an answer; the time the subjects required to type in their answers was not recorded. The answers were categorized as correct or incorrect with respect to the causal event chain underlying the text.

Separate analyses of variance were performed on the sentence reading times, the question-answering latencies, and the proportion of questions answered correctly. Passage difficulty (easy versus hard) and version (intact versus abridged) were within-subject factors in all analyses. For the analyses of the question-answering latencies and the proportion of correct answers, question type (factual versus inferential) was an additional within-subject factor. The results are summarized in Fig. 8.1.

TABLE 8.2
A Fragment from an Easy Passage Designed to be Appropriate for
Tenth-Grade Readers

Mudflows originate on hillsides (A) [when rain saturates the soil]. (A) Rain makes shallow soil layers liquid. (PS) The liquefied soil flows like streams of water down gulleys, canyons, and valley bottoms (A). Steep slopes, loose soil, and heavy rains can produce large mudflows (A). [There may be so much mud (PS) that] the mud spills out of stream channels. (A) The mud can spread about across nearby low ground (A).

Factual Question: What happens to the liquefied soil?

Inferential Question: Why are hillsides required for mudflows?

Each clause or sentence is identified as an Action (A) or Physical State (PS) according to the causal taxonomy; there are no Mental States in this fragment. The bracketed clauses were deleted in the abridged version of the passage. The underlined sentences were the targets. The passage was adapted from Spargo and Williston (1980). One factual and one inferential question accompany the fragment.

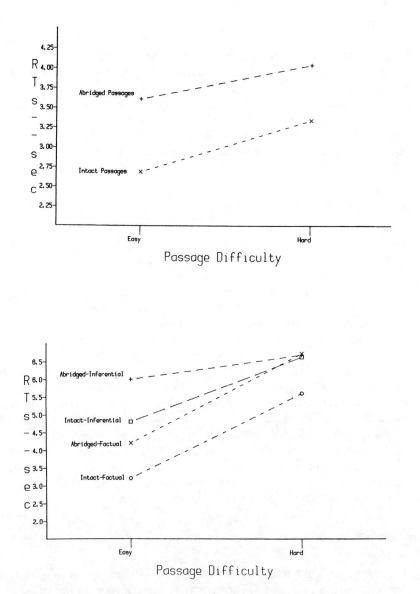

FIG. 8.1   Mean reading times for target sentences in passages with intact and abridged causal chains and mean question-answering latencies for factual and inferential questions.

Reading Times

Target sentences were read more rapidly in the easy passages designed for tenth-grade readers than in the hard passages designed for college-level readers, $p < .05$. However, target sentences in the passages with intact causal chains were read significantly more rapidly than those in the versions with the abridged chains, $p < .05$. Both effects suggest that readers must actively infer causal connections among the actions, physical states, and mental states of a text's causal event chain. These causal connections are more rapidly established in easy passages and in passages with relatively intact causal chains.

Question-answering Latencies

Answers were formulated more rapidly for the easy than the hard passages, $p < .05$, for the passages with intact causal chains compared to those with abridged chains, $p < .05$, and for the factual questions than for the inferential ones, $p < .05$. The interactions between passage difficulty and question type and between passage difficulty and version were both significant, both $p < .05$. For the easy passages, designed for tenth-grade readers, factual questions were answered significantly more rapidly than inferential ones, $p < .01$. However, for the hard passages, this advantage for factual over inferential questions was reduced, $p > .05$. For the easy passages, questions about the versions with intact causal chains were answered more rapidly than for those with abridged chains, $p < .01$. This difference was reduced for the hard passages, $p < .05$. This pattern of results suggests that difficult passages, including those with abridged causal chains, are understood less well than easy passages or those with intact causal chains. As a consequence, readers are unable to directly access information in order to answer questions about the hard or abridged texts. This information must be inferred and the inference process increases the question-answering latencies.

Accuracy

The only significant finding was that the subjects answered more factual questions (mean = 3.2 of 4) correctly than inferential ones (mean = 2.9), $p < .05$. This indicates that the subjects' recall of the passages contained more correct information derived from stated facts than derived from inferences made either during comprehension or during question answering. The absence of other main effects and all interactions indicate that the subjects understood the easy and hard passages with intact and abridged causal chains equally well.

Discussion

These results support the causal event chain analysis of texts by demonstrating that readers actively infer missing causal connections between the links of a causal event chain. These inferences are triggered during comprehension by gaps in the causal event chain underlying a text and increase the reading time for subsequent sentences. The overall memory representation of difficult texts, such as those with many missing causal connections, is less coherent than that of easy texts with intact causal chains. One consequence is that not all of the connections between the actions and states of the causal chain are directly accessible. As a result, readers must infer the missing causal connections in order to answer questions about the text. These inferences take time and increase the latency to read questions and formulate answers.

The event chain approach to text comprehension suggests that comprehension may be impeded when readers are required to detect and infer missing causal connections between the actions, physical states, and mental states described in the text. However, the event chain approach relies on a general taxonomy of possible causal relations between actions, physical states, and mental states to guide this inference process. More specific inferences may be derived from other types of general background knowledge or from special expertise. By using general background knowledge of scripted events and cultural schema, readers may be able to rapidly and accurately infer missing causal connections as they read texts and answer questions.

QUESTIONS ABOUT SCRIPTED ACTIONS

Inferences about the goals and actions of story characters may be derived from scripted knowledge. A script is an organized memory representation of the set of actors, roles and events that frequently co-occur in highly familiar situations (Bower, Black, & Turner, 1979; Schank & Abelson, 1977). Scripted knowledge may facilitate inferring answers to questions about vignettes by making available causal connections between the stated actions and states. Scripted knowledge about restaurants, sporting events, and gas stations is actively used by readers to understand and remember texts (Graesser, 1981; Sanford & Garrod, 1981).

Texts rarely describe the entire sequence of actions in a scripted event. Rather, key scripted actions are typically embedded within other, less predictable events. Consider the following two vignettes:

2. (a) Mary's car ran out of gas on the freeway. She walked to the gas station on the corner. She looked around and picked up a can.

(b) Mary's car ran out of gas on the freeway. She walked to the church on the corner. She looked around and picked up a can.

In both vignettes, the most likely explanation for Mary's final action is that she wants to fill the can with gasoline for her car. This inference should be more obvious and therefore faster in 2a than in 2b if scripts facilitate inferring causal explanations for characters' actions. In vignette 2a, "gas station" triggers relevant scripted knowledge about pumping and storing gasoline. No such relevant knowledge is triggered by "church"in vignette 2b; however, information about Good Samaritans and the power of prayer might be activated.

Relevant scripted knowledge may facilitate reading times for script-based events and facilitate the speed and accuracy of answering questions about those events. Two aspects of scripted knowledge were investigated: First, a script must necessarily list the causal preconditions for its execution. These preconditions describe initiating mental states and enabling physical states that must be met if the script is to be successfully employed. Second, a script can be summarized by a "script header" or key phrase. Script headers provide setting and location information for the occurrence of the scripted event. Both script headers and preconditions may trigger scripted knowledge and consequently enable readers to rapidly bridge gaps in the underlying event chain.

Six different versions of 18 vignettes were prepared. Each vignette described a common situation that led to a scripted action involved in, e.g., visiting a dentist or going shopping. To test the effectiveness of script preconditions and script headers, different versions of each vignette were created from a common set of elements. First, the vignette might provide a causal precondition. If a precondition was included, it was either appropriate or inappropriate to the scripted action. Second, the vignette also included a script header; the header was either relevant or irrelevant to the scripted action. Third, the final sentence of each vignette was common to all versions. This target sentence described an action that commonly occurs as part of a script. Finally, each vignette also included a question about the action in the target sentence. The question required the reader to infer a cause or consequence of the action. A sample set of script elements is presented in Table 8.3.

The subjects read each vignette one sentence at a time and then answered the question about it. The vignettes were presented via a computer-controlled system that permitted the subjects to regulate the presentation of each sentence. After reading the two or three sentences of the vignette, they read the appropriate question. The subjects were instructed to read each question and to formulate an answer. When they had formulated their answers, they pressed a control key that presented an answer prompt. In response to this prompt, they typed in their answers. The reading times for the target sen-

TABLE 8.3
The Elements of a Scripted Vignette

Script precondition

None

Appropriate: Phil's back hurt.

Inappropriate: Phil's teeth hurt.

Script header

Relevant: Phil went to his chiropractor's office.

Irrelevant: Phil went to his laywer's office.

Target Sentence

There he undressed and lay down on the table.

Question

Why did he lie down on the table?

Six versions were created by different combinations of these elements.

tences, the question-answering latencies, and the subjects' answers were automatically recorded. The question-answering latencies reflected the time required to read the question and formulate an appropriate answer. The answers were scored as correct or incorrect with respect to the script corresponding to each vignette.

A multivariate analysis of variance was performed on the three dependent variables: mean reading times for the target sentences, mean question-answering times, and the proportion of questions answered correctly. The MANOVA main effects for the type of script header (relevant versus irrelevant) and the type of precondition (none versus inappropriate versus appropriate) were all significant, all $p < .05$. There were no significant multivariate interactions. These results are summarized in Fig. 8.2.

Script Header

The presence of relevant script headers facilitated reading the target sentences $p < .05$, reduced the question-answering latencies, $p < .05$, and increased the proportion of correct answers to the questions, $p < .05$.

Script Precondition

The type of precondition had no effect on the reading times for the target sentences, $p > .05$. However, the question-answering latencies and the pro-

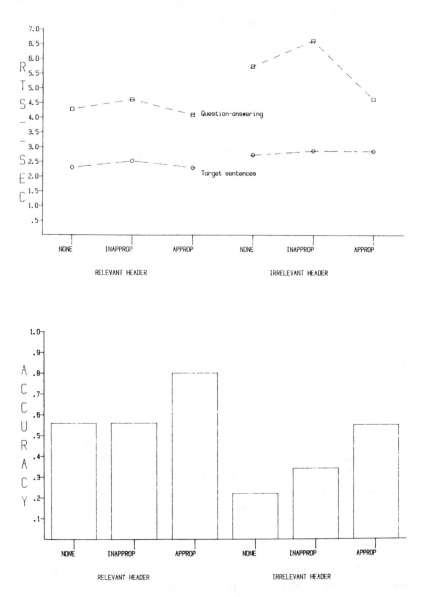

FIG. 8.2 Mean reading times for target sentences, question-answering latencies, and the proportion of questions answered correctly about the scripted vignettes with no, inappropriate, or appropriate preconditions.

portion of questions answered correctly were affected by this manipulation. Questions preceded by appropriate preconditions were answered more rapidly and more accurately than those with no precondition, both $p < .05$. Inappropriate preconditions increased the question-answering latencies, $p < .05$, while decreasing the accuracy of the answers, $p < .05$.

Discussion

Shared background knowledge of typical causal sequences of actions can significantly facilitate the speed and accuracy of inferential answers to questions about characters' actions. This shared causal knowledge, organized as scripts, can be triggered by the presence of cue words in a text. Script headers that summarize location information for a scripted activity and script preconditions that provide initiating mental states and enabling physical states are two such cues to the scriptal nature of a causal event chain. By using the specific causal information about the chain of events that typically occurs in a scripted activity, readers can rapidly infer causal connections between the stated elements of a vignette. A direct consequence is that a sentence describing a character's actions can be more rapidly read and understood if its causal relation to the preceding text is known. An indirect consequence of the use of scripted knowledge to infer missing causal connections is that the speed and accuracy of question answering improved. Scripted information, triggered by the relevant script headers and appropriate preconditions, provides causal information about the causes and consequences of the character's actions that is necessary to correctly answer questions about those actions.

QUESTIONS ABOUT CULTURAL STEREOTYPES

Cultural stereotypes about behavioral norms are a second source of information for causal explanations of characters' actions. For example, removing one's shoes upon entering a house is appropriate behavior in Japan but is inappropriate in the midwest. Why? This polite gesture has evolved from a need to protect traditional Japanese tatami floors. This causal explanation forms the background for a cultural convention that does not hold in Kansas. Cultural conventions such as this may be integrated to form cultural stereotypes or schema. Thus, cultural schema may provide the basis for predictions about and explanations for characters' actions. Cultural schema may facilitate comprehension of causal event chains and affect the speed and accuracy of question answering.

   Three hypotheses about the role of cultural schema during text comprehension were proposed. First, text reading times were assumed to reflect, among other comprehension processes, the time required to infer causal explanations for characters' actions. Information relevant to the appropriateness of cultural schemas was predicted to facilitate such causal inferences and lead to significant decreases in text reading times. Second, specific causal inferences may be made only in response to questions about the text. Consequently, cultural schema were expected to facilitate inferring answers to questions but not the retrieval of factual answers. Third, any facilitation by cultural schema on question answering may be restricted to only those actions whose interpretation is culturally determined. Thus, cultural schema were predicted to have no effect on the process of answering questions about actions with invariant "universal" explanations.

To test these hypotheses, four narratives about events that might typically occur in Bogata, Vienna, Kyoto, or the rural Amish area of Ohio were written. Each narrative mentioned at least eight actions with causal explanations that were dependent on the prevailing cultural milieu and eight other actions with causal explanations that were more invariant across cultures.

For each narrative, eight factual and eight inferential questions were created. The answers to the factual questions were explicitly stated in the narratives, whereas those for the inferential questions needed to be inferred. Half the questions were based on the culturally determined actions and half were based on the culturally invariant actions. The questions were balanced for word and syllable length and type of information asked, e.g., why or how an action was done.

Two versions of each narrative were then created. In the biased versions, the place and character names were appropriate to the geographic and cultural settings. In the neutral versions, these names were replaced by ones appropriate to the midwest. Preliminary testing evaluated the success of this manipulation. Judges recognized the cultural milieus of the biased stories and accepted the appropriateness of both the culturally determined actions and the culturally invariant actions. However, the judges found only the culturally invariant actions to be appropriate in the neutral versions; culturally determined actions were judged to be unlikely and inappropriate in the neutral versions. An excerpt from one biased narrative and example factual and inferential questions are presented in Table 8.4.

There were three specific predictions. First, the culturally appropriate place and character names were expected to facilitate reading the biased versions of the narratives. Second, the cultural cues were also expected to facilitate answering questions about the narratives. However, this facilitation was expected to occur only for inferential questions about the biased versions of the narratives. Third, the culturally appropriate place and character names were expected to faciliate answering questions about actions that are culturally determined but not those with culturally invariant explanations. These predictions were tested by examining the speed and accuracy of readers' answers to questions about the neutral and biased narratives.

TABLE 8.4
Excerpt from a Culturally Biased Version of One Narrative

Sr. Gomez closed the door of his small leather-goods shop and locked it. He was tired. It had been so hot that noon that he hadn't been able to sleep at all. He was angry, too, because his customers had haggled endlessly all morning. They didn't want to pay even half his original price. He muttered to himself as he walked down the almost empty street toward his favorite bar.

At home, his daughter, Maria, had just finished dressing. She was getting ready for her first date. She was very nervous.

"How do I look, Mother?" she asked.

"Pablo will be very proud," her mother replied. "With my lace shawl over your head, you look like a madonna."

"No, she doesn't." her little brother piped up. "She looks like a dope and I won't be seen dead with her."

"You most certainly will be seen with her. I won't let my daughter go on her first date alone Think what the neighbors would say!"

Just then Pablo arrived. He was nervous, too, but he said and did all the right things. He even brought some flowers for Sra. Gomez. He said they were going to the movies and he promised to have Maria back home by ten o'clock sharp. Then the three of them started off down the street as Sra. Gomez watched from the doorway.

Factual questions:	What did Sr. Gomez do as he walked down the street?
	What did Pablo bring for Sra. Gomez?
Inferential questions:	Why was Maria nervous?
	Why wouldn't Sra. Gomez let Maria go on her first date alone?

The subjects controlled the presentation of the narratives and questions, using a computer-driven system for studying self-paced reading. They were instructed to read each narrative at their natural reading rate; the narratives averaged six pages (approximately 1500 words) in length. After reading a narrative, the subjects answered a series of 16 questions about it. For each question, they were to first read the question and then formulate their answer. When they were ready to answer, the subjects were instructed to press a control key to receive an answer prompt and then type in their answer. The total time to read each narrative was automatically recorded along with the question-answering latencies and the subjects' answers. The question-answering latencies included the time to read the questions and that required to formulate an answer. The answers were scored as correct or incorrect with respect to the causal event chain underlying each narrative.

Narrative Reading Times

A univariate analysis of variance was performed on the narrative reading times. Story version, e.g., those with neutral versus those with culturally biased place and character names, was a between-subject factor. The narratives with neutral place and character names (mean = 164.6 sec) were read more slowly than the biased versions (mean = 147.8 sec), $p < .05$. Thus, the first prediction was confirmed as the culturally appropriate names facilitated reading the narratives.

Question-answering

A multivariate ANOVA was performed on the question-answering latencies and the proportion of questions correctly answered. In this analysis, narrative version (neutral versus biased names), question type (factual versus inferential), and question content (culturally determined versus culturally invariant actions) were factors. The results are summarized in Fig. 8.3.

Latencies

Overall, factual questions were answered no more rapidly than inferential ones, $p > .05$. Questions about culturally determined actions were answered as rapidly as those about culturally invariant actions, $p > .05$. However, questions about the versions with culturally appropriate names (mean = 5.44 sec) were answered more rapidly than those about the neutral versions (mean = 6.48 sec), $p < .05$.

There was a significant interaction between the version of the narrative and the type of question. For the narratives with neutral names, factual questions were answered more rapidly than inferential ones, $p < .05$. However, the culturally appropriate place and character names facilitated answering inferential questions. Thus, for the biased versions of the narratives, factual and inferential questions were answered equally rapidly, $p > .05$.

The interaction between the type of question and the content of the questions was marginally significant, $p = .06$. For questions about culturally invariant actions, factual questions were answered more rapidly than inferential ones, $p < .05$. However, for questions about culturally determined actions, factual questions were answered as rapidly as inferential ones, $p > .05$.

Accuracy

The subjects answered more factual questions (61%) correctly than inferential ones (55%), $p < .05$. More questions were answered correctly about the narrative with culturally appropriate names (69%) than those with neutral names (47%), $p < .05$. And more questions about culturally invariant actions (60%) were correctly answered than ones about culturally determined actions (56%), $p < .05$.

There was a significant interaction between the version of the narratives and the type of question, $p < .05$. For the neutral versions, answers to factual

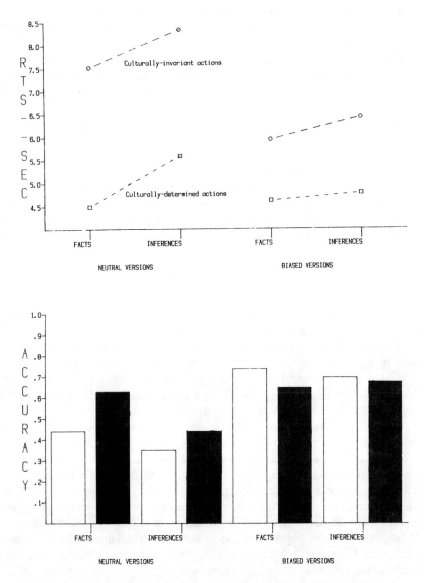

FIG. 8.3 Mean question-answering latencies and the proportion of correct answers to questions about culturally determined actions (open bars) and culturally invariant actions (solid bars).

questions were more accurate than answers to inferential ones, $p < .05$. In contrast, for the stories with culturally appropriate place and character names, answers to inferential questions were as accurate as answers to factual ones, $p > .05$.

However, there was a significant interaction between the version of the narrative and the content of the question, $p < .05$. For the narratives with neutral place and character names, more questions about culturally invariant actions were correctly answered than ones about culturally determined actions, $p < .05$. In contrast, for the narratives with culturally appropriate names, questions about culturally determined and culturally invariant actions were answered equally accurately, $p > .05$.

Overall, the question-answering latencies and accuracy measure confirmed the second and third predictions. The culturally appropriate place and character names improved both the speed and accuracy of answers to inferential questions. And the culturally appropriate place and character names also improved the accuracy of answers to questions about culturally determined actions.

Discussion

These results demonstrate that place and character names are powerful triggers for causal explanations for characters' actions. By activating cultural schema for appropriate and inappropriate actions, the culturally appropriate names facilitated making causal inferences during text comprehension. Once activated by the names, the cultural schema provided information about likely causes and consequences of the characters' actions and thus enabled the readers to infer missing causal connections.

Cultural schema facilitate not only immediate comprehension of the sequence of events in a narrative but also question answering. Overall, answering factual questions is both more rapid and more accurate than answering inferential questions. Cultural cues, such as the place and character names, can enable readers to infer answers as rapidly and as accurately as they can retrieve factual answers. The cultural schema, triggered by the names, provide accurate causal information that can be readily retrieved. While the culturally appropriate place and character names did not increase the speed of answers to questions about culturally determined actions, the cues did improve their accuracy. This suggests that cultural schema are heavily weighted toward accurate information about the causes and consequences of actions that are unique to the cultural milieu. Such unique, culturally determined information is retrieved no less rapidly than is more general, culturally invariant information.

CONCLUSIONS

In order to answer questions about characters' actions, readers must understand the causes and consequences of those actions. They must know or infer the complete causal event chain underlying a text in order to answer a question about what a character did, why it was done, or how it was accomplished. These causal explanations may be directly stated in the text or inferred using relevant background knowledge. Our research has explored the utility of two such sources of causal information, scripts and cultural stereotypes, for answering factual and inferential questions about texts.

The answers to factual questions need only be retrieved from information directly available in memory. However, the answers to inferential questions must be inferred from the available information. By examining both the speed and accuracy of inferential answers, relative to factual ones, we were able to identify the kinds of information readers use in this inference process.

Overall, readers are more rapid and more accurate when they must simply recall directly stated, factual answers to questions about characters' actions. Inferring an answer to a wh-question is a time-consuming process that is subject to error. However, scripted knowledge of causal sequences and cultural stereotypes about appropriate and inappropriate actions can improve the speed and accuracy of question-answering. These two sources of background information for causal explanations can be triggered by information in the text and facilitate both reading the text and inferring answers to questions about it.

Answering questions about texts draws upon causal inferences processes that are similar to those used during immediate text comprehension. Consequently, background causal knowledge can facilitate both question answering and text comprehension. Scripted knowledge and cultural schema facilitate inferring causal explanations for why and how characters act as they do and causal expectations about the consequences of actions and events. Other kinds of background knowledge may also interact with information in texts to facilitate causal inferences and question answering. Special expertise such as knowledge of mechanics, physics, or cooking may, like cultural stereotypes and scripts, facilitate comprehension and question answering.

ACKNOWLEDGMENTS

Preparation of this chapter was supported by grant IST-81110439 from the National Science Foundation. Thanks to David Gleue and Roseanne Marney-Hay for their assistance with developing the causal event chain analysis and to Tom Cocklin for his comments. Portions of this chapter were presented at the Midwestern Psychology Association meeting in Chicago, May 1983.

REFERENCES

Bower, G. H., Black, J. B., & Turner, T. Scripts in text comprehension and memory. *Journal of Experimental Psychology,* 1979, *28,* 511–534.

Camp, C. J., Lachman, J. L., & Lachman, R. Evidence for direct access and inferential retrieval in question-answering. *Journal of Verbal Learning and Verbal Behavior,* 1980, *19,* 583–596.

Graesser, A. C. *Prose comprehension beyond the word.* New York: Springer-Verlag, 1981.

Kemper, S. Filling in the missing links. *Journal of Verbal Learning and Verbal Behavior,* 1982a, *21,* 99–107.

Kemper, S. *The event chain analysis of texts.* (Tech. Rep No. NSF-R-81-12). University of Kansas, 1982b.

Kemper, S. *Causal inferences in text comprehension and production.* Paper presented to the Midwestern Psychological Association, Chicago, May 1983a.

Kemper, S. Measuring the inference load of a text. *Journal of Education Psychology,* 1983b, *75,* 391–401.

McCall, W. A., & Crabbs, L. S. *Standard test lessons in reading.* New York: Teachers College Press, Columbia University, 1979.

Nicholas, D. W., & Trabasso, T. Toward a taxonomy of inferences for story comprehension. In F. Wilkening, J. Becker, T. Trabasso (Eds.), *Information integration by children.* Hillsdale, NJ: Lawrence Erlbaum Associates, 1980.

Omanson, R. C., & Formosa, M. J. *An analysis of narratives: Scoring manual.* Unpublished document, Learning Research and Development Center, University of Pittsburgh, 1982.

Omanson, R. C., Warren, W. H., & Trabasso, T. Goals, inferential comprehension, and recall of stories by children. *Discourse Processes,* 1978, *1,* 355–372.

Sanford, A. J., & Garrod, S. C. *Understanding written language: Explorations in comprehension beyond the sentence.* Chichester, Great Britain: John Wiley, 1981.

Schank, R., & Abelson, R. *Scripts, plans, goals, and understanding: An inquiry into human knowledge structures.* Hillsdale, NJ: Lawrence Erlbaum Associates, 1977.

Spargo, E., & Williston, G. R. *Timed readings* (Books 7 & 10). Providence, RI: Jamestown, 1980.

Warren, W. H., Nicholas, P. W., & Trabasso, T. Event chains and inferences in understanding narratives. In R. O. Freedle (Ed.), *New directions in discourse processing* (Vol. 2). Norwood, NJ: Ablex, 1979.

9 Inferential Reasoning In and About Narrative Texts

Susan R. Goldman
University of California, Santa Barbara

We have been using questioning procedures to examine various aspects of narrative understanding. In most theories of comprehension, a distinction has been made between understanding the causal and logical relationships represented in the narrative and understanding a more general level theme or message in the narrative (e.g., Kintsch & van Dijk, 1978; Rumelhart, 1977). For either type of understanding to occur, connections must be made among different aspects of information, an inferential reasoning process. When the causal and logical relationships among the various elements of a narrative are understood, the narrative representation may be said to be internally coherent. We refer to this type of understanding as Text-Internal Reasoning. When the message or theme of a narrative has been understood, the comprehender may construct relationships among the narrative and previously experienced narratives and situations, or previously acquired concepts. Thus, connections may be formed between the narrative and aspects of knowledge that are external to it. We refer to this type of understanding as Text-External Reasoning.

Questions that ask about text-internal relationships have expected responses that reflect inferential reasoning about the specifically questioned information. An example of a question of this type is the following: "The story says, *Bill stole John's bike. John hit Bill.*Why did John hit Bill?" The expected response, "because Bill stole his bike" involves making the causal inference that Bill's action directly caused John's action. When asked questions that are text-external, expected responses reflect reasoning about the story as a whole in relationship to abstract rules of behavior, morals, and principles that the particular text might exemplify. Using the previous example, a text-external question might be "Was it okay for John to hit Bill? Why?" The answers might reflect a situation specific response, e.g., "Yes, because Bill stole his bike" or a more generalized response, e.g., "Well, you shouldn't hit but you also shouldn't steal" or "Yes, because stealing is wrong."

The distinction between text-internal and text-external reasoning reflects two common functional outcomes of narratives in a culture: the acquisition of story-specific knowledge and the transmission of societal values, norms, and caveats on appropriate behavior (see Stein's discussion, 1982). Even if the primary function of storytelling is entertainment (see Brewer & Lichtenstein, 1982), these outcomes might occur. Both functions have strong ties to understanding the development of cognitive processes, memory functioning, problem solving, and social cognition. It is clear from the many analyses of children's stories that the content of narratives reflects social interpersonal problem solving (see discussions in Goldman, 1982; Johnson & Mandler, 1980; Rumelhart, 1977; Stein & Goldman, 1981).

The core of interpersonal problem solving and social interactions is the behavioral episode, consisting of intentional, purposive action(s) and its (their) consequences (see Bruner, 1973; Damon, 1981). Analyses of stories have shown that the behavioral episode is the basic structural unit (e.g., Mandler & Johnson, 1977; Stein & Glenn, 1979; Stein & Goldman, 1981). In well-formed stories, the episode has four primary components: information that (1) conveys the character's intention or goal, (2) the reasons for that intention, (3) an attempt sequence consisting of actions designed to accomplish that intention, and (4) the consequences of the attempt with respect to the goal and original reasons for the goal. These components are illustrated by the example in Table 9.1. The original reasons for the goal are motivating conditions, consisting of states and/or events that occur in the character's physical or mental environment and/or affective responses to these states and events. These motivating conditions cause the character's intention, the goal. The existence of the goal causes the character to attempt to satisfy the goal. The attempt causes some result, the consequence. To understand this

TABLE 9.1
Example of a Behavioral Episode

Type of Information	Text Sample
Motivating Events/States	Jimmy came home from school and finished his homework. He was bored
Goal	and wanted a dog to play with.
Attempt actions	He emptied his piggbank and went to the pet store.
Consequence	He bought the dog and played with it in the store.

chain of causal and logical relationships in a story, individuals probably rely on a naive theory of human action (Heider 1958) that applies outside of the story context as well as in the story context.

Thus, when we assess children's reasoning and text-internal relations we are examining a combination of knowledge: knowledge about the social world in general and about the particular social world depicted in the text. When we assess children's conceptions of the theme or message of a story we are examining understanding of story functions as well as how the child might be acquiring or recognizing more general principles for operating in a societal context.

The research reported in this chapter assesses developmental similarities and differences in responses to questions requiring text-internal reasoning and to those requiring text-external reasoning. The original rationale for the text-internal work was based on predictions derived from story grammar and schema frameworks for story memory and representation. In one study, we presented stories in which we manipulated logical connections among the components comprising a behavioral episode. These manipulations affected the type of causal relationship between the attempt and consequence. In a second investigation we manipulated the type of logical connection between behavioral episodes in a multi-episode story. These manipulations affected the degree to which one episode was causally related to the others in the story. In both research projects, recall and why-question techniques were used to assess understanding of the relationships. Story grammar and schema frameworks predict that both types of manipulations have consequences for story memory and representation. In general for both projects, story memory predictions, as measured by free recall of the presented stories, were not supported, whereas the why-question data revealed that the representations were characterized by the presence of the predicted differences in logical relationships (see Goldman & Varnhagen, 1981 and 1983 for further discussion). Thus, in both projects why questions revealed aspects of understanding not evident in recall protocols. The nature of the responses to the text-internal questions is discussed in the next section of this chapter. This is followed by a discussion of the work we are conducting on aspects of text-external reasoning. Two aspects are discussed: conceptions of the lessons taught by Aesop's fables (Goldman, Reyes, & Varnhagen, 1983) and children's explanations of their own story-sorting behavior (Johnson, 1983). The story-sorting experiment tested the degree to which children's story similarity judgments reflected the understanding and use of story themes.

TEXT-INTERNAL REASONING

A number of researchers have conducted theoretical analyses of the underlying logical relations between events in a behavioral episode. Some researchers take a problem-solving approach and concentrate only on goal-action relationships (e.g., Lichtenstein & Brewer, 1980) while others have examined behavioral episode relationships as they occur in simple stories (e.g., Stein & Trabasso, 1982). Both approaches specify that actions are caused by the existence of a goal. That is, actions in a behavioral episode are connected to the goal by an *in-order-to* logical connection. Thus, for the sample in Table 9.1, *Jimmy emptied his piggybank* in-order-to accomplish his goal, *wanting a dog*.

As discussed above, behavioral episodes that occur in stories typically include two components other than the goal and attempt action sequence, namely motivating conditions that psychologically and often sequentially precede the goal and consequences. The motivating conditions cause the goal to be formulated in the first place. They lead to the characters' specific intention in the episode. Attempts result in consequences and when an attempt works, it causes a consequence that is consistent with the goal of the episode. Thus, the logical structure in a behavioral episode in which the actions do lead to success (goal attainment) is relatively straightforward: (1) motivating event/state leads to goal, (2) actions in-order-to accomplish goal, and (3) action cause consequence = goal attained. For the example in Table 9.1, Jimmy's having finished his homework and being bored leads to his formulating a specific goal, namely he wants a dog to play with. He then empties his piggybank and goes to the pet store *in-order-to* get a dog. These actions cause the consequence that he buys the dog and plays with it. Simple episode stories having this logical construction have been examined frequently in comprehension studies (e.g., Mandler & DeForest, 1979; Nezworski, Stein, & Trabasso, 1982; Stein, 1979).

Goldman and Varnhagen (1983) were interested in comparing understanding of this logical structure with the understanding of episodes where the actions did not lead to goal attainment. Specifically we examined episodes in which an obstacle external to the protagonist prevented goal attainment. In Table 9.1 we provided an example of an episode in which the goal was attained. The obstacle, non-goal attainment version of this episode is shown in Table 9.2. The obstacle appears in the consequence category and conveys the information that the attempt does not cause goal attainment, whereas in the no-obstacle scenario the consequence information does imply that the attempt causes goal attainment. The second statement in the no-obstacle version, *and played with him* (puppy), is an explicit statement of meeting the goal of the episode. Likewise, the second consequence statement in the obstacle scenario explicitly states that the goal could not be met.

These differences between the consequence information in the two scenarios have implications for the logical structure of the one-episode stories that Goldman and Varnhagen (1983) presented. The no-obstacle and obstacle stories have the same causal structure up to the occurrence of the obstacle. In the

TABLE 9.2
Sample of Obstacle Scenario and Reactions to an Episode

Type of Information	Text Sample
Motivating Events/States	Jimmy came home from school and finished his homework. He was bored
Goal	and wanted a dog to play with.
Attempt actions	He emptied his piggbank and went to the pet store.
Consequence = Obstacle	The puppies were too expensive
Consequence = Goal not attained	and Jimmy couldn't buy one.
Reaction	Jimmy was very angry and stomped out of the store.
Reaction for No-obstacle scenario given in Table 9.1	Jimmy was very happy and carefully carried the puppy home.

obstacle case, the causal link between the actions and goal attainment is interrupted and the motivating conditions and the goal continue to be "active." The conflict of the episode is unresolved and subsequent behavior by the character might still be governed by these active states. In the no-obstacle case, where the conflict is successfully dealt with, the character is essentially free to pursue some other activities. Table 9.2 also shows one additional category of information, the reaction. This category is typically considered to be optional in a well-formed story, but when it does occur, it conveys the character's response to the outcome of the attempt, as described in the consequence category. This response may be feelings or actions. In the two scenarios, the reactions differed so that they were consistent with the information conveyed in each scenario. That is, in the no-obstacle scenario, where Jimmy gets his puppy, he is happy and takes the puppy home. However in the obstacle scenario, Jimmy gets angry and the action reflects that anger. Thus in each scenario, the reaction is caused by the consequence of the story.

Goldman and Varnhagen (1983) offered some general predictions about comprehension and answers to why questions asked about the motivating states, goals, actions in the attempt, consequences and reactions to the consequence. Children in second and fifth grade and college students were each presented with two examples of one-episode stories of the obstacle type and two of the no-obstacle type. In addition to the Jimmy-dog story three other story themes were used: (1) a girl who wants to make a home for some ants; (2) a horse who wants to eat some carrots; and (3) a beaver who wants to patch a hole in his dam. Following each story a free recall was elicited. This was followed by a series of why questions. We focus here on the responses to the why questions because they proved to be far more sensitive to the difference in the logical structure than did the free recall data (see Goldman & Varnhagen, 1983, for details).

For both obstacle and no-obstacle stories we expected to find similarity in responses to why questions about the motivating states, goals and actions in the attempt category. This prediction was based on the assumption that these three categories have the same causal structure in the two scenarios. Table 9.3 illustrates the questions asked about each of these three categories of information and also provides sample responses and the scoring categories into which the responses to the three questions were classified. The data suported the prediction that the responses to these three questions would be similar: Comparisons between no-obstacle and obstacle scenarios of the types of responses to these questions were nonsignificant. Furthermore, the most frequent responses to each question were the same for the college students and the children. The sample responses in Table 9.3 are the most frequent ones.

When asked why Jimmy was bored, 72% of the college students' responses and 54% of the children's referred either to the presented motivating event or

TABLE 9.3

Sample Why Questions and Types of Sample Responses for Motivating State, Goal and Attempt Information in Obstacle and No-Obstacle Scenarios

Sample Question	Type of Response	Sample Response
1. Motivating State Why was Jimmy bored?	Motivating Event	*He had finished his homework.*
	State resulting from Motivating Event	*He had nothing to do.*
2. Goal Why did Jimmy want a dog to play with?	Anticipated consequences of goal attainment	*So he would have something to do.*
	States and Events active at the time of goal formulation	*He was bored; He had finished his homework; He had nothing to do.*
3. Attempt actions Why did Jimmy empty his piggybank and go to the pet store?	Goal	*He wanted a dog; He wanted to get/ to buy a dog.*

to a state resulting from that event, e.g., *he had nothing to do.* This type of response indicates that the state of being bored is understood as causally linked to the event that preceded it, consistent with the causal structure analysis of an episode. Responses to why the protagonist had a particular goal were classified into three categories and the proportions of responses in each were not significantly different from one another. For children and adults, 34% of the responses occurred in the category "Anticipated consequences of goal attainment." These are statements that explain that the protagonist formulated the goal in order to obtain a desirable resultant situation by removing the explicitly and implicitly negative circumstances specified in the motivating state information presented in the story. For example, the response shown in Table 9.3, *so he would have something to do,* will be the result of getting the puppy and will remove the state of being bored and not having anything to do. Essentially, the goal is being explained by its potential for removing the conditions that led to it in the first place. It may represent a forward rather than backward causal connection (see Stein & Trabasso, 1982). The other two response categories refer to states or events that could be assumed to be active at the point in the story when the goal was formulated, essentially leading to the goal (see Graesser, Robertson & Anderson, 1981; Lichenstein & Brewer, 1980). Children and adults gave these equally often. These responses indicate that the state of the story world prior to goal formulation causes goal formulation, either directly or by the potential of goal attainment to remove these prior states.

The hypothesized causal link between the goal and the actions in the attempt was reflected in the responses of both the children and college students: 87% of the responses explained the characters' attempts by their goals, e.g., *because he wanted a puppy.* Thus, from second grade there is evidence that the basic intentional action schema, consisting of motive leads to goal and goal causes attempt, underlies the representation of the initial portion of these one-episode stories. These data support story grammar proposals regarding the logical relationships among the categories of information that comprise the beginning and middle of an episode in a story and the prediction that representations for the no-obstacle and obstacle scenarios would not differ up to this point in the story.

Goldman and Varnhagen (1983) also predicted differences in the representations of the remainder of the no-obstacle as compared to the obstacle scenarios. These differences were predicted on the basis of the goal being met and therefore neither it nor the motives for it remain active after the first statement in the no-obstacle consequence. However, in the obstacle scenario, the original episode goal is not met and it and the motives causing it remain active in the story world. Differences between the representations of the two scenarios were found, and there were also developmental differences in the representations within each scenario. Four story statements occurred after the attempt in both the no-obstacle and the obstacle stories. Two of these constitute the consequence category and two the reaction category, as shown in Tables 9.1 and 9.2. Why questions were asked about each of these statements and are illustrated in Table 9.4.

For the no-obstacle scenario, the first statement in the consequence category was an action that conveyed the fact that the episode goal had been met, e.g., he bought the dog and now has one. Since Jimmy now has a dog, the reasons for wanting one are no longer active. The removal of the motivating conditions was the type of response that the children gave most frequently, 58% of the responses. This proportion of the responses is significantly greater than the proportion of the college students' responses that were in this category, 36%, $z = 2.37$, $p < .05$, and suggests that the causal connection between the beginning-middle and consequence of the episode is more salient to the children than to the college students. Equally often, 32% of the responses, college students gave a new goal that could be interpreted as a superordinate of the original episode goal, e.g., *he wanted a friend*. This is superordinate in the sense that *wanting and buying a puppy* is a subset that satisfies the higher-order wanting-a-friend goal. The college students' frequent use of this type of response may indicate that they have a greater tendency to explain actions by goals than children have: There is no goal "active" once the dog has been bought, since the original episode goal is met and the motives removed by the action; therefore the college students provide a new "active" goal. This developmental difference in the responses to this question may imply a difference in the elaborateness of the representation of a simple episode, with college students providing embellishments that add greater complexity, whereas children tend to "stick" more to the presented information.

For the second statement in the no-obstacle consequence, which was also an action, providing a new goal was the dominant response for the children (.72) as well as for the college students (.92) but the college students gave this response more frequently than the children, $z = 2.43$, $p < .05$. The children explained this second action by talking about personal properties and attributes of the protagonist 21% of the time. Thus, in explaining the two actions in the no-obstacle consequence, actions that imply that the original episode goal is no longer active, children supplied new goals for the actions less frequently than the college students. More frequently than the college students, the children stayed within the original story by relating the actions back to the beginning or to the protagonist's character. Information of the latter type would fall within story-setting information and can be interpreted as part of the original episode.

The responses to the questions about the information in the reaction category also indicated some developmental differences in the representation, at least for the final story action. The two questions on reaction category information are shown in Table 9.4. The positive emotional state in the reaction

TABLE 9.4

Sample Why Questions and Types of Responses for Information in the Endings of the
No-obstacle and Obstacle Scenarios

Sample Question	Type of Response	Sample Response
No-Obstacle Scenario		
1. Consequence - action₁		
Why did Jimmy buy a puppy?	Removes motivating conditions or accomplishes story goal	*Then he would have one.* *He wanted one.*
	New goal	*He wanted a friend.*
2. Consequence - action₂		
Why did Jimmy play with him in the store?	New goal	*He wanted to be friends.*
	Property of protagonist	*He was lonely.*
3. Reaction - emotion		
Why was Jimmy happy?	Goal attained	*He had his puppy.*
4. Reaction - action		
Why did Jimmy carefully carry the puppy home?	Previous emotion	*He was happy.*
	New goal	*He didn't want the puppy to get hurt.*
Obstacle Scenario		
1. Consequence - obstacle		
Why were the puppies too expensive?	States or events external to the protagonist	*The storeowner was greedy.* *They only had fancy dogs.*
	Protagonist's faulty attempt	*He went to the wrong store.* *He didn't bring enough money.*
2. Consequence - goal not met		
Why couldn't Jimmy buy a puppy?	Obstacle	*The puppies cost too much money.*
3. Reaction - emotion		
Why was Jimmy angry?	Original goal and motivating conditions still exist	*He wanted a dog.* *He still had nothing to do.*
4. Reaction - action		
Why did Jimmy stomp out of the store?	Previous emotion	*He was angry.*
	Original goal not met	*He wanted a dog.*

was represented similarly by each age group: 65% of all responses indicated that Jimmy was happy because he had a puppy, i.e., because he attained his goal. Responses for the final story action showed a tendency for the youngest children to supply a new goal at this point (78% of the responses) more frequently than any other type of response. The fifth graders and college students divided their responses between new goal responses and the positive emotional response in the reaction category. Despite these differences between age groups, both relationships do relate the final action to a motivating state or goal that is different from those in the original episode. This is consistent with predictions about actions following episodes in which no obstacle is encountered: Since the original goal has been met, some new purpose is needed to guide the action. All age groups indicated a sensitivity to the need for a new purpose, although the story statement that elicited this aspect of the representation differed across age groups: College students tended to provide the protagonist with a new purpose earlier in the episode than the children did. The representations for the endings of the no-obstacle versions generally indicated two phenomena. First, as predicted by story grammar analyses, consequence information is causally related to the beginning-middle of the episode. Second, when a story action occurs in the absence of an active goal, the action is causally related to a motivating state or inferred goal. The latter finding is a second piece of supporting evidence for the previously discussed conclusion that by second grade, the basic intentional action schema is used to guide the interpretation and causal explanation of story actions.

The continued presence of an active goal is one of the major differences between the no-obstacle and obstacle versions of the stories. This difference has several implications for the predicted causal relationships between the beginning-middle of the episode and the ending in the obstacle stories. First, as was pointed out previously, the first statement in the consequence conveys the obstacle or stumbling block to the success of the attempt. These obstacles were conditions over which the protagonist had no control. When asked to explain why these states existed, 88% of the children's responses were states and events external to the protagonist. This was a significantly greater percentage than the adults (60%). An example of this type of response is shown in Table 9.4. The other 40% of the adult responses constructed a causal link between the character's actions and the obstacle: These responses talked about what was wrong with the protagonist's actions to meet the goal. Thus, the adults tended to assign more control and responsibility to the story character than did the children, thereby constructing a direct causal link, similar to that in the no-obstacle stories. The second statement in the obstacle consequence directly stated that the character could not attain the goal and 70% of all subjects said this was caused by the immediately preceding story statement, i.e., the obstacle state.

Thus, for the children the predicted differences in causal structure between no-obstacle and obstacle stories were clear-cut. For adults this differentiation was significantly attenuated by making the protagonist responsible for the obstacle. These data may indicate that adults tend to interpret a wider range of obstacles as avoidable with appropriate planning than do children. The data may also reflect a phenomena analogous to one found in the attribution literature: Developmental differences have been observed in how situational and stable personality trait information are used and weighted in predicting an individual's subsequent behavior (e.g., Ross, 1981).

Although there was this developmental difference in assigning responsibility for failure to the protagonist, the responses to the reaction category questions clearly showed the predicted differences between the representation of the no-obstacle and obstacle stories. Since the original goal and motivating conditions were still active, the reaction should be connected to them rather than to new ones. The negative emotion was explained by the continued existence of the original episode goal or motivating states in 72% of the responses, with no developmental differences. There were also no developmental differences in the responses to the final story action: It was causally connected to the whole episode by all groups; either the directly preceding negative emotional state was given (38%) or the original and still unmet story goal was given (37%).

Thus, in our examination of children's understanding of the relationships among motivating states, goals, actions, and their outcomes we found a basic understanding of the causal in-order-to relationship between actions and goals in a simple episode. We also found that when a goal has not been met, that goal and its associated motivational states are still active, and potentially may guide subsequent behavioral episodes. In a subsequent study we pursued the issue of causal relationships between, as well as within, episodes by examining logical relationships in multi-episode stories.

MULTI-EPISODE STORIES

The logical relationships between episodes comprising a multi-episode story are of three types, And, Then, and Cause (Mandler & Johnson, 1977; Stein & Glenn, 1979). An And relation is a temporal simultaneity relation; the order in which the episodes occur is essentially arbitrary. A Then relation is a temporal succession relation between episodes, with no direct causal relation: episode$_1$ preceded in time episode$_2$ but nothing that occurred in episode$_1$ motivates episode$_2$. An example of such a relation might be an adventure story describing a series of heroic deeds that occur over time, but each deed is essentially independent of the others. Episodes are causally related when something in one episode directly motivates the next episode. Cause relations define episode embedding. There are, however, different types of cause relationships and therefore different types of embedding (see Johnson & Mandler, 1980).

Goldman and Varnhagen (1981) examined memory for and representations of stories having two different types of multi-episode relationships. These are referred to as goal-subgoal and goal-sequential stories. Recall and why questions were examined. As they found in the no-obstacle/obstacle research, the why questions were more sensitive to representational issues than were the recall protocols. College students and children in third and firth grades were tested to examine developmental similarities and differences in the understanding of interepisode relationships. Half of the subjects at each age group listened to the stories and half read them, and each subject received one example of each type of story. Children and one group of college students were tested immediately after story presentation. This immediate condition represented a minimally difficult task for the college students, since the vocabulary and content were appropriate for the youngest children. Therefore, to increase the difficulty of the task and to examine the stability of the representations over time, a second group of college students was tested at a 48-hour delay.

The goal-subgoal type of story is an everyday type of situation in which a person has some goal, but in order to attain the goal, various preconditions must be met. So the person systematically meets the preconditions and finally meets the original goal. An example of this type of story is given in Fig. 9.1. The statement numbers indicate order of presentation in the story. A boy named Jimmy wants a bike but needs money to buy the bike, so he gets a job and saves the money until he can buy the bike. The goal-sequential type is also an everyday type of situation in which a person's ability to attain a particular goal is affected by previously attained goals, although the previously attained goals may have been met for reasons totally divorced from later goals. An example of this type of story is shown in Fig. 9.2. Jimmy wants a job so he gets one. Then he decides he wants to save a lot of money so he does his job in a certain way. Having saved a lot of money, he is in a position to meet the last goal in the story, buying a bike.

There are a number of differences between the two types of goal structures, including the relationships between episodes. The goal-subgoal case represents a relatively stronger causal connection between episodes than does the goal-sequential case. In the goal-subgoal case $episode_2$ is motivated by the goal in $episode_1$ and $episode_3$ is directly motivated by the goal in $episode_2$ and less directly by the goal in $episode_1$. Furthermore, $goal_1$ remains active or unresolved until $goal_2$ is resolved; $goal_2$ remains active or unresolved until $goal_3$ is resolved. In problem-solving terms, the goal of the third episode is a subgoal to the goal of the second episode and the goal of the second episode is

(1) Setting: There once was a boy named Jimmy.

Episode$_1$

(2 & 3) Motivating Events:
  One day Jimmy met Tom
  and saw Tom's new bike.

(4) Motivating State:
  Jimmy thought the bike was neat.

(5) Goal:
  He wanted one like it.

Episode$_2$

(6 & 7) Motivating Event:
  He called the bike shop
  and asked about the price of bikes.

(8) Motivating State:
  Jimmy was still interested.

(9) Goal$_2$ = Subgoal$_1$:
  He wanted to save money.

Episode$_3$

(10 & 11) Motivating Event:
  He talked to his mother that night.
  She said Jimmy should get a part-
  time job.

(12) Motivating State:
  Jimmy liked to work.

(13) Goal$_3$ = Subgoal$_2$:
  He decided to get a paper route.

(14 & 15) Attempt$_3$:
  He went to the newspaper office
  and talked to the sales manager.

(16 & 17) Consequence$_3$:
  Jimmy got a list of customers
  and began to deliver newspapers.

(18 & 19) Attempt$_2$:
  He put the papers near each door
  and range every doorbell.

(20 & 21) Consequence$_2$:
  Jimmy earned a lot of tips
  and saved all the money.

(22 & 23) Attempt$_1$:
  Jimmy counted the money one day
  and went to the bike shop.

(24 & 25) Consequence$_1$:
  Jimmy picked out the bike he wanted
  and gave the man the money.

(26 & 27) Reaction: Jimmy was very happy
  and rode the bike to Tom's house.

FIG. 9.1   Sample goal-subgoal story. Numbers correspond to presentation order in the stories.

a subgoal to the highest-order goal in the story, the goal of the first episode. The most deeply embedded goal must be attained as a precondition to attaining the next goal, and meeting that goal is a precondition to meeting the highest-order goal. Hypothesized logical links between the three goals are as follows: subgoal$_2$ (e.g., get a paper route) in-order-to subgoal$_1$ (e.g., save money) in-order-to goal (e.g., buy a bike). Note further that the particular sub-goals that the character selected in these stories are not the only ways to meet the preconditions of the highest-order goal. The particular selected goals are also motivated by the events and states that were presented between the goal statement of episode$_n$ and the goal statement of episode$_{n+1}$. Thus each of the episodes shown in Fig. 9.1, with a few minor wording changes, constitutes a complete, single-episode story. Goldman and Varnhagen (1981)

```
                    (1) Setting:   There once was a boy named Jimmy.

           Episode₁

(2 & 3) Motivating Event₁:
           One day Jimmy was talking to his mother.
           She said Jimmy could get a part-time job.

(4) Motivating State₁:
           Jimmy liked to work.

(5) Goal₁:
           He decided to get a paper route.

(6 & 7) Attempt₁:
           He went to the newspaper office
           and talked to the sales manager.

(8 & 9) Consequence₁:
           Jimmy got a list of customers
           and began to deliver newspapers.

                         Episode₂

           (10 & 11) Motivating Event₂:
                      Jimmy met Tom along the route.
                      Tom told Jimmy how to please the customers.

           (12) Motivating State₂:
                      Jimmy was interested in the idea.

           (13) Goal₂:
                      He wanted to save a lot of money.

           (14 & 15) Attempt₂:
                      He put the papers near each door
                      and rang every doorbell.

           (16 & 17) Consequence₂:
                      Jimmy earned alot of tips
                      and saved all the money.

                              Episode₃

                 (18 & 19) Motivating Event₃:
                            Jimmy was taking the money to the bank
                            and saw Tom's new bike.

                 (20) Motivating State₃:
                            Jimmy thought the bike was neat.

                 (21) Goal₃:
                            He wanted one like it.

                 (22 & 23) Attempt₃:
                            He counted his money
                            and went to the bike shop.

                 (24 & 25) Consequence₃:
                            Jimmy picked out the bike he wanted
                            and eagerly gave the man the money.

           (26 & 27) Reaction:
                      Jimmy was very happy
                      and rode the bike to Tom's house.
```

FIG. 9.2   Sample goal-sequential story. Numbers correspond to presentation order in the stories.

were particularly interested in whether the representations for the goal-subgoal stories connected the episodes through the goals. To examine this question, why-goal questions were asked about each of the three goal statements, e.g., *Why did Jimmy want to get a paper route?*

The goal-subgoal interepisode relationships can be contrasted with the interepisode relationships in the goal-sequential stories. In these stories, the state of the world that exists at the end of $episode_n$ allows or enables $episode_{n+1}$. Referring to the example in Fig. 9.2, the state of the world that exists after the consequence of $episode_1$ is that Jimmy has a paper route. Having the paper route enables the occurrence of motivating $event_2$ meeting

Tom. Similarly, if Jimmy hadn't saved a lot of money (consequence$_2$) he couldn't have been taking it to the bank, seen Tom's bike, nor been able to buy a bike. Thus, interepisode relationships are similar to those between a setting and an episode in a one-episode story: episode$_n$ allows or enables episode$_{n+1}$ but really does not *cause* episode$_{n+1}$. Goldman and Varnhagen (1981) therefore expected that responses to why-goal questions would indicate the intraepisode causal relationship between that episode's motivating conditions and that episode's goal.

Responses to why-goal questions were of two types: a goal, or a motivating state/event. The two types of responses reflect different logical connections. A goal response essentially reflects an in-order-to causal relationship, e.g., The response *Jimmy wanted to save money* to the question *Why did Jimmy get a paper route?* reflects the previously discussed subgoal$_2$ in-order-to subgoal$_1$ relationship. A motivating state or event response reflects a leads-to causal relationship, e.g., The response *he thought Tom's bike was neat* to the question *Why did Jimmy want a bike?* reflects the causal, motivational relationship between goal formulation and the states and events in the episode. Both leads-to and in-order-to are types of causal relationships.

The responses to the why-goal questions did indeed reveal representational differences between the goal-subgoal and goal-sequential stories. Furthermore, developmental and listening versus reading differences were found for the goal-sequential representations but not for the goal-subgoal representations. Figure 9.3 shows the representation based on responses to the why-goal questions in the goal-subgoal stories. The types of responses given by college students at both testing times did not differ from those given by the children. Nor did listening to as compared with reading the stories lead to significant differences in the frequencies of types of responses. The proportions shown along the links in Fig. 9.3 represent the frequency of that response divided by

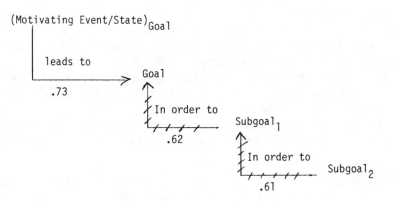

FIG. 9.3   Dominant responses to Why goal questions in the goal-subgoal stories. Interepisode links are shown with ─/─/─/─ lines.

the total number of responses given by all subjects. (The total number of subjects was 148. However, occasionally some subjects did not respond to a question and the bases vary from 140 to 148.) These proportions represent the dominant response to each question.

The data in Fig. 9.3 indicate that the three episodes in the goal-subgoal stories were connected through the goals. These goal relationships reflect the in-order-to structure: the most deeply embedded goal (subgoal$_2$) is formulated in-order-to attain the next highest goal (subgoal$_1$). This subgoal is formulated in-order-to attain the highest goal (goal). The only time the particular goal's motivating events and states were the dominant responses was for the episode$_1$ goal, the highest-order goal in the story. This is the case despite the fact that when one has some goal in mind, the particular subgoals and plans constructed to meet that goal are probably jointly determined by the goal plus other events and states that bias the choice of a particular course of action. These kinds of information were given as reasons why the subgoals were formulated, but only about 22% of the time. In the context of these stories, which did not involve any focus on the selection of a particular method of attaining the highest-order goal, the factors affecting planning choices clearly take a back seat to the logic of the goal-subgoal relationships. Thus, as expected, the interepisode goal-subgoal connections were quite salient, and a dominating logical connection for each group of subjects.

The representations derived from the responses to the why-goal questions for the goals in the goal-sequential stories should be different from that of the goal-subgoal stories for the reasons described previously. The representations differed to varying degrees, depending on age, time of test, and task. Therefore six representations are needed to understand the patterns of responses that characterized the six groups [College Immediate ($n = 32$), College Delay ($n = 32$), Fifth Reading ($n = 24$), Fifth Listening ($n = 28$), Third Reading ($n = 12$), and Third Listening ($n = 20$)]. The general trend reflected across these six groups from college immediate to third listening is an increasing tendency to connect the three episodes through the goals of each episode. The evidence for this conclusion is based on making sequential comparisons of the representations shown in Fig. 9.4.[1]

The representation derived for the college students at immediate test is shown in Fig. 9.4a. This is the group for whom task difficulty is minimal since the stories are easy and they are answering questions on stories presented 10–15 minutes earlier. Two aspects of this representation are important. First, there were no interepisode connections made by these subjects.

---

[1]The proportions shown in this figure, as well as in Figs. 9.3, 9.5 and 9.6, are those that occurred with a frequency significantly greater than 0. Z score tests have been used to test for difference from 0, as well as to test for differences between proportions. A two-tailed significance level of $p < .05$ was adopted, $z > 1.96$.

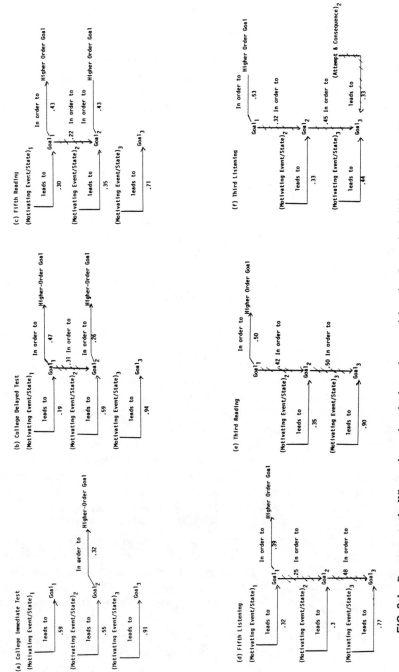

FIG. 9.4 Responses to the Why goal questions in the goal-sequential stories. Interepisode links are shown with ///// lines.

The overwhelming tendency was to explain each goal by the motivating event or state from that goal's episode. Only for $goal_2$ is that not the dominant response. For that goal, 32% of the responses gave a higher-order goal: Jimmy wanted to save a lot of money ($goal_2$) in-order-to be rich (higher-order goal to $goal_2$). The higher-order goal response still maintains the independence of the three episodes. Thus, as was predicted from the analysis of the goal-sequential stories, the episodes are not causally connected through the goals.

The representation for the college delay group is given in Fig. 9.4b. This group had somewhat increased task demands due to the 48-hour interval between presentation and test. The result of the delay was a tendency to connect $episodes_{1 \text{ and } 2}$ through the goals: one-third of the explanations for why Jimmy wanted a paper route ($goal_1$) were because he wanted to save money ($goal_2$). Thus, whereas the independence of $episode_3$ was maintained over delay, there was a tendency to causally connect $episodes_{1 \text{ and } 2}$ with the type of link appropriate to a goal-subgoal story, $goal_1$ in-order-to $goal_2$. The fifth-grade readers' representation essentially matches the college delay group, as is shown in Fig. 9.4c. However, when the fifth graders listened to the stories, the resulting representation showed interepisode connections through the goals for $episode_{1 \text{ and } 2}$ and for $episode_{2 \text{ and } 3}$. This representation is shown in Fig. 9.4d. The listening task represents a situation of greater processing load than the reading task in that readers could control the rate of input while listeners could not. The greater demands placed on working memory capacity in the listening task as compared to the reading for the fifth graders appear to lead to a different representation of the interepisode relationships.

The same interepisode relationship was reflected in the responses of the third graders who read the stories, Fig. 9.4e: $goal_1$ in-order-to $goal_2$ and $goal_2$ in-order-to $goal_3$. The explanations for $goal_3$ however stayed within $episode_3$ for both fifth listeners (77%) and third readers (90%) in that motivating event/$state_3$ was the dominant response. Finally, the data in Fig. 9.4f indicate that none of the episodes are represented as independent of one another by the third-grade listeners. In addition to the goal connections for the three episodes, $goal_3$ is explained equally often by the attempt and consequence of $episode_2$ as by the motivating events/states of $episode_3$. For this group of subjects, task demands were greater than in any other group. Not only could they not control the rate of input as their reading peers could, but since the vocabulary was third-grade level, it probably required greater auditory processing by this group than by older children or adults. The third-grade readers could compensate for decoding load by slowing down the rate at which they were reading.

The tendency to increasingly connect the three episodes as task difficulty increased may reflect differential loss of information or it may reflect a mnemonic strategy in which the subject responds to task difficulty by coding the input in such a way that it will be easier to remember, i.e., as three connected episodes with goal-subgoal relationships rather than three relatively independent episodes. While these speculations require further empirical testing, over the six groups, the current data indicate a clear trend toward the construction of interepisode connections in goal-sequential stories. These connections appear to be based on the in-order-to relationship manifested by a story that is explicitly a goal-subgoal story.

Thus, the hypothesized differences between the role of goal relationships in connecting the episodes in these multi-episode stories were observed. However, the differences tended to decrease as the difficulty of the task increased. Task difficulty was increased either by the time of test or by the combination of age and listening versus reading. Goldman and Varnhagen (1981) were also interested in the role of the attempt and consequence information in the representation of the episodes. Because of the goal-subgoal relationships in that type of story, successful attempts and consequences that meet the deepest subgoal, e.g., $subgoal_2$, help meet less deeply embedded subgoals and the higher-order goal. Thus, attempts and consequences in the goal-subgoal story might be additional sources of interepisode connectedness. In the goal-sequential stories attempts and consequences also have the potential for providing links between successive episodes. As discussed above, in the goal-sequential stories the state existing after $(attempt and consequence)_n$ allows $episode_{n+1}$ to occur and to have a successful goal attainment result. The attempt and consequence is therefore a potential interepisode link in the goal-sequential series. At the same time $(attempt and consequence)_n$ are related to motivating $event/state_n$ and $goal_n$, in the same way as in single-episode no-obstacle stories. Responses to why (attempt and consequence) questions were analyzed to determine the relative salience of interepisode versus intraepisode connections as explanations for the attempts and consequences.

Several types of responses to why (attempt and consequence) questions occurred. These responses reflect somewhat different links in the representations of the two types of stories. For example, for *Why did Jimmy go to the newspaper office and get a paper route?* three types of responses occurred: (1) *because he wanted to save money;* (2) *because he liked to work;* (3) *because he wanted a paper route.* In the goal-subgoal structure, the links reflected by these responses are as follows: (1) $(attempt and consequence)_{episode_3}$ accomplishes $subgoal_1 = goal_{episode_2}$; (2) $(attempt and consequence)_3$ caused by motivating $event/state_3$; (3) $(attempt and consequence)_3$ accomplishes $subgoal_2 = goal_{episode_3}$. The first type of response represents an interepisode link while the second and third represent intraepisode links, similar to those reported for the no-obstacle stories. In the goal-sequential stories, the first type of response also represents an interepisode link but it is an *enables* connection: $(attempt and consequence)_1$ enables $goal_2$ = saving money. The second and third types of responses represent intraepisode links: $(attempt and consequence)_1$ accomplishes $goal_1$ and $(attempt and consequence)_1$

caused by motivating event/state$_1$. As with the no-obstacle stories, a successful attempt and consequence neutralizes or removes the conditions that motivated these actions. Since we wish to focus on interepisode versus intraepisode links, and to simplify data presentation, frequencies for response types two and three have been aggregated and links of this type are labeled "to satisfy" links.

As with responses to the why-goal questions, age and task differences did not occur for responses to the why (attempt and consequence) questions for the goal-subgoal stories. As shown in Fig. 9.5, almost all the responses explained the attempt and consequences with respect to a goal or motivating state that was satisfied by the attempt and consequence. However, for the attempts and consequences that satisfied both an intraepisode and an interepisode goal, only one-third of the responses stayed within the episode. About 60% of the time the attempts and consequences linked one episode to the next. Thus, the different episodes in the goal-subgoal stories are connected both through goal relationships and through the attempt and consequence connections to the next highest goal in the story. This connectedness among the episodes is understood by both children and adults. Thus, in addition to the intentional action scheme in a simple episode, children as young as eight also understand embedded intentional action schemes in a manner equivalent to older children and college students.

The consistency across task and age groups that was found for the goal-subgoal structures was also found for responses to the why (attempt and consequence) questions in the goal-sequential stories. However, in contrast to

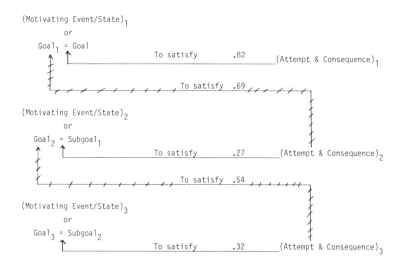

the dominant goal-subgoal responses, the dominant response to each why (attempt and consequence) question was within rather than across episodes. Responses to why (attempt and consequence) in the goal-sequential stories reflected two types of links, to-satisfy and to-enable.

The to-enable links are explicit cross-episode connections that reflect the fact that the success of (attempt and consequence)$_n$ allows episode$_{n+1}$ to begin and to be successful. The to-satisfy link relates (attempt and consequence)$_n$ back to the beginning of episode$_n$. In each of the six groups of subjects, the intraepisode link was the dominant one (z's > 2.83). For example, *Jimmy got a paper route* because *he wanted one* or because *his mother said he should get a part-time job*. The proportion of responses of this type for each of the episodes, aggregated across the six groups, is shown in Fig. 9.6.

The other type of response that occurred with frequency significantly greater than 0, was the cross-episode connection: (attempt and consequence)$_n$ to enable the beginning of episode$_{n+1}$. For example, *Jimmy got a paper route* (attempt and consequence)$_1$ *so he could save money* (goal$_2$). This cross-episode connection was reflected in an average of 20% of the responses as shown in Fig. 9.6. However, the frequency with which the to-enable type of response was given appeared to be subject to the effects of task demands: The delay test college students and children gave this response more frequently (26% of the responses) than the immediate test college students (7% of the responses) for (attempt and consequence)$_1$. The children gave the to-enable response more frequently (34% of the responses) than the college students (13%) for (attempt and consequence)$_2$. Thus, as task demands increased, the attempt-consequence links tended to be used more frequently as interepisode links, a tendency that is similar to that discussed for the goal links. The tendency was reflected more strongly through the goal than through the attempt-consequence links.

If the representation based on responses to both of these questions is considered, the following conclusion emerges: the three episodes in the goal-sequential case were represented with no interepisode links when task demands were minimal, i.e., for the college students at immediate test; with an increase in task demands due to delayed test, college students connected episode$_{1 \text{ and } 2}$ by goal$_1$ in-order-to goal$_2$ links and by an enable link from (attempt and consequence)$_1$ to goal$_2$. For the older children, the listening condition led to more cross-episode links through the goals then did reading but both listening and reading led to cross-episode links from (attempt and consequence)$_{1 \text{ and } 2}$ to goals$_{2 \text{ and } 3}$. The youngest children reading the stories behaved as the fifth-grade listeners did. Finally, the third-grade listeners connected the three episodes through the goals and through the (attempt and consequence) nodes to a greater degree than the other groups. In comparison with the goal-subgoal stories, the younger children's representations for goal-sequential stories were as tightly connected, with relatively little evidence of

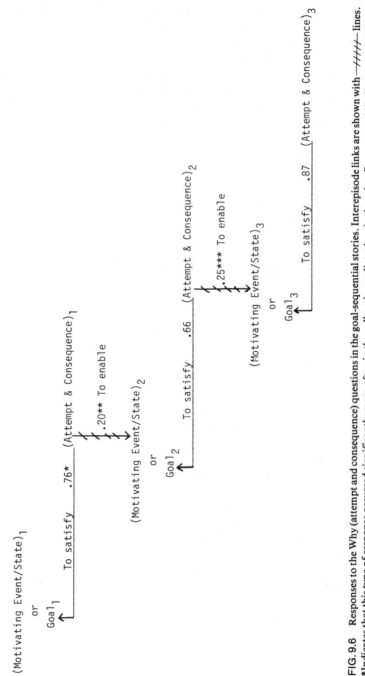

FIG. 9.6   Responses to the Why (attempt and consequence) questions in the goal-sequential stories. Interepisode links are shown with —////— lines. *Indicates that this type of response occurred significantly more often in the college immediate than in the other five groups. **Indicates that the children and college delay groups gave this type of response more frequently than the college immediate group. ***Indicates that the children gave this type of response more frequently than the college students.

episode independence. The similarity, in conjunction with the absence of developmental and task differences in the goal-subgoal stories, may indicate that the embedded intentional action scheme is used to interpret and understand sequences of behavioral episodes more generally than is appropriate. Younger children may be attributing greater intentionality to behavior than older children and adults and their conceptions of when behavioral episodes are independent from one another may be more restricted.

The investigations of text-internal reasoning, using why questions to assess the representations, indicate that the intentional action scheme as manifested in a story episode is readily understood by 7- and 8-year-olds. More complex multi-episode stories, the core of which is an extended intentional action scheme organized around a topmost goal or purpose, also pose no particular difficulties for children in this age range. Difficulties and differences among younger and older children and children and adults are associated with multi-episode stories in which the episodes are organized around different goals but where there is a sequential enables relationship between successive episodes. In this case, there was a tendency to credit the story character with knowing what he would later want to do and viewing this temporally later goal as cognitively prior to the entire episode sequence.

Knowledge about goals and actions and the intentional nature of their organization appears to be a type of learning that occurs "naturally," i.e., through exposure to everyday events and to stories of the sort discussed above. Text-internal inferences are based on this knowledge and seem to require little in the way of formal instruction. These types of inferences may be contrasted with text-external inferences. As a whole, text-external inferences require the comprehender to deal with the story as a whole, to make connections between different stories and to draw generalized conclusions from the story based on everything that happened in it.

TEXT-EXTERNAL REASONING

An important function of narratives is the transmission of rules of social conduct and the moral conventions and values of society. Certain types of narratives accomplish this function by relating a particular set of events in order to illustrate a more abstract principle. This section deals with our research that has examined children's understanding of these more abstract principles. Children are essentially being asked to reason *about* story material rather than *on* presented story material. We have employed two different types of narratives for this purpose: Aesop's fables and Bible stories.

Both Aesop's fables and Bible stories share an important characteristic: Even exact memory for the information in the story does not ensure that higher-order generalizations about the story can be or will be made. Such generalizations may depend on the construction of a more abstract-level macrostructure of the text (Kintsch & van Dijk, 1978; van Dijk, 1980), formulated around the general theme of the story.

In the case of Aesop's fables, each story theme is in the form of a moral that states the general principle illustrated by the story, usually in the form of a tagline at the conclusion of the text. Familiar morals are "A bird in the hand is worth two in the bush," "One good turn deserves another," "Little people are often capable of great things," and so forth. The morals represent a generalization from the concrete activities depicted in the stories. They are not content-specific nor tied to the particular characters or events in the story. Sayings such as these typically are not included when a person is asked to recall a story. Mandler and Johnson (1977) pointed out that such morals are optional to a well-formed story. In order to elicit children's understanding of these messages, we explicitly asked "What lesson or lessons does this story teach?"

In the case of biblical stories, the situation is similar, except the the themes are often abstract concepts that deal with behavioral tendencies, e.g., being helpful, obeying God. They are more ill defined than the morals associated with Aesop's fables in that the concepts taught mention no concrete actions. In some sense they are stated in terms of personality characteristics, which still need to be translated into particular behaviors in a particular situation. That is, one can understand that you ought to be helpful but be unable to determine what would be helpful in a particular situation.

We examined two levels of children's understanding of these types of themes: a nonverbal and a verbal. The nonverbal level was operationalized as a similarity-based sorting task and the verbal level as an explanation of the sorts the child had constructed. In this task, why questions elicit children's reasoning about their own behavior rather than the behavior of characters in a story. Unlike the findings of the text-internal questioning, asking children about these higher-order aspects of text revealed a number of developmental phenomena.

LESSONS STORIES TEACH

As part of a larger research project (Goldman, Reyes, & Varnhagen, 1983), monolingual English-speaking children in kindergarten through fifth grade listened to or read modified versions of Aesop's fables. Two fables, manifesting different morals according to Aesop, were presented. The two target morals were "One good turn deserves another" and "Little friends may prove great friends." In addition to recalling the fables, children answered the question "What lesson or lessons does the story teach?" Note that the presented stories did not include the tagline moral. The answers reflected some interesting changes in the interpretation of the question as well as in the level of generalization from the story.

The responses were classified into the categories shown in Table 9.5. *Target Moral* refers to responses that were judged to be meaning preserving of the moral associated with each of the fables while *Other Moral* refers to responses that had the form of a moral but were typically more general than the target moral. For example, "If someone helps you, you should try and help them" was scored as *Target Moral* for "One good turn deserves another," while "Help your friends and family" was scored as *Other Moral*. In contrast to these two categories, the *Do's and Don'ts of Behavior* category encompasses responses having the form of proscriptions for appropriate or inappropriate behavior, e.g., "Never steal," "Be good," "Don't talk to people you don't know." Responses of this sort reflect an understanding of generalizing from the story but the lesson seems to us to be tied to more concrete aspects of behavior than the responses scored as morals. The remaining categories do not reflect an understanding that the lesson relates to moral conventions. Some responses indicated acquisition of factual information, e.g., "how to save a person who's drowning," and were scored in the *Facts* category. In the *School Lesson* category were responses such as "letters," "reading," "to remember." This reflects a classroom-context interpretation of the term "lesson" in the question. Finally, there were responses that were specific to the text, relating events directly from the story or naming the characters. Comparisons of these responses with the same individual's recall protocols indicated little differentiation between the lesson question and the request for story recall. That is, in response to the what lesson question, one kindergarten child said, "The ant bit the hunter." This statement was also the only thing the

TABLE 9.5
Response Categories and Distributions for Responses
to Lesson Question

Category	3, 4, 5/6	K, 1, 2
Moral convention lesson	.89	.26
Target Moral	.27	
Other Moral	.41	.05
Do's + Don't's of Behavior	.20	.21
Fact Lesson	.01	.01
School Lesson		.08
Story specific information	.06	.19
No response	.04	.43

child said when he had been asked to tell everything he remembered from the story.

The distribution of responses across these categories for each of the grades indicates several developmental phenomena. First, the patterns obtained from the third, fourth and fifth graders were similar and differed from the patterns obtained from the children in second and first grades and kindergarten. Among the older elementary children, 90% of the responses reflected some level of generalizing from the text to moral convention lessons. In contrast, this was the case for only 26% of the younger children's responses. Further, of this 26%, the responses tended to be concentrated in the most concrete category, Do's and Don'ts of Behavior. Further, for the younger children, in about 60% of the cases, the question was either not meaningful (no response) or interpreted in the same way as the questions asking for recall of the story.

These data suggest that the function of stories to communicate societal and moral conventions is not understood by most children until it is explicitly taught in language arts curricula. As such it appears to be a developmental phenomena of instruction either in school or at home. That the children could not state a lesson may, however, underestimate the level of their understanding of nonliteral aspects of the text in the sense that certain types of higher-order information may be encoded but not available to verbal expression. The ability to verbalize what one knows and understands often appears later than the understanding per se. Our investigation of story themes as a basis of similarity judgments strongly supports this notion.

THEMATIC SIMILARITY JUDGMENTS

The motivation for this study originated in a task commonly used in religious education curricula for the specific purpose of teaching ethical values (see Johnson, 1983). A typical lesson for 4- and 5-year-old children involves the presentation of two stories conveying the same theme, one a Bible story and one a story in a modern day setting. The goals of these lessons are that the similarity in themes will be recognized and subsequently applied to behavior in children's own lives. A prerequisite to the attainment of these lesson goals involves the ability to use story theme as a basis for similarity judgments between stories. One aspect of Johnson's work involved testing the degree to which themes were in fact used to make similarity judgments as well as the degree to which children used thematic explanations when asked why they thought particular stories were similar.

Nine Bible stories, depicting three different themes, were presented to 18 third-grade and 18 fifth-grade children enrolled in a Christian day school. Each story had an accompanying picture. Eighteen kindergarten children were also tested but they heard only two stories for each theme. Children were asked to "put the pictures together that tell the same kind of story" and were then asked why they had constructed the various groupings.

The degree to which the sorts were thematically based was evaluated using matrix correlation techniques. Observed matrices were derived from each child's sort and compared to a predicted matrix, which represented groups based on the three story themes. The degree of similarity between observed and predicted matrices was evaluated by the Quadratic Assignment Paradigm (Pellegrino & Hubert, 1982). Note that a pre-story sort was also administered to determine if sorting based only on the pictures yielded matrices significantly close to the predicted matrix. This was not the case.

The post-story sorts indicated that 50% of the children's sorts in grades three and five were significantly close ($p < .05$) to the predicted thematic sort. Only 22% of the kindergarten children behaved in this way. However, the verbal justification behavior of these children indicated little awareness of theme as a basis for the grouping.

The justification responses were classified into three categories: abstract thematic (these are about helping, kindness, sharing, obeying), similarity of actions (these all have been put in some place, the man is talking to people in these) and similarity of characters/objects/locations (all have animals, food, traps). The first salient point about the answers to these questions is that children were not terribly consistent in the type of justification they used across the groups in their sorts. This was true regardless of whether or not the sort was similar to the thematic sort. Therefore, a criterion for consistency was adopted and consistency was defined in the following way: Two-thirds of the justifications for the groups in an individual's sort had to fall into the same justification category. Thus, if a child made the three predicted groups, at least two of these three groups had to be justified in the same way.

Among the kindergarten children, 50% were consistent justifiers but no one type of justification was prevalent. Among third graders, only 17% were consistent while among fifth graders 44% were consistent, and this difference was significantly related to grade, $\chi^2 = 3.27$, $df = 1$, $p = .06$. Task complexity is also implicated as a factor in children's ability to be consistent in the basis of similarity judgments. For the simpler task, involving only six stories, kindergartners demonstrated the same degree of consistency as the fifth graders.

However, consistent thematic justifications were few and far between: .17 for the kindergarten and fifth graders and .11 for the third graders. Furthermore neither consistency of justification nor type of justification was found to be related to the sort behavior. It was the case that significantly more children sorted thematically than gave consistent thematic justifications in third grade (10 vs. 2) and in fifth grade (9 vs. 3). These results indicate that while the sorting behavior of third and fifth graders may be thematically based, their verbal justifications do not reflect this basis. Thus, while a thematic level of understanding does appear to guide the sorting behavior of at least 50% of the older children, these same individuals rely more on concrete aspects of the texts to justify their behavior.

At this point, our general conclusion from these studies of reasoning about narratives is that questions that ask children to deal with more abstract aspects of stories reveal an area in which developmental change over the elementary and probably secondary school years is the rule. Such Text-External reasoning requires a consideration of the narrative as a whole rather than a consideration of the specific components within a narrative. Seeing the bigger picture or point of a narrative involves making generalizations from the specifics of the text. The generalizations allow an individual to examine how a particular narrative relates to events and situations that are already part of what the person knows about the world. Furthermore, to decide that two narratives are similar thematically, an individual must generalize beyond the instances presented in any one narrative. Our investigations of the development of inferential reasoning that requires operating with generalizations about a narrative suggest that these generalizations are not a necessary or natural outcome of exposure to stories. Rather, for this type of reasoning to emerge, a child may need more explicit instructional activities, whether these are formal or informal. Many children may fail to spontaneously realize that stories have functions other than entertainment. That they might concurrently learn about what is expected of them as members of a society or culture from a "story" may be a realization that arises only with the help and guidance of others. To illustrate this point, an anecdote is useful.

> Mark, a 7-year-old, lives with his mother who has recently divorced Mark's father. One day, Mark's mother scolds him for not doing his chores when he was supposed to. Mark says, "I want to live with daddy. He never makes me do chores." Mark's mother tells him a story that goes something like this: "There was once a bear who lived on a mountain. He wanted desperately to live on a different mountain, one that was very hard to get to. The bear thought everything would be perfect on that other mountain. Eventually, and after many sacrifices, the bear got his wish to live on that other mountain. But the bear found out that everything was not perfect on the other mountain and he started wanting to move to a third mountain." Mark's mother finishes the story by saying, "The moral of the story is that the grass is always greener on the other side of the street." Mark responds, "I don't want to live on a green mountain. I want to live with daddy." Mark's mother might then say, "I didn't mean it exactly that way. Isn't your wanting to live with daddy like the bear thinking things would be better if only he lived in a different place?"

It is pretty obvious that Mark has missed the point of his mother's message. However, this use of a story in an informal interpersonal interaction may be the kind of experience that contributes to the development of an understanding of the multiple functions of stories. This type of knowledge may be far more subject to individual, developmental, and sociocultural differences than other sorts of story knowledge because of the potentially greater importance of experiencing and participating in interactions of the type illustrated in the anecdote.

SUMMARY AND CONCLUSIONS

The investigations of Text-Internal inferential reasoning revealed that a basic understanding of motivated, purposive behavior is acquired relatively early. People take actions in order to accomplish certain purposes. The research on multi-episode stories indicated a tendency for younger children to overapply this relationship. Children appear to be learning when it is inappropriate to interpret behavioral episodes in this way. Knowledge of motivated behavior forms the basis for inferential reasoning in stories. In comparison to inferential reasoning about stories, inferential reasoning in stories appears to require less direct instruction. The acquisition of more abstract levels of understanding what stories are about appears to require experiences beyond mere exposure to narratives. Going beyond the up-front literal message involves active and conscious effort. This is true from multiple perspectives: that of the comprehender, that of the teacher attempting to use narratives for more than decoding practice and entertainment, and that of the researcher attempting to understand developmental patterns associated with the concept of a story.

REFERENCES

Brewer, W. F., & Lichtenstein, E. H. Stories are to entertain: A structural-affect theory of stories. *Journal of Pragmatics,* 1982, *6,* 473–486.

Bruner, J. S. The organization of early skilled action. *Child Development,* 1973, *44,* 1–11.

Damon, W. Exploring children's social cognition on two fronts. In J. H. Flavell & L. Ross (Eds.), *Social cognitive development.* New York: Cambridge University Press, 1981.

Goldman, S. R. Knowledge systems for realistic goals. *Discourse Processes,* 1982, *5,* 279–303.

Goldman, S. R., Reyes, M., & Varnhagen, C. K. *Utilization of knowledge acquired through the first language in comprehending a second language: Narrative comprehension by Spanish-English speakers.* Paper presented at National Association for Bilingual Education, Washington, DC, 1983.

Goldman, S. R., & Varnhagen, C. K. *Comprehension of multi-episode stories.* Paper presented at Psychonomics Society, 1981.

Goldman, S. R., & Varnhagen, C. K. Comprehension of stories with no-obstacle and obstacle endings. *Child Development,* 1983, *54,* 980–992.

Graesser, A. C., Robertson, S. P., & Anderson, P. A. Incorporating inferences in narrative representations: A study of How and Why. *Cognitive Psychology,* 1981, *13,* 1–26.

Heider, F. *The psychology of interpersonal relations.* New York: Wiley, 1958.

Johnson, D. *Children's use of themes in story similarity judgments.* Master's Thesis, University of California, Santa Barbara, 1983.

Johnson, N. S., & Mandler, J. M. A tale of two structures: Underlying and surface forms in stories. *Poetics,* 1980, *9,* 51–86.

Kintsch, W., & van Dijk, T. A. Toward a model of text comprehension and production. *Psychological Review,* 1978, *85,* 363–394.

Lichtenstein, E. H., & Brewer, W. F. Memory for goal-directed events. *Cognitive Psychology,* 1980, *12,* 412–445.

Mandler, J. M., & DeForest, M. Is there more than one way to recall a story? *Child Development,* 1979, *50,* 886–889.

Mandler, J. M., & Johnson, N. S. Remembrance of things parsed: Story structure and recall. *Cognitive Psychology,* 1977, *9,* 111–151.

Nezworski, T., Stein, N. L., & Trabasso, T. Story structure versus content in children's recall. *Journal of Verbal Learning and Verbal Behavior,* 1982, *21,* 196–206.

Pellegrino, J. W., & Hubert, L. J. The analysis of organization and structure in free recall. In C. R. Puff (Ed.), *Handbook of research methods in human memory and cognition.* New York: Academic Press, 1982.

Ross, L. The "intuitive scientist" formulation and its developmental implications. In J. H. Flavell & L. Ross (Eds.), *Social cognitive development.* New York: Cambridge University Press, 1981.

Rumelhart, D. E. Understanding and summarizing brief stories. In D. Laberge & S. J. Samuels (Eds.), *Basic processes in reading: Perception and comprehension.* Hillsdale, NJ: Lawrence Erlbaum Associates, 1977.

Stein, N. L. How children understand stories: A developmental analysis. In L. Katz (Ed.), *Current topics in early childhood education* (Vol. 2). Norwood, NJ: Ablex, 1979.

Stein, N. L. The definition of a story. *Journal of Pragmatics,* 1982, *6,* 487–508.

Stein, N. L., & Glenn, C. G. An analysis of story comprehension in elementary school children. In R. O. Freedle (Ed.), *New directions in discourse processing* (Vol. 2). Norwood, NJ: Ablex, 1979.

Stein, N. L., & Goldman, S. R. Children's knowledge about social situations: From causes to consequences. In S. Asher & J. Gottman (Eds.), *The development of children's friendships.* New York: Cambridge University Press, 1981.

Stein, N. L., & Trabasso, T. What's in a story: An approach to comprehension and instruction. In R. Glaser (Ed.), *Advances in the psychology of instruction* (Vol. 2). Hillsdale, NJ: Lawrence Erlbaum Associates, 1982.

van Dijk, T. A. *Macrostructures.* Hillsdale, NJ: Lawrence Erlbaum Associates, 1980.

10 Questions and Children's Cognitive Processing

Michael Pressley
University of Western Ontario

Donna Forrest-Pressley
Children's Psychiatric Research Institute
London, Ontario

Most of this chapter is concerned with the issue of whether answering questions increases memory of materials that children are asked to learn. It may be surprising to readers of a volume devoted entirely to the psychological effects of questions that there are few programmatic efforts on strategic questioning in the child development literature. On a more optimistic note, recent data and theory, including research programs in progress at the time of this writing, suggest tantalizing possibilities.

Unfortunately, research that has occurred has usually been conducted at single-age levels, an approach that precludes developmental conclusions. The question types tested and the issues addressed often have been derived in a straightforward fashion from the adult literature rather than from cognitive-developmental theoretical positions. Typical research questions are of the following type: "Question type X works in context A with adults. Will it do so with children?" Even when results obtained with children have been different from those obtained with adults, the designs of the studies usually have not permitted evaluation of why the child data differed from the adult data or whether the data patterns produced by children might be obtained in some learning situations but not others. For example, there is the question of whether slight variations in tasks or instructions are sufficient to make children's behaviors look more like those of adult learners.

Despite the general lack of developmental data on questioning effects, there are some documented developmental differences. Experiments conducted by Pressley and Bryant (1982) are reviewed to illustrate this point. In that series of studies, there were dramatic age-related differences in the learning gains produced by questions. Pressley and Bryant (1982) also demonstrated that questioning effects can depend on how the task is presented to children. Research on the effects of self-questions, teacher questions, and text questions on children's learning also are considered in the main section of the chapter. The chapter is concluded with an overview of interrogative metamemory acquisition procedures (MAPs). Interrogative MAPs are questions designed to increase metamemory, and thus, they are hypothesized to increase self-control of cognitive processes and strategies. This research on the role of questions in producing metamemory is in its early stages. The possible implications of such work to general theories of cognitive functioning and regulation (Pressley, Borkowski, & O'Sullivan, in press) and to cognitive strategy training (e.g., Meichenbaum, 1977; Pressley, 1979; Pressley, Reynolds, Stark, & Gettinger, 1983) are great enough to motivate much research.

DOES ANSWERING QUESTIONS REALLY PROMOTE CHILDREN'S LEARNING?

As suggested in the introduction to this chapter, data do not exist that allow an exhaustive, fine-grained answer to this question. However, there are many occasions when questioning children about to-be-learned materials has been shown to be effective in promoting acquisition of knowledge. Nonetheless, questioning effects can be situationally specific, as illustrated by recent work on children's associative learning.

Experiments by Turnure and his colleagues (e.g., Buium & Turnure, 1977; Turnure, Buium, & Thurlow, 1976) suggested that a questioning strategy might be even more potent than verbal elaboration, a technique known to be a powerful facilitator of children's associative learning. Verbal elaboration entails placing to-be-remembered associates into either phrases or sentences (e.g., "The *soap* is hiding in the *jacket*," for the pair *soap-jacket*). Elaborations probably promote learning by providing common, meaningful contexts for elements usually not associated one with the other (Rohwer, 1973). The power of elaborations to promote associative learning in children is indisputable (see Pressley, 1977, 1982). The Turnure experiments included two types of conditions. In sentence repetition conditions children repeated verbal elaborations as pairs were presented. In labeling control conditions children repeated the names of the paired objects. Recall levels in these two conditions were compared to recall when subjects answered elaborative questions (interrogative condition) about the pairings. For instance, for the *soap-jacket* pair, the question was "Why is the *soap* hiding in the *jacket*?" In general, interrogative recall was higher than sentence repetition recall which exceeded performance in the labeling control condition. Kestner and Borkowski (1979) replicated the superiority of the interrogative over the sentence repetition procedure. Turnure theorized that the interrogative procedure increased recall by increasing the semantic "depth" to which the materials were processed.

There were three motivations for Pressley and Bryant (1982) to conduct additional study of the interrogative technique and its effects. First, all children included in the prior experiments were 6 years of age or younger. Perhaps the children under six did not process elaborations as meaningfully and completely as they did when responding to the interrogatives. Yet older children might do so, since spontaneous meaningful processing increases with increasing age during childhood (e.g., Brown, 1978; Moely, 1977; Paris & Lindauer, 1977; Vurpillot & Ball, 1979). Second, all prior studies of the interrogative technique involved incidental learning, although most verbal elaboration research with children has been conducted when learning was intentional. Finally, in research with adults, depth-of-processing supplements, such as instructions to increase the personal meaningfulness of elaborations, have generally not increased the potency of mnemonics (e.g., Bellezza, Chessman, & Reddy, 1977; Nelson, Greene, Ronk, Hatchett, & Igl, 1978; Pressley, Levin, Kuiper, Bryant, & Michener, 1982) — outcomes seemingly inconsistent with benefits associated with the interrogative procedure.

Pressley and Bryant (1982) conducted three experiments on the interrogative method to provide data relevant to the above three concerns. In their first study, first- and sixth-grade children were randomly assigned to interrogative, sentence repetition, and labeling control conditions and were presented 31 picture-paired associates. The children were given an incidental learning set; that is, the children were not told that associative recall would subsequently be tested. At the grade one level the pattern of significant effects was identical to the pattern produced in previous research on the topic, interrogative recall > sentence repetition recall > labeling control recall. At the sixth-grade level, however, the outcome was different. Cued recall in the interrogative and sentence repetition conditions was higher than recall in the labeling control condition, with only a small, nonsignificant difference favoring the interrogative condition over the sentence repetition condition.

What mechanism mediated the closing of the performance gap between interrogative and sentence repetition conditions with increasing age? One hypothesis was suggested by informal observation of the children during Experiment 1. The children had been instructed to answer the questions, repeat the sentences, or repeat the verbal labels. The first-grade children took the task quite literally, doing what was required and then tuning out. Since answering questions required more effort, this actively engaged the children more than repeating the sentences or verbal labels. In contrast, the sixth-grade children attended to the task for the entire study period in all of the conditions. A second experiment was conducted in order to evaluate the possibility that the interrogative-sentence repetition difference at the younger age level might be due to more diligence in the Interrogative condition.

Experiment 2 included kindergarten children in three conditions. Two of the conditions were the interrogative and sentence repetition conditions. The third condition was identical to the sentence repetition condition except that before repeating the sentences they heard, children were required to wait 5 sec. The 5-sec delay was intended to keep children on task longer than the simple sentence repetition instruction did. Again, in Experiment 2 the children were unaware during study that a test would occur. As in the first experiment, recall in the interrogative condition was significantly superior to recall in the sentence repetition condition. More importantly, however, recall of sentence repetition-delay subjects was more comparable to interrogative recall than sentence repetition performance, again with a slight advantage for interrogative condition subjects. The results were consistent with the hypothesis that the reduced recall of young children in a simple sentence repetition condition may be due to reduced attention.

A third experiment was conducted to determine interrogative strategy effects when learners knew that a recall test would occur. The experiment was identical to Experiment 1 in the series, except that before the study the children were told about the associative recall test. In Experiment 3 Pressley and Bryant (1982) predicted that recall of first-grade sentence repetition subjects might be comparable to the recall of interrogative subjects, since by the time children are in the early grade school years, an intentional learning instruction does increase attention to learning tasks (e.g., Flavell & Wellman, 1977; Salatas & Flavell, 1976; Yussen, Gagné, Gargiulo, & Kunen, 1974). Thus, the explicit learning instruction was expected to increase attention of sentence repetition subjects to the elaborative mediators, and thus, accomplish sustained processing just as the delay instruction did in Experiment 2. The results were consistent with that expectation. At both the first- and sixth-grade levels, interrogative and sentence repetition subjects performed at roughly the same level, with greater recall in these two conditions than in the labeling control condition.

In summary, Pressley and Bryant (1982) showed that statistically significant positive effects produced by the Interrogative procedure relative to sentence repetition instructions do not occur consistently. When significant recall differences between these two conditions were observed, they were probably mediated largely by an attentional mechanism, rather than more complex semantic processing. On the other hand, it should be pointed out that interrogative recall was always slightly greater than sentence repetition recall, with at least a quarter standard deviation difference in favor of the interrogative condition in every comparison. Thus, if one were to choose between the interrogative strategy and sentence repetition, one would always select the interrogative procedure. The Pressley and Bryant data illustrate that questioning effects with children can involve complicated interactions with developmental level, processing variables, and instructional variables. Although this general point is true about many psychological phenomena, it is important to emphasize in this context. Research designs of studies on questioning in children usually have not been analytical enough to detect such interactions. In the next section these design deficiencies are illustrated with respect to three sources of questions that children encounter.

Questions in the World of Children

Study materials can have questions placed at a variety of locations. Questions can be inserted in the main body of the text. Questions can be printed before the study text to set the stage for subsequent information (see Levin & Pressley, 1981). Questions can be placed after text to stimulate additional study and review of the material (Rickards, 1979). Teachers can ask questions, ranging from queries that require recall of very specific facts to very open-ended questions — questions that may have no "correct" answer, but do require substantial comprehension and processing of to-be-learned content. Finally, children often pose their own questions. In reviewing the literature on test-, teacher-, and self-questions, we identified studies that we consider to be especially interesting and well conducted. These studies are used to illustrate questioning research with children.

Text Questions.   For the past 20 years the study of questions in text has been dominated by techniques and theories popularized by Rothkopf (e.g., 1966). A plethora of experiments followed from the original Rothkopf studies. Much of the relevant literature has been summarized by Anderson and Biddle (1975) for readers interested in extensive coverage of this approach. The experiment that we selected to highlight here involved children in grades 7, 8, and 9 who read science material, specifically a programmed learning unit on mechanics. In a study by Yost, Avila, and Vexler (1977) there were five groups of subjects. Three groups responded to questions in the programmed text. The questions in the three question groups varied in the degree of complexity. In the condition that received very complex questions, more pieces of information had to be taken into account to answer the questions than in the other two question conditions. There was a condition that included questions of intermediate complexity and another that involved simpler questions requiring recall of isolated facts. The questions in each condition were placed at the same points in the programmed text and dealt with the same topics. In an explanation condition subjects did not respond to questions but instead read explanations of the content questioned in the other three groups. Control subjects were not presented the programmed materials, but merely took the posttest. The posttest included questions relevant to the content probed by the experimental questions. However, the posttest questions were not identical to the questions included in the text. Other posttest questions (incidental questions) probed information in the text not covered by the questions in the experimental conditions. Recall performance among the five conditions was consistent with the following pattern for both relevant and incidental questions: control recall < explanations recall < low complexity question recall < intermediate complexity question recall < high complexity question recall. Treatment effects were more pronounced for relevant questions than for incidental questions.

Yost et al. (1977) interpreted their findings within Rothkopf's (1970) theory of inspection behaviors. They reasoned that the more complex questions increased the amount of text the subjects inspected and reinspected. This interpretation was supported by study time data. The greatest study time occurred in the high complexity question condition. In general, greater study time by subjects in a condition was associated with higher recall in the condition. Yost et al. (1977) also reasoned that the increase in recall of the incidental material in the question conditions occurred because a subject could not decide if a piece of information from the text was relevant for the question posed unless the information was inspected. However, Yost et al. (1977) assumed that incidental material was not considered further after its irrelevancy was determined, whereas relevant material was processed additionally. Thus, increases in recall were greater for material tapped by in-test questions than for material irrelevant to those questions.

As suggestive as the Yost et al. (1977) data are for the situation that they studied, more information is required before general conclusions about question complexity and its effects on text recall in children could be drawn. There are many possible directions for future research on the phenomenon studied by Yost et al. (1977). For instance, differences in study time alone across conditions could account for the differences observed by Yost et al. (1977). Question complexity should therefore be examined with study time controlled (see Faw & Waller, 1976, for additional commentary). In addition, there have been substantial technological refinements in recent years which permit fine-grained measurement of where attention is deployed in a text (e.g., Reynolds & Anderson, 1982). These advances should be incorporated into future research with children in order to document more directly the attentional modifications produced by various types of questions. Although it is not possible to review the Reynolds and Anderson findings in detail, we note in passing that they have observed question-induced changes in attention in adult samples, modifications consistent with the attentional shifts that Yost et al. (1977) assumed mediated the recall differences in their data.

Moreover, two types of manipulations are suggested in light of the Pressley and Bryant (1982) analysis of the interrogative strategy. First the most salient task requirement for the children in Yost et al. (1977) was not preparation for the posttest, but rather to work through the programmed text. The study was more concerned with incidental learning, in the sense of Pressley and Bryant (1982) experiments, than with intentional learning. Notably, Andre (1979) has recently proposed a model of questioning in which he suggests that higher-level questioning effects are much more likely in incidental than in intentional learning situations. Given both the theoretical and practical relevance of research comparing patterns of outcomes when learning is intentional versus incidental, work on questioning effects as a function of incidental/intentional set should be a high priority.

Would the pattern of results obtained by Yost et al. (1977) occur with younger children? There are data suggesting that slightly younger children (i.e., fifth graders) learn more from responding to higher-order questions than to simple rote-recall questions (e.g., Rickards & Hatcher, 1978). However, we guess that at some point down the age scale, youngsters cannot coordinate all of the information required to respond to complex questions requiring integration of several pieces of information. Executing complex information processing is more difficult with decreasing age (e.g., Pressley & Levin, 1978). For example, compared to older children (i.e., 11- to 13-year-olds), young children (e.g., 6- to 9-year-olds) experience diffculty in integrating information across units of text (e.g., Grueneich, 1982a, 1982b; Grueneich & Trabasso, 1981; Omanson, Warren, & Trabasso, 1978; Paris & Upton, 1976; Schmidt, Paris, & Stober, 1979; Wagner & Rohwer, 1981). Thus, we hesitate to offer general conclusions about the effects of questions of various complexity on children's learning. On a more optimistic note, efforts are now in progress aimed at teaching children how to identify and answer questions that require differing amounts of inferencing. Preliminary analyses suggest that children can be taught to integrate across text elements even if they experience difficulty doing so initially (Raphael & McKinney, 1983). Results such as these suggest an exciting research future for workers interested in text questions; they also suggest the possibility of many educational applications of such questions.

In concluding this subsection, we note that it is somewhat surprising that there has been so little developmental research on the effects of questions in text, especially because across-experiment comparisons suggest great differences in the effects of text questions with children versus adults. For instance, questions placed after text usually increase adults' learning of both the questioned material and text material not probed (see Rickards, 1979). In contrast, positive post-question effects have been obtained less consistently with children (e.g., Fischer, 1973; Richmond, 1976; Rowls, 1976; Watts, 1973). It is hoped that multiple-age experiments soon will replace the single-age approach to the study of questions in text.

Teacher Questions. Teacher questions are a fact of classroom life. Their efficacy in promoting learning has been assumed since classical Greece (see Dillon, 1982). The scientific evaluation of teacher questioning, however, began only recently. We selected as our example of teacher-questioning research one of the most recent studies on the topic. In the second experiment reported by Gall, Ward, Berliner, Cahen, Winne, Elashoff, and Stanton (1978), teachers taught nine units on ecology to sixth graders in intact classrooms. In three of the experimental conditions, the teachers asked questions in conjunction with the units. The three question treatments differed with respect to the proportion of higher cognitive questions (i.e., questions requiring integration of material and going beyond the information given) relative to lower-level questions. Teachers presented either 25% higher cognitive questions, 50% higher cognitive questions, or 75% higher cognitive questions. Sixth graders in the control condition read the ecology units, but received no teacher questions, performing an ecology-related art activity instead. A strength of the study compared to other experiments on teacher questioning (see Winne, 1979) was the careful counterbalancing of teachers and treatments. Also, compared to many other studies of teacher questioning (again, see Winne, 1979), the teachers were faithful to the treatment manipulations, closely following scripts provided for each condition.

In general, students in the question group exhibited greater knowledge of the ecology materials on post-treatment achievement tests than did control subjects. This was true both for recall of facts and recall of higher-order information. Fact recall levels in both the 25% and 75% higher-level question conditions tended to be higher than in the 50% condition. Also, in general, fact recall in the 25% condition was slightly better than in the 75% condition. On measures requiring integration (thus, higher cognitive knowledge), the outcomes in the 25%, 50%, and 75% conditions were generally comparable.

The Gall et al. (1978) study suggessted that teacher questioning improved learning. For fact recall, either a relatively low (25%) or a relatively high (75%) proportion of higher cognitive questions was better than an equal distribution of higher-order and lower-order questions. Although the mechanisms determining this difference as a function of percentage mix of question types were not clear, Gall et al. (1978) suggested that the teacher's goal of either fact learning or higher-order learning may have been less obvious to the children in the 50% condition. Thus, one student tactic may have been to focus on only the higher-order questions. This interpretation should be accepted tentatively, however, given the ad hoc nature of it.

The concerns raised by Gall et al. (1978) are familiar ones in the teacher-questioning literature. Do teacher questions make a difference in learning?

Are fact questions or "thought" questions more effective? Despite a long history of speculation that teacher questions promote learning, the research literature on the topic is small and not consistently of high quality (see Redfield & Rousseau, 1981; Winne, 1979). The one consistent conclusion that does emerge is that student achievement is increased by teachers asking questions (e.g., Gall et al., 1978; Ryan, 1973, 1974).

Whether there are differences in achievement due to fact versus higher-order questions has been debated recently. In reviewing the literature, Winne (1979) used a voting method of analysis. Studies were sorted into the following categories: (1) those supporting the effectiveness of higher-order over fact questions, (2) those that obtained the opposite effect, and (3) those that reported no significant difference in performance due to higher- and lower-order questions. No significant effects were obtained in the preponderance of studies, leading Winne (1979) to conclude that higher-order questions were not more effective than lower-order questions. In contrast, Redfield and Rousseau (1981) conducted a meta-analysis (Glass, 1978) of the relevant research, since small consistent effects go unnoticed with the voting method. For each experiment on the topic, Redfield and Rousseau determined the size of the question-order treatment effect by calculating the difference of the treatment means divided by the square root of the mean square within $[(\overline{X}$ Treatment $- \overline{X}$ Control$)/\sqrt{MS_w}]$. Higher-order questions produced an average .7 standard deviation advantage over lower-order questions. Redfield and Rousseau (1981) concluded that higher-order questions were more effective than lower-order questions. It it easy to make a case that educational treatments that produce .7 standard deviation advantages are producing meaningful and important learning gains (see Cronbach & Snow, 1977, Chapter 1). A learner who consistently enjoyed the learning edge implied by such a difference would be far ahead of the child who did not. Thus, we endorse Redfield and Rousseau's (1981) conclusions and would recommend the use of higher-order questions over fact questioning.

At the same time we do have reservations about the teacher-questioning research. Virtually all teacher-questioning research has been conducted at single-age levels. In most instances, the instructors have not emphasized the goal of preparation for a posttest. Thus, the need for multiple-age studies that include a variety of learning sets is as great in the teacher-questioning arena as it is in text research. Even though there has been very little study of the longer-term effects of teacher questioning, some have argued that teacher questioning alters the course of students' subsequent "thinking" strategies (Taba, 1965). For instance, a long-term observational learning effect has been hypothesized—students are expected to begin self-questioning as a function of experiencing teacher questioning (Singer, 1978). Longitudinal investigations are required which are sufficiently analytical to determine the adequacy of this interesting hypothesis.

Children's Self-Questions.   Hildy Ross from the University of Waterloo initiated an especially fascinating line of research on children's self-questions. Ross and her associates were concerned with the effects on learning of questions that children generate. It was hypothesized that question-generating activities would increase meaningful processing of the study materials over what children do spontaneously.

Ross and Balzer (1975) presented a series of slides to children in grades 1, 3, and 5.[1] Each slide was based on a picture found in a children's book and each was accompanied by a brief verbalization. For instance, one showed Eskimo children performing a Mexican hat dance. When this picture was first presented, the experimenter commented, "These children live in the far North. They are playing a new game which they just learned in school." Children viewed the slides in same-sex, same-grade pairs (e.g., two grade one boys, two grade five girls). The children were told that they were going to play a detective game in which they could ask questions about the pictures they were seeing. The children were additionally instructed that not all of the questions they asked would receive responses, although children were not informed which questions would be answered. Actually, the experimenter responded to questions from only one of the two children, answering all of that child's questions and ignoring the other child's inquiries. Three days after presentation of the pictures, the subjects were tested one at a time. The test questions were ones asked during the study session by the child who was answered by the experimenter. (Tests were tailored for each pair of children.) There were two main results in the study. Children who received replies asked more questions than children who did not receive responses to their queries. Also, the children who received answers, who had originally generated the posttest questions, made more correct responses on the posttest than did no answer children.

In a follow-up study Ross and Killey (1977) presented the same materials to pairs of same-sex grade three and grade four children. Again, the children were instructed to ask questions about the pictures as they were presented. In this study the questions generated by both children were answered. Half of the test for each child was based on questions posed during study by that child, and the remaining test items were based on queries made by the pairmate during study. The most important result was that posttest performance was better for own questions versus questions generated by the pairmate.

There are several possible mechanisms that might have produced the effects in the Ross studies. It is almost certainly the case that the personally generated questions were more congruent with the child's own schemas about the

---

[1]There were not enough subjects at each age level for a powerful statistical analysis of developmental effects.

study pictures than were the questions of the child's pairmate. Thus, answers to self-inquiries may be easier to assimilate to one's own schemas than answers to pairmate's questions. Ross and Killey (1977) reasoned, alternatively, that children may pay more attention to their own questions and answers to those questions because the inquiries stem from their own curiosity. Singer (1978) offered a similar explanation of the potency of self-interrogation. Ross and Killey's (1977) attentional hypothesis is reminiscent of Pressley and Bryant's (1982) attentional account of their data. Additional work aimed at determining the relative roles of children's schemas and their attention during self-questioning would be welcomed and would probably produce a much more detailed understanding of self-questioning effects than currently exists.

Just as with other questioning research discussed, additional work needs to be conducted on the generality of the effects reported by Ross and her associates. We feel that Ross's work tapped a dimension that is potentially very important in children's real-world learning. Ross's data suggest that it may be important to persuade children to make inquiries about study materials as well as important to answer children's questions once posed. We hope that researchers will busy themselves in the near future with determining how pervasive these effects are. This seems especially critical because children often engage in low rates of questioning during instruction (see Dillon, 1982).

Summary: Acquiring Information with Questions

A variety of studies have reported increases in children's learning due to questioning procedures. However, much research needs to be conducted before finely articulated formulations about developmental questioning effects can be put forth. With increasing age children's knowledge bases increase, their strategies multiply, and achievement motivations change (e.g., Brown, 1978; Chi, in press; Dweck, 1983; Pressley, Heisel, McCormick, & Nakamura, 1982). Given these age-related properties of cognition it is not possible to conduct single-age studies that are very informative. What is required in the near future are studies that are explicitly aimed at providing information about potential instruction × age interactions. This requires expertise in both instructional and cognitive-developmental issues. That premier programs of development-educational research exist makes it obvious that such a combined approach is possible (e.g., Case, 1978; Levin, 1976; Yussen, Mathews, & Hiebert, 1982).

Questioning effects may be consistent, even if they are not always large (e.g., Pressley & Bryant, 1982; Redfield & Rousseau, 1981). Researchers need to be sensitive to this possibility, simply because small advantages can snowball. Even though the higher-order questions about today's lesson may only be a little more helpful than lower-order questions, if a child enjoyed this advantage every day, the learning increase should be tremendous. Unfortunately, conventionally designed single-experiment studies usually are not sensitive to consistent, small effects. Meta-analysis procedures, such as those used by Redfield and Rousseau (1981) are capable of detecting subtle effects. At a minimum, question researchers should be alert to small advantages and provide a formal analysis of the size of these effects across studies whenever possible. The possibility of modest but pervasive effects is one of the best reasons for independent replications of the major issues in the psychology of questioning. We offer one caution in prescribing meta-analytic procedures. In our view efforts must be made to separate the wheat from the chaff before submitting the data to the meta-analysis. See Eysenck (1978), Glass and Kleigl (1983), and Strube and Hartmann (1983) for commentary related to this point. Redfield and Rousseau (1981) is a good example of a meta-analysis which dealt explicitly with the issue of the quality of studies included in the review.

In addition to increasing memory and processing of to-be-learned materials, questioning strategies can also be used to improve knowledge of how to do things, that is, procedural knowledge. Specifically, questioning strategies can enrich knowledge of our cognitive processes. For more on this distinction see Wong's (1982) discussion of questions for information versus questions for regulation. For the present, attention turns to the latter types of questions, ones that increase knowledge of various approaches to cognitive processing.

SELF-QUESTIONING AND METACOGNITION

We will now focus on the use of questioning strategies for regulating other cognitive strategies. Strategies are intentional plans or actions undertaken for particular cognitive goals (Brown, 1978; Flavell, 1970; Meacham, 1972; Miller, Galanter, & Pribram, 1960) and entail basic cognitive processes organized in specific ways (e.g., Borkowski & Büchel, 1983; Pressley, Heisel, McCormick, & Nakamura, 1982). For instance, one strategy for remembering text is to pose and answer questions about the material. An additional aspect of strategic action is knowledge that a learner must have about the value of a strategy, its range of applicability, and mode of execution. This strategic knowledge is referred to as *specific knowledge* (Pressley, Borkowski, & O'Sullivan, in press). Such information is particularly crucial because it has been hypothesized that specific strategy knowledge plays a large part in directing strategy deployment (e.g., Flavell & Wellman, 1977; Pressley et al., in press).

How can knowledge about strategies, a type of metacognition, be acquired? One way is to use techniques explicitly designed to produce such knowledge (Pressley et al., in press). These activities have been termed meta-strategies (Chi, in press) and *m*etacognitive *a*cquisition *p*rocedures — for short MAPs, the term used here (Pressley et al., in press). Self-questioning is a principal vehicle for actualizing MAPs. Self-questioning MAPs include, "Is the study strategy that I am currently using helping me to learn?" "What am I getting out of this strategy?" and "How could this strategy be modified to fit other tasks and situations?" The learner who consistently asks such questions and answers them while executing cognitive strategies should produce a rich body of knowledge about strategies, knowledge that could be used to orchestrate subsequent strategy use.

The study of MAPs is in its embryonic stage. For instance, there is no research that has unambiguously separated the effects of self-questioning MAPs from the effects produced by the strategies monitored by the MAPs. We know of no self-questioning studies that contain one condition in which cognitive strategies were trained and another in which cognitive strategies were trained with self-questioning MAPs. If MAPs are effective, then there should be performance differences in favor of the latter type of condition over the former type. Although analytic studies of self-questioning MAPs have yet to appear, it is possible to point to occasions when self-interrogation MAPs have been combined with other cognitive strategies. Discussion of three such occasions will clarify how MAPs can be distinguished from other cognitive strategies as well as illustrate how MAPs and cognitive strategies can be combined.

The Use of Self-Questioning MAPs

Let us consider what happens when a mature learner confronts a difficult cognitive problem, in this case understanding one of Shakespeare's plays. The first author of this chapter recently tackled *Henry IV, Part 2*. A good learner often has a lot of prior knowledge about the topic and related topics. In the present case, Pressley had read a lot of Shakespeare and had previously attended many productions of Shakespearean work. Thus, he anticipated the complex interweaving of stories in *Henry IV, Part 2,* because of encounters with similar structures in previous plays. He also knew about Falstaff, Prince Hal, the King, and some of the other characters from reading *Henry IV, Part 1,* and seeing the *Merry Wives of Windsor*. Some of the information relevant to the play automatically came to mind while reading the opening scenes, but other background was intentionally and strategically retrieved by the reader. Pressley also generated an imagery mnemonic to remember which characters were on each of the two warring sides. He also constantly monitored the effects of the strategies he was using as well as kept asking himself which parts of the text were not understood more easily due to the use of the comprehension and memory strategies. These monitoring self-inquiries resulted in changes of strategies on occasion. For instance, Pressley detected that he did not really remember much about the historical backdrop of the play. To remedy this deficiency he reviewed the Lamb's (1950) version of *Richard II* and *Henry IV, Part 1,* as well as consulted an encyclopedia article about King Henry IV. After returning to the play, Pressley continued to ask himself, "Did that background reading help?" "Do I understand how this most recent scene fits in?" and "Did those imagery mnemonics really assist in reading the play?" All three of these self-questions are MAPs, producing information about strategy effectiveness and information about the need for additional processing. Pressley's struggle with Shakespeare illustrates how a learner confronting a demanding intellectual task can deploy strategies for encoding, exploit available prior knowledge and external sources of knowledge, and use MAPs to monitor ongoing cognition. The product of such MAP activity is specific strategy knowledge and information about the effects of ongoing processing.[2] Thus, Pressley knew more about when and how to use prior knowledge retrieval and imagery strategies after his encounter with King Henry IV, Part 2, than before because of the MAP activities.

What can be done for the learner who does not spontaneously use all available cognitive resources? What about the learner who does not use available knowledge and strategies? What about the learner who does not monitor his ongoing cognitions to decide if the current processing is producing the desired cognitive end product? Still again there is the learner who does not capitalize on any of these capacities. Such a person needs a multiple-component remedy for all his/her cognitive processing ills! Unfortunately, much training research conducted by cognitive psychologists has focused on particular processes and single strategies, and usually, fairly simple strategies (see Pressley, Heisel, McCormick, & Nakamura, 1982). Nonetheless, multiple-component strategic packages are becoming more common in cognitive interventions and research. There have been a few such treatments devised for increasing reading comprehension. These aim to exploit the learner's world knowledge, increase the deployment of strategies, and ensure that cognitive evaluation takes place. Such packages (e.g., ReQuest, Manzo, 1969; SQ3R, Robinson, 1961) invariably include what we refer to as MAP components. A recent example of such work was provided by Wong and Jones (1982).

Wong and Jones (1982) hypothesized that a multiple-component treatment might aid the text learning of learning-disabled boys. The learning-disabled subjects were assigned either to a self-questioning training condition

---

[2]The second author points out that she is not sure that the first author ever did understand *Henry IV, Part 2,* despite all of the strategies. She contends that independent measures of strategy effectiveness are needed to substantiate self-report data. Although Pressley endorses the general methodological point, he feels that in the case of his introspections, the independent assessments can be bypassed.

or to a no-training control condition, with participants in both conditions reading short passages as the main activity in the study. Notably, only one type of probe question included in Wong and Jones's training package qualifies as a MAP. The training package consisted of instructing children first to ask themselves why they were studying the passage, an instruction intended to provide a self-reminder that they would be asked questions later. The children also were taught to find the main ideas in the paragraph and to think about questions relevant to those main ideas. All subjects in the study had been given pretraining on finding main ideas. They were instructed to learn the answers to their questions and, most critically for the present discussion, to "Always look back at the questions and answers to see how each successive question and answer provides you with more information." Of course, this was the MAP component — a self-inquiry MAP producing efficacy information. Although no training control subjects were exposed to the same text materials used during self-questioning training, they were not given the self-instructional training.

The main dependent variable considered in the study was correct responses to short-answer questions, and training did increase short-answer recall over that obtained in the control condition. Presumably, using the MAP of probing one's own increments in learning as a function of use of the global strategy should have increased subjects' awareness of the efficacy of the study routines that Wong and Jones (1982) used in their training package. Presumably, the MAP would also produce increased use of the strategies on subsequent tasks. Subjects would be expected to stay with something that they knew worked, a fact revealed by application of the MAP. Unfortunately, Wong and Jones (1982) did not include assessments of post-training maintenance or direct measures of metacognitive change as a function of using the self-instructional package. These measures are required before the metacognitive significance of the Wong and Jones (1982) study can be established definitively. See Forrest-Pressley and Gillies (1983) for additional discussion of cognitive and metacognitive self-questioning strategies in reading.

Perhaps the most prominent and extensive psychological research on multiple-component, strategic interventions has been conducted by researchers interested in cognitive behavior modification (for summaries, see Meichenbaum, 1977; Pressley, 1979; Pressley et al., 1983; Reynolds & Stark, 1983). Most critically for the present discussion, self-questioning MAPs similar to those employed by Pressley reading Shakespeare play a prominent role in some of these cognitive behavioral packages. In particular, cognitive behavior modifiers have hypothesized that monitoring of cognitive processes can be improved, and subsequent self-regulation increased, by posing to oneself and seeking answers to appropriate self-questions.

A study by Camp, Blom, Hebert, and Von Doorwick (1977) illustrates well how self-questioning MAPs can be employed in cognitive behavior modification with children. The procedures in Camp et al. (1977) were based on self-instructional routines developed earlier by Meichenbaum and Goodman (1971) and Spivack and Shure (1974). Camp et al. (1977) trained aggressive boys to use a self-questioning routine designed to increase their facility on cognitive tasks, such as the WISC-R and the Matching Familiar Figures task. During training the boys were first taught to ask themselves "What is my problem?" followed by the question, "What is my plan?" The boys were also instructed to think "Am I using my plan?" and at the end of the solution sequence, "How did I do?" The first two strategies were directed at getting the boys to orient to and retrieve strategies that they already possessed. The third and fourth questions, which qualify as MAPs, provided information about the match of behavior to the cognitive plan and information about the cognitive plan's effectiveness. This knowledge should be useful in regulating ongoing cognition (e.g., getting subjects to return to the plan if they had strayed) as well as useful in directing future cognition. For instance, the likelihood of using the plan in a similar situation should be increased if the subject noted that the plan was effective and decreased if the subject determined that the plan had failed to produce the desired outcome. That trained subjects exhibited more adequate cognitive processing than control subjects after the Camp et al. (1977) training bolsters the position espoused here. The case would have been much stronger, however, if there had been actual assessments of metacognition accompanying the cognitive performance measures.

Final Comments on MAPs

Self-questioning MAPs, once acquired, should be useful in developing metacognitive knowledge about diverse strategies in diverse problem areas. Given that increased metacognition has frequently been associated with more consistent and effective use of cognitive strategies (Pressley et al., in press; Schneider, in press), the study of MAPs should be a high priority. They hold great promise for the development of greater autonomy in learners, especially disadvantaged children as illustrated by Camp et al. (1977) and Wong and Jones (1982). We feel, however, that the full potential of MAPs will not be realized until research efforts evaluate self-questioning MAP effects distinct from the effects produced by the cognitive strategies monitored by MAPs. Also, the effects of self-questioning MAPs on metacognition per se need to be determined in order to specify more precisely how information produced by self-questioning MAPs determines future strategy use. The study of self-questioning MAPs is a challenging new direction in the psychology of questioning.

ACKNOWLEDGMENT

The writing of this chapter was supported by a grant to Michael Pressley and a grant to Donna Forrest-Pressley, both fundings provided by the Natural Sciences and Engineering Research Council of Canada.

REFERENCES

Anderson, R. C., & Biddle, W. B. On asking people questions about what they are reading. In G. Bower (Ed.), *The psychology of learning and motivation* (Vol. 9). New York: Academic Press, 1975.

Andre, T. Does answering higher-level questions while reading facilitate productive learning? *Review of Educational Research,* 1979, *49,* 280–318.

Bellezza, F. S., Cheesman, F. L., II, & Reddy, B. G. Organization and semantic elaboration in free recall. *Journal of Experimental Psychology: Human Learning and Memory,* 1977, *3,* 539–550.

Borkowski, J. G., & Büchel, F. P. Learning and memory strategies in the mentally retarded. In M. Pressley & J. R. Levin (Eds.), *Cognitive strategy research: Psychological foundations.* New York: Springer-Verlag, 1983.

Brown, A. L. Knowing when, where, and how to remember: A problem of metacognition. In R. Glaser (Ed.), *Advances in instructional psychology.* Hillsdale, NJ: Lawrence Erlbaum Associates, 1978.

Buium, N., & Turnure, J. E. A cross-cultural study of verbal elaboration productivity and memory in young children. *Child Development,* 1977, *48,* 296–300.

Camp, B. W., Blom, G. E., Hebert, F., & Von Doorwick, W. J. "Think aloud": A program for developing self-control in young aggressive boys. *Journal of Abnormal Child Psychology,* 1977, *5,* 157–169.

Case, R. Intellectual development from birth to adulthood: A neo-Piagetian interpretation. In R. Siegler (Ed.), *Children's thinking: What develops?* Hillsdale, NJ: Lawrence Erlbaum Associates, 1978.

Chi, M. T. H. Representing knowledge and meta-knowledge: Implications for interpreting metamemory research. In R. H. Kluwe & F. E. Weinert (Eds.), *Metacognition, motivation, and learning.* Hillsdale, NJ: Lawrence Erlbaum Associates, in press.

Cronbach, L. J., & Snow, R. E. *Aptitudes and instructional methods: A handbook for research on interactions.* New York: Irvington, 1977.

Dillon, J. T. The multidisciplinary study of questioning. *Journal of Educational Psychology,* 1982, *74,* 147–165.

Dweck, C. S. Achievement. In E. M. Hetherington (Ed.), *Carmichael's manual of child psychology* (4th ed.). New York: Wiley, 1983.

Eysenck, H. J. An exercise in mega-silliness. *American Psychologist,* 1978, *33,* 517.

Faw, H. W., & Waller, T. G. Mathemagenic behaviors and efficiency in learning from prose materials: Review, critique, and recommendations. *Review of Educational Research,* 1976, *46,* 691–720.

Fischer, J. A. Effects of a cue synthesis procedure and postquestions on the retention of prose materials. *Dissertation Abstracts International,* 1973, *34,* 615–B.

Flavell, J. H. The development of mediated memory. In H. W. Reese & L. P. Lipsitt (Eds.), *Advances in child development and behavior* (Vol. 5). New York: Academic Press, 1970.

Flavell, J. H., & Wellman, H. W. Metamemory. In R. V. Kail, Jr., & J. W. Hagen (Eds.), *Per-

spectives on the development of memory and cognition. Hillsdale, NJ: Lawrence Erlbaum Associates, 1977.

Forrest-Pressley, D. L., & Gillies, L. A. Children's flexible use of strategies during reading. In M. Pressley & J. R. Levin (Eds.), *Cognitive strategy research: Educational applications.* New York: Springer-Verlag, 1983.

Gall, M. D., Ward, B. A., Berliner, D. C., Cahen, L. S., Winne, P. H., Elashoff, J. D., & Stanton, G. C. Effects of questioning techniques and recitation on student listening. *American Educational Research Journal,* 1978, *15,* 175-199.

Glass, G. V. Integrating findings: The meta-analysis of research. *Review of research in education* (Vol. 5). Itasca, Ill.: Peacock, 1978.

Glass, G. V., & Kleigl, R. M. An apology for research integration in the study of psychotherapy. *Journal of Consulting and Clinical Psychology,* 1983, *51,* 28-41.

Grueneich, R. Issues in the developmental study of how children use intention and consequence information to make moral evaluations. *Child Development,* 1982a, *53,* 29-43.

Grueneich, R. The development of children's integration rules for making moral judgments. *Child Development,* 1982b, *53,* 887-894.

Grueneich, R., & Trabasso, T. The story as social environment: Children's comprehension and evaluation of intentions and consequences. In J. Harvey (Ed.), *Cognition, social behavior, and the environment.* Hillsdale, NJ: Lawrence Erlbaum Associates, 1981.

Kestner, J., & Borkowski, J. G. Children's maintenance and generalization of an interrogative learning strategy. *Child Development,* 1979, *50,* 485-494.

Lamb, C. *Tales from Shakespeare.* New York: Macmillan, 1950.

Levin, J. R. What have we learned from maximizing what children learn? In J. R. Levin & V. L. Allen (Eds.), *Cognitive learning in children: Theories and strategies.* New York: Academic Press, 1976.

Levin J. R., & Pressley, M. Improving children's prose comprehension: Selected strategies that seem to succeed. In C. Santa & B. Hayes (Eds.), *Children's prose comprehension: Research and practice.* Newark, DE: International Reading Association, 1981.

Manzo, A. V. ReQuest: A method for improving reading comprehension through reciprocal questioning. *Journal of Reading,* 1969, *13,* 123-126.

Meacham, J. A. The development of memory abilities in the individual and in society. *Human Development,* 1972, *15,* 205-228.

Meichenbaum, D. *Cognitive behavior modification.* New York: Plenum Press, 1977.

Meichenbaum, D., & Goodman, J. Training impulsive children to talk to themselves: A means of developing self-control. *Journal of Abnormal Psychology,* 1971, *77,* 115-126.

Miller, G., Galanter, E., & Pribram, K. *Plans and the structure of behavior.* New York: Holt, Rinehart & Winston, 1960.

Moely, B. E. Organizational factors in the development of memory. In R. V. Kail, Jr., & J. W. Hagen (Eds.), *Perspectives on the development of memory and cognition.* Hillsdale, NJ: Lawrence Erlbaum Associates, 1977.

Nelson, T. O., Greene, G., Ronk, B., Hatchett, G., & Igl, V. Effect of multiple images on associative learning. *Memory and Cognition,* 1978, *6,* 337-341.

Omanson, R. C., Warren, W. H., & Trabasso, T. Goals, inferential comprehension, and recall of stories by children. *Discourse Processes,* 1978, *1,* 337-354.

Paris, S. G., & Lindauer, B. K. Constructive aspects of children's comprehension and memory. In R. V. Kail & J. W. Hagen (Eds.), *Perspectives on the development of memory and cognition.* Hillsdale, NJ: Lawrence Erlbaum Associates, 1977.

Paris, S. G., & Upton, L. R. Children's memory for inferential relationships in prose. *Child Development,* 1976, *47,* 660-668.

Pressley, M. Imagery and children's learning: Putting the picture in developmental perspective. *Review of Educational Research,* 1977, *47,* 585-622.

Pressley, M. Increasing children's self-control through cognitive interventions. *Review of Edu-*

cational Research, 1979, *49,* 319–370.

Pressley, M. Elaboration and memory development. *Child Development,* 1982, *53,* 296–309.

Pressley, M., Borkowski, J. G., & O'Sullivan, J. Children's metamemory and the teaching of memory strategies. In D. L. Forrest-Pressley, G. E. MacKinnon, & T. G. Waller (Eds.), *Metacognition, cognition, and human performance.* New York: Academic Press, in press.

Pressley, M., & Bryant, S. L. Does answering questions really promote associative learning? *Child Development,* 1982, *53,* 1258–1267.

Pressley, M., Heisel, B. E., McCormick, C. B., & Nakamura, G. V. Memory strategy instruction with children. In C. J. Brainerd & M. Pressley (Eds.), *Progress in cognitive development research* (Vol. 2): *Verbal processes in children.* New York: Springer-Verlag, 1982.

Pressley, M., & Levin, J. R. Developmental constraints associated with children's use of the keyword method of foreign language vocabulary learning. *Journal of Experimental Child Psychology,* 1978, *26,* 359–372.

Pressley, M., Levin, J. R., Kuiper, N. A., Bryant, S. L., & Michener, S. Mnemonic versus nonmnemonic vocabulary-learning strategies: Additional comparisons. *Journal of Educational Psychology,* 1982, *74,* 693–707.

Pressley, M., Reynolds, W. M., Stark, K. D., & Gettinger, M. Cognitive strategy training and children's self-control. In M. Pressley & J. R. Levin (Eds.), *Cognitive strategy research: Psychological foundations.* New York: Springer-Verlag, 1983.

Raphael, T. E., & McKinney, J. *Developmental aspects of training students to use information locating strategies for responding to questions.* Presented at the annual meeting of the American Educational Research Association, Montreal, April 1983.

Redfield, D. L., & Rousseau, E. W. Meta-analysis of experimental research on teacher questioning behavior. *Review of Educational Research,* 1981, *51,* 237–245.

Reynolds, R. E., & Anderson, R. C. Influence of questions on the allocation of attention during reading. *Journal of Educational Psychology,* 1982, *74,* 623–632.

Reynolds, W. M., & Stark, K. D. The clinical application of cognitive strategies. In M. Pressley & J. R. Levin (Eds.), *Cognitive strategy research: Psychological Foundations.* New York: Springer-Verlag, 1983.

Richmond, M. G. The relationship of the uniqueness of prose passages to the effect of question placement and question relevance on the acquistion and retention of information. In W. D. Miller & G. H. McNinch (Eds.), *Reflections and investigations on reading.* Twenty-fifth National Reading Conference Yearbook, Clemson, South Carolina, National Reading Conference, 1976.

Rickards, J. P. Adjunct post questions in text: A critical review of methods and processes. *Review of Educational Research,* 1979, *49,* 181–196.

Rickards, J. P., & Hatcher, C. W. Interspersed meaningful learning questions as semantic aids for poor comprehenders. *Reading Research Quarterly,* 1978, *13,* 538–553.

Robinson, F. P. *Effective study* (Revised Edition). New York: Harper & Row, 1961.

Rohwer, W. D., Jr. Elaboration and learning in childhood and adolescence. In H. W. Reese (Ed.), *Advances in child development and behavior* (Vol. 8). New York: Academic Press, 1973.

Ross, H. S., & Balzer, R. H. Determinants and consequences of children's questions. *Child Development,* 1975, *46,* 536–539.

Ross, H. S., & Killey, J. C. The effect of questioning on retention. *Child Development,* 1977, *48,* 312–314.

Rothkopf, E. Z. Learning from written instructive material: An exploration of the control of inspection behavior by test-like events. *American Educational Research Journal,* 1966, *3,* 241–249.

Rothkopf, E. Z. The concept of mathemagenic activity. *Review of Educational Research,* 1970, *40,* 325–336.

Rowls, M. D. The facilitative and interactive effects of adjunct questions on retention of eighth graders across three prose passages: Dissertation in prose learning. *Journal of Educational Psychology,* 1976, *68,* 205–209.

Ryan, F. L. Differentiated effects of levels of questions on student achievement. *Journal of Experimental Education,* 1973, *41,* 63–67.

Ryan, F. L. The effects of social studies achievement of multiple student responding to different levels of questioning. *Journal of Experimental Education,* 1974, *42,* 71–75.

Salatas, H., & Flavell, J. H. Retrieval of recently learned information: Development of strategies and control skills. *Child Development,* 1976, *47,* 941–948.

Schmidt, C. R., Paris, S. G., & Stober, S. Inferential distance and children's memory for pictorial sequences. *Developmental Psychology,* 1979, *15,* 395–405.

Schneider, W. Developmental trends in the metamemory-memory behavior relationship: An integrative review. In D. L. Forrest-Pressley, G. E. MaKinnon, & T. G. Waller (Eds.), *Metacognition, cognition, and human performance.* New York: Academic Press, in press.

Singer, H. Active comprehension: From answering to asking questions. *Reading Teacher,* 1978, *31,* 901–908.

Spivack, G., & Shure, M. *Social adjustment of young children: A cognitive approach to solving real-life problems.* San Francisco: Jossey-Bass, 1974.

Strube, M. J., & Hartmann, D. P. Meta-analysis: Techniques, applications, and functions. *Journal of Consulting and Clinical Psychology,* 1983, *51,* 28–41.

Taba, H. The teaching of thinking. *Elementary English,* 1965, *42,* 534–542.

Turnure, J. E., Buium, N., & Thurlow, M. The effectiveness of interrogatives for prompting verbal elaboration productivity in young children. *Child Development,* 1976, *47,* 851–855.

Vurpillot, E., & Ball, W. A. The concept of identity and children's selective attention. In G. A. Hale & M. Lewis (Eds.), *Attention and cognitive development.* New York: Plenum, 1979.

Wagner, M., & Rohwer, W. D. Age differences in the elaboration of inferences from text. *Journal of Educational Psychology,* 1981, *73,* 728–735.

Watts, G. H. The "arousal" effect of adjunct questions on recall from prose materials. *Australian Journal of Psychology,* 1973, *25,* 81–87.

Winne, P. H. Experiments relating teachers' use of higher cognitive questions to student achievement. *Review of Educational Research,* 1979, *49,* 13–50.

Wong, B. Y. L. *Self-questioning and the processing of prose.* Unpublished manuscript, Simon Fraser University, Burnaby, B.C., Canada, 1982.

Wong, B. Y. L., & Jones, W. Increasing metacomprehension in learning-disabled and normally achieving students through self-questioning training. *Learning Disabilities Quarterly,* 1982, *5,* 228–240.

Yost, M., Avila, L., & Vexler, E. B. Effect of learning of postinstructional responses to questions of differing degrees of complexity. *Journal of Educational Psychology,* 1977, *69,* 399–408.

Yussen, S. R., Gagné, E., Gargiulo, R., & Kunen, S. The distinction between perceiving and memorizing in elementary school children. *Child Development,* 1974, *45,* 547–551.

Yussen, S., Mathews, S., & Hiebert, E. Metacognitive aspects of reading. In W. Otto & S. White (Eds.), *Reading expository text.* New York: Academic Press, 1982.

11 Notes on the Efficacy of Questioning

Don Nix
IBM T. J. Watson Research Center

INTRODUCTION: QUESTIONING AND QUESTIONNAIRING

This chapter focuses on the use of questioning techniques for the purpose of directly teaching inferential reading comprehension and meta-comprehension skills to children in classroom settings. Various researchers and educators have stressed the inadequacies of questioning as a means of instruction in that such a method does not teach children how to perform underlying processes needed to answer questions. Recent articles by Durkin (1978-1979, 1981) have emphasized this issue in relation to the teaching of reading comprehension.

There are at least two central problems with questioning as typically practiced in classrooms. First, the quality of the questions themselves does not lead to the development of an awareness of inferential comprehension. Secondly, the instructional followup to the answers given does not effectively focus on the critical features which distinguish the answer's relationship to the question, and the question's relationship to the text itself. These problems will be exemplified in turn. It is assumed that inferential comprehension is a complex process: the child must actively transform what, on the page, is a string of symbols into an inferentially integrated network of meaning. The nature of classroom questioning is viewed in terms of what impact it can have on a child's ability to perform this complex process.

A pervasive quality of questions is that the ones spontaneously asked by teachers tend to be "detail" questions (e.g., Guzak, 1968). That is, in order to answer the question it is not necessary to inferentially integrate various parts of the text. The student simply needs to repeat a proposition or part of a proposition. A typical classroom question for the following *Whole Wheat Dan* passage, then, would be, "What did Whole Wheat Dan say?"

(1)
Whole Wheat Dan was disappointed. Rayette and Loretta had not showed up. They always played all of his favorite songs, like "I call her darlin' but she calls me collect." They can even play "Mama's out of prison again." Whole Wheat sighed. "I guess they just don't care", he said.

From the standpoint of the teaching of inferential comprehension, this question has several obvious shortcomings. It has little, if any relevance to inferential comprehension itself. Worse, such questions may teach the student that comprehension consists of mere recall of specific facts from a text. For example, when children are given the task of *asking* "good comprehension" questions for a given text, they generate predominantly detail questions (Nix, 1981a, 1981b). This response type can not be expected to lead to effective inferential comprehension.

A different problem with question quality exists when questions are inferential rather than detail. The question type is characterized inexplicitly, and in typical classroom practice the procedure for answering such a question is ineffable. For example, consider the text about Whole Wheat Dan. If a teacher is asked to generate a good comprehension question about this text, and is not allowed to generate a question which simply requires an answer overtly stated therein, the teacher may generate a "main idea" question, that is, "What is the main idea in this passage?" Clearly, a student can not simply retell a specific proposition. Instead, it is necessary to inferentially integrate several propositions along with what one already knows about the world. The difficulty is that the procedure for doing such an integration is ineffable, the concept of a main idea is not itself defined in a teachably explicit manner. The teacher does not have access to a set of components which can be explained and taught in a step-by-step manner, and which together constitute main "ideaness." Thus, regardless of whether or not the question is answered adequately; the evaluation of the answer can not be made in terms that explicitly teach the student how to answer such questions in the future.

The same difficulty exists with other typical classroom conceptualizations for inferential questions. Most of these concepts are "specific skills" (Davis, 1968) such as: main idea, sequence, author's intent, characterization, and predicting outcome. These notions are not explicitly defined so that given text instances can be designated as one or the other (Nix, 1983a). Teachable rules for answering such questions are difficult to specify, in part, because the question types are not actually defined, and in part, because given text instances can often be classified simultaneously as more than one type.

A final point on question quality is that questions are not bundled together in order to effectively cover a given passage. This is true of questions of a detail type or an inferential type. Given a text, it would be possible to cover the points in the text with a series of questions, even with questions that themselves are not individually effective. For example, in the Whole Wheat Dan paragraph, one might ask enough detail and inference questions (How did Whole Wheat feel? What happened after the girls didn't show up? What happened after Whole Wheat was disappointed?) to take a student through a process of text integration. If such coverage were assiduously done over series of texts, a student might learn through questioning that each component of a text has an importance, and that components are experientially linked together. In such a case, question analyses that, from an educational viewpoint, are somewhat elaborate (Graesser & Murachver, this volume; Lehnert, 1978; Nix, 1983a), might not be needed. However, questions are not grouped in such a way. It is typical for questions about the meaning of a given text to refer to isolated aspects of the text and to be interspersed with questions only marginally related to comprehension, such as questions about pronunciation, spelling, punctuation, and grammar.

To summarize, the quality of classroom questions does not lead to the development of an awareness of inferential comprehension. Questions tend to be predominantly detail oriented; inferential questions tend to be based on teachably inexplicit conceptualizations; and questions tend to only sporadically cover the important aspects of a given text.

The second central problem with classroom questioning is the lack of an integrated instructional followup after a question has been asked and answered. The following excerpt adapted from Nix (1983a), provides an example of this problem. It is a transcript of an interaction between a teacher and small group of 3rd-grade students. The teacher had been instructed to have the students read the text about Whole Wheat Dan, ask them a good, inferential comprehension question, and finally, help the students answer the questions and understand the answer.

(2)
Children: (read silently) Whole Wheat Dan was disappointed. Rayette and Loretta have not showed up. . . .
Teacher: Now, what is the main idea in this story? Who knows?
   (no answer) Let's see. Student-1, what do you think?
Student-1: Umm. . .
Teacher: What's the story all about?
Student-1: Oh, it's about Whole Wheat Dan and Rayette.

Teacher: Well, yes — but what's the main thing it's about? Do you know, Student-2?

Student-2: It's about . . . Whole Wheat being disappointed?

Teacher: Good, good — yes, because the story is mainly about Whole Wheat Dan being disappointed. Now (points to quotation marks), what do we call these?

It can be seen in protocol (2) that the teacher asked a main idea question. When the first student was unable to answer the question, it would have been useful if the teacher could have rephrased the question in terms of component parts of the holistic notion of main idea, and then lead the student into discovering the main idea. Such a componential notion, however, is not available in educational materials. Instead, the teacher asked another student what the story was about. Student-1 does answer that question on one level: the story is about Whole Wheat Dan and Rayette. Because the relationship between these two versions of what the teacher intends to be the same question is not explicated, it becomes awkward to show the students how the second answer is not the answer being sought. Finally, once Student-2 answers in a way acceptable to the teacher, the teacher immediately skips to an unrelated topic — quotation marks.

Consider, now, the experience of Student-1, who had not mastered the notion of main idea. This experience might be summed up as, "What happened?" What was the teacher asking in the first place? What, if anything, was wrong with Student-1's answer? What was right about Student-2's answer? How are question marks related to main ideas? The process is a mystery, a mystery due, in part, to the lack of instructional followup. The students' answers were not discussed in terms of an explanatory framework, nor was the notion of main idea pursued, even superficially. In this example, then, it is easy enough to doubt the efficacy of questioning.

The reader unfamiliar with classroom environments may not be able to place the excerpt in protocol (2) in perspective. Classroom observational studies (Durkin, 1978–1979; Duffy, 1982) convincingly demonstrate that such interactions are typical rather than unusual, as far as comprehension instruction exists.

The aforementioned examples are intended to illustrate that the efficacy of questioning can be doubted because the questions themselves are not explicitly related to inferential comprehension, they are not organized to cover important points in a given text, and they are not followed up with explanatory instructional interactions.

An analogy that points out some of the shortcomings of classroom questioning is that of psychotherapy. Suppose the interaction in (3) took place.

(3)

Whole Wheat Dan:	Rayette and Loretta didn't show up. They don't like me.
Psychotherapist:	Who didn't show up?
Whole Wheat Dan:	Rayette and Loretta.
Psychotherapist:	What's wrong with you?
Whole Wheat Dan:	They don't like me.
Psychotherapist:	What is Rayette's last name?
Whole Wheat Dan:	What?
Psychotherapist:	Time is up.

This type of questioning should not be referred to as questioning at all. The term questionnairing is more appropriate.

A SYSTEM FOR QUESTIONING

The remainder of this chapter will sketch a system explicitly depicting aspects of inferential comprehension and its application to classroom instructional settings. The system, referred to as "Links," and its application, have been presented in more detail elsewhere (Nix, 1983a). The focus here concerns how this system is used for instructional questioning in contrast to questionnairing.

The motivation for developing Links was to provide a means for directly teaching inferential reading comprehension and metacomprehension skills. Comprehension skills refer to the reader using his or her prior knowledge of the world to link together propositions in a given text, in terms of various inferences. In terms of the Whole Wheat Dan text, inferential comprehension might be something like:

Whole Wheat was disappointed because the girls had not shown up; the reason that their not showing up was disappointing was that they played his favorite songs, and since they had not shown up, they would not be able to play them for him; examples of his favorite songs are "I call her Darlin' but she calls me collect" and "Mama's out of prison again"; Whole Wheat must like country music, given the song titles, and given his name, and the girls' names; Whole Wheat sighed because he was disappointed and felt sorry for himself; he commented that the girls didn't like him because he felt sorry for himself, and perhaps in general was the type of person who did a good job of feeling sorry for himself, since he liked dreary songs, and since in this case he reacted more strongly than most people would.

Are younger school children able to make such inferences, either during or after reading? In educational settings there has been a tradition of skepticism about this. The types of comprehension questions found in basal series reflect such skepticism, even as late as 3rd- and 4th-grade levels. However, an excellent article by Stein and Trabasso (in press) provides considerable evidence that children, under various conditions and often at much younger ages, can and do make inferences before, while, and after they read or listen to text. The conditions under which children are observed often preclude the discovery of what the children can actually do. Furthermore, there is at least preliminary evidence that children can be taught to more readily and consistently use inferencing as a consistent way of dealing with meaning in text.

In order to teach children to perform inferential comprehension like that in the text in (1), and to do so in a manner that would generalize to other paragraphs, an explicit system of links was developed (Nix, 1978b; in press). They have the characteristic that they are teachably explicit, that is, they are componentially defined. Each component is common sense based, and can be directly taught in a step–by–step manner with critical positive and negative examples. Specific links were defined and then introduced in interview sessions to 3rd-grade children. The purpose of these interviews was to determine which links were sensible, and whether questions could conveniently be generated therefrom. In general, a link is retained if: (a) children could use a given link concept to discuss a text under consideration, that is, if it could be the basis for a questioning type of interaction; (b) if the link could be broken down into teachable components; and (c) if the link was relevant to tying a text together.

For purposes of a brief illustration, protocol (4) is an example of the Whole Wheat Dan text partially analyzed in terms of a Links map. Only 4 of the approximately 40 links are used in this example. These four links are: the *Feeling Reason Link,* the *Action Reason Link,* the *Thinking Reason Link,* and the *Example Link.* Definitions of these links are summarized in Table 11.1.

In general, all links consist of teachable components. For example, the Feeling Reason Link consists of a *Feeling,* a *Feeler,* a *Feeling Reason,* and *What a Feeler Might Do.* In the first sentence in (4), the Feeling is disappointment and the Feeler is Whole Wheat Dan. The Feeling Reason is the combination of the Feeling and Feeler. The purpose of the Feeling Reason component is to overtly characterize the Feeling and Feeler as a reason for some subsequent activity or mental state, whether or not such an activity or mental state actually occurs in the text, or covertly in inferential additions to the text. The notion here is that Feeling and Feeler are together a psychoactive trigger for expectations. The What a Feeler Might Do that goes with the first sentence in (4) is Whole Wheat's sighing. One knows from one's knowledge of the world, and from the current context, that sighing is a possible meaningful response to disappointment. A Feeling Reason Link, then, is the link between the Feeling Reason and What a Feeler Might Do. The other links in (4) are similarly defined in Table 11.1.

TABLE 11.1
Sample Links Definitions

Feeling Reason Link = Feeling Reason + What Feeler Might Do
Feeling Reason = Feeling + Feeler
Example: Syrup was mad at Ms. Spiffy. She threw her eraser at her.

Wanting Reason Link = Wanting Reason + What Wanter Might Do
Wanting Reason = Wanting + Wanter
Example: Beanbag the cat doesn't want to be thrown around any more. She is hiding under the rug.

Thinking Reason Link = Thinking Reason + What Thinker Might Do
Thinking Reason = Thinking + Thinker
Example: Jammy looked for Beanbag in the closet. She figured Beanbag was hiding there.

Action Reason Link = Action Reason + What Might Happen
Action Reason = Action + Acter
Example: Snerdpot threw Beanbag at Ms. Spiffy. Ms. Spiffy ducked.

Example Link = Group Name + A Kind Of
Example: Snerdpot always gets into trouble. He threw his eraser out the window. He broke Whole Wheat Dan's guitar.

---

(4)

W. W. wanted them — FRL — W. W. likes
to come   country music

WRL → Whole Wheat Dan was disappointed.
Rayette and Loretta had not showed
ARL   up. They always played all of his
      favorite songs, like "I call her   FRL
EGL   darlin' but she calls me collect."
      They can even play "Mama's out of
      prison again." Whole Wheat sighed.
TRL   "I guess they just don't care",
      he said.

W. W. thinks
they don't
care

Aspects of the text in (4) can now be read in terms of links.

Whole Wheat Dan sighed because he was disappointed. The reason he was disappointed is the girls had not showed up and he had wanted them to show up. One reason he wanted them to show up is that they played his favorite songs. Examples of his favorite songs are "I call her darlin' but she calls me collect," and "Mama's out of prison again." The fact that the girls have not showed up makes Whole Wheat think they will not show up and they do not care, and so he says "I guess they just don't care."

It can be seen, then, that a set of links can be used to explicitly depict certain important aspects of how a text is inferentially connected. Viewing the text through links (as through any explicit representation system) transforms the text from a string of words or phrases into a semantically connected map of relationships. What is critical from a teaching perspective is that the links themselves are common sense oriented, explicit, componentially defined, and teachable and transferable—that is, they are teachably explicit. When mastered, these links are like a fixed bag of tricks a student can use as an aid in comprehending a text. This is somewhat analogous to solving addition problems with a set of rules (addition, alignment, carrying, etc.), rather than by simply trying out answers and being told right or wrong.

The specific links and how to apply them to texts are inferential comprehension skills that can be taught to children. Links are taught individually and in chains. Children are taught to recognize, generate, and discuss various links and link combinations. A recurrent aspect of the teaching situation is the necessity for the student to provide evidence, based on his or her knowledge of the world and knowledge of the context and of links, for the choice they make in a given text instance.

Partially as a result of this type of experience with text, students appear to make a transition in their metacomprehension point of view. They begin to conceptualize text as a network of inferentially related statements, rather than a linear phenomenon. Furthermore, the perceived locus of the meaning of a text moves from the text itself to the mind of the reader. The links teaching methodology is dogged. It is based on systematic questioning, and the requirement that the students use evidence from their knowledge of the world to justify an answer or hypothesis. Thus, comprehension is represented and practiced as a trajectory through the reader's own mind, whereby the meaning is imposed on the text by the reader.

The rationale for the development of links is as follows. Inferential reading comprehension is a complex process. Many children, including children performing at grade level and above, have difficulties with this process, particularly as the reading task shifts from *learning to read* to *reading to learn*. This process is a mystery to both the children and their teachers. Teachers do not have access to an explicit system of conceptualizations with which they can verbalize what they already tacitly know about comprehension to children who are having difficulties. The intention of links is to provide a means for effectively demystifying the process enough to enable teachers to improve students' comprehension abilities. So far, initial teaching attempts have been encouraging.

QUESTIONING WITH LINKS

Two specific teaching methodologies based on Links have been developed. The first methodology is based exclusively on asking questions motivated by a links analysis of a passage, with extensive followup discussion. A map of a passage is constructed, showing the links that are involved, similar to the abbreviated map in (1). Questions are then asked about each link line. The subsequent discussion requires the students to relate their answer to their knowledge of the world.

The second methodology introduces links components and their combinations and uses questioning as a systematic procedure for highlighting critical attributes of the various concepts, and for the justification of instances of these in specific texts. In this approach, students learn the names of links and their components.

The focus of both of these methodologies is on directly teaching inferential skills; this constitutes the training in inferential comprehension. As this progresses, links are taught in combinations, and what is referred to as the "necessity for linking" becomes a more dominant focus. That is, students learn that the process of inferentially linking text together as they read and discuss it is part of their role as a reader. This constitutes the addition of a metacomprehension level to the results of the training.

First Questioning Approach

The first type is based on a systematic "clinical" dialogue procedural model. A core set of questions for use in a dialogue was based on the content of a map of a text under consideration. The text was then covered, using this core set and any other questions which might come up as the dialogue ensued. A Links map is constructed for each paragraph to be used in a dialogue. These maps have more detail than the map for the Whole Wheat Dan paragraph shown in protocol (4.1). The map in (4.1) is a simplified map of the Whole Wheat Dan paragraph. Numbers have been added for each clause, rather than for each proposition, in order to simplify the discussion.

(4.1)

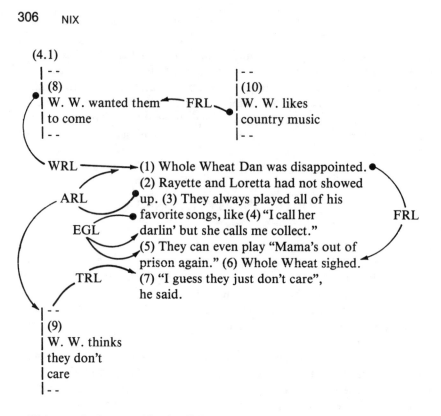

This map is then used in the dialogue setting by an interlocutor, with questions generated directly from the map. Four different types of questions are identified based on: (a) whether they refer to propositions that are overtly stated in the text; (b) whether they refer to propositions that are not in the text itself, but are covertly needed to connect the text; (c) whether they refer to a link between two propostions; and (d) whether they refer to information within a proposition. Table 11.2 shows the four types with examples based on the map in (4.1).

Question Type 1 asks for the content of an overt proposition. Type 1 questions are symbolized as "(?)" to indicate the questioned element is inside an overt proposition. The particular element questioned is not further noted in the Type designation. Question 2 in Table 11.2 is an example of a Type 1 question about part of proposition 2 in the map. Question Type 2, symbolized as "( )?" to indicate the questioned element leads to an overt proposition, asks for a link to an overt proposition, symbolized as "( )-?-". Questions 3, 4, and 5 in Table 11.2 are Type 2 questions. Question Type 3 ("[?]") asks about the content of a covert proposition. In general, for each covert proposition several Type 3 questions can be asked, each providing a different amount of information. The approach is to ask a question that provides the least amount of new information in relation to what the text overtly states

TABLE 11.2
Sample Questions for Whole Wheat Dan Passage

Question	Type	Proposition
1. What does W. W. Dan think about country music?	3	10
2. How did W. W. Dan feel?	1	1
3. What's an example of his favorite song?	2	4
4. Why did W. W. Dan sigh?	2	6
5. Why was he disappointed?	2	1
6. Why did W. W. Dan say "they don't care"?	4	7
7. What did W. W. Dan want from the girls?	3	8

Type 1 (?)	Content of an overt proposition
Type 2 ( )?	Derivation of an overt proposition
Type 3 [?]	Content of a covert proposition
Type 4 [ ]?	Derivation of a covert proposition

and in relation to what has already been discussed in the dialogue. What is considered as given in the situation depends on the text as well as the dialogue interaction. Questions 1 and 7 in Table 11.2 are Type 3. Finally, question Type 4 ("[ ]-?-") is similar to Type 2, except that Type 4 refers to a link to a covert proposition. Question 6 in Table 11.2 is Type 4.

In addition to the types of questions that can be read off the map, a set of dialoguing gambits was identified by studying transcripts of the original set of dialogues. There were three goals in identifying gambits: (1) to have techniques with which to maintain a dialogue; (2) to have techniques that can be used by classroom teachers, with or without Links; and (3) to have techniques which focused on and made salient various difficulties children have in reading comprehension.

It is difficult to conduct a discussion about what inferential knowledge of the world one must use to integrate a text with a 3rd grade child who has reading comprehension problems. Not only does the child not have an answer, but the question itself is not relevant to a child's view of what reading a passage entails. Conversational techniques for reducing the number of dead ends that otherwise occur in such a dialogue setting were iteratively developed. Transcripts were studied to determine interaction sequences which resulted in children reflecting on what evidence they could give to support or reject an interpretation of the text and, ultimately, identifying and verbalizing additional text elements as being linked to a specific element in the text.

The conversational techniques that were selected are referred to as "gambits." Gambits that were identified as being particularly useful are listed in Table 11.3 (see Collins, 1977). This set is not intended to be exhaustive, it is a workable set which can be used by classroom teachers (Nix, 1981a). An extended example of gambits follows the descriptions of each individual gambit.

Clarify asks for a clarification or explanation of what the child said. The notion that comments can be explained, and that someone is interested in an explanation, is important. *Evidence* asks the child to support a statement and to do so by relating the statement to their larger knowledge. Thus, the locus of authority is now the child's point of view — the meaning of the text is not in or of itself, or in a teacher, but in how that text is inferentially related to the child's experience. Children developmentally acquire this metacomprehension awareness. A central focus of teaching children who are developmentally stalled is to teach this.

Show, Counter-eg, and *GEN* compare children's responses in order to focus on some critical aspect. Show points out a consistency or inconsistency with a previous response; if inconsistent, it leads to a resolution. Counter-eg presents to the children a counter example to a statement they have made. A counter example can then be used to show a problem with various components of a statement. GEN makes a generalization based on some aspect of a response and, in the case where the generalization is not acceptable, explicitly resolves it.

A *Between* gambit focuses on sequential propositional links. A proposition in a map is usually linked to many other propositions. A map is not a list of proposition-to-proposition transitions, but rather a means for depicting the weblike relationships of propositions. It is important to cover the links to a given proposition in a text. Thus, if X and Y and Z are linked as $X \rightarrow Y \rightarrow Z$,

TABLE 11.3
Dialogue Gambits

---

1. *Clarify:* ask for clarification or explanation of a response.
2. *Evidence:* ask for evidence to support or contradict a response.
3. *Show: CON/INCON:* point out how a response is consistent (*CON*) or inconsistent (*INCON*) with a previous response.
4. *Counter-EG:* introduce an example that contradicts a response.
5. *GEN: VAL/INVAL:* introduce a generalization from a response that is either (*VAL*) valid or (*INVAL*) invalid.
6. *Between:* ask if there are intermediate factors.
7. *Enough:* ask if a given response is sufficient.
8. *Required:* ask if a given response is necessary.
9. *Return: New/Old/Text:* ask to return to a previous point, either one that was brought up and not pursued (*New*), or one that was previously pursued (*Old*), or to the text (*Text*).
10. (?), ( )?, [?], [ ]?: use question Type 1, 2, 3, or 4.

and the child explains $X \to Z$, then Between asks for intermediate factors in a link chain. If $(X \& Y) \to Z$, where X and Y together are linked to Z, and a child has explained $X \to Z$, then *Enough* asks if X is sufficient, and thereby probes for Y. Such probing would be in terms of other gambits. If $X \to Z$ and/or $Y \to Z$, where either X or Y is sufficient, and a child has explained $X \to Z$, then *Required* probes whether or not X is required for Z. Again, such probing would be gambit oriented. For example, a Counter-eg might be used to investigate the possibility of another factor that would also be sufficient for Z.

The *Return* gambit returns one's attention to a point that was brought out earlier. If, for example, it was a point that was mentioned but not pursued, the point would be pursued via gambits and Type questions. A point might be returned to because of its particular importance in the map, or because it has taken on a particular importance due to subsequent points discussed. A point may also be returned to that which was previously discussed. For example, such a point may have a meaning that was not relevant at the time it was first covered, or its implications were ignored at the time of introduction in order not to interpret an ongoing path.

(5)
1. I: Why was W.W.D. disappointed? (TYPE 2)
2. P: They hadn't showed up. [(2)-ARL->(1)]
3. I: Why would that disappoint him? (ENOUGH)
4.   I mean, sometimes I don't want people to
5.   show up. (COUNTER-EG)
6. P: Me neither— like, my sister.
7. I: Then why? (RETURN)
8. P: Well, W.W.D. likes that country music.
9.   [(10)-FRL->(1)]
10. I: I see. So? (BETWEEN)
11. P: So, he wants them to come [(10)-FRL->(8)]
12.   'cause they play like Mama's out of jail
13.   again [(5)-ARL->(8)].
14. I: Why does that song make him want them to
15.   come? (EVIDENCE)
16. P: It's one of his favorites. [(3)-EGL->(5)]
17. I: That's a country music song. (SHOW:CON)
18.   Do you think he'd want them to come if they
19.   didn't play that song? (REQUIRED)

The questioning strategy model consists of first selecting a question from one of the four question types and asking it. The student's answer is then discussed by using a gambit to follow it up. The links map of the passage is covered in this way. The abbreviated excerpt in protocol (5) shows an example of using most of the gambits to discuss a Type 2 question. In the excerpt, "I" refers to the interlocutor and "P" refers to the student participant. The information in parentheses indicates question type, gambit type, and link type information. In Line 1 the interlocutor asks the question. The participant's response covers the Action Reason Link between propositions 2 and 1 in the map of the Whole Wheat Dan passage shown in (4.1). Line 3 uses the Enough gambit, exploring whether proposition 2 is enough of a reason for Whole Wheat Dan to be disappointed. The map indicates that he was disappointed because they had not showed up, and that he had wanted them to show up (proposition 8). Lines 4 and 5 show the use of a Counter Example gambit, focusing on the possibility that the participant's response was not in itself enough. Line 6 personalizes the counter example to the participant's sister. Line 7 uses the Return gambit to direct the question back to the situation in the text. In Line 8 the participant gives proposition 10 as an additional reason for Whole Wheat Dan's disappointment, in terms of a feeling reason link. Line 10 uses the Between gambit to focus on proposition 8, that is, Whole Wheat Dan wanted them to come because he likes country music. In Line 11 the participant produces the link between propositions 10 and 8. Furthermore, in Lines 12 and 13 he adds the link between propositions 5 and 8. (This additional link could have been probed with an Enough gambit.) Lines 14 and 15 use the Evidence gambit to focus on why that particular song would be important. The participant in Line 16 produces the Example link in response. Line 17 relates that response as being consistent with the participant's response in Lines 8 and 9. Lines 18 and 19 use a Required gambit to explore whether that particular song is in itself a reason for Whole Wheat Dan's wanting them to come.

The interlocutor's behavior in (5) is based on an attempt to cover most of the links in the map of the Whole Wheat Dan passage. The particular excerpt shows coverage of a subset of the links in the map. As can be seen, the coverage consists of asking a question and following it up with the various gambits. There is no fixed amount of detail. For example, line 10 might have been omitted. The interlocutor might have decided that it was not necessary to pursue the intermediate link between propositions 8 and 10. An example of including more detail concerns line 8. The participant stated that Whole Wheat Dan likes country music, proposition 10. The interlocutor does not pursue this statement by, among other things, asking for evidence. If this were done, a part of the meaning of the Whole Wheat Dan passage not shown in the map in (4.1) could have been covered.

The gambits are straightforward and common sense oriented. Nevertheless, it does not appear that teachers customarily use such techniques. Excerpt (2), which is not an atypical example in Nix (1981a), shows the teacher primarily using question repetition. No effort is made to relate the students' responses to the text or to what the students know about anger, slamming doors, and not answering when one's mother asks a question. Classroom observational studies such as Durkin's (1978–1979) and others report similar results.

The gambits are an implementation of the notion that text does not make sense on its own. Text must be interconnected, and the interconnections are based on world knowledge. They are useful not only in teaching comprehension, but also metacomprehension skills. In the dialogue setting, the interlocutor, using a map and gambits, explores with the child what is relevant to tying it all together. The goals in assiduously doing this are to improve the child's comprehension abilities and to change the way the child thinks of text. In such an effort it is easy to get lost, confused, mixed up, and confounded by an unclear view of the intricacies of the text in question, and the vicissitudes of the child's answers and inabilities to answer. Much of this is overcome or attenuated by using a map of the text as an anchor, and by using the gambits as a means for navigating through the map.

As an application of this questioning approach, we selected 20 children from a school in New York City who were approximately 9 months below grade level in a standardized comprehension measure (SRA, 1971) supplied by the school. Children were given a 40 item Links test that consisted of short passages taken from various basal series and comprehension tests. The children were then divided into two groups equated on the SRA test and the Links test. Children in each group were seen individually for 24 sessions over a 2 month period. The control group was instructed in comprehension using the Barnell Loft *Specific Skill Series* (1977) according to the instructions given in the Teachers Manual.

Each training session for the Links group began with the children reading a short passage aloud and then retelling the passage in their own words. Passages were either story or content passages, taken mainly from 3rd-grade basals. After the retelling, a dialogue was conducted based on a map of links for the passage and the various gambits. When the dialogue ended, children reread the passage and retold again. The sessions were audio taped and subsequently transcribed verbatim.

The dialogues with the children consisted of the interlocutor using questions such as those in Table 11.2 as a starting point for a text. Then, using gambit techniques from Table 11.3, each answer was normally pursued in terms of its relevance to and justification by the text, and what the child knew about the world of experience related to the text. Other questions that were not directly generatable from the Links map were used at times, principally as followup to answers via the gambits. These dialogue sessions had a somewhat dogged aspect (Nix, 1978b), due to the interlocutor's discussion of almost every answer.

for teachers. For example, a question such as "Why did Whole Wheat Dan sigh?" might be a typical inferential question a teacher might ask. Aspects of the preceding dialogue technique which make it radically different from normal classroom activity involve: (a) the nature of the questions; (b) the type of followup; and (c) the perceived role of the child. The questions as a group cover the salient parts of the text and their relationships, while the followup ties the discussion to the child's inferential knowledge of the world. In this way, the role of the child changes from that of a questionnaire answerer to an active discussant.

Transcripts for different participants for the same areas of a map are similar in some ways and dissimilar in others. The main differences are in the specific sequence in which statements and links are covered, in the types of responses, and in the degree to which interlocutor prompting is necessary. Each excerpt, however, is similar in the sense that there is an attempt on the part of the interlocutor to doggedly cover the map and to sensitize the child to the notion that they must actively link the text together in terms of their knowledge of the world.

Specific link names were not used, but the link maps formed the basis for sensitizing the child. The Links analysis transformed natural text into a non text entity that focuses on the necessity for integrating text in terms of inferential connections to certain types of world knowledge. The dialogue methodology, using gambits, then implements this orientation in order to teach the child both how to think about and implement comprehension. This constituted the instruction for the Links group.

At the conclusion of the training the Links group and the control group were measured in various ways in order to ascertain group differences in both comprehension and metacomprehension skills. One set of measurements was based on five paragraphs consisting of an average of 18.6 propositions (statements) each. None of these paragraphs had previously been seen. Three paragraphs were stories, and two were expository materials. Each child read a passage, aloud, read a distractor paragraph aloud, and then retold the target passage in their own words. Retellings were audiotaped and transcribed with the number of propositions and the number of links in the retelling recorded for each group.

Scoring based on these five paragraphs is described in terms of the example in protocol (6). Here, the left-hand side contains a passage read and the right-hand side shows an excerpt from a retelling. Three types of features were scored in the recalls. First, the number of propositions retold that were also in the target text was counted. For example, in lines 10–11 in the example in (6), the text to be read contained "they didn't raise families." Lines 5–6 in the retelling contain "they wouldn't raise any families." Lines 5–6, were counted as a retold proposition.

The surface aspect of the starting point questions was no different from inferential questions observed in classroom studies and in published materials

Second, the number of explicitly tagged links in both the retellings and the target text were counted. Explicitly tagged links in the target text are indicated in (6) by uppercase type. For example, in the target text, "THAT" in "THAT they didn't raise any families" (lines 10 and 11) indicates that the FLR between being afraid and not raising families is explicitly tagged by the word, "THAT." This link is explicitly tagged in the retelling (lines 5 and 6) using the word "SO" in "and SO they wouldn't raise families." Thus, this part of the retelling would be counted as an instance of an explicitly tagged retelling link for an explicitly tagged target text link.

(6)

Target Text	Retelling Excerpt
1. Fifty years ago there were	....And then with all the new
2. twenty times AS MANY wild	cities and noises and stuff
3. animals in Africa as there are	and roads and all the noise
4. now! The African people	the animals — they got scared
5. killed some FOR food. Others	BY THAT and SO they wouldn't
6. were killed BY hunters from	raise any families. Um, they
7. other countries. Some of the	probably thought it wouldn't
8. animals were so frightened BY	be safe for their babies.
9. all the new cities, roads, and	SO + the African people were
10. noise THAT they didn't raise	afraid there'd be no more
11. families.	wild animals left to eat and
12.	kill, you know, FOR + their food
13. More and more African people	And um SO they fenced off a
14. were worried THAT soon there	large area....
15. would be no wild animals at	
16. all. SO they fenced off large	
17. jungle and forest areas,	
18. called game parks. The	
19. animals are safe there. It is	
20. against the law to shoot or	
21. hurt an animal in a game park.	

The third measure was an explicitly tagged retelling link for a link in the target text that was not explicitly tagged. These are indicated in the retelling by uppercase type followed by "+". For example, in line 9 of the retelling, the "SO+" tags the link between the animals not raising families and the Africans becoming afraid there would be no more wild animals. This was not explicitly tagged in the target text (lines 7–16). The target text states, "Some of the animals were so frightened (lines 6–7). . .more and more African people were worried. . .there would be no wild animals at all (lines 13–16)." There is no explicit word or phrase that links these statements together; one simply follows the other. This type of occurrence, then, would be counted as a link explicitly tagged in the retelling that was not explicitly tagged in the target.

Table 11.4 shows differences between the two groups on these three variables. As can be seen, the Links group retold more propositions that were in the target text, and also included in their retellings more explicitly tagged links, both ones that were explicitly tagged in the target text, and ones that were not.

A fourth type of measure was noted, but not formally counted. This is the number of unmarked links in the retelling that were not marked in the target text, or not overtly in the target text at all. For example, the example in (6), lines 6–8 of the retelling are "they probably thought it wouldn't be safe for their babies." This is linked to the noise reported in line 2 of the retelling. Furthermore, this does not appear in the target text. Presumably, the student generated this link on his or her own. However, it is difficult to determine in a testing mode why the student actually made this statement. For this reason, this type of measure was not formally counted. Such links were frequent in the Links group. Some were not explicitly tagged, as in lines 6–8, and others were explicitly tagged. They were infrequent in the control group.

The three measures actually reported in Table 11.4 stress staying closer to the text. When links such as these in lines 6–8 are measured, it is likely that the Links group will "outlink" the control group by a significant margin, because that is the specific type of linking the teaching methodology stresses.

In addition to comparing the two groups in terms of the above retelling task, a question generation task was also used. In this task, children were given a series of five short paragraphs and were asked to generate three good comprehension questions for each paragraph. These questions were then judged as being either inferential or noninferential questions. A typical noninferential question for the example in (6) would be, "Were the animals frightened by the noise?" Over 90% of the Links group questions were infer-

TABLE 11.4
Average Propositions and Links Retold

Group	Propositions	Links tagged in Target	Links not tagged in Target
LINKS	55.0	13.6	18.5
Control	41.4	9.0	8.0
p value	p < .05	p < .05	p < .01

ential, mirroring the type of questions and responses stressed in the dialogues. Fewer than 30% of the control group questions were inferential.

Finally, the transcripts of the teaching sessions for the Links group were analyzed in order to identify any changes over time. Transcripts from the first third of the sessions were compared to transcripts from the last third. Two types of differences emerged which were particularly salient, thus warranting more systematic investigation.

The first type of difference may be classified as "knowing when there is a problem." In the early sessions, participants were not always aware of the fact that they did not understand the material they were reading and discussing. This was particularly noticeable for two of the more difficult paragraphs. The paragraph in (7) is an example.

(7)
An advertising tailor put a sign on the ballpark fence. The sign announced that he would give away a suit of clothes for each home run. Biff took notice. He began to hammer out a wardrobe at such a terrific pace that the owner of the little shop trembled when he heard the news of the game.

Excerpt (8) is from a child who had the Biff paragraph in an early session, and (9) is from a child who had it in a late session. Clearly, the child in the early session could not verbalize the fact that the text did not make sense. The responses are brief, localized, and, in general, show that the participant does not understand how to integrate the material and does not overtly explicate this situation. The final comment by the participant (P: It says s.) typifies a very common attitude among children with reading comprehension problems: The meaning, if there is any, is viewed as being in the text, not in the reader.

In protocol (9), however, the child who had the Biff paragraph in a later session does detect and verbalize the problem that the text is not clear. She does this at the point of retelling, whereas the child in (8) does not do this even during discussion. The participant in (9) can be seen attempting to make sense out of the text, making various hypotheses, asking the interlocutor for an opinion, and generally in control of the situation, although unable to actually comprehend the text. The behavior in (8) is more typical of early sessions whereas (9) is more typical of later sessions. Participants appear to become sensitive to a need to make more sense of the text, and to be able to verbalize the situation when they are having comprehension difficulties.

A second type of difference that emerged between early and late sessions may be classified as "spontaneous explanation." This is exemplified in protocol (10).

(8) *Earlier Session*	(9) *Later Session*
P: Biff hammered out a wardrobe to make a closet	P: [She reads the text]
I: Ok—ok, so—so making a closet caused the tailor to tremble	I: Ok, good. Now tell me the story.
	P: I don't get the story.
P: Yes	I: You don't? Ok. . . .
I: I don't see how that makes sense—I mean if you look at it—make a closet.	P: I get it up to about homerun and then that's Biff took a notice yes, and then he began to hammer out a wardrobe—I don't get that part.
I: What else could it mean?	
P: Homerun	I: Well, ok. Tell me as much as you can about it—just as much as makes sense.
I: Would that make sense?	
P: Yeah	
I: So, if it said that Biff began to make homeruns at such a terrific pace that the tailor trembled at the news of the game—would that make sense?	P: Well, this tailor put out a sign on the fence, and I guess this maybe another tailor wanted to copy of do a better buy or something—do you think that could be Biff?
P: Yeah	I: Just tell me what you think and then we'll talk about it.
I: Ok, what would happen if Biff started making homeruns?	P: Well, maybe Biff is um maybe Biff is a ballplayer and he hammers he's trying to get up the—well that's the problem—like his best ball playing outfit or something and he could run better because he was comfortable. . . .
P: He'd finish the closet.	
I: What would the tailor think about that?	
P: Then he would take down the sign.	
I: But he wouldn't tremble?	
P: No.	
I: Well, why do you think he trembled	
P: It says so.	

(10) At last we were getting to the city. We saw apartment houses and sidewalks. I felt a funny thing, I mean not really funny, only I had never felt it before. I was *glad* to see the city. You see, out in the country I kept thinking if only we could stay there. And now I was thinking, "This is my place, I know the streets and the stores and where things are."

In earlier sessions, as shown in the transcript in protocol (11), children tended to answer questions flatly, without providing explanatory support for their particular answer. They did not attach importance to a need to orient their answer to any experience of their own, and did not see any need to make sure the interlocutor clearly understood their responses. This type of answering is reinforced by standard classroom practices.

In contrast, the participant in protocol (12) takes a different view. She offers explanations of several kinds for her responses. Some are straightforward links; some are general observations within which a particular response fits; and some are exemplary cases. Presumably, as a result of training in the

(11) *Earlier Session*	(12) *Later Session*
I: Ok. Do you think she liked the country? P: Yes. I: Ok. And then she came back to the city—how'd she feel when she got there? P: Funny. I: Something to laugh at? P: No.	I: How did she feel when she got back to the city? P: At home. I: Ok. P: Because she knows where everything is—and "this is my place". I: Was she um, what did she think about being glad to be back? P: She didn't think she was gonna be because she wanted to stay in the country. I: What tells you that? P: She says she wanted to stay in the country—usually when you want to stay in one place you're not gonna be happy when you go. I: In the country she said she wanted to stay in the country? P: Yes, because she I guess then she was in the country she liked the country better than she did the city because she met new friends and out in the country you can just push the screen door open and you're gone.

dialogue sessions, she sees it as necessary to tie the material together as well as help the interlocutor do this.

The dialogue procedure is arduous, but it is also quite revealing. The procedure gets the participant to think and explain aloud. It will be worthwhile to refine this procedure and to more carefully analyze the interactions. The above results indicate a potential for improving comprehension and meta-comprehension skills in children. In terms of comprehension skills, Links-trained children retold more propositions after reading than the control group. There is also evidence (Nix, 1981c) that Links training, similar to that described here, leads to improvement on standardized reading comprehension tests and on an experimenter designed links comprehension test. The teaching methodology requires the student to clearly focus on the material in the text, and to relate it to their own experimental background while justifying responses about the text.

Metacomprehension, like comprehension, can be defined and measured in various ways. A critical element is that the reader is aware of the necessity for linking a paragraph together. The reader needs to see the task of reading, in part, as one in which one needs to actively "think between the lines." Instead of conceptualizing text as a set of sentences strung together, one needs to view the text as "triggers" for inferentially tying it and their own experience together.

The above results indicate that aspects of these skills may be taught. The fact that the Links group produced more inferential statements in retellings, and that they also produced more inferential questions in a question generation task, tends to support this contention.

An analysis of the dialogue sessions also indicates that students were learning the necessity for linking. In the early sessions, children tended not to provide explanatory connections to the responses they made about the text under discussion. They appeared to see their role as one of answering questions, without explaining the text in their answers. This is similar to the role that is supported by teacher classroom behavior, and by teaching and practice materials which the students themselves use. This role changed, however, as the sessions ensued. In the later sessions, the participants spontaneously provided explanatory information, both for the responses they were giving and for the way the material in the text was integrated. They understood it was necessary to do this, presumably as a result of the experience of the dialogue sessions themselves.

Another important aspect of comprehension is the ability to monitor how well one comprehends what one reads and hears. Children do not typically show such an ability (Brown, 1978; Markman, 1979). This was true of children in the present study, during the early sessions. However, during the later sessions, there was a tendency for children to covertly comment that something did not make sense when they were having comprehension difficulties.

The dialogue interactions stressed that all aspects of the text and all responses in the discussion were to be dealt with in terms of whether they made sense and why or why not. The children presumably learned from this that text must make some sense, and that it is up to them to make it make sense.

All of these comments need further empirical support. The variables used need further refinement, and additional variables need to be included: for example, nontagged links, covert links, and ability to selectively retell only important or central points of a passage. However, even at the current exploratory level, the simple phenomenological fact of sitting and discussing passages with children, and seeing changes in the way they approach the dialogue setting, and the passages around which the settings center, has been enlightening.

Second Questioning Approach

Despite the preliminary nature of the Links teaching approach, the outcomes are encouraging from the standpoint of attempting to assist children who have difficulties with comprehension skills, especially when viewed within the perspective of what is now available to such children in classrooms. The approach uses specific links as the unexpressed basis for what is to be learned, and through questioning maintains a high time on task level. Students have been taught to use the gambits among themselves, while teachers have been taught to perform the role of interlocutor (Nix, 1981a).

However, the approach which is now being pursued involves more structured materials for teacher use. These materials will be easier for the average classroom teacher to use. They consist of teaching specific links explicitly by name and of doing so in such a way that remediation can be performed in terms of clearly defined subordinate skills. The teacher works interactively with groups of children using a Teacher Presentation Book (TPB) which provides a path through the materials. The materials have two goals: (1) to teach linking, and (2) to teach an explicit awareness of the necessity for linking. First, the general approach will be described, and then several examples of preliminary empirical investigations will be discussed.

Each of about eight links is a specific topic, with four instructional phases for each topic. First, each topic has lessons which teach the component pairs of a link. Second, the link itself is taught. Third, various uses of the link are taught. Fourth, various combinations of this link with other links already covered are taught. The TPB is constructed so that, at any point at which the children are having difficulties, the teacher is lead through a process of determining where these difficulties lie. This determination of the loci of the difficulties is in terms of component parts. Repair points are then provided in the materials for remedial use. A high degree of student participation is consistently maintained. The resultant interactive sessions are a stylized outcome of the dialogue sessions already described.

For example, the Feeling Reason Link involves several components: Feeling Words (FWs), Feelers (Fs), Feeling Reasons (FRs), What Feelers Might Do (FMDs), and Feeling Reason Links (FRLs). This is shown in protocol (13). Thus an FR is an F plus an FW, and an FRL is an FR plus an FMD. FW, F, and FMD are defined in terms of experiential examples.

```
(13)
    (- - - - - - - - -FR- - - - - - - - - - - - - - - - - - -)- -
    (- - - - -F- - - - - - -)      (- -FW- - - - - -)
    Whole Wheat Dan was disappointed.          FRL
    He sighed.
    (-FMD- - -)<- - - - - - - - - - - - - - - - - - - - - - - -
```

The following basic set of lessons typifies the way in which the concept of the FRL can be taught:

a. Doing and Finding FWs.
b. Doing and Finding Fs.
c. Doing and Finding FMDs.
d. Using World Knowledge.
e. Doing and Finding FRs.
f. Doing and Finding FRLs.
g. More Doing and Finding FRLs.

Each lesson contains a Teacher Introduction, followed by a series of interactive sections: student introduction; definition and examples of new concepts; practice; and recap. The point is to clearly define what is to be taught, present sufficient positive and negative examples in order to discriminate the critical attributes of each concept, that is, the links and their components, (Tennyson & Park, 1980), and maintain a high degree of time on task (Rosenshine, 1978). The use of links as the taxonomic base makes this possible.

Repair points are integrated, and each point is in terms of components that have already been covered. For example, a student may have difficulties with More Doing and Finding FRLs, which uses more complicated paragraphs than Doing and Finding FRLs. These difficulties are not conceptualized in terms of not being able to make inferences, or some other inexplicit skill, and then dealt with another similar question. Instead, the TPB leads the teacher and students through an interactive, constructive determination of where the problem exists. The problem may be the complexity of the paragraph, in such terms, for example, as distance between FR and FMD, competing FMDs, direction of the FRL, type of FW. It may be finding FRLs, FMDs, FRs, Fs, or

FWs. The TPB detects this, goes back up the scale to show how the original FRL questions can be answered, and then requires the teacher to continue with More Doing and Finding FRLs, or go to a repair point.

After FRLs have been learned, additional FRL lessons follow to implement various applications. These lessons include, following lesson (g) above:

h. FRLs and Main Ideas.
i. FRLs to Do Pronoun Reference.
j. FRLs and Comprehension Questions.
k. FRLs and Filling in the Blanks (as in close formats).
l. FRLs and Writing Inferentially Coherent Stories.
m. FRLs with Invisible FRs.
n. FRLs and Invisible Main Ideas.
o. FRL Chains.

Lessons (h) = (l) are designed to explain certain tasks that students are routinely required to do, but for which no explanation is normally given. Instead of giving unexplained practice items without followup, this approach systematically leads to the concept, for example, of main idea, in terms of FRL (and other links). Then, the concept is defined in terms of how one uses FRLs to identify or produce exemplars of it, and repair is done as an explicit component of the process. This notion is extended to various comprehension tasks with which a student is faced in a school setting. Lessons (m) = (o) deal with additional complexities in text.

As stated, the type of teacher–student interaction promulgated by the TPBs is intended to be a stylized extension of the technique described earlier. The orientation is for the dominant mode of the interaction to be in terms of questions to the students, and discussion oriented answers by the students, with explicit followup in terms of links components, gambits, and knowledge of the world, and with component-specific and text-specific diagnosis and remediation. This type of instructional methodology is imposed on the content structure.

As an example, consider for the sake of simplicity the text in protocol (14) below about Snerdpot and Ms. Spiffy. Assume that this text is being used in a section of the instructional sequence on teaching students to find Feeling Reason Links. This means that the students have already successfully completed the earlier components: Feeling Words, Feelers, Feeling Reasons, and What Feelers Might Do. Several modes would be used to teach the Feeling Reason Link component, beginning with having the students step through the components of the definition, and ending with simply asking them to find Feeling Reason Links and then justifying or refuting their answers by using the components.

(14)

    Snerdpot broke Ms. Spiffy's vase.
Ms. Spiffy was furious!- - - - - - - - - - - - -FRL- -
She said she was going to <- - - - - - - - - - - - - - - -
call Snerdpot's mother.
Then she got her broom to clean up the mess.

A sample canonical teacher–student group interaction for asking students to find a Feeling Reason Link in (14) is outlined in Table 11.5. This outline is one of the models that has been implemented in various ways in actual teaching materials. The teacher (T) asks the group to find an FRL after the text has been read. In this mode no explicit mention of the components of an FRL is made. Next, students (Ss) provide answers. The teacher picks one of the student answers to pursue. If the answer the teacher has picked is the one being sought (which is that Ms. Spiffy's being furious is FRLed to her intending to call Snerdpot's mother), the teacher uses the Ss-FIT gambit (Case A in Table 11.5). This gambit interactively leads the student group through the process of justifying the answer in terms of the components of the FRL concept. The justification is that we know being mad is a feeling, and that when people like Ms. Spiffy are mad at people like Snerdpot, they might call one's mother.

A student answer that is not the answer being sought can diverge in several ways. One critical way is that the answer may contain a Feeling Reason, but not what the Feeler Might Do because of that reason (such as Ms. Spiffy is mad, and so she picked up the broom to sweep the floor), for example, Case B in Table 11.5. Case B has 4 steps:

1. If the teacher picks such an answer, then the strategy is for the teacher and the student group to show that the answer does not fit because of the FMD. The basis for doing this is one's knowledge of the world.

2. Next, the FMD in the text itself is located.

3. According to the rule than an FRL is an FR plus the FMD, the FRL is found. In this instance there is a repair point.

4. The teacher considers whether to continue with the new concept under discussion (FRLs), or to review FMDs.

Another critical way in which a student's answer can diverge from what is being sought is that the student may select an FMD but not link it to an FR. A student might link it to another statement to which it actually is linked (Ms. Spiffy was going to call Snerdpot's mother because Snerdpot broke her vase), or to a statement to which it is not linked. These are Cases C and D, respectively, in Table 11.5. In Case C:

TABLE 11.5
Canonical Teacher–Student Group Interaction Example

Case	Condition	Followup Steps
A. If Ss = FR → FMD:		(1) Ss-FIT(FR(F + FW) + FMD(KOW))
B. If Ss = FR not → notFMD:		(1) T&Ss-NOFIT(notFMD(KOW))
		(2) Find FMD(KOW)
		(3) Find FRL(FR + FMD)
		(4) REPAIR?(FMD)
C. If Ss = X → FMD:		(1) T&Ss-NOFIT(notFR(FW + F))
		(2) Show X-LINK(KOW)
		(3) Find FR(F + FW)
		(4) Find FRL(FR + FMD)
		(5) REPAIR?(FR)
D. If Ss = X not → FMD:		(1) T&Ss-NOFIT(notFR(FW + F))
		(2) Show notX-LINK(KOW)
		(3) Find FR(F + FW)
		(4) Find FRL(FR + FMD)
		(5) REPAIR?(FR)
E. If Ss = notFR → notFMD:		(1) T&Ss-NOFIT(notFR(FW + F), not FMD(KOW))
		(2) T&SSs-REVIEW(FR + FMD)
		(3) Find FR(F + FW)
		(4) REPAIR?(FR)
		(5) Find FMD(KOW)
		(6) REPAIR?(FMD)
		(7) Find FRL(FR + FMD)
T → CHALLENGE		

T: teacher, Ss: student group, FRL: Feeling Reason Link
FR: Feeling Reason, FW: Feeling word(s), F: Feeler
FMD: What a Feeler Might Do, KOW: knowledge of the world

1. The teacher and students show it does not fit the FRL concept because it is not linked to an FR, and because it is not linked to an FW and F.
2. They then show that it is however linked to the statement they chose (that is, to the student's answer that the teacher chose to pursue), based on what is known about the world.
3 & 4. The teacher and students find the FR and, thus, the FRL.
5. The repair point is in terms of FRs.

Case D is the same as Case C with the exception that in step (2) the teacher and students use their knowledge of the world to show that the student answer is not an instance of a link.

In Case E, the answer which the teacher decides to pursue does not contain either component of an FRL. In this case, teacher and student show the answer does not fit, and then the teacher leads the students step-by-step through the components of the FRL rule in a manner similar to an earlier mode of teaching FRLs. Repair points occur after each major component.

The transcript excerpt in protocol (15) is an example of how a teacher-student group interaction progresses on the basis of the type of logic shown in Table 11.5. It can be seen that, despite the programmatic nature of the underlying logic of the teaching methodology, the interaction itself has the characteristic of conversation. The teaching methodology is the background model, or ghost in the machine, rather than necessarily a visible component of the actual interaction on which it is based.

The excerpt in (15) represents a point in the proceedings at which the students were asked to find an FRL for the text in (14). The answer the teacher selected to pursue indicated that the students were having difficulties finding FMDs. The answer was that the FRL was from Ms. Spiffy's *being mad,* to her *picking up a broom to sweep.* Being mad is a valid FR. However, picking up a broom to sweep the floor, in this context, is not what one would normally expect a Feeler to do. This excerpt illustrates Case B in Table 11.5:

If S = FR not → not FMD.

That is, the student picked an FR that is not linked to a statement that is not an FMD.

The first step in Case B is:

T&Ss - NOFIT (FMD (KOW)).

(15)
Section 1
T: OK, we've got the first part of what we need for a FRL — what have we showed on the page?
S1: The check mark. The FR.
T: What do we need next — look at our rule.
S3: What a Feeler Might Do.
T: Is there one in the paragraph?
S2: She might do anything, knowing Ms. Spiffy!
T: Does the paragraph say she did something?
S3: She got the broom to hit him with 'cause she's so mad.
S2: No, no — she won't hit him — she'd get in trouble.
S4: She's going to call his mother.
S3: No, she's not going to really hit him with the broom. I mean she's going to scare him a little bit.
T: OK, let's see. I don't know. We know about Ms. Spiffy — what tells us she might do that?

S2: She never hurts people — I don't think she'd do that.

S3: Well, she might want to.

T: Did she get the broom because she was mad? What does our knowledge of the world tell us?

S4: You could, but not here.

S1&S3: Yeah.

T: OK, so she probably didn't get the broom because she was furious — Did she do anything because she was mad?

S4: She's going to call his mother.

T: How do you know that — it doesn't say in the paragraph "She's going to call his mother *because* she was" — so how do we know?

S2: Well, if you have a teacher, see, and she's mad at a kid, then she's going to get them in trouble with the principal or you know like her parents —

S4: Yeah, teachers always do that — remember yesterday when you got in trouble, S2. You're just like Snerdpot.

S2: Forget it!

T: So, what are we using to see that calling Snerdpot's mother is the FMD?

S1: Our knowledge of the world.

Section 2

T: Right, right. Now, let's look at our rule. Do we have a FRL?

S1&S2&S3&S4: Yes.

T: How do we know?

S4: A FRL. A FR and a FMD, calling his mother.

T: OK, where does the arrow go?

S3: To calling Snerdpot's mother.

T: Yes. . . .

This indicates that the teacher and students together show that the answer selected does not fit the requirements of an FMD. The basis for determining an FMD is what people know about the world (KOW). This step is now shown in excerpt (15). The second step in Case B is:

Find FMD (KOW)

Here, the teacher and students find an FMD for the FR that has already been established. In the example in (14), the FMD for Ms. Spiffy's being mad is that she is going to call Snerdpot's mother. This is shown in Section 1 in excerpt (15).

The next step in Case B is:

Find FRL (FR + FMD).

This step comes after both the FR and the FMD have been identified. It consists of conceptualizing the FRL as the connection between these. This is shown in Section 2 of excerpt (15).

The final step in Case B is:

REPAIR? (FMD).

The purpose of this step is to make a decision whether to continue with the current topic, or to go to a repair point in the materials. The repair point in this case reviews FMDs.

The students interact with the teacher and with each other under the auspices of the TPB. It should be noted that, of course, the actual materials the teacher is using do not themselves look like Table 11.5. Instead, they implement the Table 11.5 logic in a teacher-useable format. The students also engage in other activities of the program, such as: playacting; mapmaking; scavenger hunts for various links in bodies of text (such as newspapers); detective games in which the solutions are based on clues in terms of links; and materials which follow up and extend specific exercises initially conducted with the teacher.

The other links are similarly segmented for instructional presentation. Each one has its own idiosyncratic subdivisions, sequence of presentation, and repair features. As more links are presented, more stress can be placed on combinations of links, and the repair points can diagnose a greater range of well defined problems.

In general, the buildup is carefully conducted, from simple to complex. For example, there are text transitions based on several categories.: In terms of text genre, there is a transition from simple narrative texts to more complicated expository texts, from shorter to longer text, and from more to less familiar subject matter. In terms of text structure, as viewed through Links, several transitions take place. Earlier texts use links whose components are contiguous, and for which the direction is from the first to the second component. Later texts have noncontiguous links, with various components being invisible. An example of an early type of text was shown in (14); An example of a later type of text (16) follows.

(16)
Two or three crossed sticks, some string, some glue, a piece of paper, and some rags are all a person needs to make one of the best toys in the world—a kite. The grandest kite of all is the dragon kite. A person seeing it for the first time might be scared by the sight. A typical dragon kite has horns on its head. It may make a growling or humming noise!

It is important to sensitize the child to the fact that text is psychoactive rather than passive. The child is to learn the metacomprehension point of view, it is their job, in a reading situation, to actively inferentially integrate the text in terms of what they know about the world, and to do so in terms of links. As the material becomes more complex, there is a place to go for repair, based on what they have been learning. Although the child is faced with complexity, the complexity is teachably explicit rather than ineffable. This helps to demystify the process.

Several empirical teaching studies, (Nix, 1983b; Peters & Wixson, 1981; Peters, 1982a) based on the aforementioned content representation and methodology, are sketched using the Links approach with various student populations and outcome measures. Aspects of these studies are indicated in Table 11.6, in which entries indicate either level of significance when comparing outcomes to groups trained in a different method. The *ns* signifies that no significant differences were found, and *na* signifies that the measure was not used in the particular study.

The objective of the 4th-grade study (Nix, 1981b) was to directly teach, in a classroom environment, certain inferential comprehension and metacomprehension skills. In this study, metacomprehension referred mainly to a reader's awareness that it is necessary to inferentially tie a text together in terms of his or her knowledge of the world. This use of the term overlaps, somewhat, with knowledge of cognition and regulation of cognition, as in Baker and Brown (in press). The first step was to directly teach Links so that children became more proficient in comprehending passages, and use Links to resolve pronoun reference, find main ideas, predict outcomes, and so on. The second step was to teach the necessity for linking. This refers to sensitizing both teachers and children to the fact that the task of reading is, to a considerable extent, based on inferentially integrating information in the text.

Control and experimental groups of 4th-grade children with poor comprehension skills were equated in terms of both the Gates–MacGinitie Reading

TABLE 11.6
Direct Teaching Studies

Group	Ques Gen	Comp Test	Meta-Cognitive	Inferences Recalled	Ideas Recalled	Major Ideas Recalled	Probe Qs
Low 4th grade	.01	.05	.01	.05	na	na	na
Low 8th grade	.001	.001	.05	na	.001	ns	.015
H.S. college prep	na	.01	na	na	.02	.01	na

Tests, Form D–1 (1978), and the SRA Achievement Series, Level D, Form 1 (SRA, 1978). The experimental group was trained in links, using a methodology based on the one sketched previously. Teaching materials were developed to teach five specific links, their justification, and their uses. They were used in highly interactive sessions in which a teacher works with a small group of students. Each link was taught in steps, the steps comprising the specific subcomponents of a link. At each step, the relevant concepts are explicitly defined, and positive and negative examples are presented to highlight critical attributes of the concept. The control group was trained using the Specific Skills Series (1977), a widely used series in actual classroom practice. The control and experimental groups received the same time on each task. The total training time was ten weeks, three or four times per week, for about 20 minutes at each session.

Inferential comprehension was measured in several ways using post-training differences between control and experimental groups, and analysis of covariance, with pretraining measures as covariates (see Table 11.6). First, a question generation task was used to determine what the child saw as a relevant comprehension question for a given passage. The children themselves were asked to generate such questions for a text. Then, the questions were analyzed in terms of whether they were detail questions or inference questions. The experimental group showed a higher inferential to detail ratio. This can be interpreted as a change in how the children conceptualized the types of questions that they see as relevant to comprehension of a passage. Second, a metacognitive task was given in which children read passages that were poorly written and were asked to explain the passages. Instances where they overtly stated that the passage did not make sense, or was confusing, were counted. Such instances were more numerous for the experimental group. During the course of the study, children became more overtly aware of text confusions, rather than passively accepting them. Third, children read short passages and retold them in their own words, as if they were telling them to someone who had never read the passage. The retellings were transcribed and scored for explanatory additions, referred to as *inferences recalled*. These included linking keywords (such as *so*) which did not occur in the text, and explanatory sentences which connected and/or clarified material actually in the text. Instances of explanatory additions were higher for the experimental group. Children assumed that such additions were part of the retelling task, and that simple repetition was no longer satisfactory. Fourth, the experimental group also recalled more propositions or ideas from the original texts. And fifth, the experimental group scored higher on Form D–2 of the Gates–MacGinitie Reading Test (a form equivalent to D–1), given in an untimed mode.

The objective of the 8th-grade study (Peters, 1982a) was to investigate the effects of direct comprehension instruction on standardized reading test scores and on number of ideas recalled, both in terms of amount and type of ideas. The teaching approach consisted, for the Links Group, of teaching 6 links, using a step-by-step approach. In addition to teacher-lead sessions similar to (15) above, students were given other activities, such as sorting cards, and completing links closelike structures. The control group was instructed using traditional remedial materials, including Skill Builders, SRA materials, Jamestown Specific Materials, Scholastic, and so on.

The control and Links experimental groups were equated in terms of the Stanford Diagnostic Test (1976) and teacher recommendations. Each group was taught for three months, three times per week, about 45 minutes each time. At the end of the training period, several tasks were completed and scored (see Table 11.6). Comparisons were made between groups on these tasks.

Several dependent measures were used in order to provide a range of meaning to the results. First, a question generation task, similar to the one in the 4th-grade study, was used. Children were given a passage and asked to generate four questions that "get at important ideas." The questions were analyzed in terms of their level in a Links map of the passage. The experimental group showed a higher number of major ideas in their questions. This can be interpreted as a difference in how children conceptualized the important versus less important ideas in a passage. Second, a metacognitive task was given in which children were asked to rate their own comprehension of passages they read. Third, a retelling task was given to both groups. The experimental group retold more propositions, or ideas, from the original texts than the control group. Fourth, there was no difference in the number of major ideas retold. Fifth, the experimental group scored higher on Form D-2 of the Stanford Diagnostic Reading Test. Sixth, probe questions were asked. Again, the Links group had a higher number of correct responses.

The purpose of the High School study (Peters & Wixson, 1981) was to investigate the effects of Links training on comprehension test scores and on the number and type of ideas recalled. Expository social studies materials were initially used, with a subsequent transfer to a difficult, college level text that was actually being used in the classroom, *History of the Modern World* (Palmer & Colton, 1978). The Links training consisted of the gradual introduction of and training on five links. The use of these links for mapping texts was stressed. The students were high school seniors in a college preparatory class who were good readers, but who were having difficulties with the text they were using. The entire class participated in the study, so no separate control group was used. Post training measures (Table 11.6) were between students who scored high on a Links posttest and who scored low on the same test.

Table 11.6 indicates differences between the two groups. First, the group that scored high on the Links posttest scored higher on Social Studies Critical

Reading Test (Peters & Harris, 1978). Second, the high Links group scored higher on number of ideas recalled on the recall task, and the number of important ideas recalled. The lack of a control group that received no Links training makes these results somewhat unclear. Furthermore, the differences obtained could be based on a variable such as verbal aptitude, rather than the actual training. However, these outcomes suggest areas for further study.

Other measures were made in both the 8th grade and high school studies, with results similar to the ones already outlined. However, the measures in Table 11.6 present a general impression of the types of effects that may be obtained with a teaching methodology based on Links and an assiduous, step-by-step instructional methodology. Other studies (e.g., Peters, 1982b, 1983) extend these results.

In summary, the results support attempts to directly teach inferential comprehension in terms of linking and the necessity for linking. Children with reading problems tend to read from one word, fragment, or sentence to the next, unaware that the meaning must come from their own heads, and that they have to actively inferentially impose this meaning on the text. Their view of comprehension is passive. They see relevant questions as repetition of detail. They are not actively aware when a text does not make sense. They conceptualize retelling a passage as simply repeating a string of sentences. They do not see reading as thinking between the lines. After direct training, their view of comprehension becomes more active. They produce more inferential questions. They are more actively aware of a text that is confusing. They see retelling as requiring explanatory additions, and they recall more of the original text. Finally, they see reading as thinking between the lines.

PERSPECTIVE

Large numbers of children have difficulties in reading comprehension skills. Classroom practice, both in terms of teacher behaviors and published materials, does not systematically help. The Links teaching methodology represents an attempt to deal with the constellation of problems underlying this classroom situation.

The Links approach is not intended to be a knowledge representation system or a processing model, although it is possible to pursue it in such directions (e.g., Nix, 1978a, in press). The value of Links is more a set of conceptualizations from which is called a systematic questioning procedure that improves reading comprehension and metacomprehension skills. In contrast to other approaches in cognitive science, Links is somewhat atheoretical, that is, it is justified if it teaches. This is independent of whatever characteristics it may or may not have in terms of theoretical predictions relevant to text processing. This point of view has been referred to as a "clownsuit" epistemology.

Secondly, the goal of Links is practical. This imposes on it the necessity to deal with a wide range of realistic text. The standard basal reader typically contains many different text genres, including, at a general level, such types as narrative, expository, poetic, drama, and how-to. Within each of these broad divisions appear various subdivisions. For example, a narrative may be a traditional fable, a detective story, or a history lesson in disguise. Discourse processing systems which are more theoretically motivated, such as ones based on story grammars or plot units, can not effectively deal with this range of text. This is not a defect in such systems, rather a result of the research goals of the users of those systems. Links, on the other hand, directly deals with a wide range of text, and does this in terms of a training rather than a predictive orientation.

A third point which characterizes the motivation behind Links is the intimacy between the conceptualizations and the questioning technique built on these conceptualizations. The iterative development of the system was keyed, to a significant extent, to the issue of whether or not questions could be generated from the divisions made salient by the system. For a question to be useful in a teaching situation, it should make sense in several ways. For a question to make sense, according to the approach taken in Links, the question must be answerable in terms of a set of teachably explicit components. Thus, in order for a conceptualization to be acceptable as a link, it had to be defined in such a way that its common sense components could form the basis for a questioning methodology. Furthermore, this methodology had to be an effective teaching approach.

There are many unanswered questions about Links. To what extent might such a system be useful for knowledge representation, or the representation of processing strategies? Why, for example, does the questioning procedure work? What questions work better than others? Are there individual differences among students for different question types?

However, the more urgent questions revolve around the central one: How can the conceptualizations and/or question-based methodology be improved in order to improve comprehension instruction? Returning to epistemology, the point can be crystallized as follows: if wearing a clownsuit helps a teacher teach, then, given the difficulties so many children have with comprehension skills, we first learn where to get such a suit, next, how to wear it, and finally, how to fix it when it rips. Theoretical developments in cognitive science (and particularly in artificial intelligence) have made systems like Links possible. It seems very likely that systems like Links, as well as theories of questioning and question answering such as by Graesser and Murachver and others in this book, can provide a basis for better clownsuits.

ACKNOWLEDGMENTS

I thank Florence Coulter, Mary K. Monteith, Charlie Peters, Bob Rodgers, Pete Rynders, and Aaron Stander, of Oakland Schools, Pontiac, Michigan, and Judy Phillips and Susan Zinar of Teachers College, Columbia University, for their significant and indispensible help in converting Links as a theory into Links as a set of teaching materials.

REFERENCES

Baker, L., & Brown, A. L. (in press). Metacognitive skills in reading. In D. Pearson (Ed.), *Handbook of reading research.* New York: Longman.

Brown, A. L. (1978). Metacognitive development and reading. In R. J. Spiro, B. C. Bruce, & W. F. Brewer (Eds.), *Theoretical issues in reading comprehension.* Hillsdale, NJ: Lawrence Erlbaum Associates.

Collins, A. (1977). Processes in acquiring knowledge. In R. C. Anderson, R. J. Spiro, & W. E. Montague (Eds.), *Schooling and the acquisition of knowledge.* Hillsdale, NJ: Lawrence Erlbaum Associates.

Davis, F. B. (1968). Research in reading comprehension. *Reading Research Quarterly, 4,* 499–545.

Duffy, G. (1982). *Invited Address.* American Reading Forum Annual Meeting, Sarasota, December.

Durkin, D. (1978–1979). What classroom observations reveal about reading comprehension instruction. *Reading Research Quarterly, XIV* (4), 481–533.

Durkin, D. (1981). Reading comprehension instruction in five basal series. *Reading Research Quarterly, XVI* (4), 515–544.

Gates—MacGinitie Reading Tests. (1978). Boston: Houghton Mifflin.

Guzak, F. (1968). Teacher questioning and reading. *The Reading Teacher, 21,* 227–234.

Lehnert, W. G. (1978). *The process of question answering.* Hillsdale, NJ: Lawrence Erlbaum Associates.

Markman, E. M. (1979). Realizing that you don't understand: Elementary school children's awareness of inconsistencies. *Child Development, 50,* 643–655.

Nix, D. (1978a). Linking-mediated syntax in children's sentence comprehension. *Journal of Reading Behavior, 10* (1), 79–90.

Nix, D. (1978b). *Toward a systematic description of some experiential aspects of children's reading comprehension.* Unpublished Doctoral dissertation. Columbia University.

Nix, D. (1981a). *Teaching LINKS to teachers.* Manuscript in preparation. IBM T. J. Watson Research Center.

Nix, D. (1981b). *Using LINKS to teach comprehension and meta-comprehension skills to elementary school children.* Paper presented at National Reading Conference Annual Meeting, Dallas, December.

Nix, D. (1981c). *Inferencing and direct teaching of reading comprehension.* Paper presented at NYU Psycholinguistics Circle, New York.

Nix, D. (1983a). A teaching approach to developmental progress in children's reading comprehension and metacomprehension. In J. Fine and R. O. Freedle (Eds.), *New directions in discourse processing.* Norwood, NJ: Ablex.

Nix, D. (1983b). *Direct teaching of inferential comprehension skills.* Paper presented at American Educational Research Association Annual Meeting, Montreal, April.

Nix, D. (in press). *Difficulty rankings of different Link types.*

Palmer, R. R., & Colton, J. (1978). *History of the modern world.* New York: Alfred Knopf.

Peters, C. (1982a). *Improving metacomprehension and comprehension skills in disabled readers.* Paper presented at National Reading Conference Annual Meeting, Clearwater, FL.

Peters, C. (1982b). *Improving metacomprehension skills through the systematic teaching of comprehension.* Paper presented at American Educational Research Association Annual Meeting, New York.

Peters, C. (1983). *The effect of systematic reading instruction on the comprehension and metacomprehension skills of poor comprehenders.* Paper presented at American Educational Research Association Annual Meeting, Montreal.

Peters, C., & Harris, D. (1978). *Social Studies Critical Reading Test.* Pontiac, MI: Oakland Schools.

Peters, C., & Wixson, K. (1981). *Facilitating comprehension and metacomprehension skills by utilizing a systematic process for representing macro level ideas in text.* Paper presented at National Reading Conference Annual Meeting, Dallas.

Rosenshine, B. V. (1978). Academic engaged time, content covered, and direct instruction. *Journal of Education, 160,* 38–66.

Science Research Associates. (1971). *SRA Assessment Survey.* Chicago: Author.

Science Research Associates. (1978). *SRA Assessment Series.* Chicago: Author.

Specific Skill Series. (1977). New York: Barnell Loft.

Stanford Diagnostic Reading Test. (1976). New York: Harcourt, Brace, Jovanovich.

Stein, N. L., & Trabassso, T. (in press). What's in a story: An approach to comprehension and instruction. In R. Glasser (Ed.), *Advances in the psychology of instruction* (Vol. 2). Hillsdale, NJ: Lawrence Erlbaum Associates.

Tennyson, R. D., & Park, O. (1980). The teaching of concepts: A review of instructional design research literature. *Review of Educational Research, 50* (1), 55–70.

12 Classroom Questioning Strategies: Directions for Applied Research

Thomas W. Bean, Ph.D.
California State University, Fullerton

Questions are a natural part of reading. If the text departs from the reader's background knowledge, a wide array of questions arise. There may be a need to define technical terms or a desire to discuss the material with someone who can explain discordant information. For example, the following poem may elicit any number of spontaneous questions. They may relate to the mood of the poem, its diction or syntax. At a more basic level a reader might simply ask, "What's grouting?" (Bean, 1972).

Grouting

> out the library of the window
> the day trundles by
> in Keaukaha
> a friend drags a bucking grout hose
> across a hollow tile wall
> up high
> filling holes
> other workers hide out in the rooms
> that all look the same
> smoking
> filling holes
> my eyes move back from a sky that is clouding
> to my book
> one of poems
> one that was not assigned in my courses
> filling holes

Children approach reading in the same inquisitive fashion you did in this poem. At its best, early classroom instruction capitalizes upon students' natural curiosity (Bean & Drew, 1983). A vibrant classroom may be characterized by discussion and debate among the teacher and students. Yet studies of teacher-student interaction in the middle and secondary grades suggest an absence of divergent questions that truly challenge students' thinking (Au & Mason, 1981; Durkin, 1978–1979; Goodlad, 1983; Lindfors, 1980). This is not surprising since genuinely challenging questions are difficult to test using conventional multiple-choice measures (Johnston, 1983). Alternative means of evaluating student responses to divergent questions include recording and mapping interaction patterns and engaging students in summary or essay writing. Regardless of which response measure a teacher or researcher chooses, the central problem is how to best use questioning in classrooms to capitalize on students' natural curiosity. This is a problem that remains difficult to explore.

Field-based research on classroom questioning is in its infancy. Most of the studies conducted thus far have been of short duration, usually spanning just a few weeks. Unlike more controlled laboratory studies involving single subjects, classrooms represent a new challenge to the researcher. Change in classrooms occurs slowly amidst many variables that may influence the results of a study but are out of the researcher's control. Weeks and sometimes months are required to introduce an instructional treatment, observe its effects, and sort out intervening variables. Sources of data on the value of an instructional treatment in questioning include tests, observations, interviews, and attitude measures. Any effort to measure the transfer effects of an instructional treatment beyond the immediate classroom studied entails further interviews and observations sometimes spanning an additional year of field work. Classroom research is clearly not an enterprise for an impatient doctoral student.

The studies considered in this chapter represent some of the recent attempts to field-test intuitively attractive questioning strategies recommended in many methods texts for teachers. At this early stage of the enterprise, researchers are borrowing methodology from experimental psychology, text linguistics, sociology, and anthropology. The classroom as a unit of study requires investigative strategies gleaned from a variety of disciplines. Perhaps the best approach involves a team of researchers representing experimental psychology and other disciplines.

In this chapter, I want to review what we currently know about the age-old process of classroom questioning and point out some possible directions for future applied studies. Figure 12.1 provides a graphic organizer for the chapter (Barron, 1979).

The first section of the chapter considers classroom questioning designed to probe students' unguided reading of a text. This form of teacher ques-

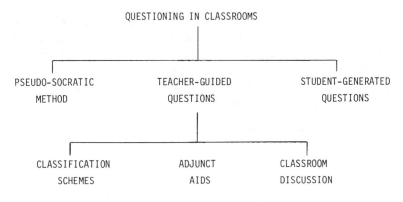

FIG. 12.1   Questioning in Classrooms

tioning places tremendous demands on students to second-guess what the teacher deems important in the text. Hyman (1974) refers to this as the "pseudo-Socratic method." Herber (1978) called it "assumptive" teaching and recommended a more guided approach to classroom questioning.

The second section discusses a more guided approach to classroom questioning. This approach is characterized by a teacher trained in question classification, the development of adjunct question guides, and strategies for guiding discussion. This guided teaching approach is just beginning to receive some research attention.

The third section reviews recent efforts to train students in question generation. Studies completed with single-subject treatments suggest that students in middle, upper, and college levels benefit from direct instruction in question generation (e.g. Andre & Anderson, 1978–1979; Brown, 1981). This training appears to benefit below-average readers more than average or above-average readers. At least one classroom-based study suggests that classroom teachers can instruct high school students in a step-by-step process for generating questions based on lengthy narratives (Singer & Donlan, 1982). These and other studies are considered in the last section of the chapter.

QUESTIONING IN CLASSROOMS

The Pseudo-Socratic Method

The classical Socratic method of instruction is undoubtedly the most misunderstood yet widely attempted questioning scheme in most classrooms (Hyman, 1974). For example, an English teacher might assign the poem "Grouting" as independent homework with the instructions to "read the poem and we'll discuss it tomorrow." Students are left to their own devices to read and attempt literary "exegesis" on the poem in preparation for whatever questions are looming in the wings the following day. A highly skilled teacher might successfully guide Socratic post-reading dialogue based on this assignment. A more probable outcome in a class of 40 eleventh graders is the following pseudo-Socratic exchange.

Teacher: "Can anyone tell me what grouting is?"
Sam: "Filling holes."
Teacher: 'Well, yes, but it's more than that in this poem. What's the significance of the grouting metaphor? Janet?"
Janet: (who did not read the poem) "Ummm . . ." (five seconds pass)
Teacher: "Melvin?"
Melvin: " Grouting—at least the way it sounds in this poem is pouring cement into a tile wall that must be high up on a new building. I've watched construction workers do that before. They pump the concrete up the building through a hose."
Teacher: "Yes, that's a literal definition of grouting but what does it really mean in this poem?"

This brief exchange is far from a Socratic dialogue. It's more of a traditional recitation converging on a single, acceptable answer. The exchange can be characterized as an intellectual "fishing" expedition (Lindfors, 1980). Moreover, it was based on an unguided purpose for reading the poem in the original assignment. How is a Socratic dialogue different from this exchange?

A true Socratic dialogue requires tremendous skill on the part of the teacher in guiding students toward self-doubt about their current knowledge structure or belief system. Once self-doubt is evident, the teacher then skillfully guides students to question their existing view. Finally, as a result of this cognitive dissonance, students may decide to revise a previously held belief or to modify their knowledge structure (Hyman, 1974; Santas, 1979). In Rumelhart and Norman's (1978) terminology, a finely orchestrated Socratic dialogue ought to result in a "restructuring" of one's schemata for a particular topic rather than simply assimilating information.

A Socratic dialogue is best reserved for complex metaphysical questions where no single answer is obvious. Unlike questions related to particular texts, Socrates' questions relied on the individual's world knowledge and belief system for a reasoned response (Hyman, 1974).

Many classrooms, particularly at the secondary and college levels, rely heavily on a lecture, read, and discuss method. Yet contemporary findings in text comprehension and a wealth of teaching strategies available offer more carefully guided approaches to reading assignments and follow-up discussion (Herber, 1978; Readence, Bean, & Baldwin, 1981). These issues are explored in the following section.

TEACHER-GUIDED QUESTIONS

Classification Schemes

Effective teacher questioning presupposes a high level of awareness concerning ways in which questions may be classified. A teacher must have a finely tuned analytical sense of question types and their correspondence to sources of information used in a class.

For years, teachers have been introduced to any number of classification schemes or taxonomies (Hyman, 1979). In my own efforts to use various taxonomies with teachers I have found that the more elaborate the scheme, the more "fuzzy" demarcations become between question types. Once we leave the reasonably solid ground of text-based explicit information, most efforts to classify "higher levels of thinking" become pretty subjective.

During the last few years I have been using a classification scheme for questions proposed by Pearson and Johnson (1978) and modified by Readence et al. (1981) to help teachers become more aware of questions they pose for discussion and on tests. Our scheme includes source of information as an integral part of the overall classification of question types. Four question types and two information sources are used in this scheme (Bean, Singer, Sorter, & Frazee, 1983). The "Grouting" poem is used to illustrate each level.

Grouting

1. out the library of the window
2. the day trundles by
3. in Keaukaha
4. a friend drags a bucking grout hose
5. across a hollow tile wall
6. up high
7. filling holes
8. other workers hide out in the rooms
9. that all look the same
10. smoking
11. my eyes move back from a sky that is clouding
13. to my book
14. one of poems
15. one that was not assigned in my courses
16. filling holes

Table 12.1 presents an example of each question type with reference to its source of information when that information is available in the poem. Source of information is classified according to its level based on Kintsch and van Dijk's (1978) model of text comprehension. Their model distinguishes higher-level macrostructure-text information abstracted by a reader from more lower-level microstructure details.

The first question is text explicit since the answer is supplied by the title of the poem. This question elicits macrolevel information, since titles usually bind together or subsume supporting details.

Question 2 requires some inferencing to determine the role of "filling holes" in the poem. The effect of this repetition relies on the reader's sense that the poet is dissatisified like the high rise construction workers and this feeling is manifested in the phrase "filling holes."

Question 3 moves outside the poem to explore the reader's experiences. Finally, question 4 requires a critical judgment of the poem's intended impact.

Figure 12.2 provides a version of this classification scheme used by Bean et al. (1983) in a study of 10th graders' expository text summaries and question-generation.

TABLE 12.1
Question Type and Source of Information

Question	Type	Source	Line
1. What is the title of the poem?	text explicit	macrostructure	0
1.1 What town is mentioned?	text explicit	microstructure	3
2. Why is the phrase "filling Holes" repeated three times?	text implicit	macrostructure	7-11-16
2.1 What kind of building is described?	text implicit	microstructure	6- 8- 9
3. Have you ever been bored with your life?	experiential	macrostructure	—
3.1 How does this feeling relate to the poem?	experiential	macrostructure	—
4. Does the poem, in your opinion, convey a feeling of dissatisfaction?	evaluative	macrostructure	—

Text: _____

Class: _____
Date: _____
Quiz Number: _____ Text Chpts. _____

ITEM CLASSIFICATION

| Question No. | Type | | | Information Source | | |
	Text Explicit	Text Implicit	Experiential	Evaluative	Macrostructure	Microstructure	Page Ref.
1.							
2.							
3.							
4.							
5.							

FIG. 12.2 Classification Scheme for Questions

Our classification scheme has several advantages for the researcher and teacher. A researcher can use this scheme to develop questions that are likely to be sensitive to a particular instructional treatment. Student answers to questions that elicit macrolevel versus microlevel information can be contrasted in a frequency analysis. This form of analysis is of particular interest in studies of summarization training aimed at guiding students in the selection of major ideas from a passage. The effect of this training on students' success at answering main idea questions can be explored in some detail with our classification scheme.

Informal interviews with teachers indicate that they typically develop quizzes and tests without a classification scheme. Most teachers are familiar with comprehension taxonomies and may use these in test development. They are less familiar with recent studies of text structure or prose analysis. This is not surprising, since classroom practice usually runs somewhat behind research in the reading process. Using the classification scheme does require a well-developed knowledge of recent insights concerning text comprehension (e.g., Graesser, 1981; Kintsch & van Dijk, 1978). We have found that training in some form of prose analysis provides a good foundation for our classification scheme.

Adjunct Aids

Efforts to guide students learning from text often include the development of adjunct aids. The most basic form of adjunct aid consists of questions to be answered in conjunction with a reading assignment. A teacher may use prereading, reading, or postreading questions (Ford, 1981; Readence et al., 1981). Each has advantages and disadvantages.

Prereading questions have a tendency to encourage selective reading to find just those answers that are required. Certainly selective reading is the hallmark of an expert reader, but prereading questions may reduce a student's overall understanding of a text chapter.

Interspersed questions designed to encourage spaced learning of text concepts may be helpful for students who are unable to maintain the attention required for reading longer segments of text. For others, breaking a text chapter into segments followed by questions may interfere with their efforts to integrate ideas. Conversations with high school students reveal that they often disregard publisher-provided interspersed questions. They regard these questions as extraneous text to be skipped unless the teacher specifically includes these same questions on the test.

Postreading questions may enhance overall retention of ideas in a text. This is especially true if they are used as a stimulus for discussion. If the questions are exclusively text-based they may discourage critical reading and encourage rote memorization.

The advantages and disadvantages of prereading, reading, and postreading questions need further study, especially in applied settings. A popular research question is whether students' text comprehension is optimal when questions are asked before an assignment, during reading, or after reading. Perhaps a combination of all three is most facilitative.

One promising alternative to questions has been proposed. The "anticipation-reaction" guide relies on prereading and postreading statements rather than questions (Bean & Peterson, 1981; Herber & Nelson, 1981; Moore, Readence, & Rickelman, 1982). In this form of adjunct aid students are introduced to a series of statements representing explicit, implicit, experiential, and evaluative information. The level of statement included usually depends upon the level of comprehension a teacher is trying to encourage. Before reading, students consider each statement and indicate whether or not they agree or disagree with its content. After reading, they reconsider their original position and revise it if such restructuring is needed. This is a particularly attractive strategy that treats comprehension as the integration, modification, and evaluation of a reader's knowledge structure in relation to a text.

Table 12.2 using the "Grouting" poem contrasts a lesson based on prequestions with one based on anticipation-reaction guide statements.

TABLE 12.2
Pre-Questions Versus Anticipated Guide Statements

Pre-Questions	Anticipated Guide Statements		
Directions: Read to find out:	Directions: Before reading, take a moment to read each statement. Decide whether you agree or disagree and place a (ν) in the appropriate column. After reading, reconsider your initial response.		
	Agree	*Disagree*	
1. Where is the setting of the poem?	_____	_____	1. People control the quality of their lives.
2. Why do the workers hide-out?			
3. What is the significance of the grouting metaphor?	_____	_____	2. Manual labor is boring.
4. Have you ever felt like the poet?	_____	_____	3. University courses include what you want to read.
	_____	_____	4. Poetry is too abstract.

Both prequestions and guide statements focus students' attention on key ideas in the poem. The major difference is the way in which this depth of processing is achieved (Craik & Lockhart, 1972). The anticipation guide starts with what the reader currently knows and believes about a topic. Yet it also develops some conceptual conflict by using statements that are antithetical to the poem (Bean & Peterson, 1981). For example, statement 3 may be challenged by the content of the poem. Anticipation guides may combine text-explicit and more divergent statements. Students defending a cherished belief before reading may decide to modify their original position in the face of new information.

Anticipation guide statements are developed by first identifying the major concepts in a text selection, lecture, or film. Three or four statements are then created with one or two of the statements presenting information that will be challenged by the text. Deciding whether or not a particular anticipation guide is effective requires a trial run in the classroom. If the guide helps generate discussion and retention of content it may be a worthwhile alternative to prequestions. Anticipation-reaction guides are intuitively attractive, but we need applied studies contrasting questions versus statement-based adjunct guides to fully understand their advantages.

Bean and Soderberg (1983) conducted a descriptive study using guide statements. They developed a three-stage series of guide statements designed to foster critical discussion of a sixth-grade ecology filmstrip. In the first stage, students simply put a check next to any concepts mentioned by the narrator as they viewed the filmstrip (e.g., "DDT is an insecticide that does not break down"). Following this recognition task, students reacted to implicit statements linked to the filmstrip (e.g., "Algae are harmless to any ecosystem"). Finally, they discussed statements related to local ecological problems (e.g., "Oil wells off the Santa Barbara Channel are necessary to provide energy for Americans even if the wells change the ecosystem there").

Once students had a grasp of the foundational information in the filmstrip, they discussed statements related to local ecological issues. Field notes charting their discussion of experiential statements concerning oil exploration off the Santa Barbara Channel provide some measure of the guide's value. Good classroom discussion may be characterized by an absence of teacher prompting and an abundance of student participation (Lindfors, 1980). Students in this class contributed 10 out of 16 comments charted or 62% of the discussion. These data indicate that students had a good grasp of the filmstrip concepts beyond a recognition or explicit level. However, their discussion pattern followed the turn-taking conventions of a typical teacher-directed lesson. They directed their ideas to the teacher for evaluation. A more active discussion might consist of students directing questions and comments to each other. Students are not accustomed to viewing filmstrips in this active fashion nor are they familiar with directing their own discussion with minimal teacher prompts. Bean and Soderberg speculated that students would exchange ideas and opinions more readily as they gained experience with anticipation-reaction guides and follow-up discussion.

Reading and Postreading Questions

Questions that follow major sections of a text chapter, sometimes called "interspersed" questions, have received a good deal of basic research attention (Rickards, 1979; Rickards & Hatcher, 1978; Rothkopf, 1966). Possibly as a result of the facilitative effects of inserted questions observed in basic research, authors and textbook publishers in the late 1970s began to include these in texts.

Although we know little about student use of publisher-provided questions, we have some indication that teacher-devised study guide questions enhance text comprehension. For example, Reynolds and Anderson (1982) found that questions altered perceived task demands in text reading by encouraging college students to attend more to the questioned material. Using a carefully controlled, on-line computer presentation of text, they found that less time was devoted to irrelevant text segments. Students selectively attended to question-specific segments of the text. Their results suggest that students are likely to allocate processing time and resources differently when study guide questions accompany reading assignments.

Study guides undoubtedly have a subtle influence on student attitude toward the material. The fact that the teacher felt the topic under consideration warranted her time to develop an adjunct guide suggests to students the relative importance of this material and the teacher's effort to ensure that they understand the text. Indeed, in a survey of students' attitude toward a university history course in western civilization, students in classes using guide material had a significantly more positive attitude toward history than students in a lecture, read, and discuss section (Mend, 1981).

Austin (1983) contrasted posttest comprehension scores of students using study guides in history with a control group in a read and discuss condition. Her study involved 225 community college freshmen for 14 weeks. The groups were matched on pretest knowledge of history. The experimental group completed a two-page study guide for each of 20 text chapters. Austin's "study guide" included a combination of items on defining key vocabulary, anticipation guide statements, instructor-devised questions, and a section for student-posed questions.

Austin found a significant difference on the history posttest favoring the study guide group. This facilitative effect for the guide is not surprising, especially in a freshman course where students' prior knowledge and metacognitive abilities are not well developed. What we cannot discern from this study is the differential effect of questions versus statements, teacher-posed versus student-posed questions, and the effect of calling students' attention to key vocabulary. Austin's findings are encouraging. Applied researchers should continue exploring the effect of study guide questions within carefully defined theoretical parameters that allow other investigators to replicate their work.

Classroom Discussion

The flow of classroom discussion is influenced in large measure by the form and style of teacher-posed questions. For example, a teacher may "fish" for a convergent, text-explicit answer or encourage more divergent responses (Lindfors, 1980). Recent efforts to observe and analyze classroom discussion typically employ techniques gleaned from cultural anthropology (e.g., Au & Mason, 1981). Participant observations, interviews, anecdotal records (e.g., study guides), and field notes of classroom interaction can be mapped and analyzed for salient patterns (Green & Wallat, 1981). Thus, in addition to traditional recall comprehension measures used to contrast experimental and control groups in applied studies, vivid classroom data can be collected through field notes and related maps. The relative effects of guide material on participation in classroom discussion can be explored through conversational maps.

Thus far, conversational maps have been confined to descriptive rather than experimental studies. For example, Bean and Drew (1983) created a simple discussion map to analyze the level of thinking and sociolinguistic function of teacher questions and statements in a first-grade basal reader lesson. Figure 12.3 illustrates the discussion map we used.

The discussion map in Fig. 12.3 includes background information and a detailed record of the discussion. It specifies lesson characteristics, including the text being used and the classroom instructional context, i.e., large group or small group, learning centers, films and so on. If students have been working in guide material prior to the discussion, the specific type of guide is indicated. Since the map is constructed from field notes, each statement or question in the notes is assigned a sequential line number to be included on the map.

The discussion map identifies the source of a statement or question (i.e., form) as well as its level and function. The following guidelines are useful in transferring field notes to the discussion map.

Source: Use a dot (.) or initials to indicate whether or not a student
            or instructor generated a particular question or statement.
Form: Use a dot (.) to indicate a question or statement.
Level: Questions or statements may be classified as:

DISCUSSION MAP

Meeting: _____ Date: _____ Text: _____

Context Description: _____ Guide: _____

| Source | | Form | | Level | | | Function | | | | | |
Instructor	Student	Ques.	Stat.	L	I	A	E	Focusing	Controlling	Ignoring or Rejecting	Extending	Clarifying	Raising
001													
002													

FIG. 12.3 Discussion Map

347

Literal: Repetition of a text or lecture concept.

Interpretive: Generating inferencess or expanding upon the literal information presented in the text, lecture, or film.

Applied: Making a connection or transfer to other similar or divergent contexts.

Evaluative: Making a judgment about text or lecture concepts.

Function: Discussion may be facilitated or inhibited by the quality of participants' statements or questions.

Focusing: Initiate discussion or refocus on an issue; e.g., "Who is Taco in the story we just read?"

*Control-   Direct or dominate the discussion; e.g., "Mike, would you
ling:*   read question 2 on our comprehension sheet so we can finish our discussion of this story today?"

*Ignoring or   Maintain current trend in discuussion. Disregard a stu-
Rejecting:*   dent's interest; e.g., "My questions are based on the part you were supposed to read yesterday, not on the part you read ahead."

Extending: Obtain more information at a particular level of discussion; e.g., "Besides turtles, what other animals hibernate in winter?"

Clarifying: Obtain a more adequate explanation. Draw out a student; e.g., "Why would the author use the word 'turtle' instead of the word 'tortoise?' "

Raising: Have discussion move from factual to interpretative, applied or evaluative levels; e.g., "What could we do to let the author know that Taco is a tortoise instead of a turtle?"

In using a discussion map, some distinctions among categories are problematic. However, clear divisions do exist between literal and higher-level questions or statements be they applied, interpretive or evaluative. Similarly, clear divisions exist between questions or statements that focus, control, or reject and those that extend, clarify, or raise.

We used the discussion map during two sessions to see if the use of higher-level questions with first graders produced critical discussion of a basal reader story. A single reading group was selected for observation so that it would be fairly easy to identify participants on the tape. The reading group consisted of 5 students judged to be average or above-average readers out of a class of 27.

The first session centered on a review of a story read the day before entitled, "Something New for Taco" (Castellanos, 1975). During the review, two children felt that the author called Taco a turtle yet he is actually a tortoise since he lives in the desert. The transcription for this discussion and a summary of the discussion map results follow. The teacher, Mrs. Drew, is identified by the letter *T* throughout the discussion and the children are identified by their first initials.

001 T: Who is Taco?

002 M: He is a turtle.

003 T: What has he been doing all winter?

004 A: Sleeping.

005 T: What is the scientific word for animals that sleep through the winter?

006 M: Hibernate.

007 E: Hibernation.

008 T: What other animals hibernate?

009 A: Bears.

010 K: Squirrels.

011 E: But Taco's not really a turtle. He lives in a desert and he's a tortoise.

012 M: That's right. A turtle lives in the water.

013 E: Yeah! A turtle can come out on land but it needs to be near the water. A tortoise is like a land turtle. It doesn't need to be in water. But a turtle really lives in the water.

014 T: Then why would the author use the word "turtle" instead of the word "tortoise?"

015 S: Maybe because the tortoise belongs to the turtle family.

016 T: That's a good idea.

017 T: I have a hypothesis about why the author used the word "turtle." Do you know what a hypothesis is?

018 E: Yes.

019 T: What does it mean, E?

020 E: It means having an idea about something.

021 A: What is your idea, Mrs. Drew?

022 T: Actually, I have two ideas but I have no proof nor disproof for either. First, perhaps the author didn't know the difference between a tortoise and a turtle. Or, second, perhaps the author was using words you already know.

023 All: Yeah! That's probably why!

024 T: Do you agree with this if it's true?

025 A: That's not right!

026 T: Should the author use the word "turtle" or introduce the new word "tortoise?"

027 A: Use the word "tortoise!"

028 T: Should the authors be careful about the facts?

029 All: Yes!

030 T: Even in a make-believe story?

031 All: Yes!

T: Tomorrow we will discuss what you as readers can do about things you read that you do not think are true.

Figure 12.4 provides a completed discussion map for this session.

By plotting this discussion on the map, the following characteristics shown in Table 12.3 are available for analysis.

An analysis of this session reveals that there were 12% more student responses (i.e., questions plus statements) than teacher responses. Although the lesson began as a review with literal questions and answers focusing on the factual content of the story, 84% of the functions were in the higher-level areas when the digression to explore students' concerns was actively pursued. The mapping shows that most of the discussion involved three of the five students and the teacher. At one point, five student responses were made before the teacher again participated in the discussion. Student-generated questions which continued the discussion at a high level accounted for 8% of the total questions asked.

During a second class session, students explored ways of letting the author know about the possibility of Taco being a tortoise rather than a turtle. They used their prior knowledge and information contained in their basal reader to locate the publisher's address. Then they decided to compose a group-dictated letter to the author questioning the accuracy of the "turtle" label for Taco.

Field notes and discussion maps provide a means of enhancing the data collected in applied studies. For example, if we discovered that students in classes using study guide questions were more willing to engage in classroom discussion than students in a non-guide condition, that would indicate the efficacy of guides beyond the level of a comprehension test. In addition, discussion maps can be used by a teacher as an analytical scheme to discern how well she is guiding classroom discussion in terms of the level of understanding students achieve, appropriateness of the text material, and "wait time" the teacher provides for students to respond to her questions (Gambrell, 1980).

STUDENT GENERATED QUESTIONS

The notion of "active comprehension" posited by Singer (1978) relies on systematically shifting from teacher questioning to student-generated questions. Based on a few studies completed thus far, it appears that student-generated questions can increase understanding and retention of narrative selections (Brown, 1981; Cohen, 1983; Singer & Donlan, 1982). Some of the success in getting students to generate questions related to stories is undoubt-

DISCUSSION MAP

Meeting: Kim's Reading Group Date: ______ Text: Macmillan R; Z' Level

Context Description: Review/Discussion Guide: ______

	Source		Form		Level				Function					
	Instructor	Student	Ques.	Stat.	L	I	A	E	Focusing	Controlling	Ignoring or Rejecting	Extending	Clarifying	Raising
001	T		•		•				•					
002		M		•	•				•					
003	T		•		•				•					
004		A		•	•				•					
005	T		•			•						•		
006		M		•			•					•		
007		E	•				•					•		
008	T		•				•					•		
009		A		•			•					•		
010		K		•			•					•		
011		E		•				•					•	
012		M		•			•						•	
013		E		•			•						•	
014	T		•					•						•
015		S		•			•						•	
016	T			•				•					•	
017	T		•			•						•		
018		E		•			•		•					
019	T		•				•						•	
020		E		•			•						•	
021		A	•				•						•	
022	T			•				•					•	
023		All		•				•					•	
024	T		•					•						•
025		A		•				•						•
026	T		•					•						•
027		A		•				•					•	
028	T		•					•						•
029		All		•				•					•	
030	T		•					•					•	
031		All		•				•					•	

FIG. 12.4 Story Discussion Map

TABLE 12.3
Discussion Map Analyses

SOURCE		FORM		LEVEL				FUNCTION					
Teacher	Student	Question	Statement	Literal	Interpretative	Applied	Evaluative	Focus	Control	Reject	Extend	Clarify	Raise
14	18	12	20	4	2	12	14	5	0	0	7	14	6

edly a function of the familiar, predictable structure of narratives. Moreover, the level of interest and attention associated with reading a good story also encourages student-generated questions. For example, Singer et al. were able to train eleventh-grade students to generate story-specific questions at key points in lengthy adolescent narratives. The researchers modeled this process with a generic scheme for asking wh-questions about the setting, characters, and story events. Eleventh graders trained in this procedure achieved significantly higher comprehension scores than a control group responding to traditional, teacher-posed prequestions.

The few studies conducted to date on student-generated questions with narrative material are promising. Additional applied studies are needed to answer questions related to developmental issues. For example, is active comprehension best introduced and trained before high school? Are poor readers gaining more from this training than fluent readers? Indeed, most fluent readers prefer not to be interrupted when they are deeply involved with the movement of a good story.

Although student-generated questions seem to facilitate comprehension of narrative material, much less is known about how to interest students in question-asking with expository text. Moreover, few long-range studies like the Singer and Donlan research have been conducted with high school students reading expository text. Unlike a story, expository text typically includes a variety of rhetorical patterns. For example, a world history text may shift from a narrative essay to a standard chronological survey within the same chapter. In addition, the volume of material students must cope with in expository text is typically greater and more diverse than following the perils of a few protagonists in a story. Despite these problems a few studies have been completed that shed some light on strategies for training students in active comprehension of expository text.

Andre and Anderson (1978–1979) explored the effects of a two-day, self-questioning training scheme on 29 high school students' comprehension of brief, 450 word passages from psychology. They found that student-generated wh-questions enhanced low and middle verbal ability students' comprehension of the material. Higher verbal ability students not trained in the question-generation procedure performed as well as the experimental group. Apparently high verbal ability students managed their study reading effectively, perhaps because they had independently acquired appropriate strategies for processing text that was not overly difficult.

In an effort to explore student-generated questions in a classroom setting over time, Bean et al. (1983) conducted a study aimed at training students in question generation in 10th-grade world history. In order to solve the problem of diverse macrostructures within a single expository text, an experimental group of 30 average and above-average students were taught a summarization strategy based on Kintsch and van Dijk's (1978) macrorules as a prelude to question generation. Students in our study used the following four macrorules to generate questions:

1. Selection or Invention: Write a topic sentence that organizes the ideas in this section of the chapter.
2. Generalization: Write a statement that organizes the ideas in this section of the chapter.
3. Question: Write up to three questions based on the general statement in step 3.
4. Conclusion and Evaluation: Write the position you support and, if possible, how you might test the truth of this position.

Students in the experimental group applied this strategy to four lessons in their world history text, *Echoes of Time: A World History* (Ostrowski & Kemper, 1977), for 14 weeks. A control group responded to teacher-posed questions in a traditional read and discuss classroom dialogue.

Eight multiple-choice quizzes consisting of 20 text-explicit items and a ratio of 7 macrolevel questions to 13 microlevel items were used to assess students' comprehension over the 14 weeks. There were no significant differences in experimental and control students' comprehension on any of the eight quizzes. However, on a summarization task, experimental group students wrote significantly more succinct summaries than their control group peers. Interviews with students revealed a positive attitude toward the summarization steps in the strategy. However, they had a great deal of difficulty with the self-questioning step, in part because they already answered the selection and generalization items making the questioning step somewhat redundant. Moreover, students tended to ask implicit or experiential questions that departed radically from the text-explicit questions required for success on the quizzes (e.g., "How did Spartan parents feel about putting a deformed baby to death?").

Balajthy (1983), in a study designed to train college freshmen enrolled in a basic skills reading course, also found that students typically generated higher-order questions that were interesting but of little help on a text-explicit measure. Perhaps a more focused self-questioning strategy involving prediction and listing of possible quiz questions would be more beneficial for these average and above-average students.

In a study involving a six-step questioning heuristic for studying text, Adams, Carnine, and Gersten (1982) found that fifth-grade students who were deficient in study skills were able to benefit from systematic self-questioning instruction. The six steps in their self-questioning scheme parallel earlier heuristics like SQ3R (Robinson, 1941): (1) Preview the passage by reading the headings and subheadings; (2) recite the subheading; (3) ask yourself questions about what might be important to learn; (4) read to find the important details; (5) reread the subheading and recite important details.

Students in the treatment condition were taught these steps over a 4-day period using carefully scripted lessons, systematic prompting, and instruction in the purpose of each step. They were instructed by a teacher in a one-to-one tutorial setting. Another group engaged in independent study with teacher feedback, and a third group received no study skills instruction. Students applied the strategy to their fifth-grade social studies text. Dependent measures included a free recall and a 10-wh-question short-answer test given after the training and again 2 weeks later.

Students using the six-step strategy performed significantly better than the control groups on the short-answer tests assessing immediate and delayed recall. Control groups were not significantly different in their respective performance on the dependent measures. Free recall results were not significant and they displayed a good deal of individual variability.

What is most interesting about the Adams et al. study is the observational data they collected to ascertain how students in the immediate and delayed posttest conditions studied the 800-word social studies passage. Only 50% of the students trained in the six-step strategy used the study rules they were taught; 40% took notes consisting of lists of key ideas, often verbatim from the text. Presumably the other 10% simply read the passages. By the delayed posttest 2 weeks later, only 20% used all six study rules despite their obvious ability to name each rule.

Given that reading, especially study reading, is a resource-limited process (Norman, 1976), then these results are not surprising. Students selected the most parsimonious features of the six-step strategy, preserving the rehearsal feature and deleting the more cumbersome aspects. The feature students found to be most problematic was question asking. Thus, both fifth graders in the Adams et al. study and 10th graders in the Bean et al. research chose other strategies over question-generation when studying independently. Indeed, it could be argued that any prompt causing the reader to reread and allocate extra processing attention to key sections of text is likely to assist comprehension. Students are quick to figure out that a modified, scaled-down version of SQ3R saves time and energy. Perhaps a crucial problem with many of our study strategies such as SQ3R and various "clones" is that they are too unwieldy. We need more studies like the Adams et al. investigation that trace what students actually import from our training sessions. Studies should attempt to discover optimal developmental periods for introducing metacognitive strategies that include only the most facilitative features of self-questioning procedures like SQ3R.

In an effort to control many of the intervening variables that may have confounded results in other question-generation studies, Balajthy (1983) varied length of training and difficulty of the passages. In addition, he measured immediate and delayed recall, and used two forms of dependent measures. His subjects were below-average readers enrolled in a college freshman basic reading skills class. Sixty subjects were randomly assigned to one of three conditions. The first group received 5 hours of training in self-generated questioning. They were taught to select topic sentences, detect paragraph organization, and use this information to pose questions related to the section just read. Group 2 followed the same procedure for just 1 hour. Group 3 comprised a read-reread condition. All the training relied on self-paced workbooks, which departs from other studies but conforms to individualized learning assistance modules often used in basic skills programs. Two 800-word passages at ninth- and sixteenth-grade difficulty were used for the dependent measures. The two treatment group subjects were advised to use self-questioning and the control group simply read. Eleven minutes were allowed for the session followed by the criterion measures, which were again administered 1 week later.

On the immediate test there were no significant differences among the three groups. The 5-week and 1-week self-questioning groups performed significantly better than the control group on the delayed difficult passage measure. However, the control group performed better than the treatment subjects on the easier passage. Belajthy concluded that question generation is facilitative for students when they are reading challenging text.

As in previous question-generation studies, the self-paced instructional scheme used in Balajthy's investigation prohibits generalization to a larger classroom context. Furthermore, the durability of the self-questioning scheme on the delayed test 1 week later still leaves the issue of what students actually do with self-questioning in future, unprompted contexts unanswered. Transfer of question-generation training remains uncharted territory. Results thus far related to student-generated questions and training in heuristics like SQ3R suggest these are unlikely to serve as substitutes for teacher guidance. Ford (1981), and Bean, Wells, and Yopp (1983) argue that careful teacher development of adjunct guides like those described earlier in this chapter ought to form a good foundation for students independent study of text. Simply introducing students to a questioning heuristic differs little from the "sink or swim" assignment instructing students to "read the Grouting poem for next time."

SUMMARY

We are just beginning to understand the intricate dynamics of classroom questioning. Before summarizing what we have learned, I want to comment briefly on some important methodological issues confronting applied researchers.

Applied studies of classroom questioning are most likely to provide us with useful insights if they are of long duration, use passages representative of normal text reading, and measure comprehension through a variety of dependent measures. In terms of duration, ethnographic studies suggest that adequate description of a classroom context requires ongoing observation spanning more than a few instructional sessions. Many ethnographic investigations routinely involve at least a year-long design. Brief expository passages at the secondary and college levels are not representative of lengthy reading assignments that demand parsimonious, yet helpful, text-processing strategies. Applied researchers ought to ask themselves, "When was the last time I used SQ3R for any text, especially longer texts?" If we hope to generalize to classroom contexts, stimulus materials should have context integrity as in the Adams et al. and Bean et. al. studies.

The problem of which dependent measures to use in applied studies of questioning has yet to be resolved. It is entirely possible to effectively instruct students in a questioning strategy that they seem to learn adequately with no significant effect on comprehension when it is measured using multiple-choice or free recall. Thus other measures relating to attitudes, student insights, anecdotal material, classroom discussion maps, and longitudinal follow-up need to become part of the applied researcher's repertoire. Studies that refine and build upon previous research conducted in a series are badly needed.

Since applied research in classroom questioning is relatively young, it would be premature to list many conclusions. Rather, at least four research questions seem worthy of consideration.

1. Do teachers trained in a question classification scheme emphasizing question types and source of information use this system to plan lessons, guide material, and tests?
2. If teachers use such a scheme, does this approach result in better student comprehension of text than a more intuitive approach?
3. Do anticipation guide statements tapping students' existing knowledge about a topic assist their comprehension of text as well as or better than adjunct guide questions?
4. Is it possible to teach students a parsimonious strategy for generating their own questions in expository text?

These and many other applied research questions are simply not answerable at this stage. As interest in improving classroom instruction continues to grow in the eighties we are likely to see a concomitant interest in pragmatic studies of classroom questioning.

REFERENCES

Adams, A., Carnine, D., & Gersten, R. Instructional strategies for studying content area texts in the intermediate grades. *Reading Research Quarterly*, 1982, *18*, 27-55.

Andre, M. D. A., & Anderson, T. H. The development and evaluation of a self-questioning study technique. *Reading Research Quarterly*, 1978-1979, *14*, 605-623.

Au, K. H., & Mason, J. M. Social organization factors in learning to read: The balance of rights hypothesis. *Reading Research Quarterly*, 1981, *17*, 115-152.

Austin, R. The study guide: an invaluable tool for content study and reading improvement. *Western College Reading Association Journal*, 1983, *2*, 3.

Balajthy, E. *The relationship of training in self-generated questioning with passage difficulty and immediate and delayed retention.* Manuscript submitted for publication, 1983.

Barron, R. F. Research for the classroom teacher: Recent developments on the structured overview as an advance organizer. In Harold L. Herber & Jim D. Riley (Eds.), *Research in reading in the content areas: The fourth report.* Syracuse, NY: Syracuse University Reading and Language Arts Center, 1979, 171-173.

Bean, T. W. Grouting. *Ka Leo*, 1972, *21*, University of Hawaii, Hilo, Hawaii.

Bean, T. W., & Drew, R. Using a discussion map to evaluate a basal reader lesson. *The California Reader*, 1983, *16*, 23-28.

Bean, T. W., & Peterson, J. Reasoning guides: Fostering readiness in the content areas. *Reading Horizons*, 1981, *21*, 196-199.

Bean, T. W., Singer, H., Sorter, J., & Frazee, C. *Acquisition of summarization rules as a basis for question generation in learning from expository text at the high school level.* Manuscript submitted for publication, 1983 (Technical Report No. 2 of the UC/CSU Learning from Text Project).

Bean, T. W., & Soderberg, V. Reasoning guides for critical comprehension. *Reading Horizons*, 1983, *23*, 108-112.

Bean, T. W., Wells, J., & Yopp, H. K. University students' rating of critical reading guides in history and philosophy. *Western College Reading Association Journal*, 1983, *3*, 5-7.

Brown, A. Metacognition: The development of selective attention strategies for learning from texts. In Michael L. Kamil (Ed.), *Directions in reading: Research and instruction.* Washington, DC: Thirtieth Yearbook of the National Reading Conference, 1981, 21-43.

Castellanos, J. Something new for Taco. In Carl B. Smith & Ronald Wardhaugh (Eds.), *Believe It.* New York, NY: Macmillan, 1975.

Cohen, R. Self-generated questions as an aid to reading comprehension. *The Reading Teacher*, 1983, *36*, 770-775.

Craik, F. I., & Lockhart, R. S. Levels of processing: A framework for memory research. *Journal of Verbal Learning and Verbal Behavior*, 1972, *11*, 671-684.

Durkin, D. What classroom observations reveal about reading comprehension instruction. *Reading Research Quarterly*, 1978-1979, *14*, 481-533.

Ford, N. *Recent approaches to the study and teaching of 'effective learning' in higher education.* Review of Educational Research, 1981, *51*, 345-377.

Gambrell, L. B. Think-time: Implications for reading instruction. *The Reading Teacher*, 1980, *34*, 143-146.

Goodlad, J. I. A study of schooling: Some findings and hypotheses. *Phi Delta Kappan,* 1983, *64,* 465-470.

Graesser, A. C. *Prose comprehension beyond the word.* New York: Springer-Verlag, 1981.

Green, J., & Wallat, C. Mapping instruction conversations—a sociolinguistic ethnography. In Judith Green & Cynthia Wallat (Eds.), *Ethnography and Language in Educational Settings.* Norwood, NJ: Ablex, 1981.

Herber, H. L. *Teaching reading in content areas.* Englewood Cliffs, NJ: Prentice-Hall, 1978.

Herber, H. L., & Nelson, J. B. Questioning is not the answer. In Ernest K. Dishner, Thomas W. Bean, & John E. Readence (Eds.), *Reading in the content areas: Improving classroom instruction.* Dubuque, IA: Kendall/ Hunt, 1981.

Hyman, R. T. *Ways of teaching.* New York, NY: Lippincott, 1974.

Hyman, R. T. *Strategic questioning.* Englewood Cliffs, NJ: Prentice-Hall, 1979.

Johnston, P. H. *Reading Comprehension Assessment: A Cognitive Basis.* Newark, DE: International Reading Association, 1983.

Kintsch, W., & van Dijk, T. A. Toward a model of text comprehension and production. *Psychological Review,* 1978, *85,* 363-394.

Lindfors, J. W. *Children's Language and Learning.* Englewood Cliffs, NJ: Prentice-Hall, 1980.

Mend, M. *Evaluation of program titled: Improving teaching and learning from texts in history and philosophy through systematic staff and student development.* Unpublished technical report, Long Beach, CA: Chancellor's Office of the California State Universities, August, 1981.

Moore, D. W., Readence, J. E., & Rickelman, R. J. *Prereading activities for content area reading and learning.* Newark, DE: International Reading Association, 1982.

Norman, D. A. Memory and attention. New York, NY: Wiley, 1976.

Ostrowski, R., & Kemper, J. *Echoes of time: A world history.* New York, NY: McGraw-Hill, 1977.

Pearson, P. D., & Johnson, D. D. *Teaching reading comprehension.* New York, NY: Holt, Rinehart and Winston, 1978.

Readence, J. E., Bean, T. W., & Baldwin, R. S. *Content area reading: An integrated approach.* Dubuque, IA: Kendall/Hunt, 1981.

Reynolds, R. E., & Anderson, R. C. Influence of questions on the allocation of attention during reading. *Journal of Educational Psychology,* 1982, *74,* 623-632.

Rickards, J. P. Adjunct postquestions in text: A critical review of methods and processes. *Review of Educational Research,* 1979, *49,* 181-196.

Rickards, J. P., & Hatcher, C. W. Interspersed meaningful learning questions as semantic cues for poor comprehenders. *Reading Research Quarterly,* 1978, *13,* 538-553.

Robinson, F. P. *Diagnostic and remedial techniques for effective study.* New York, NY: Harper and Brothers, 1941.

Rothkopf, E. Z. Learning from written instructive material: An exploration of the control of inspection behavior by test-like events. *American Educational Research Journal,* 1966, *3,* 241-249.

Rumelhart, D. E., & Norman, D. A. Accretion, tuning, and restructuring: Three modes of learning. In J. W. Cotton & R. L. Klatzy (Eds.), *Semantic factors in cognition.* Hillsdale, NJ: Lawrence Erlbaum Associates, 1978, 37-53.

Santas, G. X. *Socrates: Philosophy in Plato's early dialogues.* London, England: Routledge & Kegan Paul, 1979.

Singer, H. Active comprehension: From answering to asking questions, *The Reading Teacher* 1978, *30,* 901-908.

Singer, H., & Donlan, D. Active comprehension: Problem-solving schema with question generation for comprehension of complex short stories. *Reading Research Quarterly,* 1982, *17,* 166-186.

13 Data Base Querying by Computer

Steven P. Shwartz
Cognitive Systems Inc.

Wendy G. Lehnert
Univ. of Massachusetts
Amherst

The computer-human interface problem is rapidly becoming a critical concern to the data processing industry. Computerized data bases are currently available for a wide spectrum of applications ranging from marketing to law to finance. The computer systems attached to these data bases can, in principle, provide answers to an enormous number of user questions. But in fact, only a small percentage of the potential user population knows how to formulate queries to a data base, i.e., only those with data processing skills.

DATA BASE QUERYING: A BRIEF HISTORY

Natural language processing technology represents an enormous advance in the user-friendliness of computer systems. In the following section, we present a brief history of the development of user-friendly systems in order to put this new technology in perspective.

Programming Languages

The earliest computer data base query systems required queries written in machine or assembler language. To program in machine or assembler language one needs a knowledge of the physical structure of the data base, a knowledge of programming constructs such as loops, variables, and procedures, and a knowledge of the architecture of the machine on which the data base resides. Such programming skills are present in only a very small percentage of the potential user population for most data bases.

The development of high-level languages, such as FORTRAN, reduced the requisite level of programming expertise. A program written in a particular high-level language will run with virtually no modification on a wide variety of different computers. For this reason, high-level programmers do not need to be knowledgeable concerning computer architecture. However, considerable programming skill is still necessary to access a data base using even high-level languages. A high-level programmer must still know about the physical structure of the data base and have an understanding of programming concepts.

The introduction of English-like syntax, which made high-level languages easier to use (e.g., COBOL), did little to enlarge the data base user population. English-like programming languages still require a knowledge of programming (e.g., loops, variables, etc.) as well as a grasp of their restrictive syntax.

In the last decade, the need for "user-friendly" systems that minimize one's level of data processing skill has resulted in the development of (a) query languages and (b) menu systems. More recently, AI technology has made it possible for users to access data base information via natural language: A user can talk (or at least type) to the computer and pose questions to it as one would talk to another person.

Query Systems

Query languages enable users without programming skills to access data bases. That is, a query language user can access data base information without needing to know anything about loops or variables. For example, suppose a manager needs to know how many secretaries are in the marketing department. A typical query to retrieve a listing of all the secretaries in the marketing department might look like:

SLCT EMPL JT = SCTY DPT = MKTG

This query instructs the system to retrieve all of the items in the EMPL (employees) file for which the JT (job-title) field has the value SCTY (secretary) and the DPT (department) field has the entry MKTG (marketing).

Consider the degree to which this simple query format eliminates need for programming expertise. In order to write a FORTRAN or COBOL program to retrieve the information in the above example, a user would need extensive programming skills. For example, the user would need to know how to produce code to open the correct file, define variables to store temporary results, access portions of the file, test the values of fields, generate iterative procedures to process the file, and display the results.

In contrast, the user of the query language in the example above does not need to have any such knowledge of programming. However, a certain level of data processing expertise is still required. The user must have an understanding of the physical structure of the data base, which may be very different from the user's conceptual structure (i.e., the structure of the information in the data base from the point of view of the user). For example, the user may view the above data base as containing employee and job title information for each of several departments, where in fact the physical structure of this information is quite different, e.g., job title and department information for each employee. The point here is that a query language user must be aware of the physical structure of the data base.

Query-languages have since been made more English-like, but this does little to increase the size of the user-population or even accelerate the learning process. For example, the query above in an English-like system, would be expressed as

SELECT EMPLOYEES JOB-TITLE = SECRETARY
DEPARTMENT = MARKETING

Even though the query in the example above appears to have an English-like syntax, queries can only be expressed in a highly restricted subset of English that must be learned. For example, the above request could not be expressed as

LIST EMPLOYEES WORKING IN MARKETING DEPARTMENT

because this does not conform to the required syntax. The more complex the data base the greater the number of syntactic constructions that must be learned. The training period necessary to learn a query language can range from 1 day to several months, depending on the complexity of the data base. For a complex data base, the user would need a thick manual that lists the appropriate syntactic construction for each data type.

Menu Systems

Menu systems are much easier to learn than either programming languages or query systems. Menu systems present the user with a sequence of fixed choices and the user need only learn how to move through the options. Each choice can determine what sequence of choices will be presented next. When the sequence of choices has been completed, the menu system retrieves the desired information.

What could be simpler? Menu systems are easier to use than query systems because they rely on recognition of correct choices rather than recall of syntactic constructions. The user is never confused regarding what to do next, nor is the user ever plagued by the inability to recall the syntax of a particular command. Unfortunately, menu systems suffer from a very large number of pitfalls.

To illustrate some of the problems with menu systems, consider building a menu system that serves as a user interface end to a data base containing football statistics. The top-level menu might be:

What type of statistic would you like?

(1) individual
(2) team
(3) numerical

The problem illustrated here is that all of the choices in a menu system are not always clear to all users. In this example, what does "numerical" mean? The solution here is either to burden the user with a manual explaining all of the choices or to have an on-line HELP system. A manual or HELP system might tell the user the following:

Choose (1) for queries like
    HOW MANY YARDS DID WALTER PAYTON GAIN RUSHING
    LAST YEAR?
Choose (2) for queries like
    HOW MANY YARDS DID THE GIANTS GAIN RUSHING LAST
    YEAR?
and choose (3) for queries like
    WHO GAINED THE MOST YARDS RUSHING LAST YEAR?

Here, even though the choices are clear, the correct choice is not obvious. For example, suppose the user wanted to know

    HOW MANY YARDS DID WALTER PAYTON GAIN AGAINST THE
    GIANTS?

Is this under "individual" or "team" statistics? If the user makes the wrong choice, then what does he do? Another problem occurs when the desired information cannot be retrieved with the existing menu structure. For example, the user may have just gone through a whole series of menus in order to choose the type of statistic (rushing yards, passing, etc.), the position (QB, center, etc.), the time in the season, and many other screens of choices. However, if the user wanted to know about "rushing yards in the 3rd quarter" or "passing yards inside the opponent's 20-yard line," but didn't encounter a menu with these distinctions, the user query will not be able to be answered.

A critic may argue that in each case, we simply have an example of a poorly designed menu system, and that a well-designed system would have screens that more clearly communicated the semantics of the possible choices as well as screens for all of these statistics. At a practical level, however, this is typically not possible. Often, if enough screens are constructed to accommodate the entire population of possible user requests, every user might have to go through 100 screens to retrieve a single datum. Worse, suppose the user just got an answer to the query

HOW MANY YARDS RUSHING DID THE GIANTS GET IN THEIR LAST GAME?

With this type of menu system, the user will have to go through another 100 screens to get an answer to

HOW ABOUT THE JETS?

NATURAL LANGUAGE DATA BASE ACCESS

As a result of technology developed in the field of artificial intelligence, natural language query systems have emerged as the logical successor to query languages. Unfortunately, the definition of a natural language query system has been muddied by a number of commercial products that claim to permit the user to query a data base in English. By a liberal application of semantics, one might even claim that COBOL programming fits this description. We suggest below a more stringent criterion for natural language query systems. We call this the programmer-technician criterion.

The principal motivation for building natural language query systems for accessing data bases is to free the user from the need for data processing instruction. A natural language query system is a step above the English-like query systems that allow the user to phrase requests as English sentences, but permit only a restricted subset of English and impose a rigid syntax on user requests. These English-like query systems are easy to learn, but a training period is still required for the user to learn to phrase requests that conform to these restrictions. However, given the fact that the training period is often very brief, a natural language system can only be considered superior to a query system if *no* computer-related training or knowledge is required of the user.

The Programmer-Technician Criterion

This criterion can only be met if no restrictions are placed on user queries. A user who has previously relied on a programmer-technician to code formal queries for informative retrieval should be permitted to phrase information retrieval requests to the program in exactly the same way as to the technician. That is, whatever the technician would understand, the program should understand. Therefore, a natural language query system should be able to

1. Process the full gamut of syntactic constructs, including ungrammatical requests.
2. Process requests varying in complexity.
3. Process incomplete and ambiguous requests by engaging the user in an interactive dialogue.
4. Process a request with respect to its discourse context.

All of these capabilities are necessary for any system that claims to comprehend natural language and function at the level of a programmer/technician.

An Example: The EXPLORER System

The goal of the EXPLORER project (Lehnert & Shwartz, 1982) was to produce a non-fragile language analyzer suitable for industrial and business applications that require data base access. This means that the system should be accessible to users with no training in data processing whatsoever. The EXPLORER system is customized for a data base containing information about geological rock formations and oil wells. The user population consists of geologists and oil explorationists who need to use the information in the data base to help determine where to drill for oil.

EXPLORER embodies natural language analysis techniques developed at the Yale Artificial Intelligence Project. The most important component is a conceptual analyzer (Dyer, 1981, 1982) that uses expectation-driven parsing techniques (Birnbaum & Selfridge, 1979; Dyer, 1981, 1982; Gershman, 1979; Riesbeck, 1975; Riesbeck & Schank, 1976, 1979; Schank & Birnbaum, 1980). The output of the conceptual analyzer is a language-free meaning representation (Schank & Abelson, 1977). All question-answering and memory search techniques are derived from the work of Lehnert (1978) and Dyer (1982).

The philosophy behind EXPLORER is based on the notion that the language-understanding process utilizes syntactic, semantic, pragmatic and contextual cues in an integrated fashion. The EXPLORER system does *not* perform distinct syntactic, semantic, pragmatic and contextual analyses in a linear sequence, but rather attempts to utilize each type of analysis concurrently to determine the meaning of an input string. The input string is analyzed word by word, and an attempt is made to build a conceptual representation of the input string that keeps pace with the word-by-word analysis. Syntactic, semantic, pragmatic, and contextual information are all treated as cues that can aid this process. As the conceptual representation is constructed, expectations regarding the remainder of the input string are set up. The expectations can be for syntactic constructions, conceptual content, or likely inferences. When ambiguous words are encountered, expectations are generated that will resolve these ambiguities. For more detail on the parsing process, see Birnbaum and Selfridge, 1979; Dyer, 1981, 1982; Gershman, 1979; Riesbeck, 1975; Riesbeck and Schank, 1976, 1979; Schank and Birnbaum, 1980. A listing of code for a conceptual analyzer can be found in Schank and Riesbeck, 1981.

The following examples illustrate some of the input/output behavior of the EXPLORER system.

EXPLORER/EXPLORER   Version 02   9/23/81

PLEASE ENTER A MAP REQUEST:

*I want a structure map of the smackover formation for
*Bibb County, Georgia, with a contour interval of 100'
*and a scale of 1 inch to 2000 feet.

User requests a STRUCTURE map
output medium: PAPER
output device: PHOTODOT
county: BIBB, GEORGIA
top: SMACKOVER
ci = 100 feet
scale of 1 inch = 2000 feet

Would you like to make any changes or
    additions to your request? (Y or N) *y

Please input changes or additions.
*put the map on the applicon

User requests a STRUCTURE map
output medium: PAPER
output device: APPLICON
county: BIBB, GEORGIA
top: SMACKOVER
ci = 100 feet
scale of 1 inch = 2000 feet

Would you like to make any changes or
    additions to your request? (Y or N) *y

Please input changes or additions.
*and make the output medium = film.

User requests a STRUCTURE map
output medium: FILM
output device: APPLICON
county: BIBB, GEORGIA
top: SMACKOVER
ci = 100 feet
scale of 1 inch = 2000 feet

Would you like to make any changes or
  additions to your request? (Y or N) *y

Please input changes or additions.
*i really wanted an isopach from the smackover to the wilcox

User requests a ISOPACH map
output medium: FILM
output device: APPLICON
county: BIBB, GEORGIA
from SMACKOVER to WILCOX
ci = 100 feet
scale of 1 inch = 2000 feet

Would you like to make any changes or
  additions to your request? (Y or N) *n

Do you want to have a map created (Y or N)? *y

In the above example, the user requested a map of all wells that were drilled in Bibb County, Georgia, showing the depth contours of the smackover formation (a geological rock formation). The EXPLORER system responded with a paraphrase of the user's request that included default values regarding the output device and medium for the requested map. At this point, the system asked the user to verify its interpretation of the user's request and the user responded by requesting a different output device. In the subsequent dialogue the user requested EXPLORER to alter these default values and later changed the type of map to be displayed from a structure to an isopach map. An isopach map displays a different type of contour information.

The user can enter requests using any form of syntactic construction. The only restriction is that the input string be readily comprehensible to a person. For example, the initial request in the example above could have been phrased

*Using a contour interval of 100′ and a scale of 1″ to 200 feet
*please give me a structure map on the smackover formation for
*Bibb County, Georgia.

We have found that actual user requests contain almost as many ungrammatical requests as grammatical requests. A portion of these ungrammatical requests are due to carelessness on the part of the user and some are due to informal linguistic style. However, many are due to a desire on the part of experienced users to communicate a request in as few keystrokes as possible. A user who knows exactly what he wants can communicate his request quickly and easily.

PLEASE ENTER A MAP REQUEST:

*smackover bibb georgia ci 100 scale 2000.

User requests a STRUCTURE map
output medium: PAPER
output device: PHOTODOT
county: BIBB, GEORGIA
top: SMACKOVER
ci = 100 feet
scale of 1 inch = 2000 feet

Would you like to make any changes or
   additions to your request? (Y or N) *n

Do you want to have a map created (Y or N)? *y

At the other end of the spectrum is the novice who has little or no experience with the system and is not sure what constitutes a complete request. In the following example, the user desires a contour map of the smackover formation, but is not sure how to ask for it.

PLEASE ENTER A MAP REQUEST:

*Map the smackover.

A map region was not specified.

Do you wish to specify the map region
by county (C) or by geographic coordinates (G)? *c

Please enter a county (or counties) by name or number.
*bibb county

BIBB county is in the following states:
   ALABAMA GEORGIA

Please enter the appropriate state or a new
county specification.
   *ala

Please specify contour interval.
*100'

Please specify scale.
*1 to 2000

User requests a STRUCTURE map
output medium: PAPER
output device: PHOTODOT
county: BIBB, ALABAMA
top: SMACKOVER
ci = 100 feet
scale of 1 inch = 2000 feet

Would you like to make any changes or
    additions to your request? (Y or N) *n

Do you want to have a map created (Y or N)? *y

Our final example demonstrates the capabilities of the EXPLORER system with respect to the complexity of the input request.

PLEASE ENTER A MAP REQUEST:

*Contour a map of the smackover formation with 100 foot
*contours and show all producing wells that were
*drilled between January 1, 1975 and December 30, 1980
*by gulf but are now operated by Mobil and show oil
*deeper than 1000', are themselves deeper than 3000',
*and show the cookm deeper than 2000', have an
*analysis of oil from a commercial source, and
*were drilled within the area defined by latitude 30
*deg 20 min 30 sec to 31:20:30 and 80–81. scale 2000
*fest.

By FEST, do you mean FEET (Y or N)? *y

User requests a STRUCTURE map
latitude 30.34–31.34
longitude 80–81
output medium: PAPER
output device: PHOTODOT
top: SMACKOVER
filters: PRODUCING WELLS ONLY
        COMPLETION DATE> = 1/1/1975
        COMPLETION DATE< = 12/30/1980

```
        GULF ORIGINAL OPERATOR
        MOBIL CURRENT OPERATOR
        WELL SHOW OF OIL > 1000 feet
        PENETRATION OF COOKM WHERE TOP
        DEPTH > = 2000 feet
        OIL ANALYSIS AVAILABLE
        DRILLING DEPTH > 3000 FEET
    ci = 100 feet
    scale of 1 inch = 2000 feet

    Would you like to make any changes or
      additions to your request? (Y or N) *n

    Do you want to have a map created (Y or N)? *y
```

As this example shows, EXPLORER can handle long and ungrammatical requests, make inferences, and perform complicated word sense disambiguation. For example, the word "show" has two distinct meanings in the above request. The first instance of show is synonymous with "display," whereas the second and third times show is used it has a technical meaning (i.e., an indicator of something encountered during the drilling of a well). The surrounding conceptual context is used to determine which sense of show is appropriate in each case. It should be noted that each customization of EXPLORER takes advantage of the fact that words have a limited number of meaningful senses within any given knowledge domain. For example, within the domain of geology, it is hard to imagine a usage of the word "show" meaning "performance" (e.g., television show).

This example also illustrates the advantages of an intelligent spelling corrector. When a character string is encountered that is not in its dictionary, EXPLORER initially assumes it to be a spelling error and therefore tries to determine which word was intended on the basis of its dictionaries and morphology routines. If no plausible correction exists (Peterson, 1980), EXPLORER gives the user the opportunity to enter a synonymous word or phrase. In the above example, the spelling correction module picked up the typo "fest" and suggested a possible correction "feet" that was verified by the user. Note, however, that there are many English words other than feet that could have been suggested (e.g., best, jest, lest, nest, pest, rest, test, vest, west, zest, fast, fist, feat, feet, felt, feast, feist) by a less intelligent spelling corrector. Two of which (test and west) occur frequently within the geology domain. EXPLORER determines which of these possible corrections is most reasonable by examining the conceptual context in which the typo occurred. This capability is a natural by-product of the request-based parsing technique used by EXPLORER. The mechanism behind the semantic spelling corrector is a check of active requests at a time of understanding to determine whether any of the possible corrections generated by the spelling corrector are expected.

Finally, for a natural language query system to meet the programmer-technician criterion, it must be capable of understanding a request in its discourse context. For example, suppose a user produced the map from the previous example, and upon studying the map, decided that some additional contour information was necessary. Rather than typing a new 10-line request, the user would certainly prefer to type one of the following statements.

*Make the previous map an isopach from the smackover to the wilcox.

or,

*How about the same map but without showing any wildcat wells?

Evaluation of the EXPLORER System

The EXPLORER system has been undergoing testing for a period of less than a month by a variety of oil company employees, all of whom are naive users. While we have not received enough test requests to make a comprehensive evaluation of EXPLORER, some preliminary results are available (see Lehnert & Shwartz, 1982). Lehnert and Shwartz grouped the test requests into the three categories in Table 13.1.

As can be seen above, 30 out of 39 requests were processed correctly. Most of the A3 errors were due to missing or incorrect vocabulary or to programmer error in generating the target query language. We expect the percentage of errors to decrease significantly over the next 3 months as these errors are corrected.

An important and somewhat surprising finding was that of the 30 requests processed correctly, only 4 did not require some form of interactive dialogue. The majority of A2 requests required interaction because the user had not formulated a complete request. This statistic shows the importance of interactive dialogue.

DOMAIN-SPECIFIC KNOWLEDGE: THE KEY TO ROBUST UNDERSTANDING SYSTEMS

Most of the successful natural language data base access systems that have been developed over the past few years (e.g., Hendrix, 1976; Shwartz & Lehnert, 1982; Waltz et al., 1976) have been highly domain-specific. That is, these systems operate in a very specific subject area (e.g., oil well information) and rely heavily on domain-specific information (i.e., information that is specific to the subject area) to guide the understanding process. Transport-

TABLE 13.1
Performance of the EXPLORER Program

	REQUEST CATEGORY	NUMBER CORRECT (%)
(A1)	Original input is interpreted correctly on the first try—a perfect performance.	4 (10%)
(A2)	Original input is interpreted correctly after one or more clarifying interactions. These interactions may be due to typing errors, spelling errors, missing information, or system errors.	26 (67%)
(A3)	Original input is never interpreted correctly due to a system failure of some sort.	9 (23%)
	TOTAL	39 (100%)

ing a system from one domain to another is therefore a very resource-intensive process because a new set of domain-specific knowledge must be encoded for each new domain.

A great deal of recent research has focused on developing natural language access systems that are domain-independent in the sense that they do not rely on domain-specific knowledge. Such systems contain no knowledge concerning any particular subject area. We argue below that domain-specific knowledge is in fact an integral part of the understanding process, and therefore the goal of a domain-independent system is not realistic given the present state of technology. At a theoretical level, the need for a domain-specific knowledge base in a natural language processing system has been well documented (e.g., Dyer, 1982; Lehnert, 1978; Schank & Abelson, 1977). We argue below that in an applied context, a system that does not have a conceptual knowledge base can produce at best a shallow level of understanding that does not begin to approach the programmer-technician criterion specified above.

What does it mean to have a domain-independent natural language system? By definition, the system cannot have any specific semantic knowledge about the items in the data base. For example, consider the following information retrieval request:

LIST THE SALARIES OF ALL OF THE SECRETARIES

This type of query can easily be processed by a domain-independent system if in fact SALARY and SECRETARY directly reference fields, files or records in the data base. However, consider the query:

LIST ALL SECRETARIES IN THE SALES DEPARTMENT MAKING OVER $10,000.

If this request were handed to a technician, the technician would have no problem determining that "making over $10,000" referred to "secretaries" and not "the sales department." However, a domain-independent system understands "secretaries" and "sales department" only as references to data base items. To a domain-independent system, therefore, this request is equivalent to the following statement:

LIST ALL FOOBAZS IN THE GLOOMBATCH MAKING OVER $10,000.

It is not at all clear what "making over $10,000" refers to.

Another problem for domain-independent systems involves recognizing indirect references to data base items. Consider the following query:

WHAT IS BOB SMITH'S JOB TITLE?

This request is easily recognized as a reference to the JOB-TITLE field in the data base. However,

WHAT DOES BOB SMITH DO?

poses grave difficulties for the domain-independent system because it is not clear what data base field is being referred to. In a domain-specific system, this type of query can be understood by virtue of the fact that words such as "do" have very restricted meanings in the context of a specific application such as payroll.

Another major probem for domain-independent systems is generating interactive dialogue. In the EXPLORER system discussed above, when a user makes an incomplete request, the system will query the user for missing information. The statistics cited above (Lehnert & Shwartz, 1982) demonstrate the importance of this form of user dialogue. In a domain-independent system it is very difficult to identify a request with missing information because the domain determines what constitutes a complete request. Further, the content of the interactive dialogue is domain-specific.

SUMMARY

As can be seen above, natural language systems such as EXPLORER are clearly superior to query systems in every respect. The user of a natural language system can formulate a request as concisely as in a query system, but doesn't have to learn or recall the correct syntactic form of expression. In general, users will find natural language systems less cumbersome than menu systems because there is no need to process numerous screens of information. The burden is not on the user to know how to formulate a request. A natural language system that meets the programmer-technician criterion will guide the user in formulating a request as the EXPLORER system did in the examples above and free the user from the need for data processing skills.

At Cognitive Systems, we have developed several information retrieval systems like EXPLORER, each with its own set of domain-specific knowledge, for data bases containing company financial information, information on third world countries, and marketing analysis information. We are currently building systems with more knowledge than technician-level systems such as EXPLORER. For example, one system that has recently been installed provides a client with a decision support tool. This system can take a request such as

*How are we doing in San Francisco?

and answer with a report comparing sales of the company's product line this year with sales last year. The difference between a system that has the knowledge to understand simple queries and one that gives advice is merely a matter of degree (i.e., the amount of knowledge in the system). We are currently building a small business accounting system that will initially be released with a natural language query capability. After the initial release, the system will be "sent back to school" at Cognitive Systems where more knowledge will be put into the system. Thus, with each new release, the system will be able to respond to queries requiring greater and greater expertise and will appear to be getting "smarter and smarter." We hope to eventually provide the small businessman with a desktop MBA-level advisor.

REFERENCES

Birnbaum, L., & Selfridge, M. Problems in conceptual analysis of natural language. In R. Schank & C. Riesbeck, (Eds.), *Inside computer understanding*. Hillsdale, NJ: Lawrence Erlbaum Associates, 1981.

Dyer, M. G. Integration, unification, reconstruction, modification: An eternal parsing braid. In *Proceedings of the Seventh International Joint Conference on Artificial Intelligence*, August, 1981. Vancouver, B.C.

Dyer, M. *In-depth understanding: A computer model of integrated processing for narrative comprehension*. Yale University, Computer Science Dept., Research Report #219, 1982.

Gershman, A. V. *Knowledge-based parsing*. Yale University, Computer Science Dept., Research Report #156, 1979.

Hendrix, G. G. *LIFER: A natural language interface facility.* Stanford Research Institute Technical, Note 135. Dec. 1976.

Lehnert, W. *The process of question answering.* Hillsdale, NJ: Lawrence Erlbaum Associates, 1978.

Lehnert, W., & Shwartz, S. Natural language data base access with EXPLORER. *Proceedings of the Ninth International Conference on Computational Linguistics,* Prague, Czechoslovakia, 1982.

Peterson, J. L. *Computer programs for spelling correction: An experiment in program design.* New York: Springer-Verlag, 1980.

Riesbeck, C. Conceptual analysis. In R. C. Schank (Ed.), *Conceptual information processing.* Amsterdam: North Holland, 1975.

Riesbeck, C. K., & Schank, R. C. *Comprehension by computer: Expectation-based analysis of sentences in context.* Yale University, Computer Science Dept., Research Report #78, 1976. Also in W. J. M. Levelt & G. B. Flores d'Arcais (Eds.), *Studies in the perception of language.* Chichester, England: John Wiley, 1979.

Schank, R. C., & Abelson, R. *Scripts, plans, goals and understanding.* Hillsdale, NJ: Lawrence Erlbaum Associates, 1977.

Schank, R. C., & Birnbaum, L. *Memory, meaning, and syntax.* Yale University, Computer Science Dept., Technical Report #189, 1980.

Schank, R. C., & Riesbeck, C. K. *Inside computer understanding.* Hillsdale, NJ: Lawrence Erlbaum Associates, 1981.

Shwartz, S., & Lehnert, W. *EXPLORER: A natural language analysis system for information retrieval.* Cognitive Systems Technical Report 3, March 1982.

Waltz, D. L., Finin, T., Green, F., Conrad, F., Goodman, B., & Hadden, G. *The planes system: Natural language access to a large data base.* Coordinated Science Lab., University of Illinois, Urbana, Technical Report T-34, July 1976.

Author Index

Subject Index

381